First-Time Asia

written and researched by

Lesley Reader and Lucy Ridout

www.roughguides.com

Contents

◄◄ Street scene, Bhaktapur, Nepal ◄ Buddhist monk, Laos

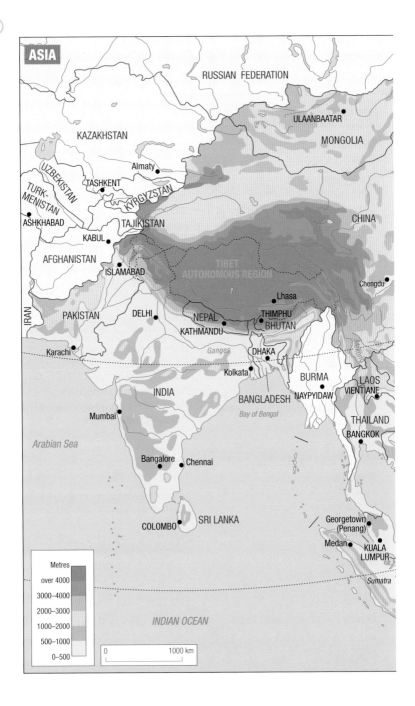

ASIA

RUSSIAN FEDERATION

ULAANBAATAR

MONGOLIA

KAZAKHSTAN

Almaty

UZBEKISTAN

TASHKENT

TURK-
MENISTAN

KYRGYZSTAN

CHINA

ASHKHABAD

TAJIKISTAN

KABUL

Chengdu

AFGHANISTAN

ISLAMABAD

TIBET
AUTONOMOUS REGION

Lhasa

IRAN

PAKISTAN

DELHI

NEPAL

THIMPHU'

KATHMANDU

BHUTAN

Karachi

Ganges

DHAKA

Mekong

Kolkata

BURMA

LAOS

INDIA

BANGLADESH

NAYPYIDAW

VIENTIANE

Mumbai

Bay of Bengal

THAILAND

Arabian Sea

BANGKOK

Bangalore

Chennai

COLOMBO

SRI LANKA

Georgetown
(Penang)

Medan

KUALA
LUMPUR

Metres

over 4000

3000–4000

2000–3000

1000–2000

500–1000

0–500

Sumatra

INDIAN OCEAN

0   1000 km

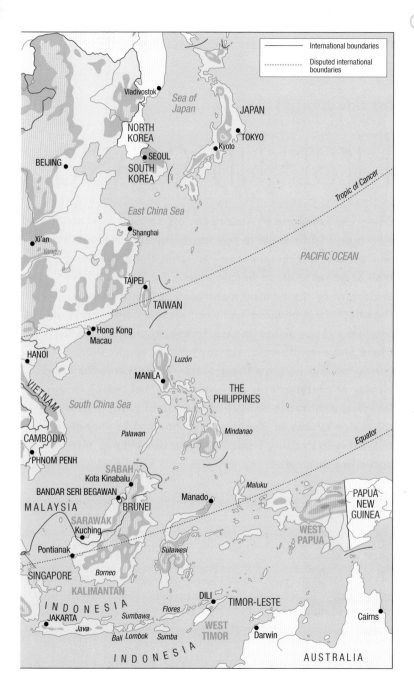

	International boundaries
	Disputed international boundaries

Vladivostok

Sea of Japan

JAPAN

NORTH KOREA

TOKYO

Kyoto

BEIJING

SEOUL

SOUTH KOREA

East China Sea

Tropic of Cancer

Xi'an

Yangzi

Shanghai

PACIFIC OCEAN

TAIPEI

TAIWAN

Hong Kong
Macau

HANOI

Luzón

VIETNAM

MANILA

THE PHILIPPINES

South China Sea

Equator

Palawan

Mindanao

CAMBODIA

PHNOM PENH

SABAH

Kota Kinabalu

Maluku

BANDAR SERI BEGAWAN

Manado

PAPUA NEW GUINEA

MALAYSIA

BRUNEI

SARAWAK

WEST PAPUA

Kuching

Pontianak

Sulawesi

SINGAPORE

Borneo

KALIMANTAN

DILI

TIMOR-LESTE

INDONESIA

Flores

Cairns

JAKARTA

Sumbawa

WEST TIMOR

Java

Bali *Lombok* *Sumba*

Darwin

INDONESIA

AUSTRALIA

Introduction to

First-Time Asia

**Every year, millions of visitors set off on their own Asian
adventure. Some want to see for themselves a few of the
world's greatest monuments – to stroll along the Great
Wall of China or stand beside India's Taj Mahal. Others
are drawn by the soaring mountains of the Himalayas,
the white-sand beaches and kaleidoscopic coral reefs of
Southeast Asia, or the chance to spot elephants, orang-
utans and even tigers in steamy jungles across the
continent. But perhaps the greatest attraction is the sheer
vitality of everyday life: you can watch Thai boxing in
Bangkok and trance dances in Bali, learn yoga in Varanasi,
drink rice whisky in Vientiane, eat dim sum in Shanghai
and satay in Penang, bargain for mangosteens in Manila
and silver in Hanoi.**

Nearly all these things are **affordable**, even for
low-budget travellers, because most of Asia is still entic-
ingly inexpensive: Western money goes much further
here than it does in Africa or South America. This has
put Asia firmly at the heart of the backpackers' trail, and
many cities and islands already boast a lively travellers'
scene, attracting young adventurers from all over the
world. Few travellers leave Asia without experiencing
at least one of its fabled hot spots: the beaches of Goa,
perhaps, the guesthouses of Kathmandu, or one of Thailand's notorious
full-moon parties.

On the other hand, **Asian travel** can also be a shocking and sobering
experience. It's hard to forget your first sight of a shantytown slum or

your first encounter with an amputee begging for coins. Many first-timers are distressed by the dirt, the squalor, and the lingering smell of garbage and drains in some Asian cities. They get unnerved by the ever-present crowds and stressed out by never being able to mingle unnoticed among them. On top of which there's the oppressive heat to cope with, not to mention the unfamiliar food and often unfathomable local customs. There's no such thing as a hassle-free trip and, on reflection, few travellers would want that. It's often the dramas and surprises that make the best experiences, and we all learn from our mistakes.

Preparing for the big adventure

We've both made plenty of mistakes during our many years of travels in Asia, and this book is a distillation of what we've learnt. *First-Time Asia* is full of the advice we give to friends heading out to

Once you've bought your ticket, you could get by in Asia on **$110** or **£70 a week**. That's for travel in the less expensive countries – such as India, Indonesia and Thailand – and for a trip that will see you spending a fair amount of time lazing on white-sand beaches and eating noodles for dinner at the local night market. Doesn't sound too bad does it? However, you will need to splash the cash a little more if you want to learn to dive, say (though that's half the price it is in the West), or go elephant trekking. A room with your own bathroom will cost more and you'll want to budget for a few nights out buying drinks as well. You'll need contingency funds too, for the unforeseen, and for shopping. The bottom line is to do a bit of **budgeting** before you go, for advice on which, see Chapter Four.

There are other ways to **stretch your funds** too: crafty planning can save on flights (see Chapter Two); it's cheaper to travel with a friend (Chapter One); and you can buy most of what you need inexpensively on the road (Chapter Six). And when all else fails you can sell your story to the press when you return (Chapter Fifteen).

Asia for the first time, and it's the book we both could have done with before setting off on our own first trips. Since then we've returned again and again, backpacking across India, China and Southeast Asia; living and working in the Himalayas, Thailand and Japan; and researching and writing guidebooks to Indonesia, Thailand and Tibet.

Camel driver, Rajastan, India

And we still choose to go back to Asia for our holidays, attracted by the chaos and drama of daily lives that, even now, seem extraordinary to us, from the food, the landscapes and the climate, to the generosity and friendship of the people and the buzz we get from hanging out in cultures that are so entirely different from our own.

This book is intended to prepare you for your big adventure, whether it's a fortnight in Malaysia or twelve months across the continent. It is not a guidebook: it's a book to read before you go, a **planning handbook** to help you make decisions about what type of trip you'd like to make. And, because we can't pretend to have explored every single corner of Asia ourselves, we've also included tips, advice and stories from lots of other travellers.

Lhasa, Tibet

Not just beaches and temples

Though it sounds unlikely, several months of undiluted beachbumming and sightseeing can get a bit dull. A satisfying way to add a different dimension is to spend a few days in a place learning a local craft or skill. Many popular tourist towns offer short, accessible tourist-oriented **courses** and these are a great way of learning more about local life and traditions. You can, for example, study woodcarving in Bali, take taekwondo lessons in Seoul and try batik painting in Indonesia. Many travellers do Thai cookery workshops, while India and Nepal are famous centres for yoga and meditation. See p.46 for more ideas.

If you wish to get involved at a deeper level, you might consider doing **voluntary work** while you're in Asia, so that your time and skills, whatever they are, benefit some of the most needy people on the planet. In return, you'll gain valuable insight into lives that are probably far removed from your own. Some travellers prefer to sign up with a volunteer-placement organization before leaving home, where opportunities can range from a week on a turtle-conservation project in Malaysia to a month helping out in a Sri Lankan orphanage; others prefer to contact local charities direct on arrival. There's advice on how to find out more about volunteering on p.23.

The opening section, **The Big Adventure**, covers the key trip-planning stage in detail. Here you'll find all the nuts and bolts info on how to choose the right ticket and what gear to pack, plus advice on how long you can afford to stay away and the best time to do it. The second half of this section looks at life on the road, advising you on how to stay safe and healthy, cultural dos and don'ts and what to expect from Asian hotels and transport.

Then comes the hard part – deciding which parts of Asia you most want to visit and which to leave out. The second section of the book, **Where To Go**, looks at your options. We focus on the 21 most accessible and most visited countries of Asia, giving you an opinionated taste of what these destinations have in store for first-timers. Each **country profile** includes a

roundup of the major highlights and tourist activities, as well as a selection of personal recommendations and lesser-known gems, plus suggestions on related books and films and contact details for tourist offices and embassies. The most remote parts of the continent, north and west of Pakistan, rarely feature on first-timers' itineraries, so we haven't included them in this book. Burma (Myanmar) is also omitted in the hope that travellers will uphold the boycott on tourism requested by Aung San Suu Kyi, the democratically elected leader of the country. Finally, the **Directory** at the back of the book is packed with useful addresses, websites and phone numbers for further information on everything from discount flight agents and travel bookshops to mosquito-net suppliers and conservation projects.

Even after you've digested *First-Time Asia,* we can't guarantee that you'll avoid every problem on the road, but hopefully you'll at least feel well prepared – and inspired. When you come back from your trip, be sure to send in your own anecdotes for inclusion in the next edition. We can promise you'll have plenty of great stories to tell.

▲ Festival dress, Kerala, India

reasons to go

Asia embraces such a range of cultures, climates and landscapes that the very diversity that makes it so appealing can also make it seem a daunting place to visit. The trick is to decide on what kinds of experiences you hope to have, rather than setting up a whirlwind tour of the major sights. What follows is a selective taste of things you could do on your adventure.

01 **Trek to the roof of the world** It's worth every iota of energy, every agonising gasp for oxygen needed to trek close to Everest from Nepal (Page **283**) or Tibet (Page **36**) or to the major peaks of the Karakoram (Page **289**).

02 Experience a local festival From Buddhist masked dancers in Bhutan (Page **222**) to Mardi-Gras style pageants in the Philippines (Page **70**), local festivals are often worth timing your visit for.

03 Paddle your own canoe Hire a kayak and set off to explore secret caves and deserted island beaches in Vietnam's Ha Long Bay (Page **336**) and Thailand's Phang Nga Bay (Page **327**).

04 Ride a tuk tuk Page **155** • These motorized rickshaws offer a high adrenalin route through the city streets. Sit back, hang on and enjoy the ride!

05 **Get a job** Page **86** • Try your luck as a Bollywood film extra in Mumbai, teach English in Korea, join a volunteer project in Sri Lanka: you don't have to be a beach bum for your entire trip.

06 **Learn to dive** Page **41** • Enter a whole new world in the tropical waters of the Philippines, Indonesia, Thailand, Timor-Leste and Malaysia.

07 **Party on the beach until sunrise** Page **327** • The Thai island of Ko Pha Ngan hosts the world's biggest beach party every full-moon night, when thirty-thousand clubbers get sandy.

08 **Hit the beach** Turquoise waters, squeaky soft sand and a fringe of palm trees – you're spoilt for choice in Malaysia (Page **271**), the Philippines (Page **293**), Sri Lanka (Page **315**) and Thailand (Page **324**).

09 **Become a surfer dude** Page **44** • Asia has caught the surfing bug in a big way – watch, learn and get wave-riding in Indonesia, Sri Lanka and the Philippines for starters.

10 **Taste the unspeakable** Page **47** • Whether it's deep-fried locusts in Thailand, snake blood in Taiwan or dried squid in Korea, Asia's night markets are the perfect place to challenge your taste buds.

11 **Do the classics** India's Taj Mahal (Page **242**), Angkor Wat in Cambodia (Page **229**), and the Great Wall of China (Page **234**) – you could see them all in a single trip.

12 **Climb a volcano** Don't tell your folks but Asia is one of the most seismically active parts of the planet and much of Asia was formed by volcanic eruptions. Climb Fuji (Japan; Page **258**), Bromo (Indonesia; Page **251**), or Pinatubo (Philippines; Page **38**).

13 **Sleep somewhere different** Page **160** • With a dozen strangers in an Iban tribal longhouse in Malaysian Borneo; in a yurt on the Mongolian plains; or in a temple in South Korea.

14 **Get armed and dang-erous**
Page **46** •
Learn kung-fu with China's Shaolin monks, Thai boxing in Bangkok or the ancient art of Kalarippayattu in south India.

15 **Survive an Asian metropolis** The sheer exuberance of life in the major Asian cities has to be experienced to be believed There's no buzz like it. Hong Kong (Page **238**), Bangkok (Page **324**), Dhaka (Page **215**) and Delhi (Page **246**).

16 Meet the ancestors Looking into the sad, knowing eyes of an orang-utan is an experience you won't forget in Indonesia (Page **253**) and Malaysia (Page **273**).

17 Find a new squeeze Page **47** • Go for an Indian head massage or a traditional Thai massage – or learn how to do it yourself.

18 Get a suit made Page **103** • Tailored to fit, and for a fraction of the cost back home. The best places to try include Hong Kong, Hoi An (Vietnam) and Bangkok.

19 Stand at the feet of the Buddha Some Buddha statues are so vast that you can only stare in awe, with neck craned as you gaze skywards. Sri Lanka (Page **314**), Taiwan (Page **321**) and Thailand (Page **324**) all feature fine examples.

First-Time Asia

The Big Adventure

Planning your trip

A vast and fascinatingly diverse continent stretches before you, so where to start? Before you come up with a shortlist of destinations you intend to visit it's worth deciding what **kind of trip** you are after as well as how long you intend to go for. Next you'll want to consider the highs and lows of **individual countries**, for which see "Where to go" in the second half of this book. Then there's the question of planning your **itinerary** – later in this chapter you'll find some suggestions for popular and creative journeys across Asia. In Chapter Five there's a roundup of pan-Asia travel literature and websites that should also be a good source of ideas. But first, consider the following:

- **The length of your trip** If money is the main consideration, check out Chapter Four to find out how far your budget will stretch.
- **The climate** Is it the right time of year to go trekking/white-water rafting/snorkelling and diving? Will it be raining all the time, or too hot to enjoy yourself? See Chapter Three for advice on this.
- **Are your proposed destinations safe at the moment?** Political turbulence and natural disasters won't enhance your trip, so consult Chapter Fourteen first.
- **Ticket options** Make some preliminary investigations into different ticket options, and check out relevant visa requirements, described in Chapter Two.
- **Think about the pace of your proposed trip** Are you going to be whizzing through places so fast that you won't have any real sense of where you are or what each country is like? Are you allowing yourself enough time and flexibility to add new places

www.roughguides.com

19

to your itinerary or linger in spots that you like a lot? Cramming too many destinations into your schedule means that you'll see far too much of the worst bits of a country, namely its bus stations and airports.

● **Is your itinerary nicely balanced?** Will you get bored if you see nothing but beaches for the next few months? Might you start longing for some hill-walking after weeks of museums and temples?

A shared experience?

Now is also the time to think about who you want to go travelling with, or if indeed you want to share your trip with anyone at all. There are obvious pluses and minuses to both options. Travelling with one or more **companions** means you always have someone to chat to and plan things with; you can mull over your experiences together and share your enthusiasms and worries; and you may well feel braver about exploring and going out in the evening if you're with someone else. On a practical level, you will save money because double and triple rooms are better value and taxi expenses will be halved; and there'll always be someone to mind the bags while one of you looks for a hotel room or nips off to buy a mango in the market.

However, travel is a surprisingly **stressful** activity: the heat, the hassle and the sheer strangeness of things are bound to fray your nerves, and guess who's going to bear the brunt of your irritability? Expect to fall out every so often, and be prepared to split up during the trip – either for a few days because you've got different priorities, or for good because your differences seem insurmountable. Bearing this in mind, you and your prospective companions should take a long hard look at your friendship and try to imagine it under stress. Will one person be making all the plans and taking all the responsibilities, and will that annoy you? Do you have broadly the same expectations of the trip and share a similar attitude to mishaps and hassles? Does one of you have a lot more money, and will that cause tension?

If travel puts a strain on friendships, imagine what it does to **relationships**. A disconcerting number of romances crack during a long cross-Asia trip, but then perhaps they weren't meant to last anyway. If yours survives it, you will have been brought closer together and will have lots of great stories and photos to coo over for many years to come.

Going solo

Solo travel is a more extreme and intense experience. You have to face up to everything on your own, and find the motivation to move on, explore and be sociable all by yourself. There will be lonely times for sure, and scary ones, and you'll probably get tired of eating out on your own every night. But you will also be a lot more open to your surroundings and you'll make more effort to chat to new people – as indeed they will to you (twosomes often put people off because they seem self-contained). Some people find that they're more alert and receptive on their own, and most single travellers write much more interesting emails and journals simply because they're desperate to blurt out all their experiences. And, of course, you have no one to answer to but yourself, which means you can change your plans at a moment's notice or idle away your days without feeling guilty.

Finding a travel companion

If you're nervous about going on your own, but can't find anyone to accompany you, all is not lost. Travel magazines, university noticeboards, newspaper personal columns and internet travel forums are full of advertisements from people looking for **travelling companions** (see Chapter Five for some leads). Most advertisers have specific itineraries in mind and will want to meet and discuss plans quite a few times; if you don't find an ad that fits your bill, why not place one yourself – bearing in mind the obvious safety precautions. Travelling with an unknown person can bring its share of unpleasant surprises, so you should definitely discuss ground rules before you go and perhaps even set off on a dummy trip – a weekend away, for example – before the big departure. But it can also be unexpectedly fun, and with any luck you'll have made a new friend by the trip's end.

Even if no one suitable turns up before you set off, you'll find it remarkably easy to hitch up with travel companions once you've arrived in Asia. The **backpackers' scene** is well established in major Asian towns, cities and beach resorts, and guesthouse noticeboards are often thick with requests for travelmates. Bangkok's Khao San Road, the Paharganj area of New Delhi, and Thamel in Kathmandu are all fruitful places to look.

Joining a tour

For some people, joining an **organized tour** is the most appealing introduction to Asia. This takes away a lot of the more daunting elements – like arranging local transport and accommodation yourself – and often means that you're accompanied by an expert whose in-depth knowledge of the country can really enhance your stay. Hundreds of tour operators offer trips to Asian destinations (see Directory, pp.343–344, for some recommendations) and the range of packages is phenomenal, from walking and cycling tours to ones that focus on culture, wildlife or cooking; a few specialize in budget travel, featuring homestay accommodation and local transport, while some offer long, slow, overland journeys lasting six months, usually in specially converted trucks and with participants sharing the chores.

A popular compromise option is to start your trip as part of an organized tour for a few weeks, then branch off by yourself when you've gained more confidence and Asia know-how; many tour operators are used to this and offer tour-only prices so that you can arrange your own flights. This is also fairly common practice on budget-minded **overland tours** (such as those run by Dragoman and Explore) and gives you a good grounding as well as the chance to meet possible onward travel companions.

A sponsored holiday

A potentially interesting way of joining a tour and exploring a country while contributing something useful is to participate in a **fundraising activity holiday** in aid of a charity. Many of the major-league charities organize one or more of these events every year; recent examples have included a fortnight's cycle ride from Ho Chi Minh City to Angkor Wat, an eight-day horse ride across the Mongolian plains, a trek along the Great Wall of China, a climb up Malaysia's Mount Kinabalu followed by trekking through the jungles of Borneo, and a trek to Everest Base Camp in the Nepali Himalayas. For some expeditions, training in advance to get fit is part of the challenge, while for others the emphasis is more on having an energetic holiday and making some money for a good cause at the same time.

Each charity has a different way of organizing these events, but most ask for a minimum amount of **sponsorship**, typically between $4000/£2500 and $6500/£4000 for a fortnight's trip. It's up to you how to get this money, though organizers usually offer advice and sometimes even practical help. Obviously some of your money is used to cover your expenses – these are holidays after all, with reasonable board and lodging provided, as well as time set aside for sightseeing where relevant – but not everyone is happy at the percentage of the fee which goes in the charity box, so check first before registering. In addition, some people feel uncomfortable that their friends, families and colleagues are effectively financing the trip – hence the increasing emphasis on the pre-trip challenge of getting fit, which shows that you're working for your sponsorship.

If you have a favourite **charity**, contact them to see if they're planning any fundraising holidays, or browse online. The long-established organization Charity Challenge (T020/8557 0000, W www.charitychallenge.com) runs many different fundraising adventure holiday programmes in Asia, most of them treks and mountain-bike rides, and has dozens of charities on its books, or you can add your own to the list. For information on working with a charity while you're in Asia, see the section on "Volunteer programmes", below.

Volunteer programmes and placements

Organizing a place on a **volunteer programme** is an increasingly popular way of anchoring a trip and giving it substance. Programmes can last anything from a week to six months, but the emphasis is always on participation in activities that contribute directly towards your host community; generally, you pay your expenses (sometimes minimal, sometimes at a premium) plus an administration fee, which can also vary considerably, as well as donating your time and skills. The big attraction is the opportunity to get involved in local life at a deeper and potentially more fulfilling level than you would as a backpacker or on a fundraising adventure holiday. Typical volunteer programmes include coral surveying in the Philippines, working in elephant conservation projects in Sri Lanka, and teaching English in Nepal. Volunteer projects vary widely and while some are very rewarding, others can feel unsatisfying, even futile. To help choose the best one, ask lots of questions before signing up and try to contact some former volunteers – a service offered by many of the most reputable outfits.

A variation on the volunteer programme is the **placement** or **internship**, whereby you get the chance to work in, say, a local newspaper, radio station, clinic, school, law firm, animal welfare centre or hotel. These placements are generally aimed at students looking for work or study experience. You pay for the privilege but the fee includes board and lodging. In some cases you will be benefiting the community, in others you'll just be learning more about the job – and the country.

A different kind of trip

When I packed in my job, I decided to go travelling for a while, but I wasn't interested in just bumming around and wanted to try and get under the surface of things instead. Indian Volunteers for Community Service (IVCS; ⓦ www .ivcs.org.uk) fitted the bill perfectly: a three-week visitors' programme at a small rural development project in northeastern India.

On our first day, we ten new volunteers were taken to town to buy traditional north Indian dress: *salwaar kameez* for the girls and pajama for the boys. This was to make us feel and act like we weren't just tourists, and to help us blend in better with the villagers of Amarpurkashi. Back at the village, we spent the next three weeks following an informal programme of yoga, Hindi lessons, cultural lectures and rural development workshops. We also worked in the kitchens, helped with the literacy campaign and gave regular English lessons at the village school.

I couldn't have asked for a better introduction to India. Though there was quite a big group of us Westerners, we all got involved in community life and experienced things tourists rarely get to see and do. By the end of the three weeks I felt acclimatized, confident and eager to do some exploring, so I spent the next five months making informal visits to development projects in other parts of India, using contacts I'd made at Amarpurkashi.

Juliet Acock

Agencies and organizers of established short-term volunteer projects, placements and internships are listed in the Directory on pp.344–347. Other useful **resources** include handbooks and directories such as **Volunteer for Development** (World Service Enquiry ⓦwww.wse.org .uk), which features general advice and a directory; and *Green Volunteers* (ⓦwww.greenvol.com), a directory of wildlife conservation projects and organizations worldwide.

You don't always need to set up your voluntary work in advance. Some **local charities** are happy to accept volunteers who walk in off the street and have no qualifications except a desire to help out for a few days; consult guidebooks and the web for details, or check the traveller-oriented collective Go MAD: Go Make a Difference ⓦwww.go-mad .org for leads.

At the other end of the spectrum, the big **international voluntary organizations** like VSO (ⓦwww.vso.org.uk), the Peace Corps (ⓦwww .peacecorps.gov) and Australian Volunteers International (ⓦwww .australianvolunteers.com) employ people for longer periods (generally for two years, but shorter placements are also available) and require specific qualifications; these jobs are always paid. For information on finding other kinds of paid work in Asia, see p.86.

Taking the kids

Many package tours are child-friendly and offer good deals, but it's also increasingly common for independent travellers, including single parents, to take their kids to Asia. **Children** are considered a huge blessing in most parts of Asia and yours will be treated accordingly. Outside the main resorts you're unlikely to find child-oriented enter-tainments, but there's usually so much going on that this shouldn't be an insurmountable drawback. And there's always the beach. The chief worry is how to keep your child healthy, but if you follow the advice given in Chapter Twelve, there's every chance that the whole family will have a hassle-free trip. As with adult travellers, certain countries or regions make for a smoother initiation into Asia than others – notably Singapore, Hong Kong, Japan and Taiwan – while China, India, Nepal and Pakistan may be better tackled after some acclimatization. Most of Southeast Asia falls somewhere in between.

Where to start?

You probably won't have much trouble deciding where to start your trip: there'll either be an obvious geographical option, or your travel agent will persuade you with an offer too tempting to ignore.

For Europeans, the usual **gateway cities** are Kathmandu, Delhi or Bangkok. These are the nearest entry points to Asia and generally the cheapest places to fly to, though low-cost carrier Air Asia (Ⓦ www.air -asia.com) has now made Kuala Lumpur an enticing alternative. Australians usually begin somewhere in Indonesia, or in Singapore. Flying to Asia from America is a more long-winded process as you're literally travelling to the other side of the planet. From the East Coast, it's faster and nearly always cheaper to go via London, Amsterdam or Frankfurt, and then on to Kathmandu, Delhi or Bangkok. If you're starting from the West Coast, the cheapest routes will probably be to Seoul, Taipei, Tokyo, Hong Kong or Singapore.

Saving money should not be the only consideration, though, and you'd be wise to think about the stress factor of your first days and nights in Asia:

- **Start yourself off gently** Many travellers find the poverty, chaos and crowds of India, for example, a very tough introduction to Asia, so you might want to begin your cross-Asia trip somewhere calmer, like Malaysia or Bali.
- **Fly in somewhere other than the big, stressful capital city** You can fly from Europe directly to Chiang Mai in north Thailand, for example, which means that by the time you've worked your way down to Bangkok (or across to Vientiane) you'll exude the confidence of an old Asia hand. Or you could make use of the burgeoning number of budget airlines operating within Asia and buy a Los Angeles–Singapore flight, say, making an immediate connection to Cambodia's Siem Reap, perhaps, or to the beaches of Krabi in south Thailand. See Chapter Two for information on the different types of air tickets available.
- **Plan an easy schedule for the first week** See Chapter Seven for more advice.

Across Asia by air

Most people choose to do their cross-Asia trip **by air**, simply because it's faster and easier than going overland. Travel agents sort out all the details for you and everything is booked in advance, which is reassuring for anxious relatives and one less headache for you. Advice on buying the best plane ticket for your trip is given in Chapter Two.

The best approach is to work out your **ideal route** before grilling the travel agent. But once you've got your core must-sees, be prepared to be flexible about the in-between bits, bearing in mind that some routes are a lot cheaper than others. If possible, leave some extra free

www.roughguides.com

25

Fear of flying

Not everyone relishes the idea of travelling to the other side of the world in a pressurized metal box. **Fear of flying** is a relatively common anxiety – apparently seriously affecting one in six adults – making overland travel a necessity rather than a choice for many people.

Though getting to Asia by land and sea can be a very enjoyable experience (see p.27), there are a number of courses and other **resources** to help those who would like to combat their dread of air travel. The self-help website ⓦ www.anxieties.com has a comprehensive section on fear of flying, with advice, practical step-by-step programmes and plenty of comparative statistics to impress on you how safe air travel actually is.

Several airlines, including British Airways and Virgin Atlantic, run regular **therapy workshops** which aim to help you deal with your fear by taking you through a simulated flight – some even culminate in a short real flight. In the UK, prices are about £200 for a one-day course and there's a directory of them on ⓦ www.airfraid.com. For workshops and self-help courses in the US, see the US section of ⓦ www.airfraid.com. In Australia, Qantas-staffed weekend courses are run by Fearless Flyers (☎ 02/9522 8455, ⓦ www .fearlessflyers.com.au; Aus$900).

The Qantas team has produced a **book**, *The Fearless Flier's Handbook* by Debbie Seaman; other books on the subject include *The Easy Way to Enjoy Flying* by Allen Carr; *Flying Without Fear* by Keith Godfrey; and *Ask the Pilot* by Patrick Smith.

For advice on how to enjoy your flight, see Chapter Seven.

time at strategic intervals so you can be spontaneous and follow up other travellers' recommendations once you're on the ground.

Before making any firm decisions about your ticket, check out the section on **overland routes** within Asia beginning on p.27. There are all sorts of intriguing bus, train and ferry routes between countries in Asia, and this can save you a lot of money on your air ticket, as well as enhancing your adventure. It's also a greener way to travel.

Round-the-world classic: UK–India–Nepal–Thailand–Malaysia–Indonesia–(Australia)–UK

This is a **classic first-time Asia itinerary** for anyone making their way there from Europe, giving you the run of the best of South and Southeast Asia with the added option of rounding off your trip in Australia. The route can be done on a round-the-world ticket, a multi-stop ticket or even on an open-jaw return – see Chapter Two for details on which ticket would be most suitable for you. For Australians, the same route applies, but in reverse, with the option of extending to Europe if you want.

The first port of call on many round-the-world trips is **Delhi**, chiefly because it's only ten hours' flying time from London. Although the Indian capital can be a stressful place for first-timers, it is well positioned for trips to Rajasthan and the Himalayas. But if you're going to head south to the beaches of Goa or Kerala, get an international flight to

Mumbai or Bangalore instead. Kolkata is a more unusual alternative, but a useful one as you can get cheap routeings to Bangkok via Dhaka in Bangladesh. From any point in India you have the choice of flying or overlanding to Kathmandu (see p.29), but to continue to Bangkok you'll have to fly as it's currently impossible to cross Burma overland.

If you decide to leave out the Indian subcontinent altogether, your trip will begin in **Bangkok**. From there, you have a choice of flying in short hops through Thailand, Malaysia, Singapore and Indonesia, or making the long trek south overland. You may also want to factor in enough time to explore Laos, Cambodia and Vietnam from Thailand first, either overland or by local airlines. Travelling from Bangkok to Bali by bus, train and boat will save you heaps of money, but is obviously a lot more time-consuming. If you want to stop off for a while in all four countries en route then allow yourself at least two to three months for this part of the trip. There's a lot of ground to cover – Sumatra, for example, is the fourth largest island in the world – and the whole adventure becomes a real slog if you try to cram it all into three weeks.

In fact, the most popular route **south from Bangkok** is a combination of flying and overlanding. You can either weave a couple of flights into your round-the-world ticket before you go (for example, between Malaysia and Sumatra, and between Java and Bali), or buy flights in Asia as and when you get tired of long bus journeys. Bangkok is a good centre for cheap flights (visit ⓦwww.statravel.co.th for a list of sample fares), there's a growing number of budget Southeast Asian airlines (ⓦwww.airasia.com, ⓦwww.jetstarasia.com, ⓦwww.berjaya-air .com, ⓦwww.fireflyz.com, ⓦbangkokair.com), and internal flights within Indonesia are both inexpensive and extensive. Long-distance overnight trains and buses cover the Thai–Malaysian–Singapore peninsula, and you can easily island-hop all the way from south Thailand and Malaysia to Bali and even on to Timor-Leste if you have the time.

Overland routes into Asia from Europe and Australia

For some travellers, the process of getting to Asia is part of the whole adventure, and choosing to go **overland** will vastly reduce your carbon footprint. A single flight from London to Beijing for example adds 0.72 tonnes of CO_2 per passenger; doing it by rail adds just 0.23 tonnes. However, time is a major factor here, and the expense may be off-putting too: though trains, buses and boats are generally cheaper than flights, you will have spent a fair bit on accommodation and food before you even arrive in Asia.

Delhi to London on a motorbike

After six months exploring India on an elderly Enfield Bullet, bought in Delhi for £600, I thought the bike would make a good souvenir. Shipping it was an option, but somehow riding the 10,000-odd miles home across Asia seemed a lot more interesting…

My route was a fairly standard one, taking me through Pakistan (with a side-trip up the Karakoram Highway into the northern hills), and then on to Iran and Turkey. Over the next five months, I rode through some of the most stunning and least-tourisced areas of Asia, beneath soaring mountains, through barren deserts and across fertile plains. All the way along, people were exceptionally hospitable – there was always someone around to help me decipher squiggly road signs, direct me to a mechanic or, frequently, invite me home to stay with the family.

The gradual transition from East to West was fascinating: the culture, climate and terrain changed imperceptibly day by day. On top of that, there was something immensely satisfying about tracing a line on the map across two continents and actually following it on the ground.

Nicki McCormick

The overland **routes** listed below are just a handful of the possible options. Though we've described them as routes **into** Asia, they're quite feasible when done in reverse. It's almost, but not quite, possible to travel all the way from Australia to Britain (and back) without resorting to an aeroplane. The only hiatus comes when you need to cross the sea between northern Australia and Timor-Leste. Unless you cadge a ride on a yacht or a cargo boat, you'll have to get an Airnorth flight (ⓦ www.airnorth.com.au) from Darwin to Dili in Timor-Leste, after which you can island-hop all the way to Singapore. In reality, most Australians choose the easy option and fly straight into Bali, beginning their journeys from there.

Once in Asia you have the option of continuing your travels by road, rail and river (see "Overland routes within Asia", p.30), or you can buy a series of air tickets as you go.

Some people choose to travel overland to Asia under their own steam, either **in a car or on a motorbike**, typically along the route blazed by the hippie travellers of the 1960s and 70s. Though it is also possible to buy a vehicle in Asia and travel back home with your own wheels, this option entails even more paperwork; the bureaucracy involved in riding a motorbike back from India, for example, is so overwhelming that some travellers give up before they even get started.

The Trans-Siberian Railway: by train to China

The **Trans-Siberian Railway** is *the* classic overland route into Asia. Beginning in Moscow it leads you on a slow transition from Europe to Asia, via the endless Siberian wastes and Russia's vast Lake Baikal. It's a fabulous chance to watch and absorb the unfolding of lives and landscapes between continents and a great way to acclimatize yourself to the rhythm of travel. However, it's nowhere near as cheap as flying one-way to Beijing, and you need to plan your paperwork quite carefully.

Each of the three trans-Russia trains begin in Moscow and travel east to Irkutsk, beyond which the line divides into three: the **Trans-Mongolian** route branches off to Beijing via Ulaanbaatar, the **Trans-Manchurian** route also goes to Beijing, but via Harbin, while the **Trans-Siberian** proper goes to Vladivostok via Khabarovsk. Taking the Trans-Mongolian route from Moscow to Beijing means spending six days on the train, while the Trans-Manchurian route from Moscow to Beijing takes seven days. If you are patient, have lots of time and have paid meticulous attention to visa requirements, you can then continue by train from Beijing to Hanoi in **Vietnam** (2 days; see ⓦwww.seat61.com/China.htm). If you choose the Trans-Siberian route from Moscow you'll end up in Vladivostok (7 days), from where there are more or less weekly ferries to Fushiki in **Japan** (ⓦwww.bisintour.com; 39hr) and to Sokcho in **South Korea** with Dong Chun Ferry (ⓦenglish.visitkorea.or.kr; 48hr).

Standard Trans-Siberian **tickets** for any of the three routes are direct and do not permit stops or side-trips; if you want to dally en route you'll need to go through a specialist tour operator, who can also arrange all the visas and other paperwork. The main routes are very popular so booking ahead is essential, even for non-stop services: fares booked through Real Russia (ⓦrealrussia.co.uk) start at $620/£380 for non-stop journeys from Moscow to either Beijing or Vladivostok. A rail ticket from London to Moscow adds another $490/£300. Sundowners travel agency offer budget Trans-Siberia packages for 18- to 35-year-olds on their Vodka Train tour (ⓦwww.vodkatrain.com; from $1300/£795).

For a full rundown of everything you need to know about visas, life on the train and **ideas** for stopoffs, see the *Trans-Siberian Handbook,* published by Trailblazer, and the exceptionally detailed The Man in Seat Sixty-One website at ⓦwww.seat61.com/Trans-Siberian.htm.

The hippie trail: from Europe to Kathmandu via Turkey, Iran, Pakistan and India

In the flower-power days of the 1960s and 70s, the most popular route for adventurous, spiritually curious, budget travellers was to meander slowly **overland from Istanbul to Kathmandu**, taking in Iran, Afghanistan, Pakistan and India along the way. The route came to be known as the hippie trail and, almost a half a century later, it's still a fascinating way of travelling between Europe and Asia. These days, international politics permitting, the most common way to do this route is by car or motorbike, though it's also possible by public transport or with an organized tour.

With your own vehicle, if you put your foot down and ignore the temptations of the countries en route, you can reach Delhi from London in 21 days. However, doing it this way obviously involves some serious preparation, both for yourself and your vehicle. The **paperwork** is the biggest headache – visas need to be sorted out well in advance of your departure date, especially for Iran, and you will also need a special document for your vehicle known as a **carnet de passage**. Bikers should check out Trailblazer's *The Adventure Motorcycling Handbook*, which contains full details of all these requirements, as do the forums at ⓦwww.horizonsunlimited.com, which are also relevant to car-drivers and have links to many travellers' blogs and other useful resources. For an account of biking through Asia, see ⓦwww.chrison2wheels.com and its author's e-book, **Southeast Asia on 2 Wheels**.

Some **tour operators** (such as Dragoman and Exodus; see Directory, p.343) organize group overland trips along these routes in converted lorries. The trips take from four to thirty weeks, the age range is generally 18 to 40, and the all-inclusive cost is quite reasonable. If you're nervous about setting off for Asia on your own, then this could be a good way to start.

Overland routes within Asia

Before fixing your ticket routeing, think about spicing up your flight itinerary with some **overland routes** in between. It's a great feeling to watch from a train window as one country slowly metamorphoses into

▲ Travelling overland leaves a smaller carbon footprint

Long-distance cycling

Three of the world's classic cycle routes are in Asia, all of them mountain routes and all of them challenging: **Lhasa–Kathmandu**, from Tibet to Nepal; the **Karakoram Highway**, between China and Pakistan; and **Leh–Manali** in the Indian Himalayas. If you time it right, to get the most favourable weather and road conditions, this is an unbeatable way to experience these regions. Not only do you appreciate the landscape a lot more when you're pedalling every contour and reacting to every slight change in weather and altitude, but you're also off the beaten track a lot of time, stopping for food, water or lodging in villages you'd otherwise zip past. The Trailblazer **guidebook** *Himalaya by Bicycle* (ⓦwww .pocketsprocket.com) describes all three routes in great detail, and other useful Trailblazer cycling guides include *Adventure Cycle-Touring Handbook* (ⓦwww.adventurecycle-touring handbook.com), which features routes, practical advice and first-hand adventure-cycling tales for Asia and the rest of the world; and *Tibet Overland* for routes through and between Tibet, China and Nepal.

Southeast Asia is a less extreme region for long-distance cycling: the website Biking Southeast Asia with Mr Pumpy (ⓦwww.mrpumpy.net) covers cycle trips across Vietnam, Malaysia, Cambodia, Thailand, Indonesia and India and has a long list of Asian-cycling links. Another good resource is Bike Sutra (ⓦwww.bikesutra.com/asia_cycling.html), which has many links to trip reports about cycling in Asia

If you want a bit of back-up en route, several tour-operators run **cycle-tours** along some of the best Asian routes: established companies include SpiceRoads (ⓦwww .spiceroads.com) and Red Spokes (ⓦwww.redspokes.com).

another – far more satisfying than whizzing over international borders at thirty thousand feet – and in nearly every case it will be a lot cheaper than flying. It's a lot more environmentally friendly and sometimes also quicker and more convenient than backtracking to the airport in the capital city. Overlanding under your own steam, especially by bicycle can also be an exhilarating way to travel; see box above for more.

Having the right **paperwork** is essential for overland routes, as most countries demand that you specify the exact land border when applying – see Chapter Two for more advice on this, and be sure to check out the viability of your proposed overland route before making any firm flight bookings.

You'll find a detailed list of the current designated **border crossings** in Asia on pp.32–33, and there's more detail in the individual country profiles on pp.215–340.

Southeast Asia: Thailand–Malaysia–Singapore–Indonesia

By far the most popular overland route within Asia is the trip down **from Thailand into Malaysia**. Having lingered on the coasts and islands of southern Thailand (Ko Samui, Ko Pha Ngan, Ko Phi Phi and Ko Lipe to name just a few), you can cross into Malaysia quite effortlessly by bus, minibus or ferry. Train travel via Hat Yai is also possible, but

Border crossings and international ferries

All the **border crossings** listed below are open to foreign travellers and, except where stated, are currently accessible from both sides. Burma and Sri Lanka are currently the only two countries that are inaccessible to overlanders.

Indian subcontinent

Pakistan–China By bus along the Karakoram Highway from Sost (Pakistan) to Tashkurgan (China).

India–Pakistan Bus or train from Amritsar to Lahore via Attari and Wagha.

India–China No overland crossing allowed.

India–Bangladesh From Kolkata to Dhaka (via Haridaspur and Benapole) to Dhaka by train and bus; from Shillong via Dawki/Tarnabil to Sylhet by bus. Also, from West Bengal: between Burimari and Patgram; Balurghat and Hili; and Lalgola and Godagari; plus from Agartala in Tripura to Akhaura.

India–Sri Lanka Owing to the unrest in Sri Lanka, the ferry service between the two countries is suspended indefinitely.

India–Nepal Several crossings convenient for foreigners, including: by bus from Delhi, Varanasi or Gorakhpur (via Sonauli and Bhairawa) to Mahendra Nagar, Pokhara or Kathmandu; by bus from Bodh Gaya, Kolkata or Patna (via Raxaul and Birganj) to Pokhara or Kathmandu; and by bus and/or train from Siliguri, Darjeeling or Kolkata to Kakarbitta. Other borders crossings into western Nepal at Banbassa, Dhangadhi and Nepalganj.

Bhutan–India By road from Thimpu via Phuntsoling to Siliguri or Darjeeling; and by road via Samdrup Jongkhar to Assam district (this route is not permissible in reverse).

Nepal–China (Tibet) Currently not allowed for independent travellers on public transport (though it is permitted in the other direction). However, foreigners who have booked inclusive tours of Lhasa (these can be arranged in Kathmandu) are allowed to cross here; the tour companies organize the paperwork.

Southeast Asia

Thailand–Malaysia and Singapore Because of ongoing separatist violence in far southern Thailand the safest overland routes depart from Satun province: by minibus to Kangar, by ferry to Kuala Perlis or Langkawi and by boat from Ko Lipe to Langkawi. The direct trains from Bangkok to Penang, Kuala Lumpur and Singapore travel via Hat Yai, in Thailand's troubled far south, so check government travel advisories first.

Malaysia–Singapore By bus, train or ferry.

Malaysia and Singapore–Indonesia By ferry or speedboat from Penang to Medan (Sumatra); from Melaka to Dumai (Sumatra); from Johor Bahru or Singapore to Pulau Batam and Pulau Bintan (Riau archipelago). By bus from Kuching (Sarawak) via Entikong to Pontianak (Kalimantan). By ferry from Tawau (Sabah) to Pulau Tarakan (Kalimantan).

Malaysia–The Philippines By ferry from Sandakan (Sabah) to Zamboanga (Mindanao).

Indonesia (West Timor)–Timor-Leste By bus from Kupang to Dili via Batugede. By road into Oecussi via Oesilo.

Indochina

Thailand–Laos By bus or train from Nong Khai to Vientiane; by bus from Mukdahan to Savannakhet; by ferry across and along the Mekong River from Chiang Khong (via Houayxai) to Louang Phabang; by bus from Chong Mek (via Ban Mai Sing Amphon) to Pakxe; from Nakhon Phanom (via Thakhek) to Vientiane.

Thailand–Cambodia By bus and boat or share-taxi from Trat to Sihanoukville and Phnom Penh (via Ban Hat Lek and Koh Kong). By bus and train from Aranyaprathet to Sisophon and Siem Reap (via Poipet). By bus from Surin (via Kap Choeng/O'Smach) to Anlong Veng. Via Sa Ngam near Si Saket province to Choam. By chartered minibus from Pong Nam Ron to Ban Laem or Phsa Prom for Pailin.

Cambodia–Laos By boat and bus from Stung Treng to Don Khong (Si Phan Don) and Pakxe (via Voen Kham).

Laos–Vietnam By bus from Savannakhet and Xepon to Hué or Hanoi, via Lao Bao and Dong Ha. By bus from Lak Xao to Vinh, (via Kaew Nua and Cau Treo). Via Ban Nong Het to Vinh; via Na Maew to Nam Xoi; via Bo Y to Kon Tum; and via Tay Trang to Dien Bien Phu.

Vietnam–Cambodia By bus and share-taxi from Ho Chi Minh City to Phnom Penh (via Moc Bai and Bavet). By taxi, boat and bus from Chau Doc and the Mekong Delta to Phnom Penh (via K'am Samnar); and from the Mekong Delta and Phu Quoc island to Kampot and Kep (via Phnom Den and Prek Chak). From Pleiku to Ban Lung (via Le Tanh and O'Yadaw).

Vietnam–China By bus or rail from Hanoi (via Dong Dang and Pingxiang) to Nanning; by bus or rail from Hanoi and Lao Cai (via Hekou) to Kunming in Yunnan; with your own transport from Haiphong to Nanning (Guangxi) via Mong Cai and Dongxing.

Laos–China By bus from Oudomxai and Louang Namtha (via Boten/Mo Han) to Jinghong (Yunnan).

China, Mongolia and Japan

China–Mongolia By train (Trans-Mongolian Express) or bus from Beijing or Hohhot to Ulaanbaatar (via Erenhot and Zamyn-Uud).

China (Tibet)–Nepal Informal shared jeeps via Zhangmu to Kathmandu, but not allowed going from Nepal into Tibet unless on a tour.

China–South Korea By ferry to Incheon (near Seoul) from Tianjin (near Beijing), Qingdao and Weihai (both in Shandong), and Dalian and Dandong (both in Liaoning) and Lianyungang (Jiangsu).

China–Taiwan None.

Taiwan–Japan By ferry from Keelung and Kaohsiung to Naha in Okinawa.

China–Japan By ferry from Shanghai to Osaka and Kobe, from Tianjin (near Beijing) to Kobe, and from Qingdao and Suzhou to Shimonoseki.

Japan–South Korea By ferry and hydrofoil from Shimonoseki, Fukuoka and Osaka to Busan.

because of ongoing separatist violence in far southern Thailand the safest routes are via Satun and Ko Lipe instead. Not surprisingly, Bangkok–Kuala Lumpur is a common "surface sector" leg on round-the-world, Circle-Asia and open-jaw tickets (see Chapter Two). Some people round off this overland route with a few days on the island of Singapore, which is connected to southern Malaysia by a causeway.

A relatively popular extension to the Thailand–Malaysia route is to continue on **into Indonesia by sea**. There are frequent ferries and speedboats from various ports in Malaysia to Sumatra, and from Johor Bahru and Singapore to Indonesia's Riau archipelago.

Indochina: Thailand–Laos–Vietnam–Cambodia–Thailand

The overland trail **from Thailand across Indochina** is becoming increasingly well travelled, and makes an interesting circular route that can be done without ever taking to the air. There are numerous border crossings between Thailand, Laos, Vietnam and Cambodia, with through-transport available by bus or river-boat, and new routes open frequently. Visa formalities are mostly straightforward (see Chapter Two), but bear in mind that road transport in Laos and Cambodia is very slow and can be exhaustingly uncomfortable.

Overland from China to Thailand via Indochina

As China has useful land borders with both Laos and Vietnam, the Indochina circuit described above can easily be adapted into a smooth overland link **between China and Thailand**, and makes it feasible to do the entire journey from London to Ho Chi Minh City by train.

By bus from India to Nepal

Overlanding **between India and Nepal** is straightforward and popular, and a useful surface sector in Circle Asia and open-jaw tickets (see Chapter Two). There are many border crossings, but the easiest approaches are from Patna (in the state of Bihar) and Gorakhpur (Uttar Pradesh), which between them have useful train services to and from Delhi, Varanasi, Darjeeling, Gaya and Kolkata. Patna buses connect via Raxaul for Kathmandu while from Gorakhpur you go via Sonauli for bus connections to Pokhara or Kathmandu.

India to China via Pakistan and the Karakoram Highway

This unusual trans-Asia route is longer and more challenging than the classic version through India and Southeast Asia, as travel is relatively difficult in **Pakistan** (even dangerous in some regions, so check government travel advisories as outlined in Chapter Fourteen) and can be irksome in **China**. Travellers are rarer, which for many is part of the appeal. Regional politics permitting, the Pakistan–China section can be woven into all sorts of Asian and round-the-world itineraries, including as the surface sector of an open-jaw return or a Circle Asia flight (described in Chapter Two) that drops you in Delhi and then takes you out of Bangkok or Singapore a few months later.

Delhi is the obvious entry point to India if you're heading up to Pakistan: it's about seven hours by train to Amritsar, where trains and buses cross to the Pakistani city of Lahore (about 12hr).

From Pakistan you can take a bus into China along the spectacular 13,000-kilometre **Karakoram Highway** (KKH), which starts in Rawalpindi and goes via Gilgit and Hunza to Kashgar in far northwest China. The journey takes about four days but is only possible between May and October when the 4695-metre Kunjerab Pass on the border is not snowbound. The KKH is also one of Asia's best known long-distance cycling routes, taking from three weeks to complete: see the box on p.31 for more info. Kashgar is on the railway line, so from here the rest of China is but a (very long) train ride away.

Riding high

I'm not a sporty person (a school report once read "We think that Laura could enjoy PE, but we've never seen her doing any"), but since my first experience of long-distance cycling in India I haven't really looked back. I went on to complete a two-year bike trip covering the length of the Himalayas and wrote it up for *Himalaya by Bicycle* (reviewed p.31).

The cycle trips aren't about sport – it's more a way of travelling that is totally independent, and brilliantly simple: just get on the bike and ride! Buses leach energy, but travelling by bike makes you look after yourself and keeps you strong and healthy. You take in one hundred percent of what's going on around you – there's no chance to fall asleep and miss it all.

The hardest part is always leaving. I'll have the idea for the trip, tell my family about it, and then privately wonder why I want to head off for places like Pakistan by myself, on a bicycle…But the minute I sniff a new country in my nostrils, the change of heat, the light…I'm pulled in straight away.

Laura Stone

By sea from China and Russia to South Korea and Japan

If you're in eastern China, it's quite possible and inexpensive, if time-consuming, to take a **boat across to South Korea** (minimum 14hr) and then continue by hydrofoil or **ferry to Japan** (3–17hr); see the excellent South Korean tourist board website (ⓦenglish.visitkorea.or.kr) for full details. Or you could take a direct **ferry from China to Japan** (about 4hr). There are also useful ferry services out of Vladivostok, at the end of Russia's Trans-Siberian line, to the Japanese port of Fushiki, and to Sokcho in South Korea.

Themes for travel

Rather than base your trip round tourist sights and famous landscapes, you might consider planning it around specific **activities** instead. We've selected some popular highlights below. You'll find specialist guidebooks covering some of these themes, though any decent travel guide should have at least a few pointers on a country's most interesting activities.

Trekking and hiking

There's plenty of scope for interesting **treks and hikes** in Asia, and you don't necessarily have to be an experienced walker to enjoy them. In Asia, the word "trek" is generally used to refer to a long-distance walk, with one or more nights spent in tents or lodgings en route. "Hike" usually means a walk taking a day or less.

In many cases you can do hikes and treks unassisted, so long as you have a decent route map. But in some places you'd be foolhardy to go without a **guide**: jungles, for example, are notoriously hard to navigate, even with a map, and high mountain passes are usually best negotiated with a local expert. For long, arduous treks you'll probably need to hire a porter as well, to help carry tents and food. Travellers often join forces to arrange cheaper group treks, and in the more established places tour operators organize daily group treks along standard routes.

Don't forget to check on the **climate** (mid-June to late September, for example, is hopeless for trekking in the Himalayas), and remember to pack suitable clothes and footwear (see Chapter Six).

Here's a selective roundup of hikes and treks to whet your appetite:

- **Bhutan** Masses of hiking and trekking potential, from short, scenic walks along river valleys or up mountainsides to visit temples and monasteries, to the 24-day Lunana Snowman Trek across half of the country.
- **China** Highlights include the one- to three-day trek through the alpine scenery of Sichuan to the spectacular tongue of ice known as Hailuo Guo Glacier; hiking in the hills around Xinjiang's Tian Chi (Heaven Lake), surrounded by snowy peaks and pine forests and staying in Kazakh nomads' tents; and the two-day trek through Tiger Leaping Gorge in Yunnan, the world's deepest canyon. Much more arduous, but popular nonetheless, is the three-day, 58-kilometre circumnavigation of Tibet's sacred Mount Kailash, stopping at monasteries en route.
- **India** There are challenging Himalayan treks of two to twelve days through forests and valleys, alongside mountain streams, past remote

villages, and over sometimes snowy passes, with constant Himalayan views on all sides. The less difficult routes start from Dharamsala; the more strenuous ones – through the Zanskar and Ladakh regions – begin in Leh. See *Trekking in Ladakh* (Trailblazer) for a comprehensive account.

- **Indonesia** One-day volcano hikes are plentiful and rewarding, including the sunrise walk up Java's awesome Mount Bromo and the hike up Keli Mutu on Flores to see its famous three-coloured crater lakes. West Papua's Baliem Valley offers scores of flatter trails through cultivated land to Dani tribal villages. Among longer treks, one of the most popular takes you up to Gunung Rinjani's crater rim on Lombok, a two- to four-day expedition that can also include the crater lake and, for the very fit, the summit. Another highlight is the six-day route through Gunung Leuser National Park in north Sumatra, from Ketambe to the orang-utan sanctuary in Bukit Lawang.

- **Malaysia** Almost everyone who makes it across to Sabah, the Malaysian part of Borneo, attempts the two-day hike to the summit of Mount Kinabalu (4101m). Neighbouring Sarawak offers some strenuous day-hikes in Gunung Mulu National Park, through rainforest to the razor-sharp fifty-metre-high limestone pinnacles, plus access to parts of the largest cave system in the world, while the

Trekking in Tibet

Trekking to the sacred Mount Kailash in Tibet, we saw no one for days, with the exception of sheep, yaks and a few nomads. An unforgiving wind swept across the plateau, and there were no trees, just low bushes, random rocks, high mountains and rolling hills. I had been told that we would see no one until we reached the mountain, but the desolate and almost Martian landscape made me long all the more for people.

The rivers we crossed were too cold for bathing, and plumbing was nonexistent. Thinking I was an eco-traveller, I carried plastic bags in which to dispose of my toilet paper. But I soon noticed trash and human waste scattered across the land, in the middle of nowhere, like it belonged there. Perhaps it had been dropped by pilgrims on their way to Kailash, or by Western tour groups from the windows of their Land Cruisers.

When we finally reached the mountain, the home of the Hindu god Shiva, and the centre of the Buddhist universe, happy pilgrims appeared. Finally, people! Pilgrims older than my deceased grandparents had walked 56km in a single day – at altitudes of over 4500 metres. One had walked all the way from Delhi, slept out in the open and crossed the Himalayas barefoot. In contrast, I wore heavy winter gear, walked no more than ten steps before having to gasp for breath, and slept inside a tent, wrapped in a down sleeping bag. Circling the mountain took three days of walking through blizzard conditions but each step was worth it, especially as I looked at the sheer dedication of those around me.

Karen Christine Lefere

Bario Loop is a tougher five-day experience in the jungle of the Kelabit highlands near the Kalimantan border, with nights spent at longhouses en route. On Peninsular Malaysia, the biggest draw is Taman Negara National Park, which has a good selection of one- to four-day trails through the rainforest, some of them taking in observation hides en route.

- **Nepal** The Nepal Himalayas are the most popular area in Asia for trekking. Among the many highlights, the three-week Annapurna loop takes you up to a challenging 5416m, and the several Everest climbs are similarly tough, though not prohibitive if you're fit. The Langtang and Helambu routes are less demanding and there are literally scores of other options (see p.283). Independent trekking is quite feasible (though check the current security situation first), but guides, porters and organized tours are also available from Kathmandu and Pokhara. For detailed practical info, consult the relevant trekking guides published by Trailblazer, such as *Trekking in the Everest Region* and *Trekking in the Annapurna Region.*

- **Pakistan** In the north of the country, where the Himalayas, Karakoram and Hindu Kush mountain ranges collide, you'll find some of the best, and least crowded, trekking in the world. The trekking centres of Shigar near Skardu, Gilgit and Chitral all offer treks that last from one day to several weeks, with the chance to take in glaciers and 5500-metre passes.

- **Philippines** Highlights include the steep four-day ascent and descent into sacred Mount Banahaw's thickly forested crater, in Quezon National Park; the picturesque day-long hike through sculptured rice-paddy valleys to the traditional village of Batad in Ifugao; and the trek up to the impressive crate lake on eerie, volcanic Mount Pinatubo.

- **South Korea** This country has seventeen national parks, nearly all of them offering scores of well-maintained trails. One of the best is Seorak-San National Park, whose tracks run via craggy peaks and forested slopes, taking in waterfalls, Zen temples and mineral springs along the way. Other good ones are Jiri-san, which has long trails through the mountains, and the wooded valleys of Songni-san, where you'll come across lots of important temples and hermitages while hiking.

- **Sri Lanka** The night-time trek up Adam's Peak in time for the sunrise is one of the highlights of the country.

- **Taiwan** Several good trails in the central mountain ranges, especially around Sun Moon Lake, from Alishan to view the sunrise from the peak of 2490-metre Chu Shan, and the reasonably challenging trek up Yushan, which at 3952m is the highest mountain in East Asia.

- **Thailand** A huge percentage of visitors to Thailand go jungle-trekking in the northern hills around Chiang Mai, Chiang Rai and Pai, mainly to see hill-tribe villages but also for elephant rides and white-water rafting. There's more remote and less commercial trekking from Umphang, or head for the steamy southern jungles of Khao Sok National Park.

Wildlife spotting

Asia is home to some of the most unusual animals in the world, including the **tigers** and **elephants** of India and Indonesia, the **snow leopard** of northern Nepal, the **yaks** of the Himalayas and Tibetan plateau, and the **orang-utans** of Kalimantan, Sumatra and Sarawak, not to mention scores of extraordinary birds. Many of these creatures are now endangered, as the pressure from an expanding human population and the continued trade in rare species threatens their existence, so you're unlikely to happen across many of them on a random hike in the mountains or the jungle. However, Asia has a fair number of **national parks** where rare fauna and flora are, at least in theory, protected from poachers, and some are accessible to tourists.

Listed below are the cream of the pack, highlighted because you have a good chance of seeing wildlife there and can travel independently without much trouble. You'll need to be careful about the **timing** of your visit to any national park, as birds and animals tend to be more social and therefore easier to spot at certain times of the year. Consult relevant guidebooks for advice on this, or consider taking a specialist wildlife tour with one of the operators listed on pp.343–344. For bird guides to Asia, John MacKinnon's *Field Guide to the Birds of Borneo, Sumatra, Java and Bali* is a classic.

- **Bangladesh** At the crossroads of India and Southeast Asia, Bangladesh has a wide diversity of wildlife, particularly birds. The mangrove swamps and coastal wetlands of the Sunderbans are good for cranes and golden eagles (and there's a very remote possibility of seeing a Bengal tiger here, too). The Madhupur Forest Reserve is renowned for its brown wood owl and the dusky owl, and you'll see rhesus monkeys and langurs here as well. Several species of pochards and teals visit the Sunamganj wetlands in Sylhet, as do crakes and various fishing eagles.
- **Bhutan** The snow leopard is the most elusive of Himalayan creatures but you do have a chance of seeing one on longer treks. And there's always the yeti to think about while you're waiting.
- **India** The tiger population is famously in decline in India, but you've a reasonable chance of spotting one at Kanha Tiger Reserve

and in Bandhavgarh and Ranthambore national parks. Wild elephants are a little more common, and best looked for in the Periyar Wildlife Sanctuary and Corbett National Park. Kaladeo National Park is one of the most famous bird reserves in the world, with huge breeding colonies of cranes, storks, flamingoes and ibis, and the winter population of cranes in the desert village of Keechen is a similarly impressive sight.

● **Indonesia** Highlights on Sumatra include the Bukit Lawang orang-utan sanctuary, and the hornbills, Argus pheasants and numerous other birds of Kerinci-Seblat National Park. On Komodo, everyone goes to gawp at the enormous and ferocious monitor lizards known as Komodo dragons; while West Papua is famous for its spectacular birdlife, including birds of paradise (best seen in Pulau Yapen), and innumerable cockatoos, parrots and cassowaries, along with heaps of gorgeous butterflies.

● **Malaysia** There are common sightings of gibbons, macaques and monitor lizards in the easily accessible Taman Negara National Park on the peninsula. In Sabah, the big draws are the Sepilok Orang Utan Sanctuary, the flowers of Sabah's Mount Kinabalu – including a thousand species of orchid, 26 types of rhododendron, and various bizarre insect-eating pitcher plants – and the chance of seeing the proboscis monkey, found only in Borneo and most likely spotted along Sabah's Kinabatangan River. Gunung Mulu

▲ Snapping a rhino, Nepal

National Park in Sarawak is renowned for its phenomenal birdlife, which includes eight species of hornbill.

- **Nepal** Trekkers rarely see any interesting mammals in the mountains but on the plains of the Tarai there's a good chance of spotting rhinos, monkeys and possibly bears at the popular Chitwan National Park. Langurs and wild pig are frequently sighted in Bardia National Park, and there are occasional encounters with rhinos, tigers and Gangetic dolphins. Swamp deer, crocodiles and awesome birdlife, including cranes, cormorants and eagles, are good enough reasons to visit Suklaphanta Wildlife Reserve.
- **Sri Lanka** Bundala National Park is famously rewarding for bird-watching, and is especially known for flamingoes. There's a reasonable chance of spotting wild elephants in Yala National Park, but Millennium Elephant Foundation is the place to see dozens of them at extremely close quarters.

Saving the world, one reef at a time

Ok, I admit it: I'm a wimp. I'd always wanted to learn to dive but the murky, freezing waters of the UK had put me off for years. The perfect solution arrived in the form of a six-week expedition with Coral Cay Conservation – the location looked like the set of *The Beach*, an idyllic strip of white sand and palm trees off the remote island of Palawan in the Philippines, my fellow islanders a small band of local scientists and like-minded volunteers from across the globe.

The first couple of weeks were spent scuba training and memorizing the names of the countless tropical fish and coral species we were to encounter out on the reefs. Then came the actual work: 6am starts, survey dives twice a day, evenings spent inputting data on a solar-powered laptop and helping out with the chores – everything from baking bread to maintaining our eco-friendly composting toilet. While this probably isn't everyone's idea of paradise, the sense of camaraderie and the feeling of doing something positive for the environment is an experience I'll never forget; in fact, I'm saving up for my next expedition right now.

Coral Cay Conservation run forest and marine projects throughout the world, helping local people to manage their resources in a sustainable way; see Ⓦwww.coralcay.org.

Andy Turner

Diving

Internationally certified **scuba-diving courses** are cheaper in Asia than in most other parts of the world and, once you've done your training, the underwater world is yours. The reef life is as diverse, prolific and fascinating as anywhere on the planet, and as the water tends to be bath temperature you won't always need a full wetsuit. You will find reputable dive schools in all the major resorts listed below, and the same places also organize dive trips and rent out equipment. The worldwide Professional Association of Diving Instructors, or PADI (Ⓦwww.padi.com), keeps

www.roughguides.com

an up-to-date list of PADI-registered dive centres around the world, as does the National Association of Underwater Instructors (ⓦwww .naui.org). In Thailand, the four-day open-water PADI course costs as little as $295/£175, about half what it costs in the UK or US; in the Philippines, dive excursions to local reefs cost from $25/£15, including equipment and one tank, or from $1200/£735 for a week's all-inclusive live-aboard dive package to the more remote and exceptional reefs.

Though you can dive year-round in Asia, some seas become too rough and visibility drops during the rainy season (see Chapter Three), so do some research before fixing your trip. There are a number of specialist **diving guidebooks**, all of which describe and illustrate the marine life as well as detailing the best dive sites; try *Diving Southeast Asia* (Periplus) or *Diving Southeast Asia* (Footprint), or New Holland's individual *Globetrotter Dive Guides* to Thailand, Indonesia, Malaysia and the Philippines. The Diving Asia Pacific website (ⓦwww.divingasia pacific.com) is also not a bad starting point, with summaries of major sites, dive-centre ads and links.

- **Indonesia** Boasting warm, clear waters and a breathtakingly diverse marine life, Indonesia offers masses of quality dive sites. The most accessible of these are found off north and west Bali; off the Gili islands in Lombok; and in Sulawesi at the Bunaken-Manado Tua Marine Park. Flores is also becoming an increasingly popular diving destination and there's great diving at the more remote Pulau Derawan, off northeastern Kalimantan. If you're on a generous budget, live-aboard charters open up areas off Maluku and West Papua.

- **Malaysia**'s best diving facilities are centred on Pulau Tioman, but there are lots more dive centres on other east-coast islands, including Pulau Perhentian, Pulau Redang and Pulau Kapas. Aficionados head for Pulau Sipadan off Sabah.

- The thousands of islands that make up the **Philippines** archipelago are ringed by over four thousand square kilometres of reef, making this one of Asia's most important diving destinations. The main centres are at Moabal, Puerto Galera and Boracay, but the finest reefs are off the Palawan Islands and Occidental Mindoro, and there are exciting shipwreck dives off Busuangra.

- **Thailand**'s small, traveller-oriented island of Ko Tao has over 50 dive companies and is the largest dive-training centre in Southeast Asia, with access to many of the country's best reefs. Other exceptional dive sites include the island chains of Ko Similan and Ko Surin, within reach of popular dive resorts at Khao Lak, Phuket and throughout the Krabi area.

- **Timor-Leste** Still way off most beaten tracks, this tiny country offers spectacular, world-class diving without the crowds. As well as several impressive wall dives, especially near Tutuala, there are plenty of chances to swim with manta rays, sharks, turtles and dugongs.

Chasing the adrenaline rush

For most people, a bus trip on the Trans-Sumatran Highway, several hours in a tiny, overladen ferry boat in heaving seas, or a few minutes aboard some of the domestic airlines, generate quite enough excitement. But there are all sorts of other ways to **spice up your trip**, some of which are listed below. For more inspiration, and tales from the hot seat, have a look at the online version of the Hong Kong-based magazine *Action Asia,* ⓦwww.actionasia.com, which covers everything from mountaineering to kayaking in Asia. If you're planning to do any of the following adventure sports, be sure to advise your insurance company before buying your policy.

- **Kayaking** Paddle your own canoe through mangrove swamps, jungle rivers and island caves in south Thailand, north Vietnam and the Philippines.
- **Marathon-running** Take your mind off the pain of a 26-mile run by enjoying some of the finest scenery on the planet. In China, the Great Wall Marathon (ⓦwww.great-wall-marathon .com) includes a seven-kilometre stretch on the Great Wall itself, plus around 3700 steps; it's held in May. The gruelling Himalayan 100-mile Stage Race (ⓦwww.himalayan.com) takes you past four of the world's five highest mountains (including Mount Everest), is organized in five daily stages and is open to runners and walkers; it's held in late October and begins from Darjeeling in India.
- **Mountaineering** While most travellers go to Nepal to trek, the country is also the world's centre for serious mountaineering expeditions, as is the entire length of the Himalayas. The colossal Karakoram peaks of Nanga Parbat (8126m) and K2 (8900m) are both tackled from inside Pakistan. And at 5030m, Puncak Jaya in West Papua (Indonesia) is the highest peak in Southeast Asia and one of only three snowcapped equatorial mountains in the world.
- **Rock-climbing** The limestone karst that peppers the Krabi coastline of southern Thailand (ⓦwww.railay.com) and Ha Long Bay in north Vietnam is crying out to be scaled and there's also the chance to try deep-water-soloing (unaided over-water climbing with no ropes, bolts or partner). There are even more karst routes around Yangshuo in southern China (ⓦwww.chinaclimb.com). Rock-climbing's also a popular sport in South Korea, particularly

THE BIG ADVENTURE

in Bukhan-san National Park, which is nicknamed "little Yosemite" because of its many perpendicular cliff faces.

- **Skiing, heli-skiing and snowboarding** in the Indian Himalayas. Take a very expensive helicopter flight out of Manali, then do spectacular runs from around 4000m. Or set your sights and your wallet even higher for heli-ski trips in the Annapurna and Everest areas of the Nepali Himalayas. There are less dramatic, and less costly, opportunities for skiing and snowboarding in mountainous South Korea, in northeast China's Heliongjiang province, and in the Japan Alps.

- **Surfing** along the southern and western side of the Indonesian archipelago. The best facilities are in Bali but there are also world-class breaks off Sumatra, Lombok and Sumbawa, plus the famous G-Land breaks off the eastern end of Java. See Indo Surf and Lingo (Ⓦ www.indosurf.com.au) for more detail. In Sri Lanka there are surf centres in Hikkaduwa and Midigama and, in the Philippines, Luzon gets reliable waves, as does Siargao Island off Mindanao. Wanna Surf (Ⓦ www.wannasurf.com) describes and rates breaks all over Asia, from Indonesia to China, and Surfer magazine's website (Ⓦ www.surfermag.com) carries surf news and tips for Asia and elsewhere and sells online surf reports on all the major Asian breaks.

- **White-water rafting** In Nepal, you can race down choppy Himalayan rivers, through wooded canyons and jungle. It's less popular in the Indian Himalayas, but the scenery's almost as good – particularly around Leh, Manali and Rishikesh. And, in Pakistan, there's some spectacular rafting around Gilgit. Alternatively, try the rivers of west Thailand, around Umphang; or the Chico, Cagayan and Bombongan rivers on Luzon in the Philippines.

Spiritual quests

Westerners have been going to Asia on **spiritual quests** for decades, so there are heaps of foreigner-oriented courses to choose from. They're generally inexpensive and last from a few days to several weeks; most are residential.

Don't be put off by the fact that these courses are designed for visiting foreigners: the truly authentic programmes last for months (if not years), are conducted in the local language, and would be far too rigorous for first-timers. In most cases, the foreigners' **courses** are quite demanding enough: the daily programme generally starts around 5am; the food is healthy but hardly indulgent; sex, drugs and drink are all forbidden for the duration; and some course leaders ask you to stay silent for most of the day. With any luck you'll come away in a calmer and healthier state of mind and body and may also have learnt a bit more about the Asian way of looking at the world. It's quite feasible to practise your newly acquired yoga or meditation skills on your travels, especially if you're staying near a beach.

We've selected a few of the most popular centres for **yoga and meditation** instruction, but there are plenty more: have a look at Ⓦwww.buddhanet.net for links to Asian Buddhist centres catering for foreign students, and Ⓦwww.dhamma.org, which lists forthcoming Vipassana meditation courses worldwide.

- **India** is the spiritual heartland of much of Asia and the most popular place for travellers pursuing spiritual interests. Established centres for yoga and meditation courses include Rishikesh (Ⓦwww .yogaholidays.net/magazine/Rishikesh.htm) – famous as the place where the Beatles met the Maharishi – and Dharamsala, home-in-exile of the Tibetan Buddhist leader the Dalai Lama, and hundreds of his compatriots. The holy city of Varanasi is another good place to find yoga and meditation gurus. Among India's countless yoga centres (known as ashrams) some of the most popular with travellers are the Root Institute in Bodh Gaya, scene of Buddha's enlightenment (Ⓦwww.rootinstitute.com); the Sivananda ashram in Kerala (Ⓦwww.sivananda.org/neyyardam); and Shri K Pattabhi Jois Ashtanga Yoga Institute in Mysore (Ⓦwww.kpjayi.org). For some more options, see Ⓦindia.yoganet.org.
- **Japan** is the home of Zen Buddhism, and Kyoto the best place to find introductory Zen retreats catering for foreigners. Many temples across the country host half-day meditation sessions and overnight stays for foreigners: see Ⓦglobal.sotozen-net.or.jp/eng for a detailed list.
- **Nepal**, like India, attracts a large number of travellers looking for yoga and meditation courses, most of whom end up at Tibetan-Buddhist ashrams in the Kathmandu Valley. One of the most famous is Kopan Monastery (Ⓦwww.kopan-monastery.com), which holds 7- to 30-day international courses throughout the year. See Ⓦwww.fpmt.org/centers/nepal.asp for further leads.
- **Thailand**'s most popular meditation course is the ten-day Vipassana programme held every month at Wat Suan Mokkh in Surat Thani (Ⓦwww.suanmokkh.org). Other options include six-day retreats on Ko Pha Ngan (Ⓦwww.dipabhavan.com) and ten-day courses in Chiang Mai (Ⓦwww.palikanon.com). See also Ⓦwww.dhammathai .org for a general list.
- Zen (Son) Buddhism is widely practised in **South Korea** and the Korean Tourist Board (Ⓦwww.visitkorea.or.kr) posts links for the

temples whose retreats – lasting from two days to three months – are open to international students. Several temples in Seoul also run half-day meditation courses.

Learning a new skill

With all that time on your hands, why not **learn a new skill** while you're in Asia? The places listed below are renowned on the backpacker circuit for their short, traveller-oriented courses, where you might learn batik painting in a couple of days, or the fundamentals of Mandarin in a couple of weeks. Most are informal and relatively superficial, but they're a fun way to get a little further under the skin of a country. Guidebooks usually carry details about course durations and prices.

- **Arts and crafts** Design yourself a T-shirt or paint your own wall-hanging in Indonesia by taking a short course in batik design and dyeing in Yogyakarta (on Java) or Ubud (Bali). You can also learn batik making at Cherating and Kota Bharu in Malaysia. In Kyoto, the Japanese cultural capital, you can take workshops in various traditional arts, including woodblock printing, textile dyeing, calligraphy and ikebana flower arranging.
- **Cookery** Is the best way to understand a nation through its cuisine? Find out on a cookery course, outlined in "Food" on pp.47–49.
- **Diving** There are plenty of dive schools in Indonesia, Malaysia, Thailand and the Philippines, as well as in Timor-Leste, where you can do one-day introductory courses as well as internationally approved certificate courses. See p.41 for more advice.
- **Language** All Asian capitals have language institutes catering for foreign students and interested tourists; contact tourist offices and/or embassies for details, and see the list of specialist tour operators on pp.343–344 for language-learning holidays.
- **Martial arts** In China, home of kung fu and producer of a million martial-arts movies, you can do kung fu courses in the travellers' centre of Dali (Yunnan), and in Beijing or, if you're really serious, at the world-famous Shaolin Si Buddhist temple in Henan (Ⓦwww.shaolins.com), where the kung fu cult was born hundreds of years ago. Korea is the spiritual home of taekwondo, and you can take various courses in Seoul (Ⓦenglish.visitkorea.or.kr), plus there's an annual martial arts festival in Chungju, where modern taekwondo originated. In Thailand, tourists are welcome to train at many Thai boxing camps, including in Bangkok (Ⓦwww.muaythai-institute.net) and Pattaya (Ⓦwww.fairtexbkk.com). In Kerala, south India you can study the basics of the Ayuvedic martial art of Kalarippayattu (Ⓦwww.kathinayoga.org and www.kalarikovilakom.com).

- **Massage** Become a hit with fellow travellers by learning the basics of traditional Thai massage in Chiang Mai (⊛www.thai massageschool.ac.th) or Bangkok (⊛www.watpomassage.com). Or do an introductory shiatsu massage course in Japan (see ⊛www .shinzui.jp and ⊛www.shiatsu-k.com).

- **Music and dance** You'll get a lot more out of watching cultural performances if you've tried a few steps or banged out a few tunes yourself. India's Vinjana Kala Vedi School of Traditional Indian Arts in Kerala (⊛www.vijnanakalavedi.org) offers many interesting classes, including short residential courses in tabla, traditional percussion and Kathakali and Bharat Natyam classical dance. Beginners' courses in Indonesian dance and gamelan instruments are held regularly in Ubud and Yogyakarta.

- **Yoga and meditation** Open up your mind, and loosen up your limbs – a huge variety of yoga and meditation courses are held in India and Nepal; see "Spiritual quests", p.44.

Food

What could be better than slurping a bowl of **tom yam** soup in a Thai night market or tucking in to an Indian **thali** in a Delhi canteen? Once tasted, the real thing, eaten on location, is rarely forgotten – and chances are **food** will become a bit of a travel obsession. Asia is home to two of the world's greatest cuisines – Indian and Chinese – (three if you count Thai), as well as some of the weirdest and most unpalatable dishes you could ever want to be offered (Mongolian sheep's eye anyone?). Searching out special local foodstalls and restaurants is a great way to get off the beaten track when you're travelling, and eating at them can make you feel more adventurous than any jungle trekker – as you'll discover when you're given a bowl of rancid yak-butter tea in Tibet, for example, or a deep-fried Cambodian tarantula. Just be sure to follow the food hygiene advice in Chapter Twelve, and check out the dining-etiquette tips in Chapter Eight. Another good way to expand your culinary horizons is to have a go at cooking local dishes yourself, and there are chances to do that on **cookery courses** in an increasing number of travellers' centres across Asia.

For a spot of **gourmet tourism** inspiration, check out *Ant Egg Soup: The Adventures of a Food Tourist in Laos* by Natacha Du Pont De Bie; Fuschia Dunlop's *Shark's Fin and Sichuan Pepper: A Sweet-sour Memoir of Eating in China*; and Anthony Bourdain's *A Cook's Tour*, which describes his encounters with extreme cuisine in Japan, Vietnam and Cambodia.

- **China** boasts an enormously diverse and complex cuisine with meals and even individual dishes carefully constructed to achieve a

www.roughguides.com

balance in flavours, taste, texture and colour. This can be hard to appreciate if you eat alone and can only sample a couple of dishes. Regional cuisines are very distinctive, with *dim sum* the trademark Cantonese style, and rich, chilli-hot dishes the speciality of Sichuan food. You get the best of everything in Hong Kong's canteens and street stalls. If you want to learn how to make southern Chinese food, head for the travellers' centre of Yangshuo, near Guilin (Ⓦwww .yangshuocookingschool.com).

- **India** Indian food is familiar the world over but it is the variety and number of regional specialities that takes most visitors by surprise, from the tandoori cuisine of the north, where breads and meats are baked in

traditional clay ovens, through to the coconut-laced, lightly spiced dosa pancakes of the south. India is also heaven for vegetarians as pretty much every eatery offers both "Veg" and "Non-veg" menus. For an insider's take on how to create that authentic taste, try any number of cooking schools, including Gourmet Desire in Delhi (Ⓦwww.gourmetdesire.com) and Branca's Cookery Class in Goa (Ⓔedetroit_institute@yahoo.com).

- **Japan** Raw fish sashimi is the iconic dish here, and it's famously pricey, but Japan is also the home of the enjoyable budget alternative, the conveyor-belt sushi restaurant and, as elsewhere in Asia, noodle soup is a cheap and ubiquitous belly-filler. Many restaurants display plastic models of their main dishes in the window, which makes it easier to know what you're getting. For lessons in home-style cookery, adapted to suit the season, contact Uzuki in Kyoto (Ⓦwww.kyotouzuki.com).

- **Thailand** *Pat thai* fried noodles is everyone's favourite, and you can't go far wrong with the northeastern speciality of fried chicken with sticky rice, but mostly the flavours of Thai cuisine are more subtle and sophisticated – stir-fries and curries laced with lemon grass, ginger and coriander and often fired up with

Vegging out in China

The biggest surprise of our trip around China was that we didn't have to survive on noodles and pizzas for a month. As vegetarians we'd been expecting slim pickings, with the famous joke about Chinese culinary resourcefulness – using everything with four legs except a table – much on our minds. But of all the planning we'd done, the most useful was getting a Chinese friend to write "We are vegetarian; we don't eat meat or fish" on a card for us. Though we felt a bit silly brandishing the card at every waiter, it worked brilliantly and we had many delicious and memorable meals, never once having to pick out rogue bits of pork or give up and go to the pizza parlour.

Dee Ridley

chilli. The best and cheapest places to sample authentic Thai dishes are the night markets that sizzle through the night in every town. There are plenty of Thai cookery courses in Chiang Mai (Ⓦwww.thaicookeryschool.com) and Bangkok (Ⓦwww .thaihouse.com, Ⓦwww.maykaidee.com).

- **Vietnam** The national dish is *pho*, a fragrant but hearty noodle soup that's flavoured with cinnamon and handfuls of fresh herbs and is usually eaten for breakfast. It's a street food, brewed up in push-cart kitchens and eaten on stools alongside and you can find it anywhere, but most famously in Hanoi. Rice-flour spring rolls, nem, are the other classic dish, filled with vermicelli and minced shrimp and served with fresh mint and coriander. Learn to cook them in Hanoi, Hoi An (Ⓦwww.visithoian.com) or Ho Chi Minh City (Ⓦwww.expat-services.com).

Visas, flights and insurance

Very few countries in Asia refuse entry to independent travellers (the Himalayan kingdom of Bhutan being a rare example), but in many cases you can only enter via certain air- and seaports if you've obtained a **visa** in advance; in a few cases you're not allowed to enter by land borders at all. With this in mind, it's essential to start researching the visa situation for all your intended destinations as early as possible – before you pay for your air ticket, and before it's too late to get all the paperwork done. You shouldn't actually apply for your visas, however, until you've got firm bookings for your flights, as most visa applications ask for your arrival and departure dates.

Note that many countries won't let you in **if your passport is due to expire** less than six months after the date on your return ticket, and most airlines won't even let you check in with a soon-to-expire passport, even if you've got a ticket. Some countries also require that you have at least one **blank page** in your passport for immigration stamps. The A–Z list of countries on the US State Department website (W travel.state.gov) is an easy place to check the specifics.

Visas and borders

Many Asian countries issue **visas free of charge on arrival** at major airports and land-borders. You simply show the immigration official that your passport is valid for at least another six months and that you have a ticket out of the country (sometimes, you need only show you've got enough money to buy an onward ticket). However, if you want to enter the country through a less frequented route or stay longer than the statutory period granted upon arrival, you'll probably need to **apply for a visa before you travel** (though in some countries you can apply for an extension while there). Rules change all the time, especially in countries where the political climate is volatile, and often vary

Visa requirements

The following table indicates whether you need to buy a visa before you arrive. It's meant as a planning aid only and applies to entry via the most popular gateways (air, sea and land). As rules change quite often, you should double-check with the relevant embassies. In the countries that let you in without an advance visa, the number of days you're allowed to stay is given in brackets; you may be able to get a longer visa by applying in your home country before you leave. Some countries charge for visas on arrival, payable at immigration.

Do I need to buy a visa in advance?

	EU	US/Can	Aus/NZ	SA
Bangladesh*	no (15)	no (15)	no (15)	no (15)
Bhutan	yes	yes	yes	yes
Brunei	no (30)	no (US: 90; Can: 14)	no (30)	yes
Cambodia †	no (30)	no (30)	no (30)	no (30)
China	yes	yes	yes	yes
Hong Kong	no (UK: 180; most EU 90)	no (90)	no (90)	no (30)
India	yes	yes	yes	yes
Indonesia	no (30)	no (30)	no (30)	no (30)
Japan	no (UK: 180; most EU: 90)	no (90)	no (90)	yes
Laos	no (30)	no (30)	no (30)	no (30)
Malaysia	no (90)	no (90)	no (90)	no (90)
Mongolia	yes	no (US: 90); yes (Can)	yes	yes
Nepal	no (90)	no (90)	no (90)	no (90)
Pakistan	yes	yes	yes	yes
Philippines	no (21)	no (21)	no (21)	no (21)
Singapore ‡	no (30)	no (30)	no (30)	no (30)
South Korea	no (90)	no (US: 90; Can: 180)	no (90)	no (90)
Sri Lanka	no (30)	no (30)	no (30)	no (30)
Taiwan	no (90)	no (30)	no (30)	yes
Thailand ‡‡	no (30)	no (30)	no (30)	no (30)
Timor-Leste	no (30; Portugal: 90)	no (30)	no (30)	no (30)
Vietnam	yes	yes	yes	yes

* Anyone intending to arrive by land should get a visa in advance.
† You may need to buy a visa in advance if arriving overland from Vietnam or Laos.
‡ 14 days if arriving overland.
‡‡ You may only get 15 days if arriving overland; rules on this change frequently.

Déjà vu on the Karakoram Highway

We reached the front of the queue and I handed the Pakistani officer our passports, open at the Chinese visa. He glanced casually at the first, then a little more deliberately at the second and finally scrutinized the pair together, side by side. Then he raised his head abruptly and peered over the lectern.

"What is this? These have not been signed! They must be signed, you cannot use them!" he barked.

"What? Surely not!" I protested. "Where?"

"There! Can't you read?"

"Well, actually, no," I admitted. "Not Chinese. Look, it's just an administrative error. These are genuine visas, they'll see that."

But it was no good, he was adamant the Chinese would not let us enter, and therefore he could not let us leave Pakistan.

"You'll have to go back to Islamabad and get them signed. Next!"

Slightly bewildered, I sat down and tried to come to terms with the appalling prospect of going all the way back. We had just spent three weeks exploring the Karakoram Highway and now we had to retrace our steps. In the end it took us four days and a catalogue of hassles, including an unpredicted holiday at the Chinese embassy, a bus breakdown, a randy fellow passenger and an awful lot of déjà vu.

Neil Poulter

according to nationality because of specific reciprocal agreements. Land borders are especially unpredictable: see Chapter One for an overview.

The table on p.51 gives a broad outline of **visa requirements** in Asia, but you should confirm details with the relevant embassies (see pp.215–340).

Even when you have your visa, this doesn't necessarily give you *carte blanche* to roam wherever you wish. In some countries (including China, India, and Vietnam) you also need **special permits** to visit remote or politically sensitive areas; trekking in parts of both Nepal and Pakistan is subject to restrictions; and many countries have areas where foreigners are not permitted at all – some parts of Tibet and border areas of India, for example. Permits for trekking and for visiting restricted areas are usually issued in the relevant country, but it's always worth checking with embassies before you go and maybe applying in advance. For example, Inner Line Permits for access to the Indian state of Sikkim can be applied for at Indian embassies overseas as well as in India itself, whereas rules are much more stringent for access to India's northeastern hill states (Manipur, Mizoram, Nagaland and Arunchal Pradesh) and require using a registered travel agent.

Applying for a visa

Even in the most efficient embassies, **applying for a visa** is a time-consuming procedure – queues may stretch down the hallway, and most embassies and consulates keep unhelpfully short hours. Many embassy websites (see Country Profiles, pp.215–340) now have visa application forms available to download and should also carry details of application requirements (photos and documentation needed, and whether you can pay by cash, cheque or credit card) as well as opening hours. Take national holidays into consideration, both yours and theirs – not only do embassies close on these days, but queues are twice as long on the days before and after. The same advice applies when collecting your visa. Finally, get to the embassy as close to opening time as possible, and take a good book.

If you can't or don't want to apply in person or by post, you can pay a **specialist visa service** to organize it for you, which can be especially handy if you're in a hurry and need visas for multiple countries: in the UK, try Trailfinders (Ⓦwww.trailfinders.com; from £30); in the US there's VisaHQ (Ⓦwww.visahq.com; from $45); and in Australia there's Visa Link (Ⓦvisalink.com.au; from Aus$60).

A few more points to remember when applying for visas:

- **It's usually best to apply for a visa in your home country** However, most countries require you to start using your visa within three or six months of it being issued, which is hopeless if you'll be hitting India seven months after, say, leaving Australia. In such cases you'll have to get that visa en route.

- **Sometimes visas are easier to get en route** Visas for China are simplest to obtain in Hong Kong (though these are then valid from the date of issue and not from date of entry). And as Laos has no embassy in the UK it's better to apply for that visa when you're in Bangkok. On the other hand, getting an Indian visa is ridiculously bureaucratic in Nepal and much better done elsewhere.

- **Be as accurate as you can about your date of arrival** Some embassies – eg Vietnam's – issue visas with exact dates on them; if you can't be certain, delay applying for a visa until later.

- **Consider applying for a multiple-entry visa** This gives you increased flexibility (enabling you to make a side-trip into Nepal from India, for example), and is useful if you might be returning later, to catch a plane for example.

- **Occupational hazards** In some countries, the authorities regard writers, journalists and photographers with suspicion, so it's advisable to be vague about these occupations on the visa form (they're unlikely to check).

- **Some countries are hostile to passport-holders of particular nations** Islamic countries, for example, often refuse entry to Israeli passport-holders; this is true of Bangladesh and Indonesia. Check with embassies for details. You may also get questioned if you just have a visa stamp from Israel.

www.roughguides.com

▲ Anything to declare? Border guards, South Korea

- **Longer-stay visas** If you know that the statutory amount of time on a tourist visa is just not long enough for your trip, you could try applying for a special student or business visa. Sometimes it's enough to have a written invitation from someone in the host country; alternatively, try signing up with a language school or a meditation centre and getting a letter from the principal.
- **When collecting your visa, check that all the details are correct** If relevant, also check that it has been signed.

Extending your stay

Some countries offer a way of **extending your visa** once you're there; see embassy websites for details. In Thailand, for example, you can go to any provincial immigration office and get a thirty-day extension for about $55/£30; in Nepal you can apply for three consecutive 30-day extensions on top of your original 60 days, giving you up to 150 days in the country. Most extensions require two or three passport photos, and it always helps if you're dressed smartly when applying. In some countries, certain types of visa are absolutely non-extendable: Indonesian tourist visas for example.

All is not lost if you can't get a long enough visa. If you're planning to **overstay** by a few days, then – in some countries – you may as well just put aside some money for the fine that you'll be landed with when you fly out; in Cambodia it's around $5/£3 per day. In other countries, however, this is definitely not a great idea – China charges $70/£45 a day for overstaying, even by a few hours, and Indonesia threatens anyone who overstays by more than sixty days with either a five-year prison sentence or a fine of US$2000.

Alternatively, you can do what numerous long-staying travellers do: **cross the nearest border** to get a new tourist visa and come back in again. In some places this is simple: in Indonesia, for example, you can either fly to Singapore, or take the two-hour boat ride there from Pulau Batam and then back again. In Thailand you can simply walk into Laos or Burma and back; if you're in southern Malaysia you can zip across to Singapore; while from Japan the cheapest exit is by boat to South Korea. Always ask other travellers for advice on the best exit strategy, however, as immigration policies are changeable and there are occasional clampdowns to try and deter travellers from using this option instead of applying for a work visa for example.

Buying a flight

The travel industry is a hugely competitive business, so it pays to **shop around** when looking for the best fare. For simple routes, with just a couple of stops, you'll often get the best deals online, but for complicated multi-stop journeys and round-the-world-tickets, it can be easier to talk to a **travel agent**, who should also be able to come up with interesting alternatives. Staff at these places are usually well travelled themselves; they know what they're talking about and generally aren't out to rip you off. Youth- and student-oriented travel agents give significant discounts to travellers who are under 26, and some places extend their deals to anyone under 35; student-card holders of any age are often entitled to cut-price deals as well. See the Directory, p.343, for a list of agents.

If you're concerned about the legitimacy of a travel agent, especially an online-only one, it's worth checking that they're bonded with one of the big **travel-industry associations**: in the UK this means being a member of ATOL (@www.atoldata.org.uk); in Australia it means being a licensed travel agent and contributor to the Travel Compensation Fund (@www.tcf.org.au). These organizations will refund you on holiday packages if the agent goes bust, but generally not on flight-only purchases. There's no comparable outfit in the US, but here, and also in the UK and Australia, paying for your ticket by credit card is an alternative way to protect yourself against unreliable bucket shops, as the credit-card company is obliged to reimburse you if the agent doesn't; this does not extend to Visa debit-card holders. See also the section on insurance, later in this chapter.

Another factor to consider is the **safety** and comfort of the airline. The European Commission publishes regularly updated reports on airlines it considers so unsafe that it bans them from using EU airports (ⓦec.europa.eu/transport/air-ban/list_en.htm) and the web is full of sites that rate individual airlines on both safety and comfort. Many travellers understandably sacrifice a little bit of comfort for the sake of a decent discount, but if you're flying all the way to Indonesia, for example (at least 16 hours from London), you may consider the extra money well worth shelling out, not least for more leg-room, on-demand games and videos throughout the flight, and edible food.

To make your arrival as hassle-free as possible, try to book a flight that **arrives during daylight**, remembering that it could take up to two hours to get through immigration and collect your baggage and that the sun sets around 6pm in South and Southeast Asia. This will give you plenty of time to sort out your ride into the city and get to your accommodation before it's dark. For more advice on planning your arrival, see Chapter Seven.

How to save money on your flight

- **Do some serious surfing.**
- **Ring round half a dozen travel agents** Some travel agents have special discount arrangements with particular airlines, so check the price of the exact same flight with several different agents.
- **Investigate several different types of ticket** It's worth thinking laterally, even if you already think you know what you want; see opposite.
- **Book early** The best deals are always snapped up fast. If you want to fly from Europe to India at Christmastime, for example, you should book your ticket by September to ensure a reasonable fare. And if you're heading from the US to Nepal for the popular October to November trekking season, you need to make your reservations around June.
- **Be as flexible as possible on departure dates** Airlines have high, low and shoulder seasons and prices vary accordingly, so you can sometimes make a significant saving by altering your schedule by a week or two. As a general guide, high season for flights to Asia covers the busiest holiday periods, namely mid-December to mid-January, and July to mid-September; shoulder season wraps around the peak winter season, usually from November to February (when most parts of Asia are enjoying their pleasantest weather); and the remaining months are low season.
- **Avoid weekend flights** These tend to be more in demand than mid-week ones.

- **Be equally flexible about your routeing** It's generally more expensive to fly into less popular regional airports – such as Chennai in India rather than Mumbai or Delhi – simply because demand is low and competition slack. Perhaps an inexpensive overland connection (from Mumbai, for example) would do just as well, especially if it saves you $150/£90 or more. On the other hand, spending your first night in Chennai will be less stressful than kicking off with Mumbai, so the extra cost might be worth every penny.
- **Ask if you can make a provisional booking** This may be possible with RTW and long-haul tickets. However, many travel agents ask for a small deposit – transferable but non-refundable – to deter time-wasters. Full payment is usually only due six weeks before departure.

Which ticket?

Most discounted flights come with **restrictions**. For example, once you've paid for your ticket, you probably won't be able to cancel it and probably won't be able to change your initial departure date (though return dates and the onward segments of round-the-world tickets are nearly always flexible). Most holiday insurance policies (see p.62) cover unavoidable cancellations and delayed departures. However, if you simply change your mind, or decide not to use the first/outward leg of your flight (you get a lift, go overland, or buy a budget one-way instead) be warned that you will also forfeit the rest of your ticket and will not get a refund; international law does not honour return tickets when the passenger has been a no-show on the outward journey. Many discounted tickets also have time restrictions on them, with a minimum stay of seven days and a maximum of thirty or ninety days, though this varies according to the airline.

Special deals

Sometimes it's worth paying a little extra for your international flight to qualify for special perks. The **ASEAN pass**, for example, is a good deal for flights between Southeast Asian countries, the proviso being you have to arrive in Asia on one of the eight participating airlines (ⓦwww.visitasean.travel). Other individual airlines offer good **deals on domestic flights** if you fly in and out of the country on the national carrier; the airline website may not mention this so you'll need to phone to check. In all the above cases you need to buy the air passes before you go, having fixed the destinations, though dates can be left open. For more details see p.141.

Some agents throw in several **free nights' accommodation** with flights on particular airlines; this is known as an inclusive tour (IT) and is well worth considering to make your first-night experience more enjoyable; see Chapter Seven for more advice.

One-way tickets

There's nothing as liberating as **one-way ticket**. Spontaneity gets the upper hand and you're as unrestricted as it's possible to be. Sadly, not everyone sees this as a good thing: many immigration departments require you to show an **"onward ticket"** – proof that you have booked a return flight or onward transport – either when you apply for a visa in your home country, or when you arrive at the border. Similarly, some airlines won't allow you to even check in without an onward ticket; apparently this is because if you're deported on arrival it can be the airline's responsibility to transport you home again, at their expense if you have no ticket. **Rules** vary significantly with different airlines and different countries, however, and some don't worry about it at all, so it's best to contact airlines and embassies directly with specific queries. In practice, countries where it's common to continue overland shouldn't be too demanding. However, a common failsafe solution is to buy an e-ticket for a cheap onward flight with a budget carrier, and junk it once you're through immigration.

Open-jaw returns

Open-jaw tickets allow you to choose different airports for your arrival and departure, which means you can minimize backtracking during your trip. You could, for example, fly from London to Delhi and then from Mumbai back to London, making your own way overland between the two. On some airlines, it's possible to buy an open-jaw that flies you into one country (eg Thailand) and out of another (say, Singapore), leaving you a fairly lengthy overland sector to organize yourself. Open-jaw prices are generally calculated by halving the return fares to each destination and then adding the two figures together.

First impressions

I flew into Bangkok from Kolkata. I remember the light, diffuse and glowing, and the smells – exhaust fumes, jasmine and garlic edged with chilli. I checked into Charlie's Guest House, sat downstairs and ordered fried chicken and chillis with rice. It was late afternoon and tuk tuks screamed past on the street. And just like that, in a revelatory moment, I was in love with Southeast Asia.

Chris Taylor

Stopover returns

If you're only visiting one or two countries in Asia, then buying a return ticket with a **stopover option** will probably be your best deal, particularly as most stopovers are offered free of charge. Flying from Sydney to Delhi, for example, you could stop over in Singapore, Kuala Lumpur or Bangkok, depending on which airline you use; flying London–Bangkok, you could stop in Mumbai. Most airlines allow you to stop over for up to three months, and you can usually choose whether you stop off on the way out or on the way back; you may even be allowed to do both. Don't forget to find out whether you need a visa for your stopover destination.

Round-the-world and other multi-stop tickets

The next step up from a stopover return is a multi-stop ticket, most popularly a **round–the-world (RTW) ticket** that, for Europeans, takes you out to Australia/New Zealand via various Asian cities and back home again via North America. More restricted versions of RTW tickets include Circle Asia and Circle Pacific tickets. The best value RTW tickets are those designed by travel agents using their cheapest current deals with particular airlines, and those offered by the main airline groups such as Star Alliance (Ⓦwww.star-alliance.com), One World Alliance (Ⓦwww.oneworldalliance.com) and Great Escapade (Ⓦwww.thegreatescapade.com).

The cheapest way to get the most out of almost any RTW ticket is to include one or more "**surface sectors**" – sections of the journey not included in your ticket, therefore requiring you to make your own way by land, sea or locally purchased flight. The easiest and most popular international surface sector in Asia is from Bangkok to Kuala Lumpur or Singapore (or vice versa), which can be travelled as you please, either slowly, with several stops on the way, or in one swoop by overnight train, bus or locally organized flight. Overland trips between Delhi and Kathmandu are another favourite. Do look carefully at the possible surface sectors as not all of them are covered by as many transport options as Bangkok–Singapore; because of Burmese border restrictions, for example, any Bangkok–Delhi surface sector will either involve a very long journey via Tibet and Nepal or will require you doing the surface sector on a locally purchased international flight.

RTW deals are mostly priced according to mileage bands and seasons – typically from about $5000/£2300 for a 29,000-mile route during low season – with around 15 stops allowed in all. Various restrictions usually apply: journeys must be in a continuous east- or westbound direction, with no unavoidable backtracking outside specified regions, must last between ten days and one year, and must end where they began.

The main budget travel agents (see the Directory for a list) usually have half a dozen **ready-to-go RTWs**, which will be the cheapest available at the time and are easily adapted, at varying cost. As internal and short-hop flights are generally cheaper to buy inside Asia than out, and given the dramatic expansion of budget airlines within Asia, you may find it more economical to buy a skeleton RTW with long surface sectors and then add whatever extra flights you need once you've got there.

Once you've decided on your key RTW cities and paid for your ticket, you can't alter the route, but you can usually change the **dates** of component flights free of charge. The cheapest deals generally see you setting off between late April and mid-June, while the priciest time to begin your trip is in the pre-Christmas fortnight.

A few **sample prices** for travel agents' off-the-peg RTWs (low season, excluding taxes):

- **Under £650** London–Bangkok surface to Singapore–Melbourne–Auckland surface to Christchurch–Dubai–London
- **Under £1200** London–Delhi surface to Kathmandu–Singapore–Hong Kong–Sydney surface to Brisbane –Auckland–San Francisco surface to Los Angeles–London.
- **Under $1600** San Francisco–Hong Kong–Bangkok–Mumbai–Bangalore–Singapore–San Francisco.
- **Under $2000** New York–Los Angeles–Hong Kong–Ho Chi Minh City surface to Bangkok–Ko Samui–Phuket surface to Kuala Lumpur–Bali–Hong Kong–Vancouver–New York.
- **Under Can$2000** Vancouver–San Francisco–Seoul–Beijing–Delhi–Singapore–Tokyo–Vancouver.
- **Under Aus$4000 or NZ$5000** Sydney/Perth/Auckland–Kuala Lumpur–Beijing–Tokyo–Hawaii–Los Angeles–Panama–Caracas–Houston–Miami–Amsterdam–London–Dubai–Sydney/Perth/Auckland.

Charters and courier flights

Charter flights to major holiday resorts (such as Goa and Phuket) are sometimes cheaper than discounted fares on scheduled flights. Charters are sold through high-street travel agents and sometimes include accommodation as well (you're under no obligation to use the accommodation for any or all of the time if you want to move on), but you're generally limited to a two-week trip – a month at most. Some package-tour operators also offer good last-minute discounts on any plane seats left unsold in the last week or ten days before departure. These are advertised in travel agent windows, in newspapers and online.

One other way to get a cheaper flight is to become a **courier**, though this is becoming increasingly rare. A very few airlines and courier companies offer international flights for up to 85 percent off the typical fare to travellers willing to accompany documents and/or freight to the destination for them. There's nothing dubious about these companies or their goods: it's just cheaper for them to subsidize a traveller's fare than send one of their own employees. They are however only available to certain destinations (chiefly Bangkok, Hong Kong, Manila, Shanghai and Tokyo) and usually have considerable restrictions attached: you will probably have to come back within a month, may only be allowed to take carry-on luggage, and will likely have to travel on your own. Courier deals are sold through special agents such as the International Association of Air Travel Couriers (ⓦwww.courier.org); you usually need to pay a nominal joining fee to qualify. In the UK, you can also try phoning the British Airways Onboard Courier line on ☎0870/320 0301.

Now you've booked...

- **Choose your seat** An increasing number of airlines let you do this online and the earlier you log in the more choice you have (though some airlines only allow this 48 hours before departure). Everyone has their own theory about the best seat, including: aisle seats are better because you can move about freely and go to the toilet whenever you want, without worrying about waking your neighbour every time (essential for avoiding both boredom and DVT; see p.118); window seats are better because you get the views, and more privacy, and are away from the noise of the aisle; middle seats are the worst, but an inside seat in a row of four is preferable to the middle in a three, because no one will be clambering over you to get out; as infants' bassinets are always attached to the bulkheads (the plane's dividing walls), avoid any seat near this area if you want a peaceful flight. There's extensive advice on all this at ⓦwww.seatguru.com, which details the best and worst seats on a great many planes operated by a great many airlines.

- **Order a "special meal" for the flight, if you need one** All international airlines cater for a range of special diets – including vegetarian, vegan, kosher and diabetic – but these must be ordered in advance, either through your travel agent or by calling the airline yourself.

- **Buy travel insurance** If you need to change your departure date, having insurance may be the only way to avoid having to pay for an entirely new ticket. See p.62 for advice.

Insurance

Whatever the length of your trip to Asia, you're strongly advised to arrange **travel insurance** to cover medical treatment and perhaps also loss of personal possessions. If you get seriously ill or are involved in an accident, medical insurance will enable you to get the best care, which in some places will only be available in expensive private hospitals (see Chapter Twelve); you will also be entitled to free medical evacuation to your home country if necessary. Some policies aimed at backpackers exclude baggage cover to keep costs down, but that could be a false economy. You may only be taking your tattiest clothes, but the cost of replacing everything, including rucksack and perhaps sleeping bag and camera, can be very high.

- **Shop around** Hundreds of companies sell travel insurance, and there are scores of price-comparison websites to help you make your mind up. though see the points below on what to check for. One year's basic worldwide backpacker insurance can cost as little as $600/£200. Banks also sell travel insurance, as do many large travel agents; try: ⓦwww.worldnomads.com, ⓦwww.columbusdirect.com, ⓦwww.statravel.com or ⓦwww .trailfinders.com. Although some credit cards advertise travel insurance as part of their package, you must usually book the holiday using your card, and it is extremely unlikely that overall cover will be adequate.
- **Fix your dates and itinerary** It's not worth buying insurance until you know the exact specifics of your trip. But do buy as soon as you've paid for your ticket, as your policy may entitle you to compensation if you then need to cancel or delay your trip due to an emergency. If the latter happens you will most likely need to buy an entirely new ticket (most air tickets don't allow you to change the date of your outward flight) and get your insurance to refund you.
- **Consider hazardous pursuits cover** Typically, hazardous pursuits include bungy-jumping, paragliding, scuba diving, skiing and white-water rafting, but some insurance companies also view riding a bicycle or trekking in remote areas as hazardous. Paying a surcharge may get you cover for excluded activities, or you may have to choose a different insurer.
- **Check the time limits** Ask whether you can extend your policy once you are travelling or reclaim money for unused time.
- **Insurance for couples** Some insurance companies will allow travel companions or home-sharers to buy a policy for a couple, rather than two separate policies.

- **Expensive items** Note any limits on the value to which your possessions are covered. Most policies have single-item limits that don't cover camcorders, expensive cameras or laptops. It may be easier to add these items to an existing household insurance policy under an "all risks" clause that covers the item outside the home.
- **Check the "excess"** Before you buy a policy, check how high the "excess" is: this is the amount you have to pay on each insurance claim. If, for example, the medical bill you paid in Cambodia comes to $90/£55 and the excess on the policy is $50/£30, you'll only get $40/£25 back from your insurer.
- **Emergency numbers** Make sure there is a 24-hour emergency medical line in case of accident or illness, and take the number with you.
- **Check how to claim** In cases of theft, for example, you must get a police report to submit when making a claim. Claims won't usually get settled until you get home so it is wise to have emergency funds – a credit card is the easiest – to cope with reimbursement costs on the spot.
- **Particular circumstances** If you have particular circumstances (you might be over a certain age or have a medical condition, for instance), some insurers may be hesitant about covering you, so start your research early. The chances are that you will find a company who will offer cover, but it may take some time to track them down.

3

When to go

s a general rule, the northern hemisphere's spring and autumn are the mildest and most pleasant times to visit the **temperate regions** of north Asia such as Japan, South Korea, China, northern India, Nepal and Bhutan. Spring and autumn are also the seasons for trekking in the Himalayas. Summer in north Asia varies from the pleasingly warm to the stiflingly hot (air pollution and smog make cities like Shanghai and Xian almost unbearable from June to September), and winter days can get very cold, though skies are often invigoratingly blue.

As you move further south towards the equator, the weather gets warmer and the seasons become less distinct. By the time you cross the Tropic of Cancer (the line of latitude that runs just north of Vietnam and 450km south of Delhi) and enter **the tropics**, there is precious little change in temperature at any time of year: Kuala Lumpur, for example, averages 31°C in December and 33°C in May. Instead, seasons in the tropics are defined by the amount of rainfall and, to some extent, by the relative humidity. So you get a **"cool" season**, whose comparatively low humidity and little rain make this the pleasantest time to visit; a hot season (high humidity and little rain) and a **rainy season** (high humidity and lots of rain).

With careful planning it's possible to organize an extended itinerary that follows the least extreme weather across Asia, when travel is generally easiest and most comfortable. This period is also usually **peak season** for the tourist industry, with accommodation and flights at a premium. See the country profiles on pp.215–340 for individual climate charts and advice on best times to visit, and consult the BBC weather centre's website (ⓦwww.bbc.co.uk/weather/world) for a handy list of average monthly weather conditions in major cities worldwide.

The weather is only one factor, of course. You might want to time your visit around a specific **event** instead – the famous full-moon party,

Extreme measures

Travelling in extreme heat or cold can affect your **budget** as well as your state of mind and body. Most **air-conditioned rooms** cost at least a third more than fan-cooled ones, but sometimes that's a price worth paying when temperatures and humidity levels are unbearably high. If your finances won't stretch that far, take refuge in cafés and fast-food joints that can afford their own cooling systems; big supermarkets and modern shopping malls serve the same purpose. At night, try wrapping yourself in a damp sarong or sheet when you go to bed – it should keep you cool for long enough to get to sleep and by the time you wake up will have dried out. Though air-con trains and buses can be overrated (in clapped-out old vehicles it's often much more refreshing to throw open the window instead), **taxis**, whether air-conditioned or not, can be a real boon in the sweltering midday heat, so that's another expense to consider.

Conversely, you may be glad of **heating** in certain highland areas; again you will have to pay extra for this, though you might be able to get by with renting extra blankets and ensuring the showers have hot water. A cautionary note on primitive heating systems: it's essential that you check both your bedroom and the bathroom for decent **air vents** before using any gas- or coal-fired heater, as toxic fumes from these fires can and do kill.

held every month on the Thai island of Ko Pha Ngan, for example – or one of the major Asian festivals, detailed on pp.69–72.

The climates of Asia

Weather in Asia is determined in large part by two main seasonal winds, known as **monsoons**, which follow a particular timetable and itinerary. From May to October the southwest monsoon brings mostly wet weather, while from November to April the northeast monsoon brings drier, slightly cooler weather. Rains are capricious, however, and although local lore has it that they should arrive in each place on the exact same date every year, they're often late or, worse still, might not come at all to some areas, causing drought and extreme hardship.

Rainy-season travel

The southwest monsoon arrives in west-coast regions of Asia at around the end of May and by mid-July **the rainy season** will be in full swing in many parts of Asia (notable exceptions are listed below). From then on you can expect overcast skies and regular downpours across the region until October or November. To get an idea of just how wet tropical Asia can be during the rainy season, compare London's **wettest month** (80mm), or New York's (109mm), or Sydney's (135mm), with Bangkok, which gets an average of 305mm of rain every September.

This, then, is overall the **worst time to travel** in tropical Asia. Quite apart from the likelihood getting soaked whenever you leave your hotel, you'll be uncomfortably sticky in any rainproof gear (use an umbrella instead) and may also have to ward off leeches, malarial mosquitoes and other wet-weather bugs. Diseases like Japanese encephalitis spread faster in these conditions, too (but are mainly confined to rural areas; see Chapter Twelve), and you'll be more prone to fungal infections and unhealthy skin. Diving will likely be a waste of time with visibility at a minimum, and beaches often languish under the garbage washed up by the storms. Some islands, such as Thailand's Ko Similan, are impossible to get to at this time, while other regions may be **inaccessible** because the roads have turned to mud.

However, rain needn't put a damper on *all* Southeast Asian itineraries. Downpours are often limited to just a couple of hours every day for two or three months during the wet season, and in some places will arrive at the same time every afternoon. **Waterfalls** spring back to life, rice paddies flood picturesquely, and this is often the best time of year for flowers.

The rainy season is generally **low season** for the tourist industry, and this can have many advantages, including discounted accommodation and, as one of only a few visitors in town, more chance to spend time with local people. Despite the weather though, some airlines and hotels treat **July and August** as a special peak season, because this is the time the northern hemisphere takes its summer holidays.

Whenever and wherever it comes, the **end of the rainy season** is always a good reason for a party, particularly in Cambodia, where traditional boat races are held on the swollen rivers of Phnom Penh and around Angkor, and in Laos, where elegant longboats race up the Mekong River in an attempt to lure the water spirits back from the paddyfields.

Typhoons and cyclones

Fierce tropical winds are more frequent during the rainy season. Known as **typhoons** in the western Pacific and **cyclones** in the Bay of Bengal, these hurricanes hit certain parts of Asia, notably the Philippines, Bangladesh and southeast China, at speeds of over 120km per hour, leaving a trail of flattened crops, battered houses and an inevitable toll of human casualties as well. Typhoons can be especially dangerous on the coastal plains where tidal waves cause additional destruction, so you should always heed local advice about places to avoid. As forecasters usually predict typhoons a few days in advance, you should have plenty of time to prepare and protect yourself (see Chapter Fourteen for advice).

Rainy-season alternatives

The high plateaus of Tibet, northwestern China and Mongolia, and the deserts of India are some of the driest places on earth so are all options during monsoon season. Also, in Southeast Asia the **east-coast regions** of Vietnam, peninsular Thailand, peninsular Malaysia and Sri Lanka, and the southeastern region of India stay dry during the southwest monsoon and get rain when the rest of tropical Asia is having its driest period. For travellers, many east-coast beaches and islands come into their own during this time – making **May to October** peak season for Ko Samui, Ko Pha Ngan and Ko Tao in Thailand, and the best time to head for east-coast Sri Lanka; east-coast Malaysia is at its best between March and July. Off season for these coasts and islands is between November and April, during the northeast monsoon.

The other wild card is **Indonesia**, which gets the worst (or best) of both monsoons, attracting the west-coast rains from May to October, and the east-coast rains from November to February. In some parts of the archipelago – like equatorial Sumatra – barely a week goes by without a shower or two, while the islands that lie relatively far south of the equator, like Sumba, experience an annual dry season that usually runs from April to October. Nearby **Timor-Leste** also enjoys a relatively dry season from May through October.

The hot season

By February, the heat is starting to build across the plains, reaching a crescendo in May when Bangkok temperatures peak at 34°C in the shade, and it's probably 41°C in Delhi. This is the **hot season**, when travel can be surprisingly hard work, not least because the humidity is so high that it saps your energy and can make you loath to leave the air conditioning between 10am and 3pm. Heat exhaustion is more likely too (see Chapter Twelve).

The weeks **before the rains break** are a notoriously tense time: tempers are short, people are more likely to resort to violence, and the suicide rate goes up. Depleted water supplies mean many rural households struggle to keep their crops and livestock alive, and electricity in towns and villages is often rationed because there simply isn't enough water to run the hydroelectricity plants all day long. It's especially important to take a torch if travelling at this time of year, as budget guesthouses rarely have their own generators.

Many Asian cultures believe the rains are controlled by gods or spirits, so the end of the hot season is a good time to catch **rain-making festivals**. The people of Laos and northeast Thailand traditionally regard rain as the fruit of heavenly lovemaking, so in mid-May they hold an exuberant rocket-firing festival to encourage the gods to get on with it.

Places to avoid at all costs during the hot season include the Pakistani region of Baluchistan which, by the end of May, becomes one of the hottest places in the world, with peak daytime temperatures averaging 46°C; you won't get much relief across the border in India at this time, either, where the Rajasthani town of Jaisalmer swelters in the low forties throughout May and June.

www.roughguides.com

If you can't stand the heat...get out of the city

When the mid-morning mercury hits 35°C and the humidity averages ninety percent, it's time to think about cooling yourself down. If you can't get to the seaside, consider **heading up into the hills** instead.

During the Raj era, the colonial Brits decamped en masse every summer to the Indian **hill stations** of Shimla, Ooty, Darjeeling and Kodaikanal, and these old-fashioned resort towns are still pleasant places to visit, many of them reached by quaint steam trains that trundle up through tea plantations to the refreshing forested hills. Further south, in Sri Lanka, the hill resort of Kandy (488m) makes a lovely cool lakeside retreat from the roasting plains, and for a full-on chill-out you can continue up to the former colonial outpost of Nuwara Eliya (1890m), at its best in March and April. In Malaysia, hot-season temperatures up on the Cameron Highlands are a good 10°C cooler than down in the sweltering capital. Other popular upland getaways include the hills around Chiang Mai in northern Thailand, the Bolaven Plateau in Laos, Da Lat in south Vietnam, Sylhet in Bangladesh, Baguio in the Philippines, and the volcanic highlands around Berastagi in North Sumatra.

Cooling down in the mountains

Temperatures plummet by 6.5°C for every 1000m you gain in **altitude**, so the higher you go the colder the air becomes – worth bearing in mind when you're sweltering on the plains (see box above for suggested upland getaways).

The **Himalayas** are Asia's major mountain range and, though the climate here is much cooler than on the lowlands, it too is affected by the southwest monsoon. The torrential rain that drenches the Punjab from June to August falls as several metres of snow in the Everest region, making this a potentially dangerous time to go trekking. At lower elevations, the rains can cause landslides on mountain roads, so it's as well to keep travel plans flexible or avoid the region altogether. The exceptions to this rule are the high plateau of Tibet and the dry mountain areas of Ladakh and north Pakistan, where summer is the best time to go trekking.

The snow is heaviest, however, during the cold **winter** months, and mountain passes above 4000m are usually blocked between December and April, with the snow line descending to around 2500m during this period. October and November are therefore the most popular months for **trekking** in Nepal and northern India: skies are clear and daytime temperatures fairly warm, especially in the sun (nights are always cold in the mountains). Lower-level trekking is also popular from February to mid-April.

Throughout Asia, mountain areas become **inaccessible to vehicles** as well as trekkers and mountaineers during the winter months. Heavy snowfall makes the 5000-metre-high trans-Himalayan Manali–Leh Highway impassable between November and April (although the road is officially shut between September 15 and June 15, public buses plough on until the last possible moment). And the similarly dramatic Karakoram Highway, which links Pakistan and China via a 5575-metre-high pass, is also closed between November and April.

If you're not trekking or driving at very high elevations, however, the northern winter is a lovely time to admire the snowcapped peaks from a warmer vantage point in the **foothills and valleys**. Though days are brisk and nights extremely cold, the air is crisp and fresh in this season, the skies are a brilliant clear blue and the mountains at their most spectacular. So long as you're kitted out with the right gear, this can be an exhilarating – and peaceful – time to be in northern India, Nepal, South Korea and northern Japan.

Festivals and events

Many **festivals and annual events** are well worth planning your itinerary around – or even changing your schedule for. Religious festivals can be especially fun, many of them celebrated with street parades, food fairs (Thailand), dance performances (India), shadow-puppet plays (Indonesia) and masked dances (Bhutan and Ladakh), which tourists are usually welcome to attend (though you should ask locally first). As Buddhists and Hindus operate on a lunar calendar, as opposed to the Western Gregorian one, these festivals occur on different dates every year, but tourist offices will be able to give you precise details. See individual country summaries, pp.215–340, for guides to the most interesting festivals.

Soaking up the atmosphere, Indian style

It was Holi, the first day of spring, and the townspeople of Puri in east India were celebrating the day in traditional style, by taking to the streets with pails of water and armfuls of paint bombs, and chucking them at passersby. The owner of the guesthouse advised us not to go out until after midday, when the water-throwing had to stop. Foreigners were popular targets, he said, and it would not be a pleasant experience.

But we had to go out, to buy tickets from the train station. From the safety of our rickshaw seat, we watched as people on the streets got sprayed, but we stayed fairly dry. Then the rickshaw driver turned down an alleyway and stopped, and the ambush began. A group of young guys rushed towards us, pelting us from all angles with buckets of water and handfuls of paint, which they rubbed into our faces and hair. It was pretty scary, and we got soaked. Our camera was sodden, I had paint in my eyes, and my clothes were stained for ever. Mission accomplished, they backed off and we drove on.

At the train station we stood soggily in the statutory queue. Just as we reached the sales counter, the ticket man's face dropped and we looked round to see another gang of water guerrillas bursting through the doors. This time everyone got soaked, not just the tourists, and files and papers were reduced to mush. Excitement over, the salesman proceeded with his form-filling, and we came away with our tickets.

Jo Mead

The biggest festivals often draw huge local **crowds**, so be prepared for packed trains and buses and overbooked hotels. If possible, reserve transport and accommodation well in advance and expect to shell out up to double the normal price for food and lodging. Occasionally, the volume and exuberance of festival crowds can become intimidating, and so may be best avoided – the water- and paint-throwing festival of Holi, which is celebrated throughout India and Nepal every February or March, is a typical example.

National **public holidays** tend to be more stuffy occasions, especially the ones commemorating political victories or rulers' birthdays, and are usually marked by military parades and speeches, if at all. Most businesses close on these days, as do markets and restaurants, though popular sights – particularly waterfalls, temples and public parks – will be chock-a-block with local people on their day off.

Good days...

We've chosen some of our favourite festivals below, but any guidebook will offer heaps more and ⓦwww.whatsonwhen.com reviews dozens of small- and large-scale celebrations in Asia and the rest of the world and gives dates for the coming year.

- **Ice Lantern Festival in Harbin, northeast China** From January 5 to February 5, when temperatures sink to a chilly minus 30°C, the excess snow and ice in Harbin's Zhaolin Park is carved into extraordinary sculptures and even replica buildings such as life-size Chinese temples.
- **Ati-Atihan harvest pageants, Kalibo, the Philippines** This small town hosts a huge Mardi Gras-style extravaganza in mid-January. The streets are packed with people in outrageous costumes, there are days and days of excessive drinking and everyone joins in the dancing.
- **Thaipusam Hindu festival of ritual body-piercing, Singapore and Malaysia** To do penance for past sins and honour the deity Lord Subramaniam, the Hindu communities of Singapore and Kuala Lumpur hold an annual festival of self-flagellation and body transcendence in which devotees pierce their skin with an array of sharp objects, including tridents and steel arches. They process through the streets to the main Hindu shrine (in KL, at the Batu Caves on the outskirts of the city), watched by vast crowds of spectators. Held at full moon in either January or February.
- **Buddhist New Year in Thailand, Laos and Cambodia** The Buddhist countries of Southeast Asia celebrate New Year in mid-April with nationwide public water fights – once symbolic

of a purification ritual, but now more of an excuse for clowning about and drenching total strangers. The most-organized people circulate town in pick-up trucks fitted with hosepipes and water cannons, while others limit themselves to more genteel sprinkling. Any passersby, tourists included, will get a soaking, though it's quite refreshing at this time of year, April being the hottest month of the hottest season. The most exuberant New Year celebrations are held in Chiang Mai (Thailand) and Louang Phabang (Laos).

The Pushkar Camel Fair

Nothing prepares you for the Pushkar Camel Fair. The streets heave with pilgrims, traders and tourists, and the bazaar spills over into a labyrinth of dim, twisting alleys and market stalls, a blaze of colour, the air thick with spices, dust and sweat. Perhaps the greatest impact is the sheer size of the place – a sea of makeshift tents, camels and assorted livestock stretched far out across the plain. Tall, regal men dressed in waistcoats and long, baggy loincloths wander among the animals, inspecting, discussing, bargaining. Even the camels are decorated with vibrant bridles of twisted cord, tasselled and beaded. Most animals stand or lie quietly ruminating, surveying their surroundings disdainfully, but every now and then a screeching and a swirl of dust will signify a runaway, pursued by groups of stick-wielding men.

Nicki McCormick

- **Cherry blossom picnics and maple-leaf viewing, Japan** Cherry blossom season begins when the first flowers appear in spring in Okinawa, the southernmost island of the Japanese archipelago, and for the next few weeks national TV broadcasts a nightly *sakura* forecast, showing how far the pink wave has progressed up the country. When the main island of Honshu turns pink (towards the end of April), the parks are packed with blossom-viewing picnic parties. Friends and families settle under the trees, getting drunk on saké, belting out karaoke songs and composing maudlin *haiku* poems about the fragile petals. Seven months later, the ancient capital of Kyoto flames a brilliant red for the last couple of weeks in November; this is also your chance to sample the bizarre local delicacy known as *momiji tempura* – fallen maple leaves fried in batter.
- **Spring fair in Dali, China** For five days every April or May, thousands of people from all over Yunnan converge on Dali for horse-trading, wrestling matches, racing contests, dancing and singing.
- **Gawai Dayak harvest festival, Sarawak, East Malaysia** Parties in the traditional Iban longhouses are always riotous, but the biggest celebration of the year happens in June to mark the end of the rice harvest. Expect all-night drinking and heaps of food, plus lots of jokes, pranks and party games.

www.roughguides.com

71

▲ Get to Mongolia in July for the Naadam festival of traditional sports

- **Naadam festival of traditional sports, Ulaanbaatar, Mongolia** Mongolian tribespeople show off their sporting prowess in horseriding (some of it bareback), archery and wrestling during a hugely popular and fiercely competitive three-day extravaganza held in nearly every town and village in mid-July.

- **Esala Perahera historical pageant, Kandy, Sri Lanka** For ten nights every July or August, extravagant torch-lit processions of costumed dancers, drummers and elephants in full regalia parade through the streets of Kandy in what's thought to be one of the oldest historical pageants in the world.

- **Pushkar camel fair, northwest India** For three days in late October or early November all roads seem to lead to Pushkar in Rajasthan, as crowds of 200,000 descend on this tiny desert town for India's biggest camel fair – part market, part religious festival. Some fifty thousand camels are paraded, raced and entered for competitions and the place brims over with market stalls and street entertainers. At night, visitors are housed in a specially erected tent city where huge marquees are equipped with camp beds and bush toilets.

...and bad days

Though the tourist industry never grinds to a complete standstill, there are certain public and religious holidays when you'll be hard-pressed to find hotels and restaurants open for business. In Bali, for example, the **Hindu New Year**, Nyepi, is celebrated in March or April with a day of complete silence and inactivity – shopkeepers are actually fined if they trade on that day, tourists are requested to stay within hotel grounds, and even the airport is closed for 24 hours.

Nor is it a great idea to land in China or Taiwan during the three-day **Chinese New Year** celebrations (in late January or early February) as everything will be closed, and you'll be unlikely to find a hotel room anywhere. The same is true of any town or city with a majority Chinese community – Singapore is an obvious example, but the hotels and restaurants in many Thai and Malaysian cities are also run by ethnic Chinese. If you want to be in one of these places for Chinese New Year (the firework displays can be unforgettable), then get to the city a couple of days early so you can stake your claim on a room and stock up on food. The same advice applies if you're in Vietnam for the Tet new year celebrations (late January or February) or Sri Lanka over the Sinhalese New Year (mid-April), when lots of hotels and restaurants close down for a whole week.

Similarly, you might want to think twice about visiting an Islamic country during **Ramadan**, a month-long period of abstinence that falls during the ninth Muslim month (starting around August 11 in 2010, August 1 in 2011, July 20 in 2012 and July 9 in 2013), when practising Muslims do without food, water and tobacco during daylight hours. This makes for a very stressed-out population, particularly by the third and fourth week, so you may not get the hospitality you were hoping for, especially in the more orthodox communities such as in Sumatra and Kalimantan. Many restaurants stay shut during the daytime throughout Ramadan, and in parts of Indonesia and Pakistan local bus services are less frequent during this month, too. If you are in Indonesia, Pakistan, Bangladesh, India, Malaysia or southern Thailand during Ramadan, be sensitive to your hosts and don't flaunt your food, drinks and cigarettes in front of them. On the plus side, as soon as darkness falls everyone heads out to make the most of their evening meal; there are some great night markets during Ramadan, and a general feeling of celebration every time the fast is broken.

Steer clear of big cities in the immediate run-up to **elections**, too, particularly in India and Bangladesh, where rallies can turn nasty and curfews may be imposed on and around polling day. It's not unknown for election results to be greeted with riots, so consider heading for safe havens in the hills or by the sea, instead of sticking around in the urban centres.

How much will it cost?

Budgeting is boring, but spending a bit of time on it at the planning stage will leave you more energy to enjoy Asia once you're there, rather than worrying about survival. Carefree and exotic as it may sound, there is actually nothing romantic about jetting off to the furthest place you can think of and realizing when you get there that you can't afford to eat or drink or sleep in a decent bed, that you've got a ticket that won't let you return home early, and you have to spend the first week investigating how you can get money wired to you. If you are seriously strapped for cash, it's worth planning a shorter trip – we guarantee you'll have a better time than if you embark on a longer, penny–pinching haul. This chapter will help you calculate your costs, give you ideas for making your cash go further and provide practical advice on how to take your money with you.

However carefully you work out your budget, though, there are bound to be unexpected expenses along the way, so try to take more

Exchange rates and currency fluctuations

Economic conditions in Asia can change fast so it's worth keeping an eye on currency fluctuations pre-departure and once you are travelling. Inflation can be equally volatile and anyone operating on a shoestring budget with no room for manoeuvre can find themselves in trouble if prices rocket – for example, in mid-2009 annual inflation in most parts of the continent was between two and six percent. If, however, inflation shoots up to 85 percent or more as it did in Laos a few years ago, it will send any pre-departure calculations haywire.

An excellent site for checking conversion rates is Ⓦ www.oanda.com. They feature useful FXCheat Sheets; print it out, stick it on a card and laminate it for a portable ready reckoner.

money than you think you'll need – the insatiable urge to ship a divine granite elephant home from Bali or the pressing necessity for a white-water rafting trip down the Sun Kosi in Nepal will throw inflexible finances into chaos.

Budgeting

One thing to remember is that **generalizations** are dangerous. "Oh, Asia's cheap", you'll hear again and again. It is true that, compared with the major expense of your plane ticket, prices in Asia can seem cheap. But while you can find a basic beach hut in Goa for about $5/£3 a night or on the islands off the southeast coast of Thailand for $8/£5, you'll be paying at least $14/£8 for a bed in Singapore or Hong Kong, while in Tokyo anything less than $25/£15 is very rare indeed. You'll find both extremes across the continent, for example a night in the Raffles Hotel in Singapore will cost you over $350/£180, which buys almost three months' accommodation in parts of Indonesia. In India, a twelve-hour train trip can cost as little as $3/£2 second-class and a cup of tea beside the road is just a few cents, but it's equally possible to spend $200/£122 or more a night staying in luxury hotels in the big cities. And while Japan's tourist board does its utmost to entice you there, giving information on economical accommodation, food and travel in all its brochures, the truth is that you can manage in Japan on a New York or London budget – but not on a Bangkok one.

How much you spend naturally depends on the sort of holiday you want to have. While rock-bottom accommodation, local transport and food from simple roadside stalls in India, Thailand, Vietnam or Laos is likely to set you back about $15/£7 daily, once you start considering travelling around more, a bit more comfort, a few beers and better-quality food, then $30/£14 is more realistic. It's relatively easy to sit at home and swear you'll manage without air conditioning, bathe in cold water and love it, and never want a private toilet, but after a week in 45°C heat, a few cold showers at 3000m, or three days with chronic diarrhoea, your priorities will certainly alter.

Bear in mind that there are also plenty of potential costs outside your daily living expenses and these can quickly add up. Cambodia is generally cheap for foreign visitors, yet the current admission charge to Angkor Wat is $20 per day, $40 for three days and $60 for a week. Entrance to the Taj Mahal for foreigners stands at Rs750 ($16/£10). Internet costs can easily add up. Internet access in tourist centres throughout Asia is about a dollar an hour. OK, it's not megabucks but over a six-month trip, a dollar a day will become $180/£110, which is worth taking into account in your calculations.

Sample budgets

Here is a rough indication of minimum daily costs in all the countries we cover; see individual country profiles for more precise figures in the Where to Go section (pp.215-340). If you are planning internal flights or adventure activities, you'll need to add these on top:

Top-end countries will cost you $40/£23 a day upwards:

Bhutan	Japan	Brunei	Mongolia	China

Mid-range countries should be manageable on a budget of $20–40/£11–23:

South Korea	Timor-Leste	Taiwan	Singapore

The **cheapest** countries can be coped with on under $20/£13 a day:

Bangladesh	Nepal	Cambodia	Pakistan	India	Philippines
Indonesia	Sri Lanka	Laos	Thailand	Malaysia	Vietnam

Three months in India

It's just about possible to manage on around $11/£6 a day ($77/£42 a week) in India by staying in the cheapest hotels, eating only rice and dhal and travelling second class on all train journeys. If you bump up your luxury quotient, have a room with your own bathroom, vary your diet slightly and throw in some more comfortable train journeys, then you're looking at $21/£13 a day ($147/£91 a week). Go further up the scale – book into mid-range hotels, eat in moderately priced restaurants and take a few excursions – and a better estimate is around $41/£25 a day ($287/£175) a week. To travel reasonably but realistically, we recommend reckoning on covering around half the trip (6 weeks) at the lowest rate, four weeks at the middle rate and then three weeks at the top-range above, giving a much more realistic total of about $1900/£1150.

A three-month trip through Thailand, Malaysia and Indonesia

To spend a month in each country, you'd need about $1350/£810 if you work out your costs using a minimum daily budget of $15/£9 a day for Indonesia, Thailand and Malaysia. Allowing for half the trip at the basic rate, and the other half at double this (a total of $2025/£1215) means you can afford some more comfortable accommodation and travel plus a few meals in pricier restaurants. However you'll need to double this total again ($4050/£2430) if you intend to explore the entire Indonesian archipelago by plane, indulge in some serious adventure sports, hardcore shopping or bar hopping in Bali.

It's also useful to realise that as some Asian countries are so vast that you'll find different **price zones** in different parts of the country. In mainland China, budget travellers can manage on $44/£27 a day in the interior areas or $88/£54 if you do it in more comfort. However, if you just explore the east-coast cities, where costs are sky-high you'll be looking at closer to $176/£108. In Thailand, it's more a question of supply and demand: unappealing guesthouse rooms on the overcrowded island of Ko Phi Phi, for example, rarely charge less than $24/£14 a night, while much more inviting beach huts on nearby Ko Jum go for half that.

Throughout Asia prices can escalate sharply in **peak season**, with hotel rooms as much as doubling in price. Peak seasons vary locally, but Christmas and New Year are popular pretty much everywhere. On Bali, June to September – coinciding with the European holiday season – is very busy, whereas in Nepal, it's October and November that see a tourist rush to take advantage of the ideal trekking weather.

Saving money before you go

Some of the biggest savings you'll be able to make are those before you go. The best flight deals sell out early and you'll find that certain routes, eg to Goa for Christmas and New Year, are booked solid several months in advance. If you're rushing to fit visas, vaccinations and shopping into a few hectic weeks, you'll have to make hurried decisions and may end up paying to cut corners. The following tips can help:

- **Plan your itinerary with your budget in mind** You may well be better off visiting a few places in one region than racing across the continent – even in Asia the cost of train/ferry/internal-flight tickets adds up. A free stopover in Tokyo may seem like a good idea, but can you afford several days of city prices? Taking a cheaper ticket that leaves you to travel from Bangkok to Singapore overland can sound appealing, but make sure you budget for the train or bus fare and the extra days on the road.

- **Arrange your own visas** Many companies offer this service but it is always cheaper to do it yourself. However, you will need to allow plenty of time, especially if you are applying by post. See Chapter Two for more on visas.

- **Ask your doctor about vaccinations** For certain countries, you'll need an armful of these (see Chapter Twelve). Travel clinics provide specialist information and are a time-saving way to get your jabs. However, many injections are cheaper – even free – from your own doctor.

- **Contact hotels direct to book your first night** This can be cheaper than deals offered through your travel agent. Also check online accommodation booking agents (listed on p.347) for good deals.

- **Do not skimp on insurance** Knowing that your medical costs and replacement gear will be paid for doesn't make a disaster OK, but it certainly makes it a whole lot more bearable. Don't consider going without insurance. For more on insurance, see p.62.

- **Wait until you arrive to buy clothes/equipment** (see Chapter Six) Lightweight clothes, insect repellent and mosquito nets, soap, shampoo, stationery, mosquito coils and detergent are cheaper once you are in Asia. Sarongs, those all-purpose coveralls, are cheap across the continent. However, sun block, tampons, hair conditioner and deodorant can be pricey and difficult to find outside tourist areas.

www.roughguides.com

- **Buy a water purifier** (see p.179). The price of bottled water, particularly in tourist resorts, can be surprisingly high and could use up a substantial part of your budget over a long period.
- **Buy secondhand gear** Keep your eyes open on Gumtree (🌐www .gumtree.com), Freecycle (🌐www.freecycle.org) and ebay (🌐www .ebay.com). Trekking equipment shops often have a board advertising secondhand gear, and outdoor sports magazines usually include a classified ads section. Try local thrift and charity shops for cotton clothes, rucksacks, waterproofs and even boots, though do check stuff carefully – you don't want a pack with holes, broken zips and detached straps (see Chapter Six for advice).

Spending wisely while you're there

While many of the major savings can be made before you even leave home, there are plenty of ways to save money on the road. These tips may be handy:

- **Take your student ID card (ISIC)** In some places it'll simply get a bemused look, but in others it can get you reduced entrance fees to museums and performances.
- **Eat local food** Western food and drink cost significantly more throughout Asia.

It's not fair?

In several Asian countries there is an official **two-tier pricing system** in operation with foreigners paying more for certain things. In Thailand, Nepal, India and Sri Lanka, foreigners are charged more than local people for entry to all national museums and historic places (and in Thailand and Sri Lanka to all national parks, too). For example, a foreigner pays Rs750 to enter the Taj Mahal, an Indian Rs20.

The reasoning behind all this is simple: foreigners can afford to pay more, therefore they should be charged more. For some national museums and monuments it's also argued that because local people pay taxes they are entitled to "subsidized" entry fees. Whatever the official line, it's a philosophy you will encounter time and again throughout Asia, from the woman selling mangoes in the market to the taxi driver. Some travellers feel it's a fair cop, others fume against it at every turn. There is usually little you can do in official situations, except pay up. However, when dealing with local people, try to find out a fair price from those around you and endeavour not to pay too much more). If foreigners consistently pay way over the top for something, there is a danger that prices will also rise for local people or that traders will prefer to provide services to foreigners. Accept that you'll end up paying somewhat over the odds on many occasions, but try not to get totally obsessed about it and feel you are constantly being "ripped off" – especially when the amount involved may be just a few pennies.

- **Eat in groups** Many restaurant dishes come in family-sized portions, especially in China, Hong Kong, Singapore and Thailand, the idea being that diners share several dishes.
- **Try coachsurfing/travel networking** You can get free accommodation this way (see Chapter Eleven).
- **Swap guidebooks and equipment** There is a ready second-hand market among travellers on the road. Many travellers' hotels and restaurants have noticeboards advertising goods.
- Hone your **bargaining skills** (see below).

Bargaining

It's important to remember that **bargaining** over the price of something is as much a ritual of social interaction in Asia as it is about saving money. Essentially it means that, with a few exceptions, the price of anything on offer is open to negotiation. However, if you offer a price and it is accepted, you are morally bound to go ahead with the purchase – so don't haggle if you haven't made up your mind whether or not you really want the item. It's perfectly acceptable, though, to wander around a market asking the prices just to get some idea of the starting figures.

If you're really into bargain-hunting, it can be worthwhile doing your shopping early in the day. In parts of Indonesia, for example, vendors believe that a good early sale establishes their fortune in trading for the rest of the day, so start bargaining at lower "morning prices".

Fixed prices and discounts

The real difficulty in Asia is knowing when and when not to bargain. Basically, prices are **fixed** (non-negotiable) in restaurants; in supermarkets and department stores; on official public transport with tickets; in metered taxis; and in museums, parks or temples. Even in shops with prices labelled, such as CD and DVD shops, you may be able to negotiate a better rate for purchases of ten or more or get a free CD thrown in.

As you move upmarket, the jargon changes slightly. So, for example, in a small guesthouse in Vietnam you might simply enquire whether they can let you have the room they offered you at 100,000 dong for 80,000 dong, whereas in a luxury hotel you could enquire about the availability of **discounts**, perhaps producing a business card for extra effect. You are far more likely to get discounts on accommodation during the low season than when the place is packed out. However, it's always worth bargaining if you're staying longer than a couple of nights as many places do good weekly and monthly rates.

Special price for you, madam

You might like the look of a pair of trousers in an Indian market. You enquire the price, the vendor asks five hundred rupees. You shake your head and offer two hundred (somewhere in the region of a third or a half the initial asking price is a good starting figure in India). He or she throws their hands up – they have a family to support, how can you expect them to survive when you are taking the rice out of the mouths of his starving children, and how about four hundred? You nod sympathetically, but you notice a tiny fault in the material, can't really see your way to paying that much, but could perhaps go as high as three hundred. The fault is nothing; here, he has another pair that are perfect, three-eighty? Ah, but you have seen similar ones at a better price down the road, what about three-fifty? He agrees, smiles, this is a special price for you, madam – the transaction is done. All this may well have taken place over five minutes, an hour or even a week! However, it's always accompanied by smiles, gentle voices and good humour. Even if you can't reach an agreement, and often you can't, you can shake your head and walk away. This can actually be a useful strategy – many a sale has been concluded halfway down the street.

Indulging yourself

It's worth bearing in mind that cheapness isn't everything. Asia is probably the best chance most people have of affording some five-star luxury – so why not join the jet set for a few days? For example, the slap-up Tiffin Curry buffet lunch at the legendary Raffles Hotel in Singapore costs around $51/£31 and a night in the Lake Palace Hotel in Udaipur, one of the world's most spectacular hotels – it's an ex-maharajah's palace on an island in the middle of a lake – will set you back $253/£154. You can see Bali or Vietnam in style, with your own car and driver for the day, for $40/£24, fly between Delhi and Chennai in India for $35/£25 (it's 33 hours or so by rail) or have a good-quality tailor-made silk suit run up in Bangkok for around $290/£175.

Whenever it's a toss-up between spending a bit of extra cash and putting your own safety at risk, you should always part with the cash.

Cash, travellers' cheques and plastic

However short your trip, never simply take a huge wodge of cash. You want flexibility and easy access to your money, but you also need security against loss and theft, and ideally some kind of back-up or emergency funds. The best solution is to travel with a **combination** of cash, travellers' cheques and credit/debit cards. In case the exchange counter at the airport you're flying into is closed when you touch down, or if the local ATM machines don't like your plastic, it's a good

www.roughguides.com

idea to change a small amount of cash into the currency of your first Asian landfall before you leave home. However, this isn't always possible: for example, you cannot buy Indian rupees or Vietnamese dong abroad; and some other currencies are partially restricted, so you can only buy tiny amounts overseas at an appalling rate.

Cash

The **US dollar** is the hard currency of choice throughout Asia, as long as the notes are clean, new issue (rather than older) and in good (ideally almost pristine) condition. Even little hotels in the back of beyond may be willing to change a few dollars into local currency if you get stuck, but they're unlikely to look at any other form of foreign currency. Many businesses, big and small, across Asia will happily accept dollars instead of local currency. Always take small denominations ($1 and $5) and avoid $100 notes, which can be hard to exchange as they are viewed with suspicion because of fake bills in circulation. The advantage of cash is that it's usually exchangeable even if you lose your passport. The big disadvantage is its vulnerability – if stolen, cash is untraceable and most insurance policies expressly exclude the theft of cash from their cover. However, if you lose your plastic cards or get your passport and/or travellers' cheques stolen, you'll be very glad of a $50 or $100 emergency stash kept hidden in the bottom of your pack.

Travellers' cheques

Although fewer people are using them these days, **travellers' cheques** can be a useful back-up and a secure way to carry money. If the cheques are **stolen** they can generally be replaced within a day or two, provided you have their missing serial numbers, information about the date and place of purchase, and your passport (always keep these things separate from the cheques themselves). **American Express** is the most widely accepted brand in Asia. However, every now and again there is a localized scare about fraud and if you are relying heavily on travellers' cheques you should take cheques from two or more companies. Some banks and moneychangers also insist that you show them the receipt from the original purchase of the travellers' cheques – it has "Agreement to purchase" written on the back.

Although travellers' cheques in most major currencies are accepted at moneychangers and banks in tourist centres, get off the beaten track and you'll find that only **US-dollar cheques** are acceptable. It pays to do some research before heading into the wilderness, as in the remotest regions – in parts of Indonesia, Laos, Cambodia and Vietnam, for example – travellers' cheques aren't always exchangeable.

www.roughguides.com

Changing money

Whether you are changing cash or travellers' cheques it is worth bearing a few things in mind:

- **Check the exchange rate and commission** Just as rates vary from bank to bank, so can the commission on the deal. You'll need to do your sums to decide on the best rate. For example, £100 of Thai baht at B56 to the pound with a one percent commission fee is a better deal than a rate of B55 to the pound with no commission.

- **Shop around for the best rates** These are usually found at licensed moneychangers in travellers' centres where there's plenty of competition. The worst rates are found at border crossings and hotels.

- **Ask for small-denomination notes** It can be extremely hard to get change for larger notes and it's always better to have small notes for bus tickets, street food, taxis, etc.

- **Always count your money** However long and tedious the process – you must be the last person to touch/count the money before you put it away. Once you've left the desk it's impossible to do anything about it. There are plenty of **scams** in operation: one involves folding notes in two so that you actually get half as much as appears to be being counted out; another is distracting you while counting out the money. Kotong gangs in Manila are notorious for ripping tourists off.

- **Keep your exchange certificates**. This is your proof that you changed the money legally and in many countries it's vital if you want to change unspent local currency when you leave the country, or want to pay for tourist tickets – for example, on Indian railways or for internal flights in China – with local currency.

- **Avoid black market moneychangers** These will only offer slightly better rates than the banks or official moneychangers. You may also be arrested for using them (occassionally by police entrapment squads).

Using ATMs

ATMs are a convenient way of accessing your money, especially if you're sticking to major towns and resorts. However, it is worth checking out the cost of using your debit card abroad with your bank as you will be charged a "**handling fee**" for each transaction. This can be around two percent, or it might be a flat fee. The flat fee is particularly irksome if the ATM you're using has an unhelpfully low maximum withdrawal amount (£40 in some cases), so you end up having to pay three lots of handling fees if you want to withdraw £100. Note that some banks also charge a "foreign exchange loading" on top of this. Credit cards incur separate charges (see p.84).

Networks are expanding, but don't expect to find ATMs on every street corner or in the more rural areas. The MasterCard website (🅦www.master card.com) contains lists, organized by country and town, of ATMs that accept Cirrus and Maestro – they are currently in all countries covered by this book except Bhutan, Timor-Leste, Laos and Mongolia; 🅦www .visa.com does the same for debit cards with the Visa Plus logo, which can be used in all the countries covered by this book except Bhutan, Timor-Leste and Laos.

Heightened **security measures** at many major Western banks means that any attempt to withdraw cash from an ATM in a country with a reputation for card fraud (which applies to many countries in Asia, including Thailand, Malaysia and Indonesia) will trigger a block on the card. Always call your card provider before you travel (and this applies to credit cards as well) to tell them of your trip. Your card may still get blocked, usually on your first night when you're desperate for cash, so it's essential to take the international access phone number of your card provider with you, preferably the direct number for the security depart-

Manila card tricks

It was the morning after the night before. Bleary eyed, I wandered the streets of downtown Manila in search of an ATM. "Ah, at last!" I thought spotting a glowing Visa sign behind glass doors across the street. I grabbed the handle but the doors wouldn't budge. "No, no you need use card!" said a helpful customer inside pointing at a swipe machine on the wall. Running my debit card down the slot the doors magically opened. As I entered my PIN I noticed the guy was still hanging around but thought nothing of it – I had a flight to catch.

Returning home I discovered that $1000 had been withdrawn from my account whilst I was in the air. The machine at the ATM had been a cloning device and the guy had simply held the door shut until I swiped my card; he had then looked over my shoulder as I entered my PIN. Armed with this information it's easy enough to create a new card and merrily withdraw cash until there's either no money left or the bank starts asking questions. Being an obvious case of card fraud I got the money back but it's left me pretty wary about using ATMs, especially when hungover.

Andy Turner

ment, so that you can speak to them if this happens. It's also another reason not to rely on just one card or just one method of taking your money for your journey.

In Asia many ATMs operate differently from those you may be used to; they give out the money first and then return the card – keep your wits about you, as it's easy to walk away without the card.

Credit cards

The extent to which **credit cards** are acceptable as payment varies across the continent. Though most top-class hotels, restaurants and shops are happy to accept them (and you often get a very favourable rate of exchange when the bill comes in, although you will be charged some sort of foreign-usage fee, typically two to three percent), they're much less use at the budget end of the market.

Credit cards are useful for major outlays such as flights, hotel or restaurant splurges or adventure sports. They can also be useful when booking and pre-paying for a hotel room over the phone, fax or internet.

Even if you don't plan on using it, a credit card is also a great emergency stand-by, since you can also use it to obtain **cash advances**. Visa and MasterCard are the most widely accepted throughout Asia, both at banks and moneychangers; you can also use their cards to withdraw cash at ATMs. See the ATM section above for countries that do not have machines. Be aware that if you use your card in this way you'll be charged the same cash-withdrawal fee that you would be at home, even if you pay your bill in full when it comes in, on top of the foreign-usage fee.

American Express charge cards are mostly useful for mid- and top-end places but their services can be useful in an emergency (see opposite).

Whichever card you take, make sure you carry the emergency phone number with you to report theft of the card, and never let the card out of your possession, even stored in a so-called safe while you're away trekking for a few days (see p.198). Also, **card skimming** is, unfortunately, very common throughout Asia; your card details are copied and then used for fraudulent transactions. There's little you can do if establishments use electronic card-copying methods that illegally duplicate the information from all the cards they process. However, many of the methods are less sophisticated and you should at least try to **keep your card in view** during a transaction. Bear in mind that, if the card does get lost or need to be cancelled as it has been copied, getting a replacement is likely to take several days, and that you'll need to organize payment of your credit-card bill while you are away.

Internet banking abroad

If you use **internet banking** at home it's tempting to imagine that you'll just carry on as usual while you are away. That's fine if you are travelling with your own laptop/notebook (see p.187) although you should still be aware that wireless networks, especially if unsecured, can still be hacked, so install all the security software possible. However, it's a very bad idea to use internet cafés for online banking. You have no way of knowing what spyware may be lurking on the computer (so that all your keystrokes are stored in the computer's memory for later retrieval), or whether the machines are networked in such a way that whatever you are doing can be snooped on from another machine. There are ways of adjusting the settings of any computer to safeguard against this but the safest advice is not to use internet cafés for internet banking, but to make alternative access arrangements before you leave home or entrust a family member at home to access the account for you.

▲ How much? The universal language of numbers

Prepaid currency cards

A number of card providers issue **prepaid currency cards**. Essentially you load the cash onto the card before you leave home (and can top up while you are travelling) and then use them like debit or credit cards to pay for goods and services or in ATM machines to withdraw cash once you are overseas. It means that you don't have to have a bank account to have a card, they are pin protected so can be stopped like other cards if they are lost or stolen and most providers will be able to send you a replacement while you are overseas, but check this (and whether there is a replacement charge) and the costs before you sign up. Just a couple of examples in a market of a great many options are the Visa TravelMoney card and American Express Travellers Cheque card.

Wiring money

It is possible to get **money wired** out to you from home and it is easy for your nearest and dearest to do it online or do it by cash or card at an agent near home. However, it is pricey and should be reserved for emergencies only. The most straightforward method is to use Moneygram (Ⓦ www.moneygram.com) or Western Union (Ⓦ www.westernunion .com), which transfer money to their overseas agents in a matter of minutes. Currently Western Union has agents in all the countries covered in this book as does Moneygram with the exception of Timor-Leste. As an example of costs, both companies charge between five and fourteen percent when sending £100 but charge a lower percentage the more money you send. It pays to check both websites before sending money as they also vary on the exchange rates so the payout at the other end can vary quite a bit.

Some types of American Express cards enable cardholders to access emergency funds at some overseas offices by cashing a personal cheque drawn on your home bank account. See Ⓦ www.americanexpress.com for the locations of their offices worldwide.

In a dire emergency the least desirable alternative is for somebody at home to get money wired to a local bank for you to collect. It is absolutely the method of last resort – it is much more time-consuming for all concerned, it takes longer and the results are far more haphazard. It doesn't even necessarily cost any less.

GI blues

The plan was to travel from London to Perth – I had $400. I sold my camera in Delhi, but by the time I got to Bangkok I was broke. Somehow I had to get to Bali. I wasn't particularly worried about it; something would turn up. And it did – I landed a role in a movie called Saigon. The screen test required a crew-cut as I was to be a GI, and I got one by marching around and saluting a bemused Thai hairdresser and saying loudly in English, "Shorter, shorter". Heading to Lop Buri, however, where some evacuation scenes were to be filmed, I was singled out. I'd been surviving on $5 a day in India and it showed. The hard-as-nails American drill sergeant took one look at me and said, "Get him out of uniform." As I sloped off in scrawny shame, he called out, "You can play a civilian, son." Still, I was officially a GI (I had the haircut to prove it), and when the GIs went on strike for higher wages I got a rise too.

Chris Taylor

Earning while you're away

There are ways of profiting from your trip. No, we're not talking drug-running; however, it may be possible to supplement your money supply with a **temporary job** of some sort while you're away, or to sell the story of your journey and/or photos of your trip. It's worth looking into these options before you leave home because a bit of planning is required.

Discretion is the order of the day here, as many tourist visas expressly prohibit employment. Depending on the job, and the employer, you might get away with working on your tourist visa for a month or two; to work any longer entails regular "visa runs" across the nearest border. For official employment you'll need a **working visa**; contact the relevant embassy about this (see the country profiles for addresses). Information on doing unpaid, short-term voluntary work in Asia is given on p.23.

Before you travel, have a look at the Asian sections in *Work Your Way Around the World* (Crimson Publishing) by Susan Griffith or *The Directory of Jobs and Careers Abroad* (Vacation Work Publications) by Guy Hobbs. Once you are travelling look out for adverts in English-language newspapers and on noticeboards in travellers' areas; also talk to other travellers or approach potential employers directly.

In Japan, many young Western women get work as **hostesses** in bars where they entertain male customers. While there is nothing inherently seedy about most of these places ("hostess" is not a euphemism for "prostitute"), drunken fumblings are not unknown, and the same risks apply as in any situation where you might find yourself alone with a relative stranger. If you're considering this sort of work, be sure to search the internet for opinions/experiences and sound out other Western women already employed in this way.

Teaching English

One of the more common jobs for foreigners in Asia is **teaching English**. Most employment is in private language schools catering for the full range of pupils, from beginners to pre-university students. The best pay is to be found in Japan and Taiwan. Classrooms are often small and the hours antisocial, as many students want classes in the evening or at weekends, but students are invariably eager and the work can be a stepping stone to employment as a private tutor or better-paid jobs in the more established schools or universities.

While there is work for those with no qualification, a **TEFL** (Teaching English as a Foreign Language) qualification is very useful and it gives access to better rates of pay. The most widely recognized qualification is the Cambridge Certificate in English Language Teaching to Adults (**CELTA**), which is designed for those with no previous teaching experience, takes four or five weeks' full-time study (it is also available part-time) and is recognized throughout the English-teaching world. Courses are widely available in the UK and cost £850–1200, but are well worth it if you are seriously contemplating teaching while you're away. The University of Cambridge (Ⓦwww.cambridgeesol.org) publishes a list of hundreds of centres around the world where the CELTA course is on offer. In the US the full-time CELTA course costs around US$2500, in Canada Can$2300–2500 and in Australia Aus$2700–3000. There are also centres in Bangladesh, China, India, Indonesia, Japan, South Korea, Malaysia, Singapore, Sri Lanka and Thailand where you can take the course once you are in Asia. This can be a pretty economical option: in Bangkok, for example, the CELTA course costs around $1600/£973 (see Ⓦwww.eccthai.com or Ⓦwww.ihbangkok.com).

For details of the profession, the different courses available and how to find work abroad, look at *Teaching English Abroad* by Susan Griffiths (Crimson Publishing), which has a good-sized Asian section, or, for North Americans, *Teaching English Overseas: A Job Guide for Americans and Canadians* by Jeff Mohammed (English International). Websites such as ⓦwww.tefl.net, ⓦwww.tefl.com, ⓦwww.eslcafe.com, ⓦwww.tefljobs.asia, ⓦwww.teachenglishinasia.net and ⓦwww.toalesl .com advertise jobs at language schools all over Asia, including a good selection in China, Indonesia, Japan, South Korea, Taiwan, Thailand and Vietnam. When you travel, don't forget to take photocopies of your qualifications and references from previous employers with you.

Working as a diving instructor/divemaster

There is a good living to be made in Asia as a **diving instructor** especially as − rightly or wrongly − many novice divers prefer to be guided or taught by a Westerner rather than a local person. Diving is especially popular in Indonesia, Malaysia, the Philippines and Thailand, and this is where most opportunities are to be found.

To become an instructor or **divemaster** (the next rung down in the PADI system), you need relevant experience and certificates from one of the internationally accredited dive organizations. Alternatively, many travellers get the diving bug while they are overseas and end up taking all the necessary courses while they are on the road. For information about the training necessary for PADI qualifications, which are accepted throughout Asia, take a look at ⓦwww.padi.com, which also gives the locations of diving centres and resorts.

5

Guidebooks
and other
resources

O nce you've planned a skeleton route, you can enjoy filling in some of the detail by scouring **guidebooks** and tourist brochures, reading **travelogues** and talking to old Asia hands. Check out some of the millions of travel-related sites on the **internet** (see p.94 for some good websites to start you off, and the online sections in the County Profiles, pp.215–340) and contact relevant tourist offices and embassies.

Guidebooks

In an alien culture where you can neither speak the language nor read the signposts, a **guidebook** will be a real comfort in the first few days. You don't have to use it slavishly, but a good guidebook can make all the difference to your trip by helping you decide what to leave out of your itinerary as well as what to include. Don't buy your guidebook at the last minute, however, as it will also contain crucial advice on travel preparation, including what visas you'll need, which inoculations to organize, and what gear to take along. See the Directory, pp.348–350, for a list of recommended travel bookstores.

On the other hand, you could waste a lot of money if you splash out on a set of guidebooks before you've settled on a definite route. Start off by borrowing a few guides from a library (even out-of-date editions

The backpacker trail

Guidebooks can have a huge influence on a town's tourist trade. If a hotel, restaurant or tour agent in a popular travellers' centre is given a favourable review in a Lonely Planet guide, for example, that business is almost guaranteed to receive a steady flow of backpackers. In a North Indian town, a tout runs through the normal routine: "Where you from? How long you been in India? Where you stay? I know cheap hotel." When we say that we've already decided to go to Dreamland Hotel, he smiles. "Ah, you must have the Rough Guide. All Rough Guide readers go to Dreamland; Lonely Planet readers go to Uphar Hotel, next door."

If a business does not appear in the guide, it will have to try harder to attract customers, possibly by resorting to touts or by making itself more competitive. On the door of a small restaurant in a tiny, but touristed, Indian village is pinned a sign that reads, "We're not mentioned in the Lonely Planet, but please give us a try anyway."

Lucy Ridout

are usually perfectly adequate for planning purposes), and then invest in a couple of new editions when your itinerary becomes more certain.

If you're planning a long trip, there's no need to buy a guidebook for every country you're going to visit: you'll save money and luggage space by buying **secondhand guides** on the road, or swapping a guide you've finished with for a book on your next destination. Don't rely on out-of-date editions though; travellers routinely complain that prices on the ground are different from what's written on the page, but it's ridiculous to expect that room rates and bus fares won't have gone up in, for example, the five years since your old guidebook came out.

Choosing a guidebook

Personal recommendation is the obvious way to go, but you can also make your own judgement in bookshops by comparing the way Guidebook Series A describes a certain town and the way Series B does it. Look up a few things you're particularly interested in – wildlife, for example, or budget accommodation – and see how different books approach the topics. Don't be swayed by sumptuous photographs, and remember that you'll be lugging your chosen book around for quite a few weeks, so it shouldn't weigh too much. (Whatever the size of the book, you can save weight by ripping out and discarding the sections you know you'll definitely not need.)

Most **guidebook series** have a particular style of travel in mind. Guides published by Rough Guides (ⓦwww.roughguides.com), Lonely Planet (ⓦwww.lonelyplanet.com) and Footprint (ⓦwww.footprintbooks .com) are all written for independent travellers and so give detailed practical information for tourists across all budgets. Trailblazer (ⓦwww .trailblazer-guides.com) produces specialist guidebooks with an emphasis on overlanding and trekking, Bradt (ⓦwww.bradt-travelguides.com) tends to cover more unusual destinations, including North Korea, and

Time Out (www.timeout.com) is good for cities. Less focused on independent travellers, Insight (www.insightguides.com) and DK Eyewitness (www.dorling kindersley-uk.co.uk) guides are known for their inspirational photography.

Whatever the focus of your guidebook, never expect it to be infallible: new editions are generally only published every two or three years, and in between things do change – prices rise, hotels shut down. Guidebook authors also have their own preferences (some series emphasize this, others play it down), so you may not always agree with their choices. And it can be worth getting a second opinion on certain things – for example, the specific direction of a mountain trail – either from other travellers, or from local people.

Bear in mind, too, that there are many **types of guidebook**. Books that cover several countries in one volume – the whole of Southeast Asia for example – are easier to carry than a set of individual books and include specific information on overland border crossings; on the down side, the smaller and less mainstream islands, towns, hotels and restaurants will have been edited out because of space considerations. If, on the other hand, you know that you'll be sticking to just one city, region or route, do an internet search to see if there's a detailed guide

Good guides and bad guides

"We're going to die."

"I know," I replied. We sat on the mountain ridge in silence. There was nothing more to say.

Dawn was approaching. The sun was rising leisurely over Lake Batur, northern Bali. I remember thinking it was the most beautiful sunrise I had ever seen. Oranges and purples filled the sky. Down below, specks of brown dotted the white sandy beach: men had risen early to prepare for the day's fishing. Life was going on as usual, unaware of our predicament. I laid back in the sun and closed my eyes.

We had begun to climb Mount Batur in the early hours of the morning, misled by a guidebook which had stated that the route was easy and a local guide unnecessary.

Two hours later, with a bruised back and a twisted ankle, we found ourselves stranded on a rock ledge. A sheer rock face loomed above us, and a steep drop onto boulders lay below. No one knew where we were. I really believed this could be the end.

Some time later, our knight in shining armour arrived in the form of an eight-year-old boy, wearing flip-flops and balancing a bucket of iced drinks on his head. We would have paid anything to have been led off the mountain but, crazily, in true Indonesian style, the bargaining began. We settled on $3; a bargain.

For the next nerve-racking three and a half hours, we scaled precipitous rock faces with no ropes or safety equipment. A couple of times we slipped, but somehow managed to hold on. To this day I cannot believe we made it.

At the summit we learnt that we'd taken the wrong path up the mountain. It was sheer luck that a local villager had spotted us and summoned our guide. I felt someone was watching out for us that day. Guidebooks contain lots of useful information, but local knowledge should always be consulted too.

Sasha Busbridge

on that area. The Rough Guide to Goa, for example, contains a lot more local information than the general India guide, and also includes access and accommodation details for Mumbai, the gateway city to the region. There are also a useful number of activity guides, some of which, like *Trekking in Ladakh* (Trailblazer), are self-contained and include enough details on gateway cities and accommodation options for you to do without any other guidebooks; others, such as *Surfing Indonesia* (Periplus), are best used in conjunction with general guides.

Maps

Most guidebooks include useful enough **maps** of major towns and resorts, but if you're planning to do much driving or long-distance cycling you may want to buy a good general country or regional map before you leave home. These aren't always available in Asia, so check your guidebook for specific advice. See pp.348–350 of Directory for a list of recommended travel-book and map stores.

Very large-scale maps for independent trekking should also be bought before you leave home (the best selection of trekking maps for Nepal and Tibet, however, is available in Kathmandu). Detailed town and city street maps, on the other hand, are often best bought on arrival, particularly big city maps that include bus routes.

▲ According to this map there is definitely a temple around here...

Background reading

Other people's **travel stories** are often inspirational and will be full of good ideas on where to go and what to do; they will help prepare you for what lies in store, too. Travel websites and blogs are fruitful places to look for first-hand, up-to-date travellers' tales, as are specialist travel magazines, which are often fleshed out with alluring photos. We've recommended a few publications and websites to get you started, plus a highly selective list of some pan-Asia books that couldn't be squeezed into our country-specific reading recommendations on pp.215–340.

Magazines

All the below-listed travel **magazines** are aimed at independent travellers and many also have great websites carrying archived features, travellers' forums, blogs and more. (They're all potential publishers for stories after your return as well; see Chapter Fifteen.) For a more detailed take on the realities of daily life in Asia, there are a number of more high-brow magazines that cover the region in greater depth than Western national newspapers.

- **Action Asia** (Ⓦwww.actionasia.com; Hong Kong). Asian adventure travel magazine covering trekking, kayaking, white-water rafting and the rest.
- **Adventure Travel** (Ⓦwww.atmagazine.co.uk; UK). Strong on trekking, mountaineering and cycle-touring features, plus gear reviews.
- **Far Eastern Economic Review** (Ⓦwww.feer.com; US). Hard-hitting, readable news features on Asia's social, political and economic issues, plus book reviews and humour too, much of it generously reproduced on the website.
- **Geographical** (Ⓦwww.geographical.co.uk; UK). Intelligent, thought-provoking features on travel and foreign cultures in this magazine of the Royal Geographic Society.
- **National Geographic Adventure** (Ⓦadventure.nationalgeographic.com; US). Predictably good on stories about wilderness travel and wildlife, plus adventure sports, explorers and expeditions; famously great photography too.
- **Wanderlust** (Ⓦwww.wanderlust.co.uk; UK). The UK's main travel magazine, with regular features on destinations, trip-planning, travel gear and travel-industry news; the classified ads are a good place to look for travelling companions, and for travel jobs.

Online resources

Among the squillions of **travel websites** out there on the web, from holidaymakers' blogs to tour operators' advertorials, we've highlighted a few general sites to get you started. Useful country-specific websites are listed in country profiles; online accommodation booking services are listed on p.347; websites for travel agents and tour operators start on p.343; and travel-health websites are on p.348.

- Ⓦ**www.bootsnall.com** Excellent travel features plus forums.
- Ⓦ**www.gapyear.com** Big on practical advice for the first-time long-haul traveller, with free downloadable guides to everything from budgeting to solo-female travel and volunteering abroad.
- Ⓦ**www.journeywoman.com** Site aimed at women travellers, with unique sections, including "What Should I Wear?" featuring firsthand tips on acceptable dress in over one hundred countries and advice for solo travellers.
- Ⓦ**www.lonelyplanet.com/thorntree** Very popular travellers' forums, divided by region.
- Ⓦ**www.roughguides.com** Digital guides to destinations around the world, with links to featured hotels, guesthouses and tour operators, plus forums, travel tips and articles.
- Ⓦ**www.travelfish.org** Straight-talking backpacker guides to Cambodia, Laos, Malaysia, Singapore, Thailand and Vietnam that are especially good on guesthouse reviews; they're available as e-book downloads too.
- Ⓦ**www.tripadvisor.com** Ignore the commercial aspect to this enormous, globally famous accommodation-booking site, and concentrate instead on the travellers' reviews of hotels all over the world. It's a fantastic resource once you've learned how to weed out the fake reviewers and impossible-to-please whingers.
- Ⓦ**www.utopia-asia.com** The top website by and for gay and lesbian travellers to Asia, with details on the gay scene in most Asian countries, plus links to gay meeting places and organizations.

Books

Recommended country-specific novels and non-fiction titles are highlighted in country profiles, pp.215–340, but below are a few good general introductions to Asia:

- **The Great Railway Bazaar: By Train Through Asia** (Paul Theroux). A travel classic, published in 1975, about a four-month train journey that begins at London's Victoria Station and continues – via the Orient Express, the Khyber Pass Local and the Trans-Siberian Express, among many others – through India and Southeast Asia to Japan and back to the UK. The book made Theroux's name, and established his style as an astute and entertaining, if grumpy, warts-and-all observer of life on the move.

- **The River's Tale** (Edward A. Gargan). A superbly written account of a year-long odyssey from the source of the Mekong River through China, Tibet, Burma, Laos, Thailand, Cambodia and Vietnam. The author's incisive observations are given context by informed background on recent history, economic and political issues and he pulls no punches in his rather sobering conclusions.
- **Introducing Buddha: A Graphic Guide** (Jane Hope); **Introducing Islam** (Ziauddin Sardar); and **Introducing Hinduism** (Vinay La). A trio of enjoyable cartoon-and-caption guides to major Asian religions that look light-hearted but are all seriously good primers. They're published by Totem Books.
- **Travelers' Tales Guides** (ed. James O'Reilly & Larry Habegger; ⓦwww.travelerstales.com). This outstanding series of travel-themed anthologies cherry-picks from travelogues, travel journalism and guidebooks to create lively, multi-faceted volumes on individual countries – including China, India, Nepal and Thailand – as well as on worldwide themes such as Food, Adventure and Self-Discovery.

Learning the lingo

English is the language of tourism throughout Asia, making it quite possible to do a six-month trip without ever consulting a phrasebook. Indeed, in India, one of the greatest pleasures is the number of Indian English-speakers who are keen to debate local and international issues with English-speaking travellers.

That said, it's well worth learning at least a few phrases – and is essential if travelling off the beaten track – as, wherever you go, people will appreciate your efforts to speak their **language**. You'll probably be giggled at, but that's as good an icebreaker as any and, in the more remote spots, being able to string a basic sentence together can make the difference between having to cope with a plate of deep-fried locusts and enjoying a tasty bowl of noodles.

Though some languages are guaranteed to turn you into a tongue-tied fool (Mandarin Chinese with its four tones and everyday alphabet of 10,000 pictograms springs to mind), others are relatively simple to learn. Bahasa Indonesia, for example, is generally considered to be the easiest language in the world. It's written in roman script, has a straightforward grammar, and is very similar to the Malay language that's understood throughout Malaysia and Singapore.

⑤

Mixed messages

Learning even a little of the language of the country you visit can vastly improve your experience there. But learning it badly can just add to the confusion.

After a week in Beijing, and several enjoyable meals at a restaurant near my hotel, I thought I was ready to order unassisted from the bewildering Chinese menu. Waving the English-speaking waiter away I ordered in Mandarin Chinese what I thought to be simple rice and vegetables. One hour later the kitchen doors swung open, and the beaming waiter returned, bearing a monstrous four-foot fish. It was the most extravagant meal in the restaurant, and too big for either my appetite or my wallet. The restaurant staff ate well that night.

Nicholas Reader

If you have the time, it's very satisfying to give yourself a proper grounding before you go. There's a huge range of **teach-yourself** language-course books with CDs and MP3 files available for most Asian languages, including Hodder's Teach Yourself series (ⓦwww.hoddereducation.co.uk), and other options from Routledge (ⓦwww.routledgelanguages.com) and Berlitz (ⓦwww.berlitzpublishing.com). The Linguaphone tape courses (ⓦwww.linguaphone.co.uk) are the most comprehensive, but are also expensive. Or go online and make use of the excellent free language courses offered by Word2Word (ⓦwww.word2word.com).

Alternatively, fix yourself up with some face-to-face **language classes** before setting off. Expatriate Asians quite often advertise lessons in local papers, or you might try setting up an informal language exchange via a community centre or even a neighbourhood Asian restaurant. Should you be planning a lengthy stay in Asia, the best way to learn the lingo is to attend a course on the ground – see Directory, pp.343–344, for details of tour operators who offer language-course packages in China, Taiwan and Japan or, once you're there, check the local English-language press for ads and ask at tourist offices, embassies or universities.

Choosing a phrasebook

The easiest way to make yourself literate in an Asian tongue is to travel with a good **phrasebook**. The language-course publishers described above all produce pocket-sized phrasebooks for tourists, as do Rough Guides, Lonely Planet and Collins. As with guidebooks, you should compare several different ones by thinking of a few situations – asking the price of a double room, for example, or saying that you're vegetarian – and seeing which phrasebook is easiest to use. Check if words and phrases are written in local script – especially important for China, Japan, South Korea, Laos and Thailand. Some phrasebook publishers also produce audio files that you can download on to your MP3 player – not a bad way to while away an interminable bus journey.

6

What to take

You could happily set off for Asia with all your belongings stuffed into a plastic bag and stock up on clothes and extra bits as and when you need them. Most of Asia is brimming over with merchandise, so you don't need to pack a year's supply of T-shirts or shampoo.

Of course a few things are best bought at home, as the quality of Asian goods is variable, and certain items will be difficult to find when you're away. But apart from these essentials, we'd advise you to take the very minimum you can and improvise on the rest. Buying on the road is nearly always cheaper, shopping for everyday stuff can enhance your travel experience and will almost certainly enhance the local economy a little bit, and, crucially, this approach means that you'll be able to **travel light**. A heavy load is a real hindrance and can spoil your trip by making you loath to stop off at places because you can't face dragging your huge pack along with you. Things really are bad when your pack begins dictating your itinerary, so start how you mean to go on and get your baggage under control right away. A few tips on how to lighten the load:

- **Mail heavy/bulky things to where you'll need them** For example, if you're doing a three-month overland from Australia to Europe and you're planning to look for office work when you get to London, send your smart work clothes direct from home to a UK poste restante. Avoid sending parcels to most Asian postes restantes though (see p.192) and plan carefully, as poste restante (general delivery) is usually only held for two months.
- **Send excess baggage back home** Your thermal underwear and wool sweater after you leave Kathmandu, for example. Better still, buy your woollies when you get there and then sell them, junk them or send them home. Surface mail from Asia generally takes about three months (see Chapter Thirteen).

- **Give away your kit when you're done with it** Many local charities welcome donations of clothes and books, even old mobile phones and spectacles; some charity websites specify what they need, or see Ⓦ www.stuffyourrucksack.com for some good leads.
- **Rent or buy any special gear on the ground** You can rent down jackets and sleeping bags in Kathmandu, and sleeping bags in Lhasa, Chiang Mai (northern Thailand) and Malaysia's Taman Negara National Park (which also rents out walking boots). You may also be able to buy secondhand equipment from departing travellers, via ads posted on guesthouse noticeboards.
- **Avoid succumbing to gadget mania** Travel equipment suppliers and the gear pages in magazines are filled with stuff you really will not need and should not buy, let alone take with you. There are lots more useful things you can spend your money on than, for example, a special banana-shaped pod that stops fruit from getting squashed in your daypack.

Backpacks

If you haven't already got a **backpack**, this is the one item that it's worth splashing out on. Choose a recognized-brand-name pack (such as Berghaus, Deuter, Eagle Creek or Lowe-Alpine) as they are hard-wearing and ergonomically designed. These cost from £85–180 in the UK, $130–450 in the US or Aus$200–600 in Australia, but think of it as an investment: a good pack could last you for many years and will certainly make your trip a more comfortable one. For details of recommended suppliers of backpacks and other travel equipment, see the Directory, p.350.

Backpack **capacity** is measured in litres or cubic inches – not that helpful really as it's hard to visualize your socks and T-shirts in liquid form. Our advice is to buy the smallest one that looks practical for you: a 40- to 55-litre one if possible, but certainly no bigger than 65 litres. Buying a smaller pack forces you to travel light, and you'll be grateful for that when you're battling with overflowing Bangkok buses or wandering up and down a roasting Colombo street. Bear in mind, though, that fully stuffed side-pockets can add a good 30cm to the width of your pack, and attaching boots, sunhat and umbrella to external loops only makes your load more difficult to carry.

Some travellers, on the other hand, claim you should buy as large a pack as you're ever likely to need, presuming that if you don't fill it to the brim on your way out, you'll certainly pick up enough trinkets on the trip to make it worth its massive size. In the end, though, it's not the capacity that matters so much as the **weight** of stuff that you cram into it. Many airlines specify a 20kg maximum for hold baggage, so that should definitely be your limit; a realistic optimum weight lies somewhere between 10kg and 15kg – it's definitely worth jettisoning stuff once the scales go over the 17kg mark.

Choosing a backpack

You won't regret the time and care you take in choosing the right backpack. Always try them on before buying, don't order blind online, and think about the following:

- The best packs are made from **heavy-duty synthetic fabrics**; avoid the ones that feel flimsy and might tear easily. Zips should be sturdy, too.
- Most travellers' backpacks are constructed round a lightweight **internal frame**. This gives shape to the pack but, most importantly, it helps spread the load across your back. The smaller packs – under 40 litres – are often considered too small to warrant a frame, but they should come with thickly padded and contoured backs which also help distribute the weight and make the whole thing more comfortable.
- A thickly **padded hip belt** is essential for carrying any load over 10kg. This transfers most of the weight off your shoulders onto your hips and legs – the strongest and sturdiest part of the body. By channelling the weight down to your lower body, you're also making yourself more stable: a full load resting solely on your shoulders will quickly tire you out.
- If you're not average size and build, check out the packs with **adjustable back systems**, where you can change the position of the shoulder straps in relation to the frame.
- Some packs are **designed especially for women**, with shorter back lengths and a differently contoured back shape and hip belt.
- Packs with more than one **compartment** are easier to use. And side- and lid-pockets are perfect for stashing items you need to get at with minimum fuss (soap and a toothbrush for overnight train journeys, for example), as well as your map and guidebook, or your rain gear. Some backpacks have detachable front pockets which are actually daypacks, of which more on p.101.
- Some rucksacks come with a **breathable mesh** layer to help minimize sweaty back syndrome.

Is it a backpack? Is it a suitcase?...

...No, it's a **travelpack**. Some backpacks can also be turned into suitcases: a special flap zips over the straps and, with the aid of a handle, you can carry it like a suitcase or a shoulder bag – a useful feature for

6

plane, bus and train journeys where dangling straps can get tangled up or ripped off. This also means that you can walk into a smart hotel without necessarily looking like a scruffy, impecunious backpacker. More handy still is the fact that most travelpacks can be unzipped all the way round to open like a suitcase, making them much more convenient than a conventional backpack, especially for overnight stopovers. They are also easier to lock.

Though all these features make travelpacks versatile, the cheapest versions rarely provide the long-distance support of a properly contoured backpack and most have a rectangular, suitcase-like shape which makes them much bulkier to carry on your back. If you choose this option, go for a travelpack with an **internal frame**, not just padding, and make sure there's a hip-belt as well as external compression straps to help secure the load. Some of the more expensive ones have really well designed harnesses that compare well with those on good backpacks.

Flashpackers: luggage on wheels

You don't have to do it the hard way. Plenty of travellers are choosing to do their trans-Asian trips with a little more cash and a little more dash – so many, in fact that they've earned a special name: **flashpackers**. Ditching the pack in favour of a suitcase on wheels means you and your clothes will probably arrive less dishevelled than many, but wheels will be a hindrance on beaches and rough tracks, in the many places that have lots of stairs but no lift, and getting in and out of boats. You may find yourself splashing out a fair bit on tips and taxis. Backpacks with wheels are generally considered to be the worst of both worlds, so if you're going to go for sophistication you may as well do it properly.

Packing up and locking up

Consider customizing your pack to make it as user-friendly, resilient and secure as possible:

- Most backpacks are showerproof, but that doesn't make them monsoon- or tropical-storm-proof. To **keep your stuff dry**, either buy a special backpack liner, or make do with a large bin liner or two. Consider buying at least one fully waterproof "**dry bag**" for your camera, iPod and other high-value gear so that you can come out laughing when your backpack gets an accidental dunk.
- Pack your backpack so that you are not being pulled backwards all the time. This means **distributing weight** as evenly as possible from top to bottom, and keeping the heavier stuff as close to your body as possible.

www.roughguides.com

100

- As well as tagging your pack on the outside, stick an **address label** to the inside of one of the side-pockets, so that there can be no dispute about whose it is. Tie a brightly coloured ribbon to one of the outside straps to make it easily identifiable in airports and bus stations. See Chapter Seven for more advice on packing for flights.
- Though many backpacks are non-**lockable** as bought, many come with useful devices like double zips so that you can use a small padlock on them. To lock the straps you can use specially designed little ladder locks.
- Some travellers go for chicken-wire-style **backpack meshes** to prevent thieves slashing open their pack, but that's overkill for most mainstream Asian destinations. Not only does it send an unnecessarily bullish message to everyone you encounter but it also makes it look as if you have something well worth stealing. The bottom line is never to leave your most valuable or important items in an unattended pack – that's what money belts are for (see p.102).
- Some travellers take a small chain and a spare **padlock** for securing their pack to luggage racks on overnight trains and buses (see p.109 & p.147).

Daypacks and shoulder bags

Unless your planning's gone seriously awry, you won't be carting your backpack around every day of your trip, so you'll probably need a much smaller bag for daily around-town necessities like your camera, guide-book, map, water bottle and sunblock.

Many travellers like to use a daypack for this purpose, but there are advantages to using a **shoulder bag** instead: they are smaller and less unwieldy, and can easily be folded away into your main pack or worn comfortably at the same time as your main pack. They are also easier to access while you're walking along, and do not mark you out so obviously as a tourist, particularly in bars and clubs.

Daypacks on the other hand are much more comfortable for longer days out. Some are also designed with a handy internal water pouch and drinking hose which saves you having to stop to get a water bottle out of your pack every few minutes. Some main packs are designed with built-in, detachable daypacks, which zip onto the outside of your main pack. If you go for this option, never carry valuables in the zipped-on mini-pack as you won't be able to tell if a pickpocket slashes it when you're on the move.

Money belts

Most travellers like to keep their valuables on their person at all times, and the safest and most convenient way of doing this is to wear a **money belt**. It should be worn under your clothes, and should be as discreet as possible – preferably invisible – so that it does not attract the attention of muggers and pickpockets. To keep it slimline, only use it for stuff that you don't need to access every twenty minutes. Keep your passport, your airline ticket, your credit card, travel insurance policy and the bulk of your cash in the money belt, but leave your petty cash, notebook and pocket torch for your daypack.

Don't confuse money belts with **bum bags/fanny packs**. A bum bag is a larger and an altogether more ostentatious item; it's worn over your clothes and can usually hold a small camera as well as sunscreen and sunglasses. As a security item the bum bag is useless and may as well be inscribed with flashing lights announcing "Valuable items inside, help yourself". It just takes one deft swipe of a knife for your bum bag to drop to the ground and into the hands of an opportunist thief.

Cotton money belts are best: unlike nylon and plastic ones, they absorb the sweat and do not irritate the skin. It is, though, a good idea to keep something waterproof at the back of the money belt nearest your skin (your free plastic-coated travellers'-cheque wallet for example) so that any excess sweat won't obliterate vital documents such as airline tickets.

Some people prefer **neck wallets** to money belts, while others find that they swing around more and therefore feel less safe and possibly more uncomfortable.

If you're planning to spend a fair amount of time on the beach, consider buying – as a supplement to your money belt – a little **waterproof canister** that you can wear when swimming. These come in varying sizes (with names like "Surfsafe") and should be able to hold your room keys and/or security box key so that you don't have to worry about leaving your money belt with all its valuables unattended on the beach.

Clothes

Once you're on the road you'll almost certainly end up wearing the same two or three outfits week-in, week-out. Ideally you'll want to work that out before you leave home, but there's always parcel post to send back any excess. Nonetheless, try to be brutal with yourself at the packing stage. Ask yourself: do I really need five T-shirts and three pairs of jeans?

Your clothes will deteriorate faster than they do at home because of the heat, the extra sweat, and the pounding and mangling they'll go through at local laundries. To some this is a reason for taking new clothes: the newer the item, the better its chance of survival. On the other hand, why waste your money if things are only going to get ruined anyway?

Asia is of course full of clothes shops selling stuff that's ideal for the local climate. However, **Asian sizes** rarely go above men's UK/US trouser size 36 and women's UK size 16/US size 14, though you can get Western sizes in touristed towns. Also bear in mind that tailoring in Asia is extremely inexpensive, and Asian fabrics are stunning, so you can always get new clothes made up, particularly in Bangkok, Hoi An in Vietnam, Hong Kong, Singapore and almost any big town in India (a tailored cotton shirt costs about $8/£5 in India). You may end up wanting to replace your entire wardrobe anyway: Asian men and women tend to dress far more colourfully than Westerners so you might feel rather drab in comparison if you wear nothing but sober blacks and khakis.

The modesty factor

Many traditional Asian cultures find **revealing dress** offensive and cheap, so you'll get a much better response from local people if you respect their views and adapt your attire accordingly. This is particularly important when visiting temples, mosques and shrines – if you're unsuitably dressed in these places you'll probably be refused entry.

Prudish (and sweaty) though it sounds, this means keeping shorts for beach resorts. Singlets are also considered low-class, especially for women, who will get a lot of unwanted attention if they reveal their cleavages or are obviously not wearing a bra. The notice above the entrance gate to Bangkok's Grand Palace sums up the (usually unspoken) **rules**; it's illustrated with photos of unsuitably dressed men and women, and forbids "leggings, shorts, singlets, fishermen's trousers, torn and dirty clothing and flip-flops".

Lots of travellers ignore **local clothing etiquette** and may not even notice that it's an issue. This is quite easy to do if you're sticking to heavily touristy ghettos – Bangkok's Khao San Road, for example, or the Gili Islands on Lombok. And in many big cities it's the norm for locals to go partying in fashionably skimpy outfits. But as soon as you deviate from the beaten track you'll start to feel more self-conscious. One young female traveller got stones thrown at her in Medan (a Muslim town in Sumatra) for walking around in shorts; another adopted local Indian dress (cotton pyjama-style tunic and trousers) for her six-month stay and found that this made villagers much less nervous of her – in fact, they would often start a conversation by complimenting her for wearing a *salwaar kameez*.

Stripping down for **swimming** and sunbathing is a Western practice that bemuses many Asians. When the Thais and Cambodians go swimming they walk straight into the water in their jeans and T-shirts; Indian women do the same in their saris or *salwaar kameez*. At established tourist-oriented beach resorts there'll always be foreigners wearing swimwear, but if you're going for a dip way off the tourist track it's sensible to check out local practices first.

For first-hand **advice** on acceptable clothing for women in about one hundred different countries, check out the "What Should I Wear?" section of the Journeywoman website (⊛www.journeywoman.com), which has sartorial tips and comments from dozens of women travellers.

Packing for the heat

For tropical Asia you will need clothes that are long, loose and light:

- **Loose trousers and long sleeves** are good for respecting local dress codes, but also for sun protection and, curiously enough, for coolness as well. The more skin you expose to the sun, the faster your body moisture evaporates and the more dehydrated and, therefore, hotter you become. You only have to picture the flowing robes of an Arab sheikh to be reminded of this. Long sleeves and long trousers are also good protection against mosquitoes.
- **Lightweight fabrics** are faster to dry and smaller to pack.
- **Cotton and linen** are the most comfortable, as natural fibres are absorbent and let your skin breathe.
- **Artificial fabrics** such as lycra, nylon and rayon tend to encourage sweat and itchiness, and may even cause heat rash and fungus. On the plus side, they don't look as rumpled as cotton fabrics do when dragged from the bottom of a pack.
- **Short-sleeved cotton shirts** dry faster than heavy T-shirts and are lighter to pack.
- **Jeans** are heavy to carry, hot to wear and take a long time to dry, though some travellers find they make them feel comfortably at home.
- **Light-coloured clothing** will help to keep you cooler (it reflects rather than absorbs the sunlight) and is less attractive to mosquitoes, but will also get dirtier faster.

Packing for a cold climate

The best way to pack for a trip that is to include a few weeks in a cold climate is to go for the **layers technique** (two short-sleeved T-shirts under a long-sleeved shirt for example), though you should also think about topping up with some of the following:

- **A fleece jacket**: very warm and surprisingly light, though they can be bulky. At the least take a micro-fleece top, which are very light, pack small and dry faster than woollen sweaters.
- **Thermal underwear**: ideally long johns and a long-sleeved undershirt, but woollen tights or thick leggings and a long-sleeved brushed cotton top will do instead. If you have money to spare, buy some silks (100-percent silk thermals), which feel incredibly light (and slinky) but are extremely warm.
- **Warm socks**: go for the hard-wearing, double-thickness ones sold in camping shops. They're good for wearing with hiking boots in hot places as well.

- **Woolly hat and scarf**, or balaclava, plus gloves are easily bought when you arrive; the yak-wool ones sold in Nepal are especially popular.

A clothing checklist

- **Two pairs long trousers/skirts/dresses**
- **Two T-shirts/short-sleeved shirts**
- **One long-sleeved shirt**
- **One micro-fleece top**, lightweight fleece jacket, sweatshirt or similar item for moderate warmth.
- **One pair shorts**
- **A sarong**
- **Swimwear**
- **Underwear**: natural fibres are most comfortable. Easily replaced all over Asia, except for bras over size 38B. Don't bring too many, as you can wash and dry them in no time at all.
- **Socks**: to stop your feet getting ravaged by mosquitoes after sunset.
- **Rain gear**: a PVC poncho or cagoule might be useful and squashes into a small space. But in the tropical heat that comes with monsoons you'll feel more comfortable using an umbrella instead (PVC makes you sweat). Buy your umbrella when you need it; don't take one with you.
- **Sunhat**: not many people wear them, but they do keep you cooler and prevent sunstroke. Broad-brimmed straw hats are a pain to carry when you're on the move, so either buy one there and then dump it, or opt instead for a baseball cap or squashy cotton number.
- **One smart outfit**: you might find yourself invited to a festival, a wedding, or even a circumcision ceremony, so you'll want to at least look like you've made an effort. Smart gear is also useful when dealing with Asian bureaucracy. Something light that doesn't crumple is best.

Cracking the dress code

A friend of mine and I were in Amritsar and decided to walk from the hotel to the Golden Temple. We were both wearing ankle-length skirts and decently modest tops, but we may as well have been sporting sequined bikinis for all the anonymity that gave us. As soon as we stepped out of the lobby we were stared at, eyes levelled unashamedly and unmistakably at crotch height. It took us a while to realize that this was not the impolite lunacy of one or two individuals, but rather the local pastime for any male aged between 10 and 80. Our skirts were neither see-through nor hip-hugging, but maybe that was the attraction: what could be hiding behind those draped floral pleats? Which just goes to show that, however hard you try to be inconspicuous, as a foreign female you are always likely to be an object of curiosity.

Lucy Ridout

www.roughguides.com

Shoes

The footwear of choice for most backpackers is the **sports sandal** or reef-walker, of which Teva are the best known: a go-anywhere sandal with adjustable straps, and sturdy, contoured rubber soles. With a pair of sports sandals on your feet, you can negotiate rough terrain, go swimming, wade through rivers and wander the streets, without having to take them off. They are, of course, not as protective as walking boots, though not nearly as heavy either.

Each extra pair of shoes adds a kilo or two to your load, so, sports sandals or not, you need to keep your shoe quotient down. Ideally this means you should take just one hardy pair for daily walking, plus a pair of **sandals** or thongs/flip-flops for beach and hotel. If you're planning to do any long-distance trekking, **hiking boots** will probably be useful enough to justify that extra space and weight, and you can always wear them rather than pack them whenever you're moving on, though some people find trainers an adequate substitute.

Above all, your shoes need to be **airy**: not only do sweaty feet stink, but they can also fester and cause flesh-rot in tropical climes. You'll also appreciate shoes that don't have laces and other fiddly fastenings: in Asia, you're forever taking your shoes off to go into temples and mosques, when visiting people's homes and in quite a lot of guesthouses too, so easy on-and-offs are a boon. Most Asians wear leather sandals for those reasons.

▲ Hiking boots – bulky but essential for serious hiking

If you have **big feet** (that is, bigger than the Asian maximum size – men's 44/US 10½, UK 10; women's 40/US 9, UK 6½), be sure that your shoes will last you the whole trip, as you may not be able to buy any more off the peg. But you will be able to get some made for you – all the big cities have reputable shoemakers.

Essentials A–Z

- **Adaptors** If you're taking a digital camera, MP3 player, mobile phone, hairdryer, laptop, or any other electrical appliance, you'll need a set of travel plugs/electrical adaptors. See ⓦ www.kropla.com for a list of the different voltages and socket types around the world.

- **Batteries** Put new batteries in your watch, camera, alarm clock, flashlight (torch) and other vital items before you leave home. Consider taking replacements as well: although you will be able to get most brands in major cities, you may not be near a major city when yours run out.

- **Binoculars** Worth considering if you're going to be wildlife-spotting in national parks, or even trekking.

- **Books** New, English-language books are relatively expensive in Asia (India and Nepal are the exceptions), but secondhand bookstores and book exchanges are usually plentiful in travellers' centres, so there's no need to carry a whole library around with you. See pp.215–340 for country-specific titles that would make enjoyable travelling companions.

- **Camping gear** Accommodation and food is mostly so cheap that you won't need a tent, sleeping bag and camping stove to eke out your budget. Exceptions include Japan and Hong Kong, and any remote wilderness areas that you plan to explore without a guide (guides usually provide food and bedding).

- **Cigarette lighter** For lighting mosquito coils, candles (during power cuts) and campfires; matches get soggy from the humidity.

- **Comfort food** Some travellers swear by Marmite, Vegemite, peanut butter or whatever – a little taste of home to soothe the stomach and the taste buds.

- **Compass** Only necessary if you're trekking without a guide.

- **Contact lens solution** You can get standard brand-name contact lens solutions, and lenses, at opticians and pharmacists in Asian capitals and major cities. Take a pair of glasses as a back-up, for dusty conditions and in case you get an eye infection.

- **Contraceptives** Condoms are available over the counter in nearly every Asian nation, but do not rely on being able to buy other contraceptives in Asia: see Chapter Twelve for detailed advice.

www.roughguides.com

107

- **Earplugs** To block out snorers, roaring all-night traffic, early-morning cock crows, music on overnight buses and many other annoyances.

- **First-aid kit** Basic first-aid kit, medicines, antimalarials and insect repellents: see Chapter Twelve for details.

- **Flashlight (torch)** You may well be staying in places with sporadic electricity supplies, or even none at all; and a flashlight is always a help on overnight trains and when walking through dark, unfamiliar streets. The more compact your flashlight, the more likely you are to carry it with you.

- **Glasses** Take your prescription with you. Any optician should be able to fit your frames with new lenses, or supply a new pair – and usually much more cheaply than at home.

> ## Earplugs
>
> Earplugs are essential for screening out the routine din of Asian hotels. Until you've been to Asia, you just can't imagine how noisy everyone is. We regularly had building work going on in the next-door room or in the one directly above us – and it always continued through the night because that's the coolest time to work! Then there's the morning throat-clearing chorus – at 5am – when the night's phlegm is hawked and spat out by every man in the locality. And in Indonesia, it's impossible to stay out of earshot of the early morning *muezzin* calls at the neighbourhood mosque; in Padang, our hotel had its very own mosque – in the room adjacent to ours!
>
> Jo Mead

- **Guidebooks and phrasebooks** See Chapter Five for advice on how to choose.

- **Journal and pens** For all your profound observations and amusing anecdotes. (Don't forget to send in the best ones for the next edition of First-Time Asia.)

- **Laptop** A laptop or notebook can be useful if you're taking lots of digital photos or compiling a serious account of your trip, but they're heavy, something else to worry about, and hard to insure. See p.187 for a discussion of the pros and cons.

- **Mobile phone** Texting home is an economical way of keeping in touch, and if your phone has wi-fi connectivity that's an even better reason to take it: for details see p.189. You'll need a travel plug adaptor for the charger, or consider a solar charger so you're not reliant on being near a power supply.

- **Mosquito coils** Buy them when you arrive, where they will be much cheaper; see p.178.

- **Mosquito net** Can be useful anywhere in Asia, though most tourist accommodation will provide nets or screened windows. Nets are much cheaper in Asia than in the West, but, if you do buy one from home, choose one which is impregnated with mosquito repellent. They're available from camping shops from about \$12/£20/Aus\$65. Also pack a handful of hooks and a small roll of heavy-duty tape so that you can fix your net to beams, bedposts, window frames and ceilings.

- **iPod** Great for long bus, boat, train and plane journeys; for the beach and the hammock; and for entertaining locals as well as other travellers. Consider taking travel-speakers as well: you can get good-quality wallet-sized travel speakers for under \$50/£30. Don't forget to take an adaptor for the battery charger, or consider a solar charger.

- **Padlocks and cable-locks** Small padlocks on your backpack serve as a deterrent and are also useful as extra security on hotel doors. Keep two sets of keys in different places, or take combination padlocks instead. A cable-lock can be handy for securing your pack to luggage racks on overnight trains, or to roof racks on long-distance buses, and also for rented bikes and mopeds.

- **Penknife** If you take one, make it a Swiss Army knife (or a good cheap copy), as you might be glad of the blade and the bottle opener. Don't put it in your hand luggage when flying, as it's considered a potential weapon and will get confiscated (see Chapter Seven).

- **Photos of home** A good icebreaker, and just as weird and interesting to the people you'll meet on buses and trains as a picture of a Dyak longhouse or a Vietnamese cycle-rickshaw would be to you.

- **Sarong** It's amazing what you can do with a 2m x 1m length of cloth: you can use it as a bath and beach towel, as a sleeping sheet or blanket, as a turban-style sunhat or a temple headscarf-cum-shawl. You can turn it into a shopping bag, an awning on a shadeless beach, or even a rope (of sorts). And, of course, like the women and men of Laos, Cambodia, Thailand, Indonesia and Bangladesh, you can also wear it! You should be able to pick one up for around \$8/£5 anywhere in Asia.

- **Sewing kit** Safety pins, needle and cotton, plus a couple of buttons for emergency repairs.

Together forever

The problem with travelling with a music keyboard in your backpack is that you don't have any room for normal things like clothes or insect repellent. But you could never make as many friends with a pair of Levi's as you could with a Casio. My keyboard was a brilliant way of meeting people and a positive effort on my part to communicate in a language other than the ones we speak.

Sometimes I used to carry my keyboard around in a bin-liner. One time, during a hand-luggage check in Vientiane Airport, Laos, they threw my money belt on top of the keyboard, setting off the demo button. Everyone stopped in their tracks and stared as this black bag emerged from the X-ray machine singing Rick Astley's "Together Forever". Naturally, I was arrested.

Chris Humphrey

- **Sheet sleeping bag** More useful in tropical Asia than a down sleeping bag, but by no means essential: if you're worried about the cleanliness of the hotel sheets you can always use your sarong instead – or change your guesthouse.

- **Sink plug** Asian sinks tend not have plugs, so a universal sink plug (available from travel equipment stores and, more cheaply, from hardware stores) can be useful, especially for wet shaving.

- **Sleeping bag** Unless you're going to spend a long time camping or trekking in the colder and more remote parts of Asia, there's no point lugging a sleeping bag around with you. In popular trekking centres (like Kathmandu and Lhasa) you can rent four-season bags for as little as a dollar a day.

- **String** To use as a washing line and to suspend mosquito nets from. Some travellers swear by dental floss instead of string – it comes in a tiny box, and, as well as helping to keep your gums healthy, is strong enough to support your wet laundry and to tie up parcels.

The ideal travelling companion

When I'm travelling on my own, I find it comforting to have a reminder of people at home, so I always take Reggie, a tiny teddy bear, along too. We have shared many adventures, but it was in India that his talent as an icebreaker came to light – children and adults seemed to find him so irresistibly cute that they just had to start talking to me!

The most memorable Reggie-encounter happened when I was trekking in Kinnaur, in the Himalayas. I was following a path up through the forest, heading for the snow line, when I heard a man's voice beckoning from below. I wandered down to the clearing, greeted the old man and his wife, and introduced Reggie, emphasizing that his Hindi was much better than mine. Beaming from ear to ear, the old man immediately grasped hold of Reggie with both hands and began to have quite an animated conversation with him. Ice duly broken, we all sat down and shared a cheroot, after which I helped them with their wood-collecting.

Juliet Acock

- **Sunglasses** Tropical light is intense, so you'll be glad to hide behind some dark glasses. The same goes for high-altitude glare in Pakistan, Nepal, Tibet, Bhutan and northern India. Buy them at home, as the quality is not as good everywhere in Asia.

- **Sunscreen** Take sun block and a bottle of high-factor sunscreen (mimimum SPF 15; 30 if you have pale skin) for the first few weeks. Don't forget that you can get burnt just as easily in the cool of the mountains as by the sea: the UV rays are just as strong and the risk of getting skin cancer just as high.

- **Tampons** Available in most major cities and resorts across Asia, though check with your guidebook. Southern Sumatra, for example, is an exception, as is most of Laos outside Vientiane, and much of Vietnam and Cambodia.

- **Toilet paper** Toilet paper is only sometimes supplied in backpackers' accommodation in Asia so it's handy to keep a small roll with you (minus the cardboard centre to aid squashing and save space).

- **Toiletries** Unless you have very special requirements, you'll be able to restock your toiletry supply anywhere you go. And there'll be plenty of new lotions to experiment with, too – like the ochre-coloured face powder that some Thai women plaster on themselves to prevent sun damage, or the pure coconut oil used in India to ensure supple skin and lustrous hair. However, beware the large number of moisturizers, very popular with Asian women, that have a "whitening" effect on the skin, as they contain bleach.

- **Towel** Normal towels get disgustingly smelly very easily, take ages to dry and use up far too much valuable backpack space. Use a sarong instead. Or, if you must, take a tiny hand towel. Alternatively, there are a range of lightweight, quick-drying, high-absorbency travel towels on the market that do a reasonable job.

- **Wallet** Most Asian currencies are based on notes and, in countries where the denominations are very big, you'll find a wallet much handier than a purse because you'll have far more notes than coins. In Indonesia, for example, there's even a note for one hundred rupiah, currently equivalent to about one US cent. Inexpensive leather and fabric wallets are available all over Asia, so you might want to buy one when you get there.

- **Washing powder (laundry detergent)** Camping shops sell expensive travel-wash suds in tubes, but you're better off buying cheap individual portions of washing powder when you get there.

- **Water bottle and purifier** If you stick to the beaten track, you shouldn't need your own water bottle, as bottled water is sold in all touristed areas. However, if you're going trekking or venturing into remote areas you should definitely take your own one-litre water bottle, with belt or shoulder-strap attachment, or better still a water bladder and hose that fits into a backpack. You should also take purifying equipment (see Chapter Twelve).

- **Wet ones (baby wipes)** Not just for babies, but for sweaty travel-worn adults too. Good for cleaning yourself up on buses and trains, and for wiping hands before eating.

Cameras

Obviously most travellers will want to take a **camera** but it's worth weighing up the advantages of taking a bulky top-of-the range SLR with a variety of lenses against a point-and-shoot compact or the compromise zoom–compact option; you may even be satisfied with the shots taken by your phone/iPod etc. Be realistic about what you intend to do with the pictures once you get home: if you're planning to sell them for publication or use them in slide shows and lectures, then an SLR is probably essential; be aware too that most publications require pictures at a minimum quality of 8MB. But, if you just want them for your personal satisfaction, you may be happier with a smaller and less ostentatious camera – cameras draw a lot of attention wherever you are and can make you feel self-conscious; they also attract thieves.

Even if they're just personal mementoes, it is worth keeping a careful **list of pictures** taken; it sounds silly, but after another six months' travelling you won't be able to remember which Cambodian temple, Malaysian island or Tokyo skyscraper is which.

For detailed advice on buying a camera for your travels and practical tips on accessories and image storage on the road, see ⓦadrian warren.com.

Accessories

- Pack cleaning equipment, at the very least a little brush and air-cleaner, and use it daily: dust will quickly ruin both your camera and your pictures.
- Take a UV or skylight filter if you have an SLR camera, as the ultraviolet light in the tropics and at altitude can give an unnatural cast to pictures that makes them look washed out.
- Carry some silica gel with your camera lenses and film. This will absorb excess tropical moisture.
- Consider taking a compact tripod.

Picture etiquette

Not everyone you see in Asia, no matter how photogenic, will want their photo recorded by you for posterity. Some tribal people in Indonesia and Thailand **hate to be photographed** as they believe that a tiny fragment of their soul dies with every snapshot taken; and for many orthodox Muslim women, to be photographed by strangers is almost tantamount to being indecently assaulted. You should therefore always ask before taking someone's picture.

Festivals and religious events may also be off limits, so check with local people first: masked festival dancers in Nepal believe they embody the deities during their performance, so taking photos of them is sacrilegious; and filming the sacred cremations in Varanasi, India, could easily get you lynched by mortified onlookers. Be equally sensitive when photographing temples, mosques and other shrines, and don't whip out your camera at an international border, airport or military checkpoint.

You'll even find that some people – like the Ifugao people in the Philippines, the Dani tribe of West Papua in Indonesia, and certain Nepalese sadhus – are now so used to having their pictures taken by tourists that they **charge** a per-picture fee.

Digital storage and photo-sharing

There are various possibilities for **storing your digital images** while travelling, but whichever you choose you should take at least two decent-sized memory cards. When one card is full, the cheapest way to save its images is by burning them on to a CD either at an internet café or, usually pricier but often more reliable, at a camera shop. The alternative is to travel with a portable storage device – some MP3 players, for example, have this facility. Don't forget to pack the battery charger, USB cable and a travel plug adaptor (see p.107).

Where internet connections are sufficiently fast, you'll be able to **upload your photos** – on to emails to friends and family, on to Facebook and your blog, should you have one (see p.187), or on to a photo-sharing website such as Ⓦwww.flickr.com, Ⓦwww.kodakgallery .com or Ⓦwww.snapfish.com. Photo-sharing websites are also a good alternative way of storing your shots, and you can also order prints and have them posted to any address you like.

Alternatively, many parts of Asia offer good-quality **printing** from digital images at very cheap prices; this is a great way of passing photos to people before you leave town rather than relying on unreliable postal systems – and your own unreliable memory.

Documents

Your most essential **documents** – passport, airline tickets, travellers' cheques, credit card and insurance policy – should live in your money belt. Make two sets of **photocopies** of the relevant pages of your passport, your airline tickets, travellers' cheques receipt and serial numbers, credit card details and insurance policy. Keep one set with you, but in a separate place from the originals (eg passport in your money belt; copies in your backpack), and leave the other set at home with friends or relatives in case of loss or theft. Or scan them and upload them online somewhere, either to a private webpage or in an email to yourself, so you can get hold of them almost anywhere on your travels, internet availability permitting.

Take an **international drivers' licence** if you're eligible, and a **student card** and international youth hostel card if you have them. Don't buy a **hostel card** just for the trip, though, as guesthouses tend to be cheaper and more convenient than hostels in most parts of Asia (see Chapter Eleven). In Bangkok you can buy fake student ID cards and press cards; no one will accept them in Thailand, but they may work elsewhere in Asia. Take eight passport-size photos with you to use for visa applications, visa extensions and any passes you might need to buy while you're travelling.

Your first night

here's nothing quite like a foreign airport for freaking you out and making you wonder why you left home. Illegible signs and unfamiliar people chatting incomprehensibly can be bewildering and scary, especially when you've just spent a night without sleep. On top of all this, you'll perhaps be anticipating extortionate taxi fares, sleazy hotels and "friendly" helpers who turn out to be predatory touts.

Rest assured, however, that even the most laid-back travellers find their first night in a new country a challenge, something that needs to be approached with a clear head and a sense of humour. After countless hours sat on a plane you'll probably be lacking both, so this chapter is designed to help you cope without them and ensure that your first experience of Asia is a positive one.

Planning your first night

If you follow only one piece of advice in this whole chapter, then it should be this: **plan your first night** before you leave home. The decisions and preparations you make in advance can go a long way to reducing the chances of trouble once you arrive.

Even if your aim for the trip is to wander where your fancy takes you, it isn't really advisable just to amble off the plane that first night in Shanghai, Singapore or Seoul trusting that something will turn up. It probably will, but the chances are you won't like it. So you should know where you are planning to stay and how you are going to get there.

As part of the planning, make sure you have all the right paperwork (tickets, passport and visas; see Chapter Two) and a rough idea of how long you intend to stay in the country – you may need to stipulate this on arrival.

Choosing where to spend your first night

Stage one is to work out in which **area** of the city you want to spend your first night or two. Any reliable, up-to-date guidebook will help you decide (see Chapter Five), but here are a few extra tips:

- Choose an area that has a lot of budget hotels close together, so that if you don't like the first one it's easy to move.
- Pick an area that's close to the sights that interest you, and/ or convenient for any onward transport connections you might be needing in the next few days.
- Check out how easy the area is to reach from the airport and, with the help of your guidebook, decide what method of transport you plan to use. Bear in mind that the cheapest accommodation options (eg some of the youth hostels in Hong Kong) may be less accessible than pricier alternatives.
- Consider booking in for two or even three nights, which

gives you time to sleep (check-out time at most guesthouses is 11am), clear your head and plan your next move.

Down and out in Delhi

Having touched down at around midnight in Delhi we rushed outside to join the long queue for taxis. A man suddenly appeared from the side offering us a ride. Surely this would be better than waiting? Once in his car we told him we had no idea where to go, but we needed a hotel. He knew just the place. Off we set through the dark Delhi streets. The first hotel was full. No matter, he knew another place. Twenty minutes later we learnt that the second hotel too was full. We became concerned that he would charge us for all this useless ferrying around and pointed out we wouldn't pay for his mistakes. He replied it wasn't his fault and demanded the equivalent of $50 for the trip so far. Thinking this was too much we eventually, after a heated argument, handed over the equivalent of $30, and set off on foot. We flagged down a motorized rickshaw and, having learnt at least one lesson, asked how much it would cost to take us all to a hotel – forty cents! We loaded ourselves and luggage aboard and were whisked away to an acceptable hotel where we got a bed for the night. The next morning we were having breakfast and another foreigner approached us. He was leaving India; did we want to buy his guidebook? We definitely did. We read that the official fare from Delhi Airport to town was less than $8. "Why didn't we buy one of these before?" we wondered.

Sang Man

Booking a room before you leave home

Even though you may be planning to do your entire trip at sub-sistence level and wander wherever you like on a whim, your first night is not the best time to start. **Booking your first night** or two in advance takes a great deal of the anxiety out of arriving and gives you time to draw breath and get over jet lag before heading off on the adventure.

www.roughguides.com

Plenty of Asian hotels employ English-speaking staff, so contacting them by phone, email or through their website should be straight-forward. Give them your flight number and the approximate time you expect to arrive at the hotel (allowing up to two hours to get through airport formalities, plus whatever time it takes to get into town) – and enquire about hotel courtesy buses as well. You might be asked for a credit card deposit. In Asia, not all of the cheaper hotels and guest-houses accept bookings without advance payment in cash but ⓦwww .hostelworld.com has plenty of cheaper options, and youth hostels are bookable in advance (ⓦwww.hihostels.com).

If you book through other online travel sites or use your travel agent this could work out more expensive, as they tend towards mid-range or expensive hotels. But remember that prices are lower in Asia than in Europe, the US and Australia, and that you can always move to a cheaper place later. Once you've made your booking, confirm it in writing by email or fax and take copies of all correspondence with you.

Women might also consider a homestay with a local woman for the first couple of nights: contact the Women Welcome Women World Wide organization (see p.162) for details.

The plane journey

If you're coming from Europe or America, the flight into Asia is almost certain to be long – NYC to Hanoi, for example, lasts a good thirty hours, while London to Mumbai takes at least eight. If you're doing things on a budget, your journey may be convoluted, involving several touchdowns and possibly long waits while changing planes. There's nothing you can do to speed the trip up, but here are a few suggestions to help make it as comfortable as possible.

Hand baggage

Handy items you might want to pack in your carry-on baggage include:

- **Something to read** Your guidebook can be useful so you can firm up your arrival strategy. Some travellers also swear by a Game Boy and/or iPod to help pass the time.
- **All valuables and fragile items** Your checked-in baggage is not only more likely to go astray but is also treated much more roughly.
- **Toiletries** Small quantities of basic toiletries, including a toothbrush: a quick wash and brush can improve how you feel very quickly.
- **A small bottle of water** (buy it in the departure lounge so it doesn't get confiscated at security) so you don't dehydrate either

on the plane (you can refill it up from the water dispenser) or in transit lounges, where you might otherwise have to shell out for soft drinks in local currency.

- **Clothes** It's a good idea to wear or take several layers of clothing so that you don't perish in your home country and boil when you arrive (or vice versa); also remember the modesty factor (see box on p.103). You may also find you need to wrap up on the flight itself (planes in tropical climates get cold at 36,000 feet) and airline blankets can be in short supply. Always pack one set of clean underwear – if your bags don't arrive you don't want to be trying to buy new underwear on your first morning in Vientiane.
- **Medicines** Include any regular medication. Painkillers are useful as flying is dehydrating and headaches are common. Air sickness is not unusual: put some medication in your hand baggage just in case.
- **A pen** for filling in immigration forms.
- An inflatable **neck pillow**, eye shades and ear plugs if you're intending to sleep during the flight.
- If you're going to spend a few hours in transit at Singapore's Changi Airport, you might consider including swimwear – the airport has its own swimming pool.

Checking in

If you've followed our advice in Chapter One, you'll already have chosen your seat, booked your meal, arranged all necessary visas and arrived at the airport with loads of time to spare. Some other tips:

- Check in your bag with every compartment locked (see p.101). Put your name, email address and destination on the inside of your luggage – when luggage gets lost the tags often get ripped off.

Memorable landings

Flights into parts of Asia offer some of the most spectacular scenery in the world:

- Planes arriving in Kathmandu make their descent within spitting distance of the soaring peaks of the Himalayas, including Everest.
- After flying across Sichuan's western mountain ranges, the landing at Lhasa seems like a miracle of faith over logic as the ground appears to rise up to meet the plane instead of the plane making a normal descent.
- Flying in to the Philippines, you get a great view of the sparkling South China Sea and the seven thousand plus atolls that make up this island nation.
- At 2700m above sea level with a mountain at one end of the tiny patch of runway and a long, long drop at the other, the arrival at Lukla, Nepal, en route to Everest is dramatic enough to excite even the most hardened traveller.

- A baggage coupon will be issued. Keep this safe. You will need it if officials want to check that you are the owner of the bag or if your baggage goes astray you need to complete lost-luggage paperwork at your destination.
- Some travellers slip a colour photograph of their case/rucksack into their hand baggage. If necessary you'll be able to show airport staff at the other end what is missing rather than struggle with descriptions in a foreign language.

Coping with the flight

The following suggestions may help the flight pass more comfortably, and safely:

- Combat **dehydration** by drinking lots of soft drinks and water.
- Go easy on the **booze**: there's often plenty of free alcohol available on long-haul flights which can help you relax but too much can result in gigantic headaches and a soaring body temperature. The other disadvantage of over-indulgence is that you'll arrive in Asia at your most befuddled, just when you need your wits about you.
- Take regular **exercise**: walk around the cabin as often as possible and follow the stretching routines suggested on board. Apart from relieving stiffness and swollen ankles, moving about helps reduce the risks of developing DVT (see next point) which can be life threatening.
- **Consult your doctor** before flying if you have an increased risk of developing **DVT** (deep-vein thrombosis); note that this can include expectant mothers and those on oral contraceptives. Always report any DVT-linked symptoms, such as leg pain and breathing problems, on arrival. See ⓦwww.nathnac.org/travel/factsheets/dvt .htm for more information.
- Some travellers swear by **sleeping pills** but they can leave you feeling even worse on arrival
- An additional point, for **divers**: always leave at least twelve hours after a dive before flying, preferably 24 hours, especially if you've done multiple dives or a dive with decompression stops. ⓦwww .aviation-health.org has more information.

The transit experience

Should you be turfed off the plane for a couple of hours' refuelling en route, or have to wait for a connecting flight, the **transit expe-rience** won't necessarily be unpleasant and some of Asia's airports are wonderful (see below). It's always worth asking your airline whether it is possible to pay to use the first- or business-class lounge – it's much quieter than the rest of the airport, the chairs are more comfortable and there'll be free coffee and newspapers. At the other end of the scale, the website ⓦwww.sleepinginairports.com provides all you'll need to know about the best (and worst) Asian airport floors and chairs on which to grab some sleep between flights.

Some of the best transit experiences in Asia can be found at:

- **Singapore**'s Changi Airport (ⓦwww.changiairport.com.sg) has a great English-language bookshop full of publications on Asia. There's free internet access throughout the terminal, a rooftop swimming pool and showers, gardens, and free two-hour city coach tours for transit passengers with sufficient time. The airport's transit hotel rents out rooms for short periods (with wake-up calls provided) so you can get some proper sleep.
- **Kuala Lumpur** International Airport (ⓦwww.klia.com.my) has the excellent **Airside Transit Hotel**, which rents out rooms for six-hour periods or, if you just need to freshen up, showers, a sauna and gym are available with toiletries, towels and hairdryer provided. There's also a reflexology and massage centre.
- **Jakarta**'s Soekarno-Hatta Airport is pleasingly laid out in pagoda-style buildings, connected by walkways that lead you through tropical gardens. There's a well-priced Asian food court.
- **Hong Kong**'s gleaming Chek Lap Kok airport (ⓦwww .hongkongairport.com) features the Plaza Shower and Relaxation Lounge offering hot showers and a Hair and Beauty Salon as well.
- The transit lounge at **Osaka**'s Kansai International Airport (ⓦwww.kansai-airport.or.jp) has massage, showers and a relax-ation lounge available.

Arriving

While many Asian international airports have the appearance and the seamless efficiency of anything in Europe, North America or Australasia, others are more basic, although the days of grass landing strips and tin shacks operating as international airport terminals are largely extinct. Remember that airports the world over, even in your own country, can be confusing, intimidating places and certainly don't reflect the country as a whole. They are, literally, a rite of passage to be gone through by every traveller – ideally as painlessly as possible.

New arrivals are prime fodder for touts; you'll be amazed just how many services you can be offered in the short walk between customs and the taxi rank – hotels, hash, sex, diamonds, tour guides, you name it. The slightest flicker of interest, or even friendly eye contact, is encouragement enough to continue the encounter and if this is your

No harm in asking...

I was nervous about doing the big cross-Asia trip on my own, but as there was no one else to go with, off I went. Standing by the luggage carousel at Denpasar Airport in Bali (my first port of call), I got chatting to a couple of hip-looking American women, and asked if I could share a ride with them into town. It turned out we got on really well and we spent the next two weeks together, travelling as a threesome all round Bali. After that I was much more confident and happy to continue through Indonesia on my own.

Debbie King

first time in Asia, it will be written all over you, from your face to the way you walk. Not only do you feel vulnerable, but this is the time when you **are** most vulnerable. Much as you may hate to be unfriendly, in arrivals you should keep your eyes fixed unflinchingly forwards, your backpack strapped firmly to your back, and your plan of action bleeping loudly inside your head.

Hopefully you've planned to arrive in **daylight** so that you have plenty of time to get into the city and find your accommodation before it gets dark (see Chapter Two). A lot of the lowlife of any city emerges after sunset; with your senses and fears heightened by the shadows it is perfectly possible, and even sensible, to assume that absolutely harmless and helpful people are out to rip you off. If the worst comes to the worst and you do arrive in the middle of the night and don't know what to do, just wait in the airport until daybreak. The website ⓦwww.sleepinginairports.com offers advice on this.

Daylight or not, if you're on your own, think about linking up with other travellers who look as if they might be on the same budget as you and therefore heading to the same area of town – there's usually plenty of time to size people up in immigration and baggage collection queues. This will save money on taxi fares and will probably make you feel more confident about the whole arrivals procedure. Nonetheless, it makes sense to retain some healthy scepticism in encounters with fellow travellers, too.

Formalities

It goes without saying, but we'll say it anyway. You shouldn't be trying to bring anything inappropriate into the country. Most countries stipulate a **duty-free allowance** for alcohol or tobacco, some do not allow the import of certain food items and all prohibit the import of hard and soft drugs. In some Asian countries the penalty for **smuggling drugs** is death and lengthy jail terms are the norm in the remainder. It is up to you to find out what the regulations are in each country and obey them – guidebooks or the official government websites of individual countries are useful for finding this out.

Solo travellers should be vigilant when collecting baggage; don't leave your hand baggage unattended on a trolley while lunging for your pack on the carousel – you risk turning around and finding it gone. Keep at least one hand on your hand baggage at all times – even if it means sacrificing your trolley.

Local currency

Unless you managed to buy some before you left home, you'll need to get some **local currency** before leaving the airport. Keep your eyes peeled for exchange facilities or ATMs as soon as you get off the plane, as in some airports they are between the runway and passport control; you won't be able to re-enter this area once you've left, so change your money while you're passing through. Rates will probably be less favourable at the airport than in town, though, so you might want to change just enough for the first couple of days. However hard it is to get your jet-lagged brain into gear, follow the guidelines for changing money in Chapter Four (see p.82).

Anarchists in the UK

The only time I've ever had trouble at immigration is when I went to Japan with my friend John. John is an archivist, which is what he told immigration officials when they asked. Unfortunately, they misheard, or at least misunderstood, and, thinking he'd said "anarchist", hauled us both off for a thorough baggage check behind closed doors. Moral of that story: either give a simple version of your job title or make one up.

Bob Williams

Arriving without a hotel booking

If you haven't pre-booked a place from home (see p.115) you are left with three options; using a booking counter at the airport, ringing around the hotels in town or chancing your luck on the streets.

Many international airports have one or several **booking counters** for local hotel rooms. The clerk rings the hotel and makes the reservation, then issues you with a voucher, which will either be the receipt for payment made at the counter or will specify the price you'll pay at the hotel. The clerk should also be able to advise you on the best way of getting there. The main drawback with this option is that only certain hotels – generally mid- to upper-range establishments – either maintain their own counters or feature at booking agent counters and if they're not described in your guidebook, you won't have any idea of what the place is like until you get there.

If you're up to tackling the local telephone system and language (and can get hold of some coins or a phone card), there is nothing to stop you **ringing hotels** yourself and finding a bed, although you should come armed with a list of options together with phone numbers – most public phones don't have directories. Remember to establish the price and make sure you get the hotel to hold the room for long enough for you to get there and claim it.

www.roughguides.com

Probably the least desirable situation on your first night is to be tramping the streets with your pack on your back, looking for a place to stay. If, for whatever reason, this happens, then you should head for an area where there is plenty of accommodation so you'll have a few alternatives and short distances to trek between places. This means that you need not be unduly concerned if the first place is full and your second closed down – particularly crucial if you arrive late in the day or if your visit coincides with the peak tourist season or a local holiday. For full details on accommodation, see Chapter Eleven. If there are two or more of you travelling together, it's easier if one of you sits in a café, bar or restaurant with the bags while the others do the trailing around to find a place.

Getting into town

The golden rule here is to put **personal safety** above everything, and that includes price. If you don't feel comfortable waiting an hour for a bus in a dark underground car park or sitting in an unlicensed cab on your own for forty minutes, then don't do it. You will have plenty of chances to save money later.

Use your guidebook or the relevant airport website if there is one (check at ⓦwww.azworldairports.com) to weigh up your transport options into town. Getting this sort of information in advance is pretty vital: for example, from Narita airport in Tokyo a ninety-minute, seventy-kilometre taxi ride into town will cost around $215/£130, whereas the sixty-minute Skyliner Airport Express train trip costs $12/£7.50 and there is an extensive choice of buses, some of which serve many of the downtown hotels, costing $15-30/£10-20.

Depending on where you are there may be a rail link (for example, Kuala Lumpur International Airport, Chek Lap Kok in Hong Kong and Narita in Tokyo), but more likely you'll be looking at road transport. The variety can be overwhelming. Your most likely options for getting into town are:

- **Official taxis** In some cases you join the taxi queue and get the next metered cab from the rank. In others there are prepaid taxi counters with fixed prices. This is generally the most expensive but most reliable method: the cabs and drivers are licensed and, in theory at least, know the city well.
- **Unofficial cabs** Touts for these hang about at most major airports and try to entice customers away from the official cabs. They may well be cheaper – providing you can haggle effectively over the price – but you'll end up at the mercy of a

▲ Local transport can be hard to tackle on your first night

car and driver with no official recognition and uncertain local knowledge. Always agree the price before you get in but on the whole they are best avoided.

● **Courtesy buses** Many of the upmarket hotels operate courtesy bus services for their customers. If you are booked into a more expensive hotel, check whether this service is available.

● **Airport buses** Many airports operate bus services, which are probably the most hassle-free and cost-effective means of getting into the city. Though slower than taxis, the buses usually have plenty of space for luggage, and often follow routes that are conveniently close to the main tourist and hotel areas. Sometimes you prepay your ticket inside the arrivals hall and sometimes you pay on board.

● **Local buses** These are the slowest but the cheapest of the lot. You'll need to have small change to pay the fare and you should be prepared to be rather unpopular if you're hauling a mountain of luggage while commuters are trying to get to or from their workplaces. Ask yourself whether you really want to tackle this on day one when you've no idea where you are, no idea where you are going, no clue how long it should take to get there and you may not even be able to see out of the windows. For more on the delights of local buses see Chapter Ten.

Jet lag for beginners

You're wide awake and feeling peckish at 3am. Try as you might, your body does not seem to understand that it's time for sleep. Though it's dark and most locals are fast asleep, you're just not tired. Chances are you've got **jet lag**. It happens because we travel too far, too fast – when travellers went by land or sea, nobody suffered from the effects of zooming across time zones and arriving at a strange time of day or night with their body clock still operating on home time.

Some of the possible **symptoms** of jet lag are disturbed sleep patterns, hunger pangs at weird times and severe fatigue and lethargy for several days. The more time zones you go through, the worse the effects are likely to be. Received opinion says that for every hour of time change it takes a day to adjust (in other words, flying from London to Delhi should theoretically take you five and a half days to adjust). If you are exhausted before you leave home the effects are likely to be worse. The younger you are, and the less rigidly timetabled your life at home is, the more adaptable you're supposed to be.

Some people find that night flights minimize jet lag, and that eastbound flights are worse than westbound (supposedly because your body clock adapts more easily to a longer rather than a shorter daily cycle). Also, being obliged to disembark during middle-of-the-night refuelling stops makes readjustment harder – check this when booking your flight.

To combat jet lag you might want to try doing one, or all, of the following:

- Change your **mealtimes** to those of your arrival country a few days before you leave home. This is easier said than done if it means breakfast at 2am.
- Adopt the **timetable** of your new country as soon as you land there. In other words, go to bed at 11pm Manila time, not 11pm Eastern Standard Time. If you're dozy at 3pm, have an espresso or go for a run round the block, but whatever you do don't lie down and have a nap – doing so will only lead to your taking longer to adjust.
- Take a couple of strong **sleeping pills** an hour before local bedtime.
- Consider **melatonin** tablets (not yet licensed for sale in the UK), a naturally occuring hormone that regulates sleep.
- To avoid late-night hunger pangs, eat high-protein foods at breakfast and lunch, and high-carbohydrate, low-protein foods such as pasta at dinner.
- Do a short (five to ten minutes' worth), gentle **exercise** programme before bed. A few bends and stretches will get the kinks out of your body after the flight and help you wind down and relax ready for sleep.

- Consider trying the **aromatherapy** method. A mix of geranium, lavender and lemongrass oils prior to travel may help you adapt, whereas geranium, camomile and lavender may be useful after arrival. For further advice, consult Jude Brown's *Aromatherapy for Travellers* (Thorsons).
- Switch on Star TV, the less-than-riveting Asian cable station.
- Soothe yourself with the thought that you'll be fully adapted in a couple of days, and meanwhile enjoy the coolness of the (very) early morning.

8

Culture shock

Do not be surprised if you don't enjoy your first few days in Asia. You might feel self-conscious, paranoid or just plain exhausted. You'll probably feel lonely and a bit frightened. You might even find yourself wishing you'd never come, hating the heat, sickened by the smells and appalled by the poverty. This reaction is quite normal: it's **culture shock**. Everyone experiences it in some form, and it's all part of the challenge of dropping yourself into an alien environment.

A few tips to help you acclimatize:

- **Take it easy for the first few days** You may well be jet-lagged (see p.124), extremely tired, and overwhelmed by the unbearable humidity. Check out the tips on coping with tropical heat in Chapter Twelve.
- **Venture out gradually** It takes time to find your bearings and get used to the ways of a new country. Start off by exploring the closer, more accessible places you want to see and save the more adventurous outings for later.
- **Buy a decent map of your new city** You'll feel far more confident if you know where you are.
- **Try speaking a few words of the local language** It will make you feel much less alien and you might even make some friends. (See Chapter Five for some language-learning tips.)
- **Don't worry if you can't face local food** If you feel like drinking smoothies and eating nothing but cheese sandwiches for the first few days, then why not? There'll be plenty more opportunities to experiment with local cuisine.

Travel talk

Once you have arrived in Asia, you'll find that the most useful, up-to-date information about where to go, what to see, where to stay, how to get there and what to avoid – in fact, stuff about pretty much every aspect of your trip – comes from **other travellers**. Sitting chatting in the guesthouse or over a beer you'll hear the latest from people who have already done it. They'll be more clued in than a guidebook, more impartial than the tourist office, and they won't be getting commission for sending you to cousin X's restaurant, shop or hotel.

However, it pays to assess the person you're talking to fairly carefully. Sooner or later, you'll bump into the long-time-on-the-road, been-there-done-it-all-on-one-cent-a-day macho-man (yes, most of them are men), who gets his jollies by insisting to newcomers that the only way to have a really authentic Asian experience is to stay in a particular rat-infested fleapit tottering on stilts over a mosquito swamp where breakfast is a grain of rice and a lentil, if you're lucky, and the toilet is guarded by a pit of writhing black mambas who can kill with a droplet of venom from twenty paces.

This kind of traveller also loves to assure you that whichever place you thought of heading for is now spoilt; you should have been here five, ten, fifteen or twenty years ago to see the real Asia. In addition, he'll claim you really need to speak the local dialect to get even a glimpse of the local culture, and any fool with half a brain could have bought whatever you've just purchased for a tenth of the price. He never takes precautions against malaria, drinks the water from the tap, doesn't believe in travel insurance and has never had an inoculation or day's illness in his life. He will spoil your holiday if you let him – avoid and/or ignore as necessary and watch out that you don't fall into the same trap of self-aggrandizement after a few months on the road.

And now for something completely different

Though your first brush with Beijing, Jakarta or Manila may be disappointingly banal – a Western-style cityscape of neon Coca-Cola ads, skyscrapers and middle-class office workers – it won't be long before you realize that the McDonald's-ization of Asia is only cosmetic.

Traditions run deep in Asia and, though urban fashions come and go, in many areas community life continues to revolve round religious practices and family units. From a Western point of view, traditional Asian values can seem stiflingly conservative, especially in relation to gender roles and social conformity. Many Asians find travellers' behaviour just as strange, not least because the whole idea of an unmarried youngster (or even a long-married oldster) sloping off around the world seems bizarre if not downright irresponsible.

Women in the traditional Muslim and Hindu communities of India, Nepal, Pakistan, Indonesia and Malaysia are encouraged to be economically dependent on fathers and husbands, and to keep a low profile in public, often hiding behind veils or scarves. This can be a shock to Western travellers, who will miss having contact with local women – and of course it has an effect on how local men see Western women, too. Asian men often address all conversation to a Western woman's male companion (if she has one), while solo women may be jeered at or worse. Advice on coping with sexual harassment is given in Chapter Fourteen.

Asia is the most populous continent in the world and your first bus ride in China or India will etch that fact indelibly in your mind. **Crowds** and queues are the norm and there's no point protesting when five more people try to cram onto an already overloaded share-taxi. Time to dust off your sense of humour and start a section on "quaint local customs" in your journal.

The same goes for the **bureaucratic tangles** involved in simple transactions like cashing a travellers' cheque, and for the haphazard timetables of most Asian buses. Indonesians have a great phrase for Asian timekeeping that translates as "rubber time" – sometimes it stretches, sometimes it doesn't.

Being an alien

As an obvious **outsider** (or "alien", as foreigners are known in Japan), you will arouse a lot of interest, for your novelty value as well as your commercial potential. What's considered nosy in the West is often acceptable in Asia, so try not to get offended by the unflinching stares, or by women stroking your oddly coloured skin and feeling your strangely fine hair. And, if you're blond-haired, get ready for movie-star treatment! Conversely, if you're of Asian stock yourself you might find you're treated with unusual suspicion, especially as a woman travelling with a white man – one of the many negative effects of the sex-tourism industry in Southeast Asia in particular.

Be prepared to answer endless **questions** about your marital status and also about your children: in most parts of Asia to be single is a calamitous state of affairs and to be childless a great misfortune. In fact, be prepared to answer questions about absolutely any private matter at

Curiouser and curiouser

We've all been stared at and had our hair stroked and muscles squeezed before, but I do remember a rather more significant experience on a long-distance bus journey in Vietnam. We had a toilet stop after about two hours, and this "toilet" just so happened to be a very large open field. Naturally I was rather surprised to find a man standing only 10cm away from me in such a spacious latrine. As I was going about my business he certainly wasn't minding his, and he saw nothing wrong in leaning over and staring directly at my penis during my efforts to relieve myself. "That's OK," I thought and looked straight ahead as if I hadn't noticed. It was only when he bent over and started touching it and wiggling it that I really had trouble ignoring him. This unbridled curiosity and complete absence of the concept of privacy is one of the hardest things to adjust to.

Chris Humphrey

all: how old you are, how much you earn and how much your air ticket cost are common conversational openers. People will read your emails over your shoulder, and eavesdrop quite blatantly, too, even if they can't understand what's being said.

Sometimes it can be easier to lie about yourself – depending on who you're talking to, it may be less controversial to pretend that you're a Christian (or whatever), as agnosticism is incomprehensible to many Asian communities and atheism almost offensive. Lies can sometimes get you into more trouble of course, as the anecdote below illustrates only too well.

You may well be asked for your home address by complete strangers who like the kudos of collecting exotic Western pals, and you'll probably have your photo taken a few times, too – now there's a cultural somersault to make you think. In short, you're as fascinating to them as they are to you – and that must have some positive influence on global relations.

"Where are you going?"

It rarely takes long to tire of being in the public eye so much. One surprising irritation is being asked the same question – in English – again and again. In India the line is nearly always "What is your mother country?", while in most parts of Southeast Asia it becomes "Where are you going?" The questions aren't meant to annoy, but are intended as friendly **greetings**: "Where are you going?" is simply the literal translation of "Hi!" or "How're you doing?" Just as in the West no one expects a full rundown on your state of health, no one in Asia really wants to know where you're heading; they just want to make contact.

Instead of getting irked by the constant chorus and more incensed still when they ignore your answer, try responding as local people do. In Indonesia,

Telling tales

Charles and I talked a lot about his travels in Indonesia. As in most parts of Asia, English-speaking Indonesians almost always ask the same four questions of every tourist: (1) "Where are you from?" (2) "How old?" (3) "You married?" (4) "How many babies?" Charles, already 62, never married, and childless, sometimes got tired of these questions. So, one day, when someone came up to him at a bus station in Sumatra and started firing away, Charles decided to make sure the guy would go away. He told him, "Yes, I am married, and sir, the reason I'm in Sumatra now is that I murdered my wife and I'm running away from the police!" The guy looked at him in awe and quickly left. Charles was satisfied, almost thrilled; he had found a way to avoid more personal questions.

An hour later the same guy came back with his whole family – about fifteen people in all – and he said to Charles, "Now you're going to tell me the story of how you murdered your wife, and I'll translate for my family!" Unfortunately, Charles' bus was delayed for ten hours, not the one hour he'd expected, and he was trapped there making up stories for the rest of the day.

Laura Littwin

for example, you should reply "Jalan jalan", which means "Walking walking"; in Thailand "Bpai teeo" means "I'm out having fun"; and in Malaysia the even more cryptic retort, "Saya makan angin", literally translates as "I'm eating the wind".

On your best behaviour

However much you dislike the notion of being an ambassador for your country, that is how local people will see you. Similarly, your view of their country will almost certainly be coloured by how they treat you. So it pays for everyone to respect everyone else. No one expects you to traipse around Asia dressed in local fashions, but it is polite – and in some places expedient – to adapt your Western behaviour to suit the local culture. Because **social rules** tend to be more rigid in Asia, it's relatively easy for tourists to do the wrong thing – nine times out of ten, you'll be forgiven for being ignorant of the niceties, but there are a few behaviour codes you should definitely follow.

- In nearly all parts of Asia men and women **dress modestly** and find exposed flesh an embarrassment anywhere but the beach (see p.103). **Shoes** are never worn indoors at home or inside temples and mosques, so remember to take them off in religious buildings and when entering people's homes – this includes some small guesthouses.
- Getting angry at anything is a very un-Asian thing to do. In fact, it's considered to be a **loss of face** and therefore an embarrassment for both the perpetrator and the recipient – a bit like being heard farting loudly in a posh restaurant. Always keep cool when expressing displeasure or making a complaint, trying to be as dispassionate as possible.
- **Canoodling** in public is frowned on in most parts of Asia (even Japan). It's quite common for friends of the same sex to wander about with their arms round each other, but passionate embraces with the opposite sex are considered rather gross, regardless of the couple's marital status.
- Throughout Asia, the **head** is considered the most sacred part of a person's body, and the **feet** are the most profane. Try not to touch anyone on the head (even kids) or to point at anyone, or anything, with your feet.
- Be aware that **making eye contact** with members of the opposite sex can be seen as an unabashed come-on.
- Take special care not to offend when **visiting temples and mosques** or attending religious festivals. Dress modestly, observe the behaviour of local devotees, and never come between people at prayer and their altar, or take photos without permission.

- Be sensitive when discussing **religion and politics** with local people. In most parts of Asia, a person's faith is inviolable and should not be questioned. Censorship is rife in some Asian countries and penalties can be severe for a resident who goes public with controversial views. This is very much the case in China at the moment, and in Tibet. Even in happy-go-lucky Thailand, anyone who makes disrespectful remarks about the royal family is liable to be put in jail. In India, on the other hand, opinionated political debate is standard fare on train journeys and in newspaper columns.
- For tips on avoiding embarrassing situations in **Asian bathrooms**, see Chapter Eleven.

Eating and food

Strange foods and bizarre eating habits are a major feature of the Asian experience, and can often be one of the highlights. After all, Asia is home to two of the world's greatest **cuisines** – Indian and Chinese – and you can be sure that tandoori chicken and Peking duck taste nothing like they do in the curry houses and takeaways of the West. Then there's the prospect of sampling real Thai food, regarded by nearly all travellers as one of Thailand's greatest assets. For some highlights of Asian cuisine so special that they're worth redesigning your itinerary for, see Chapter One. You will also probably encounter your fair share of unappetizing dishes and gut-wrenching cooking methods, but so long as you heed the advice on healthy eating and drinking given in Chapter Twelve you shouldn't go far wrong.

- Lots of Asian food is **eaten with the hand** (rather than a knife and fork). Sticky rice in Thailand is rolled up into tiny balls and then dunked in spicy sauces, and most meat and veg dishes in India, Nepal and Pakistan are scooped up with pieces of flat bread. Local people always use their right hand for eating because the left hand – which is used for washing after going to the toilet – is considered unclean (see Chapter Eleven). There's often a washbasin in the restaurant for diners to use before and after eating, or at least a pail of water and a scoop.
- Chinese and Japanese food is eaten with **chopsticks**, as are noodles in all parts of Asia. But don't panic! Though it's entertaining to watch a hapless tourist wrestling with the equivalent of two pencils and a slippery piece of spaghetti, most restaurant owners take pity on foreigners and offer spoons and forks as well.

www.roughguides.com

▲ Fast-food nation: in Japan, hot noodle soup comes out of a vending machine

- Asian dishes can be **unbearably spicy**. Just one mouthful of a Lao chicken salad or a green Thai curry could be enough to send you hopping round the room in a blaze of oral agony. Water won't cool your palate down, but yoghurt is a great palliative, and so is beer, as both contain chemicals that dissolve the chilli oils. It is possible to retrain your taste buds to actually enjoy chilli-rich food (there really is such a thing as a "chilli high"), but if you can't face that, be sure to learn the local phrase for "not spicy, please".

- Despite the strong religious culture, **vegetarians** get a mixed reception across Asia. With nearly all its restaurants categorized as either "Veg" or "Non-Veg", India is by far the most veggie-friendly nation. Many other nations, on the other hand, regard meals cooked with neither meat nor fish as poor-people's food, unbalanced and lacklustre. The best advice is to learn the phrase for "without meat or fish" (or, where relevant, the phrase for "I am a Buddhist") and to be prepared either to compromise when it comes to stocks and soups (which are nearly always made from fish or meat) or to eat mainly fresh market produce.

Some harsh realities

Poverty is a lot more visible in most parts of Asia than it is in the West, and in some places a lot more prevalent too. Asia is home to some of the poorest people in the world, destitute people who live in slums or on street corners, who sometimes disable their own children so that they can be sure of earning something from street-begging. It is also home to some of the wealthiest people in the world, and the rich–poor divide is distressingly pronounced in many Asian cities; beggars congregate outside the most upmarket hotels and in places like Hong Kong it's hard not to be shocked by the sight of glossy banking headquarters built right next door to squalid tenement slums.

For Hindus, Buddhists and Muslims of all wage brackets, the giving of **alms** to the sick, the disabled and the very poor (as well as to monks and holy men) is almost an obligation, a way of adding credit to your karma. These donations serve as an informal welfare system, as in most parts of Asia there's no national health service or financial support for the unemployed.

Western tourists tend to be less used to dealing with **beggars**, and you would not be the first one to mask your

Bitter moon

Full moon over Hoi An, an ancient port town in Central Vietnam. I gazed off into the heavens from my café table; Hoi An had me feeling mystical. I smiled dreamily at nothing. Enter Don, all energy and intellect, clever not merely for his mastery of the English language, but for his sharp wit and precocious insights. He plopped into the empty chair across from me and I waited for the standard shoeshine pitch. Instead this beautiful twelve-year-old boy asked me if I was in love. I pulled the picture of a new boyfriend (my "fiancé" for the trip) from my notebook. I kept the picture handy to ward off prospective suitors.

After twenty minutes of fluent chatter about Vietnam, America and tourism, it was clear that little Don had a crush. In the following days we shared discussions, lunches and laughs; he enjoyed practising his English and I enjoyed his energetic company. He took me to drink my first sugar cane and insistently paid for both drinks. It never occurred to me to ask Don where he got the money.

Later in my stay, I was out with a friend when we noticed Don. "Here comes my conscience", I laughed. My friend grimaced. "Don't look now, your conscience just disappeared with that German man". It was in that moment of rage and close-to-the-bone pain that I realized Don was a prostitute. He resurfaced a little while later with a fistful of money and disappeared into the night.

Andrea Szyper

discomfort with averted eyes and a purposeful stride. Giving is a personal decision, of course; you might prefer to donate to a charity instead, or to get actively involved with a local charity for a few days – see Chapter One for some suggestions. Supporting local small businesses is also a positive way of preventing the encroachment of poverty; see Chapter Nine for more about this. And it's always worth going out of your way to pay for small services – like giving kids in India a few rupees to stand in your bus queue for an hour, or agreeing to have your shoes shined by an elderly Malaysian man even though they don't really need a clean.

Time to go home

When I first arrived in Delhi, I spent some time with a guy who'd been in India for months. To get rid of the kids who would come begging around our café he used to mirror the gesture they made to show they were hungry – a jabbing finger in the mouth. I thought that was a mean, crass thing to do, but the kids usually scarpered.

Five months later, tired and strung out after many exhausting weeks of Indian travel, I was sitting in another Delhi café when a tiny girl came up and indicated she was hungry. Weary, jaded, unthinking, who knows what I was thinking, I did the finger in the mouth gesture back at her. To my mortification she fished inside her pocket and handed me two rupees.

Back at my guesthouse I cried and cried with shame. It was time to go home.

Jean-Louis Martin

Being a wealthy tourist

All over Asia, people will express amazement at the price of your air ticket – it will seem an absolute fortune to them. Regardless of how impecunious you are, or feel, to an Indian factory worker on less than a dollar a day or a Filipino waiter on the daily equivalent of $3, you are quite literally a **millionaire**. And your camera, iPod and sunglasses will do little to change his or her opinion. Small wonder that Asians can't understand why travellers dress in torn and dirty clothing – surely if they can afford an air ticket they can stretch to a new outfit?

It's always worth trying to put **money** matters in context when people ask the price of your ticket, and to emphasize how hard you had to save to buy it. For example, your ticket may have cost you the equivalent of three months' rent, or about three weeks' wages. On the other hand, there's no question that you are comparatively rich – and that was probably one of the reasons why you chose to go to Asia (just as Arabs and Japanese choose to do their shopping in Europe).

Responsible tourism

Culture shock works both ways and, with Asia playing host to tens of millions of tourists every year, it's impossible to overestimate the importance of **responsible tourism**. Travellers are increasingly alert to the impact the tourist industry has on indigenous cultures, and a number of organizations are working to help minimize some of the negative cultural and environmental effects. Chief among them in the UK is Tourism Concern (Ⓦwww.tourismconcern.org.uk), whose website features useful practical advice on 'Avoiding guilt trips'. The bottom line is never to forget that the place you're holidaying in is someone else's home. Cultural sensitivity and environmental awareness are fundamental.

In many cases much damage has already been done by multinational corporations keen to profit from the lucrative tourist trade. **Big businesses** squeeze out local enterprises and corner the market; villagers get forced off their land because a major investor wants to build a hotel or golf course there; local water supplies get wiped out by hotel complexes whose bathrooms and swimming pools make massive, unsustainable demands on local infrastructures. As an independent traveller you can't stop this happening, but you can do your bit by not supporting such projects and practices with your cash. If you can, opt instead to stay in **small-scale, locally owned** accommodation, and choose to travel with socially aware tour operators. Some guidebooks carry advice on this, or see Rough Guides' *Clean Breaks*, which reviews a selection of community-based and environmentally conscious holidays in Asia and the rest of the world.

In some cases, as in **Burma**, it is government officials who are forcing villagers to cooperate with their tourist projects. Many politically aware tourists are choosing to boycott Burma for this reason; see Chapter Fifteen for information on the Burma Campaign.

Be wary of confusing **"ecotourism"** with "responsible tourism". Many unscrupulous travel companies play on travellers' increasing desire to do the right thing and bandy around the term "ecotourism" to imply that they're a caring-sharing, environmentally responsible organization; what this often boils down to is that their trip features a walk to a waterfall or that their guesthouse is surrounded by trees. A marketing strategy otherwise known as "greenwash".

Being culturally sensitive

- Try to **learn something** about the local culture, etiquette and religion plus a few words of the local language before you arrive.
- Realize that in many parts of the world things are done and **perceived very differently** from at home. Differing concepts of time are a classic example: try to stay calm and patient however irritated you may be; an impatient, demanding tourist is not an attractive visitor.
- Take time to **talk to local people** whatever your hectic travel or sightseeing schedule. Above all, avoid falling into the all-too-common trap of seeing locals as always out to rip you off; most Asian cultures view tourists as honoured guests and it's good to behave like one, even on the occasions when you're not treated so well.
- Even if you're not planning to patronize the Hiltons and Sheratons of Asia, you may be stopping off at McDonald's and 7-Eleven convenience stores. Try to **support local restaurants**, **shops** and **hotels** instead. That way, profits stay within the community, local residents still have influence in their own neighbourhoods and the place keeps its original character – which is, after all, what you've come all this way to experience.
- Try to eat **local food**, too, so that you're not promoting a two-tier culture: one for the tourists, another for the locals. It's in your interest, anyway, as local produce – including locally produced beer and soft drinks – is always much cheaper than imported brands, and often a lot tastier too.
- Don't rule out sleeping and eating in places that aren't listed in the main **guidebooks**. Just because a guesthouse or restaurant isn't featured doesn't mean it's no good, but it does often mean that the proprietor has to work a lot harder than those places that are reviewed.

- Consider doing a homestay (see p.161 for some leads) or search the web for some **community-based-tourism (CBT) projects** at your destination. This is an increasingly popular way of adding a different dimension to foreign travel, giving visitors the chance to participate more in local activities and locals the chance to shape and profit from the way tourism affects their home environment.

- It's also important to support local initiatives when visiting **ethnic villages**, so that the people you go to see – such as the hill tribes of Laos, Vietnam and Thailand, the Dyaks of Kalimantan and Sarawak, or the Torajans of Sulawesi – profit from your curiosity. Many tour companies advertise trips to see "the primitive people" without giving travellers any chance to communicate with them and with a guide from outside who may not speak the language in any case. The ethnic communities then become little more than human zoos and exotic photo opportunities (some Thai hill-tribe villages are a depressing example of this). If possible, try to organize a tour with someone from within the community, or at least make a big effort to meet the people you've travelled so far to see.

- Some minority groups – like the Sakkudai of the Mentawai Islands off the coast of Sumatra – see tourist interest as a way of **keeping traditions alive**, of encouraging young people to learn the old ways. In Bali, too, young and old can now make a good living out of traditional performing arts. The difficult thing is for any culture in this situation to keep control of their own heritage in an increasingly voracious tourist industry.

- Think about ways in which you might be able to **help local communities**. The more rural and remote the more likely they are to benefit from your contribution. Buying local crafts in the places they are made, tipping the room boy a few cents, and engaging a local guide are just a few examples.

- However, it is vital **not to exploit** those who are so desperate to earn anything at all that they will agree to the

Just say no

One of the main tourist attractions in southern India is a six-hour boat trip along the narrow waterways of Kerala. Local kids are so used to the tourists that they now race, in relays, along the river banks yelling "One pen, one pen" at the boats. What began as a game on the boat that I took soon turned into a depressing case of bear-baiting as the tourists started to chuck pens into the water just so the little boys would dive in to grab them. The kids were just normal village boys, not destitute slum-dwellers, but they knew they could get some trinkets if they "performed" for the tourists – and that's how a demeaning relationship between locals and tourists begins. Though it's natural and generous to want to give little presents, the last thing you want to do is create a culture of beggars.

Lucy Ridout

www.roughguides.com

▲ An uphill slog? Fair pay for porters is vital.

job however meagre the pay offered and however demanding the conditions. This is especially applicable to porters in Nepal, where the International Porters Protection Group (ⓌWwww.ippg .net) advises trekkers on how not to collude in this abuse. See p.285 for more details.

- Do not just give away money or gifts willy-nilly and thus turn local people into **beggars**. Pens, pencils or books can be donated to the local school if you want to help children and many guidebooks list local charities that would benefit from your generosity. Unless you are medically trained you should certainly not dole out medicines to anyone.

- **Religious buildings and events** are minefields for the culturally unwary. For example you should never climb on Buddha statues, allow yourself to sit or stand above a Hindu priest, or enter certain temples when menstruating. And you may need to dress in a particular way, too; see Chapter Six for advice on that and consult your guidebook for information on specific taboos.

- Be sensitive when **taking photographs**: not everybody wants to end up in your photo album and some scenes are utterly taboo. See box on p.112 for more advice.

Being environmentally aware

- As a responsible tourist, you should also try to minimize your impact on the environment. In practice, this can mean anything from sticking to marked trails when you're hiking, to being careful about rubbish disposal. In particular, take your own bag shopping and decline a plastic one, and don't dump non-biodegradable stuff like **plastic bags and bottles** and dead batteries in rural areas. Advice on getting involved in conservation projects is given in Chapter One, and there's a list of relevant organizations in the Directory on pp.344–347.

- The **Himalayas** have suffered a lot from inconsiderate trekkers, but there are several ways in which you can minimize your impact. The Kathmandu Environmental Education Project (Ⓦwww.keep nepal.org; see p.285) publishes suggestions on how to trek without doing more harm than good.

- **Coral reefs** throughout Southeast Asia have also become degraded as a result of increased tourism. Reefs are extremely fragile and slow-growing ecosystems, so thoughtless snorkellers and divers have a huge impact when they tread on reefs and break bits off to take home. Souvenir-buyers have encouraged local fishermen to do the same on a larger scale, so don't fuel the trade by purchasing pretty shells and bits of coral.

- Keep your wits about you when shopping for other souvenirs, too. Many endangered species of animal and plant are (illegally) killed and harvested so that they, or bits of them, can be sold to tourists as mementos or medicines. **Animal products** on sale across Asia include sea turtle products, snake skin, ivory (from elephant tusks), tortoiseshell, and the body parts of bears and tigers. See p.210 for more on organizations that are seeking to safeguard animal populations across Asia.

- Avoid buying **bottled water** wherever possible as it creates tonnes of unrecyclable plastic waste every year. Consider filtering your own from tap water instead (see Chapter Twelve), which more than covers the cost of a water filter after just a few weeks of travel. A compromise option is to make use of the drinking-water refill service offered in some tourist centres.

- Behave as though you were paying the **utility bills** yourself wherever you are staying: don't waste resources.

- Have a think about ways you might **minimize your carbon footprint**. Flights are a major producer of carbon dioxide: try to avoid short hops by air and more harmful night flights. Consider travelling instead by bus, train, boat and even by bike or on foot where possible. See chapters one and ten for some ideas. You might also want to try and make your trip "climate neutral" via a reputable carbon-offset scheme: see Ⓦwww.roughguides.com /climatechange.

10

Getting around

Travelling in Asia can be wonderful and frustrating, often at the same time. As the entire continent is teeming with people, so it is teeming with the means of getting them around. The plains of India and China are perfectly suited to rail travel; the mountains of Nepal and northern India dictate road, air and foot travel; and the island states of the Philippines and the huge Indonesian archipelago, the mountainous jungle rivers of Borneo and the mighty Asian waterways of the Mekong and Yangzi are served by ferries and boats of all shapes and sizes. Within some cities you even have the option of rickshaws and bullock carts. Despite initial impressions in some cities, car ownership is not widespread; instead, bicycles, mopeds and scooters are common but the majority of Asians rely on public transport, and though systems may appear hideously complex and grotesquely overcrowded, they are cheap and often far more comprehensive than services at home.

However, this exciting variety needs to be set against discomfort, lateness, some of the most terrifying driving on the planet, and unreliability, all enduring characteristics of Asian transport. Look on the travel itself as part of your adventure and you'll stand a better chance of keeping it in perspective and, in fact, it is likely that some of your most memorable Asian experiences will be journeys.

The trick is to allow plenty of time to get around. Delays are inevitable at some point, and you'll be far less stressed if you've allowed for them in your schedule. The golden rule is that distance is not an indication of the time needed for a journey.

Planes

Most Asian countries have an **internal air network** and there has been an incredible proliferation of low cost, no frills airlines across the continent in recent years. Many of these offer internet booking, making it extremely easy to arrange your own flights. It pays to take a bit of time to compare routes and prices but air fares are generally a lot lower than at home, so don't rule out buying plane tickets from time to time, especially if time is tight.

You should, however, take into account the **environmental impact** of short-hop flights and the fact that you will be flying over the country rather than exploring it. Still, when it's too much to contemplate the sixty to a hundred hours on the bus along the bone-rattling 1800-kilometre Trans-Sulawesi Highway from Manado to Makassar, in Indonesia, spending a few short hours doing the same route in the skies looks decidedly appealing (and excellent value at around $54/£32). If the thirty-hour train trip between Beijing and Guangzhou is more than you can bear, then the three-hour plane journey may begin to look attractive at $154/£94. It's also worth remembering that in some countries a short plane ride means you can quickly access wilderness areas which might otherwise take days or weeks to reach. For example, the forty-minute flight between Kathmandu and Lukla in the Everest region can save you an extra five to seven days' walking, and access to many of the highland valleys of West Papua is virtually impossible without flying.

Air passes

There are a huge number of **air passes** available to tourists which might be worthwhile if you are intending to cover a lot of ground quickly but bear in mind that they tie you in a specified carrier and may well work out more expensive than sorting it out yourself. Check the website ⓦwww.airtimetable.com/airpass_asia.htm for a roundup of what passes are available. Note that many passes need to be bought before your arrival; you'll also want to find out how much the flight would cost if you bought it locally. At certain times, national airlines may even offer a free internal flight or two to tourists travelling internationally with them; check what deals are available at the time of booking your international tickets.

Some passes are for one country. For example, Indian Airlines (ⓦwww.indian-airlines.nic.in) offers 7-, 15- and 21-day Discover India passes for $400, $630 and $895. There are conditions attached to these passes and you'd need to do a vast amount of flying to make them worthwhile. Within Asia some airlines have formed **alliances** to offer more extensive passes; for example Bangkok Airways, Siem Reap Airways and Lao Airlines offer the Discovery Pass with coupons at $60 for internal sectors i.e. within one country, and $100 or $160 for international sectors. Other airlines restrict their concessions to travellers who have travelled into the country with them or their alliance partners; for example, JAL in Japan has a couple of very good value passes if you've flown in with a carrier who is part of the One World Alliance but they aren't available at peak travel times.

Stress-free flying

- Avoid airlines with poor **safety records**: check with your embassy or ⓦ www.airsafe.com, which lists safety records of many Asian airlines, before you book.
- While many airlines are perfectly safe, many are small setups so don't always expect the organization or efficiency of airlines at home.
- If you book at the airline office rather than online, get confirmation in writing, especially if your ticket will be issued later. Take a note of the name of the person you dealt with, in case of problems.
- Don't let the booking office keep your passport overnight – it can be useful to have photocopies of the key pages ready for them.
- Having booked a seat, you often need to **reconfirm** with the airline before travel. Check the rules when you book. If the airline seems to have lost your booking despite all the evidence you can produce, get them to look under your first or even your middle name, as misfiling is common.
- Some airline offices find it virtually impossible to issue confirmed tickets for flights from a city other than the one they are in. If you get a ticket under these circumstances, be sure to reconfirm with the airline when you get to the place you'll be flying from.
- The more **flexibility** you can build into your timetable, the better. Flights are often overbooked, cancelled or delayed at short notice due to monsoons, typhoons, heavy snowfall or lack of aircraft.
- Check in as early as possible; if flights are overbooked, boarding passes are often given out on a first-come, first-served basis.
- Follow the advice on **hand baggage** on p.116 – just because a flight is internal doesn't mean you can't get delayed and/or your baggage lost.
- Certain **items** are banned on Asian planes in addition to anything that may be a potential weapon. These are banned not because they could be dangerous but because they smell so bad – the durian fruit and fish sauce are the most notorious.

Long-distance buses

Bus travel in Asia is one of the most intense experiences the continent has to offer: all of human life is jammed together, often with a few animals as well, passing through the landscape slowly enough to appreciate it.

Best bus rides

The Halsema Highway, Philippines One of the most awesome roads in Southeast Asia, this highway shadows the course of the Chico river valley from Baguio to Bontoc, snaking its way up into the Central Cordillera mountains and affording panoramic views over the white-water river valleys below. The trip takes seven hours and tops 2000m at its highest point. Sit on the right-hand side of the bus, have your camera to hand, and take travel-sickness pills.

The Karakoram Highway The sheer scale of the 1300-kilometre road linking Islamabad in Pakistan with Kashgar in China is impressive enough, but the stunning and ever-changing scenery as the bus twists and curves through the Karakoram mountain range is equally magical, as is the fact that such an incredible feat of engineering was ever achieved.

Manali–Leh Highway, India The two- to three-day marathon trip between Manali in Himachal Pradesh and Leh in Ladakh, offers spellbinding mountain passes and apparently endless valleys, gorges, plains and cliffs, as the highway winds its way through the Himalayas and up onto the Tibetan plateau.

The Central Cross-Island Highway, Taiwan The road across the central spine of mountains from Tungshih to Taroko Gorge features fabulous views with misty valleys fading evocatively into the distance between fold after fold of wooded mountains. At the end of the journey is justifiably one of Taiwan's most popular tourist attractions, as the road edges between the cliffside and the river thundering below.

Bhutan by road The single track road twists and winds its way up across huge mountain passes and down into sub-tropical valleys. It takes three days from the capital Thimphu to Trashigang in the east – on the most terrifying section between Ura in Bumthang and Mongar, the road is literally blasted out of the cliff leaving a sheer rock wall on one side and a vertiginous drop into a bottomless valley on the other.

Inside, many drivers personalize their vehicles with pictures of their favourite gods and goddesses, flashing fairy lights and an incense stick or two on the dashboard. For some drivers the bus is even their home and they eat and sleep on board when it's not in use.

The quality of buses, however, is very variable – the best ones feature air conditioning and reclining seats; the worst have cracked or missing window glass, ripped seats and minimal suspension. Some "bus" services are even operated in trucks.

Many cities have separate bus stations for local and long-distance destinations, and the larger the city the more likely it is to have several long-distance terminals, often on opposite sides of town – Bangkok, Ho Chi Minh City, Jakarta and Beijing are among the most confusing. A good guidebook will provide you with enough information to orientate yourself and get into town, or vice versa.

Tickets are extremely economical when compared to travel at home – for example, the 1100-kilometre two-day/two-night trip between Jakarta and Lombok in Indonesia costs about $37/£23 including the ferry crossings between the islands en route, the 989-kilometre 42-hour-plus journey between Manila and Davao in the Philippines will set you back $54/£33, and in Cambodia the six hours (315km) between Phnom Penh and Siem Reap costs $3.50/£2.

However, don't underestimate the stamina needed to cope with several days and nights on the road. In countries with extensive train systems – India and China are prime examples – it's usually faster and more comfortable to do long-haul trips by train.

Tourist buses

In some countries private companies operate special **tourist bus services** with plenty of space for luggage and a direct, hassle-free, though generally more expensive, service between main tourist centres. Don't expect luxury though, as the vehicles themselves aren't particularly different from regular buses – many aren't even air conditioned. However, they can be useful. To get from Kuta to Ubud on Bali by public transport, for example, you have to change at least three times but a tourist bus will get you there in one go for about twice the ordinary fare. In Nepal, tourist buses between the main tourist destinations are generally faster and more comfortable than public services, again for about double the public bus fare. In Vietnam open-tour buses are a popular way to backpack around; for an $18 ticket between Hanoi and Saigon, you get to hop on and off wherever you like on the route. It pays to do some research, though – on the more straightforward routes you'll be paying a lot for little benefit. In Thailand some of the tourist buses are actually cheaper than the government buses and have tourist-friendly pick-up and drop-off points (in the main accommodation areas, for example). However, their safety record is poor, and many have a reputation for aggressive and even thieving staff; ask other travellers' advice before buying a ticket and check what your guidebook has to say.

Room on top

It is important to have the right attitude when travelling Asian-style, e.g. hanging from the side of a vehicle, teetering from the top like a flagpole in the wind or – if you are lucky enough to be inside – cramped in a fetal position with your knees in your face. These situations need meditation; releasing the mind from the perils of travel is an absolute necessity for psychological survival. We'd stepped on a few hands on the climb to the last free spaces – on the roof – but the other passengers didn't seem to mind. It took a few minutes to get the overstuffed truck moving at a reasonable clip down a one-lane road with barely a shoulder on either side and a sheer drop into the marshlands. I hoped the luggage I was holding onto was firmly attached to the roof. Several times as we moved over to the side of the road we tipped until I could see my reflection in the water all too clearly. I figured if the truck rolled over I'd be fine in the water – until the truck and other passengers landed on top of me. Swaying like a willow tree in the wind, the vehicle recovered again and again from potentially disastrous situations and continued on its way in its charmed state of existence.

Shannon Brady

www.roughguides.com

Is it safe?

There is no escaping the fact that much road travel in Asia is extremely hair-raising. Buses often travel far too fast for the conditions – overtaking on blind corners is a regular occurrence – and drivers frequently take some form of stimulant to stay awake as a lot of long-distance services travel at night. Not surprisingly, accidents are common. Remember that even once you've bought a ticket you can still decide whether or not to climb on board any particular bus. If you're seriously concerned about your own safety during the journey, you might be wise to get off at the earliest (safe) opportunity, regardless of how far you are from your intended destination.

Enjoying the journey

- Try to look at the bus before you book a seat, whatever the ticket-seller may tell you about his pristine speedmobile.

- It can sometimes appear totally impossible to get a ticket or seat on a bus – there are too many people and they are all far more adept at forcing their way through the crush than you. You could try booking through an agency for a small fee (often your accommodation will do this for you).

- Asian buses are built for generally smaller Asian physiques. Consider booking two seats if you are quite large in any dimension and can afford it, although you'll have to be pretty assertive to keep both seats to yourself as the bus gets steadily more packed along the way.

- As departure time gets close you could also consider paying a small boy to climb through a bus window and occupy a seat for you until you can get to it.

- Luggage is often put on top of the bus where other passengers may ride alongside it. As a security measure, you might consider

Karma armour

Most Asian people have a rather more fatalistic approach to accidents and misfortune than we do in the West. We are increasingly of the view that we can, and indeed have the right to, control anything nasty happening to us. In contrast, Buddhists and Hindus believe in **karma**, whereby a previous existence influences the events in their current life. Thus a traffic accident is more likely to be seen as preordained karmic retribution than a direct result of irresponsible driving. Muslims presage most plans with the word *Inshallah* ("if God wishes"), showing they accept that they do not have ultimate control over the future. This can be infuriating or even downright terrifying if you're on a bus with a maniac driver who seems intent on killing you all. It's unlikely that any of the other passengers will try to moderate any lunatic behaviour; you may want to try, or even get off and wait for the next bus.

www.roughguides.com

chaining your pack to the roof rack (see p.109) so you won't be craning your neck out of the window to see if it's still there.

- The back seats are the bumpiest, the front seats give a grandstand view of the driver's technique and an earful of his choice of music and/or video.

- Make sure you have plenty of water, food and toilet paper. Stops are often at weird times when you may not want to eat and at places with limited facilities.

- The most modern long-distance buses have toilets but if not there are toilet stops, sometimes in the countryside (men go in one direction, women in another; pretend not to see anybody and bring your own toilet paper – which you'll need to burn or take away in a plastic bag afterwards). A long skirt can be useful for women travellers to keep their modesty intact in these situations.

- Consider packing earplugs, as Asian buses usually travel with music or videos turned up full volume for the entire length of the journey.

- A neck-pillow is much better than jolting up and down on the shoulder of the person next to you.

- A blanket, sarong or jacket is useful for warmth, especially on overnight trips.

- However uncomfortable, you should keep your money belt on and well hidden: you are vulnerable when sleeping, and theft isn't unknown.

- Consider carefully whether to accept food or drink from strangers – this can be a means of drugging travellers before robbing them.

Trains

Trains offer a memorable and often safer means of travel across large tracts of Asia. Although often distressingly crowded and rather dirty, especially in the cheaper classes, train travel, like buses, thrusts you into the company of local people. You'll get brilliant views, too: the sun setting over rice paddies in central Thailand and southern India; soaring cliffs and white-sand beaches along the coast between Da Nang and Hué in Vietnam; and dizzying drops between the peaks en route from Peshawar to the summit of the Khyber Pass.

Do your research, though. Slow, stopping trains judder to a halt at every sign of human habitation; they are a lively experience with plenty to keep you entertained but they can take twice as long as the express without a corresponding halving of the fare.

You don't have to wait until you are in the country to get train information. For example, Indian Railways, one of the most remarkable setups in the world, shifting over 12 million passengers daily across more than 60,000km of track, has a website (🌐www.indianrailways .gov.in) supplying information on the entire network. Check out The Man in Seat Sixty-One (🌐www.seat61.com) for advice on train travel across Asia.

The **security issues** on trains are similar to those on long-distance buses, except that you'll have all your stuff with you and your fellow passengers have more chance to move around. In addition to the tips on p.145 it is a good idea to lock your bags and padlock them to something immovable, like the berth or seat and keep bags away from windows so they can't get rifled at stations. Solo women travellers in India and Pakistan may feel more comfortable in women-only compartments, especially on long trips.

Tickets

Ticket options vary from system to system but you'll usually have a choice between hard and soft seats or berths and between carriages with and without fan and air conditioning. Generally, the longer the trip, the more advisable it is to go for a bit of comfort.

Fares are generally good value. For example, for the twelve- to eighteen-hour journey between Beijing and Shanghai, expect to pay from $47/£29 to $135/£82 depending on the speed of the journey and the level of comfort you require, while in Vietnam, the two-day haul from Hanoi to Ho Chi Minh City on the *Reunification Express* costs $35–58/£21–35 depending on the class you choose. On Indian Railways you have an enormous choice of comfort

Hard seat hell

We boarded the train to Chengdu and our expectations for the coming journey were high. We were well stocked with fruit, chocolate and enough biscuits to see us through the coming twenty hours. We were also naively optimistic about the chances of upgrading our seats. Tickets for hard seats were the only ones available. No amount of charm, joviality or bare-faced begging could persuade our stony-faced ticket vendor to part with the more comfortable hard sleeper or even the ludicrously overpriced soft sleeper options usually reserved for party cadres. "No," he informed us, "no have." Later we discovered that a hefty hard-currency "present" would have secured a comfortable passage. Instead I waited in vain for a nonexistent legitimate bed to become available at the "next station… next station…next station". Sweat mingled freely with grime and smoke as the day turned into night and day again. My companions slept and my frustration and anger rose, aided by the neighbouring cherubic Chinese child clearing his sinuses, gulping and with an almighty hoik landing a dribble right on top of my big toe. His father looked on proudly.

Daniel Gooding

Top train rides

The Death Railway from Kanchanaburi to Nam Tok, Thailand This route is named because thousands of the World War II prisoners-of-war who built it died during its construction. It is a stunning feat of engineering. The track was blasted through mountains and rock faces and traverses numerous amazing bridges, passing along and over the River Kwai.

The Maglev train between downtown Shanghai and Pudong airport, China This is one of the fastest trains in the world on a regular passenger run reaching 431kph on its eight-minute journey.

The Shimla Toy Train from Kalka to Shimla, northern India This train winds its way through the Himalayan foothills up to the hill station of Shimla while you sit on board in armchairs, reading the morning newspapers and sipping tea served by uniformed waiters.

Peshawar to the Khyber Pass, Pakistan The steam railway passes through dramatic, barren tribal land and is unmissable. The British-built railway has 34 tunnels and 92 bridges along its fifty-kilometre route, and is so steep in places that trains need another engine at the back to push them up.

The Eastern & Oriental Express: Thailand, Laos, Malaysia and Singapore If money's no object, consider treating yourself to a ride on this deluxe train is modelled on the original *Orient Express*, with wood panelling, cordon-bleu meals and first-class service. Prices start at $1211/£740 for two days and one night (ⓦ www .orient-express.com)

Tokyo to Kyoto, Japan The Nozomi N700 is the fastest of the Japanese bullet trains or *shinkansen* averaging 270kph. It operates on the Tokaido-Sanyo line and gliding past the iconic Mount Fuji at warp speed is the classic Japanese train trip.

Golmud to Lhasa, China The railway stretches 1142km long, with 960km of it over 4000m, reaching 5072m at its peak and travelling through some of the most amazing scenery in the world as it climbs up onto the Tibetan plateau.

(seven classes of accommodation, although not all are available on every train) and price, which is calculated on distance, class of travel and type of train. For example, the Delhi–Chennai fare ranges from $11/£7 for the 33-hour haul in the lowest class to $93/£57 in the most comfortable, which is almost twice the air fare.

Buying tickets can be a major hurdle; long-distance, sleeper and first-class travel invariably need to be booked several days in advance. Although foreigners' ticket offices can cut down hassle in larger cities in China, Thailand and India, and women-only queues in India can help, you may spend hours fighting your way through a mass of people only to find the train you want is already fully booked. However, booking tickets is increasingly possible online and many travel agents and hotel staff can buy tickets for you for a small fee – this is money well spent. You won't find many ticket barriers on Asian rail networks (Japan is an exception), but your ticket will be checked on board, often several times.

Train passes

Train passes are available for travel in India, Thailand, Malaysia and Japan. Check the details before you leave home as most rail passes are only available outside the country. Consider the individual passes carefully to work out whether they are good value or not. Thai and Malaysian passes may not be worthwhile unless you're travelling a great deal and you'd need to travel far to make India's Indrail Pass – available for periods of one to ninety days first- or second-class – financially worthwhile, the chief advantages being that it saves you queueing for tickets, gives priority for tourist quotas on busy trains and allows you to make and cancel reservations free of charge. On the other hand, the seven-day version of the Japan Rail Pass ($294/£180) pays for itself in just one return trip from Tokyo to Kyoto and the fourteen-day pass ($469/£287) with a Tokyo–Hiroshima return plus a couple of side trips on the way.

Sleepers

Remember that if you book a **sleeper service** you'll be saving on accommodation costs, so it can be worth splashing out to get a good night's sleep. The sleeping areas usually consist of two or three tiers of bunks. Top bunks are marginally cheaper in some countries (China, for example), and are the safest for your luggage, but cigarette smoke

▲ Commuter joy Indian style

www.roughguides.com

Monsoon miracle

It began to rain heavily as soon as the boat left harbour on its way to Ko Tao. I established myself on a wooden bench, breathed deeply and reminded myself we'd get there somehow, sometime. We dipped and trundled into the open sea, away from land, warm hotel beds and everything safe. After half an hour we encountered not waves but swells the size of two-storey buildings which rocked and crashed our little ferry from side to side, playing with us as a cat might bat a mouse around the room. We were reassured by the crew when the engines cut for a spell that it was only engine trouble, nothing more. I sat on my bench and attempted to read as water crashed through the doorways onto backpacks and eventually onto me. The swells grew higher, meaner and quicker. Book forgotten, I looked at my white knuckles, straining to keep my body on board and in an upright position. Around me, the other passengers held on as I did to whatever they could to prevent themselves from being catapulted out of the boat. I thought of my mother. She'd be devastated to learn of my demise. No glory, no excitement - my story would end up as just a few lines in the obscure international section of the newspaper. With no life jackets on board our prospects looked grim. I began to pray and remembered, as words failed to flow, that I knew no prayers whatsoever. I wished I had been raised in some religious setting. Nonetheless, I continued: "Holy Mother of God", I chanted, "please save us". And after one hour she did. I watched the swells change from assaulting us head on, to broadside, to coming in from the stern as we slowly turned to Ko Pha-Ngan, an island between Ko Samui and Ko Tao. I was alive and thankful to walk on land.

Nicole Meyer

tends to gather up there and you may be next to a blaring radio, a light that stays on permanently, or right under a fan, which can be chilly. On the bottom bunks you'll often get people sitting along the edge and talking, smoking, eating and playing cards while you try to sleep. Thai trains are a pleasant anomaly in Southeast Asia – staff fold sleepers down out of the seats at night and make them up with fresh linen for you. Sleeper services in Japan are pretty comfortable with restaurant cars and onboard showers although it is worth checking; some trains have no dining cars or vending machines so you'll need to stock up with food beforehand. Sleeping compartments can get surprisingly chilly at night, so remember to keep your warmer clothing handy. In India you can rent extra bedding very cheaply on board. In hard or soft sleeper in China you get a thick quilt, pillow and towel to ease the journey.

Boats

One of the highlights of travel in Asia is the opportunity to make some spectacular **boat journeys**. The island nations of Indonesia, with over thirteen thousand islands, and the Philippines, with seven thousand, offer countless long- and short-distance trips, but in most Asian countries you'll have the chance to cruise on rivers and across lakes and lagoons, as well as between islands. If you have the time, boat travel is a convenient and

Best boat trips

Hong Kong island to Kowloon, China The ferry across Hong Kong harbour gives splendid views of the city's skyscraper skyline.

Puerto Galera on Mindanao, Philippines Much of the journey from Batangas City is unremarkable but the approach to Puerto Galera is incredible – a tiny entrance through a narrow strait fringed with tropical palms before opening out into a huge and picturesque bay.

Allappuzha to Kottayam Kerala, South India The two-hour public ferry service along the backwaters takes you through waterlily-choked canals and across lagoons, slicing through farmland and coconut plantations, past temples, mosques and waterfront houses.

Across the Brahmaputra (Tsangpo) River to Samye Monastery, Tibet Amid stunning high-altitude scenery, a noisy, smoky flat-bottomed boat weaves between the sandbanks.

The Bangkok *khlongs*, Thailand A ride on these inky-black canals gives an unsurpassed insight into Bangkok's watery suburbs: teak houses where longboats are the family car, half-submerged temple grounds, kids playing in the water, men bathing and women doing the washing-up.

Ha Long Bay, Vietnam Boats meander through thousands of towering and spectacularly picturesque limestone islands.

Houayxai to Louang Phabang, Laos The slow boat down the Mekong River passes through a magically shifting panorama of rice fields, limestone karst, temples and villages along the waterside.

Guilin to Yangshuo in southwest Guangxi, China A trip along the Li River is to travel through the scenery of a scroll painting with towering forested mountainsides all around.

economical alternative to flying, with the bonus of great views and the chance to see marine and river wildlife at close hand.

In some areas of Kalimantan in Indonesia, Sarawak in Malaysia and Laos, for example, river transport is the only way to get around, whereas in many cities, such as Bangkok, river ferries and taxis are considerably faster than road transport, as well as being a cooler and more pleasant way to travel.

Bearing in mind that long-distance trips can last several days, it pays to make some advance preparations:

- If you're travelling deck class, take a waterproof sheet to lie on as the floor gets very damp.
- Keep valuables, especially your camera, in waterproof bags; you can get drenched by waves or wash from other craft.
- Take your own food and water, as the quality of what's available on board – and there might be nothing – is variable. What's more, boats break down or get delayed and your journey may take longer than anticipated.
- It gets cold at sea – keep warm clothing near the top of your pack.

THE BIG ADVENTURE

- Equally, the sun can be scorching, so keep sun protection, hats and lotion to hand.
- Put some sea-sickness tablets in your pack even if you don't normally suffer. The combination of big swells and engines belching noxious fumes can affect even the most hardened stomach.
- Use your common sense and don't get on obviously vastly overcrowded boats. Ferries sink frequently in Bangladesh, Indonesia, the Philippines and Thailand.

City transport

Asian **city transport** is gloriously varied and offers you the chance to witness incredible juxtapositions of traditional and ultramodern. As well as buses, taxis and subway systems, be prepared for minibuses, motorcycle taxis, rickshaws, three-wheelers and even horse carts. You'll be flung into close, sometimes very close, proximity with your fellow passengers, who may be travelling together with their vegetables, goats and chickens for market, babies for the clinic and kids for school. A sense of humour is a prerequisite for travel this way.

Local buses

Most Asian cities have a mixture of large and small buses supplemented by a whole host of smaller minibuses, vans or motorized three-wheelers. The general rule seems to be that the smaller the vehicle, the less rigid the route and the greater the linguistic and geographical skills needed to find out where it is going; the smaller ones also stop wherever passengers want to get on and off. All these vehicles are incredibly cheap, but are very slow and packed solid with passengers, and, if the driver fancies a lunchtime break at the market en route, you'll have to wait for him to eat his noodle soup.

Women, beware!

Monks in Thailand, Laos, Cambodia and Vietnam are allowed no physical contact at all with women. If they accidentally touch or are touched by a woman they must engage in a lengthy series of purification rituals. On public transport monks often congregate in particular places such as on the back seat of buses. No matter how crowded the vehicle, women travellers should not sit next to a monk and should be very careful if passing close to one. Local people will give up their seat for a monk and you should offer to do the same.

In Laos, it's taboo for women to sit on the roof of a bus or a boat. The Lao believe that a woman has the power to ruin the potency of the amulets carried by Lao men simply by placing herself physically above him. Furthermore, boats are thought to possess a guardian spirit, and a woman riding on the roof offends this spirit, which could invite dire consequences for passengers and crew.

In some places, such as Bangkok, it is possible – almost essential – to get a map of local bus services. Otherwise, get directions at the tourist information office, your hotel or from your guidebook. Ask again for your destination when you're on board, just to be sure the bus is really going there. The following tips will help you negotiate the confusion more easily:

- Before you set off, find out the fare; check your guidebook, ask at your accommodation or check with other travellers or local people the correct fare and how to pay.
- Take a pocketful of small-denomination coins or notes – getting change is a nightmare.
- You'll find that drivers, conductors and other passengers are generally helpful and concerned to get you where you want to go, although rush-hour commuters the world over aren't the most patient of folks and Asia is no exception.
- Give yourself as much time as you can and keep calm. Remember, it doesn't really matter if you get lost.
- Be wary of pickpockets – some carry razors or knives to cut through material and the straps of shoulder bags.
- Women travelling on crowded city buses can be targets for sexual harassment ("Eve teasing" as it's called in India), and you may well experience groping hands, men squeezing past and "accidental" touches and brushes against you. It's your call whether to try to move away or make a loud public statement (though see the notes on staying calm on p.130).

Taxis

Most cities and built-up areas have **official taxis**, a convenient and usually very reasonably priced way to get from door to door. Find out what they look like and whether they should have meters or not, and you're ready to go.

There are, though, a few complications associated with using cabs. Most Asian taxis have **meters**; however, these may or may not be a true indication of the full cost. Sometimes when prices go up the meters don't get adjusted until later. In these cases, drivers carry official charts to convert from the meter price to the new fare. In other places there may be legitimate additional charges, such as entry to the central area of Singapore, tunnel toll charges in Hong Kong, expressway tolls in Bangkok, and surcharges after midnight. At many Asian airports the meter is officially suspended and taxis operate on a fixed price tariff to nearby destinations. If the driver says the meter isn't working, **negotiate the price** before you get in or find a different cab.

www.roughguides.com

153

Generally speaking, cabs in Indonesia, Thailand and India are so cheap – under $5/£3 to get across town – that if there are three or four of you with luggage, it's hardly worth bothering with a crowded bus. On the other hand, prices in Japan are sky high, ($217/£133 for a ninety-minute ride from Central Tokyo to Narita International Airport). Though taxis in Singapore and Hong Kong aren't so exorbitant, you'll still need to have plenty of spare cash to jump into them regularly.

Motorbike taxis

In many areas, **motorbikes** operate as taxis. They are a fun way to get around though a few minutes screeching through the rush-hour Bangkok traffic on the back of one and you'll understand the real meaning of fear. Motorcycles are especially useful in busy cities, though, as they can weave through traffic jams and even zoom up one-way streets the wrong way.

Negotiate the fare before you get on and, no matter how derisory the helmet offered or the means of keeping it on your head, you should still wear it. The drivers may or may not be able to manage a backpack – you might have to wear it or get it balanced between the handlebars.

Cycle-rickshaws

Rickshaws are useful for back roads where there is no other form of public transport, and for finding obscure addresses – many of the drivers know every inch of their territory. They are also a sedate way to travel, although you should be prepared to hop out on the most daunting hills and you'll be breathing in the exhaust fumes of every large vehicle on the road.

Better you take bus

I had always refused the Kolkata rickshaws despite their bell-ringing blandishments every time I set foot outside my hotel. However, one day after wandering all over the backstreets of the city I was foot-sore, worn out by the heat and flies, and found myself well off the beaten track. I approached the nearest rickshaw driver and named my hotel. He looked me up and down, took in my height and likely weight at a glance, and looked at the sun blazing down. Then he raised an arm towards the nearest main road: "Better you take bus," he decided.

Lesley Reader

A variety of different incarnations of rickshaw are found across Asia. The most ancient form, with a single man running on foot between two poles, pulling a seat perched above two wheels, has all but died out. Central Kolkata is the last outpost of such vehicles, and by the time you get there they may well have been replaced by cycle-rickshaws. It can feel morally uncomfortable sitting on the shaded, padded seat: are you shortening the poor chap's life or are you making sure his children get a meal that evening?

Cycle-rickshaws have different designs and names depending on the country: *cyclo* in Vietnam and Cambodia, *samlor* in Thailand and *becak* in Indonesia. With all rickshaws, negotiate the price before you get in and make sure it's clear whether it is for the vehicle or per person. The price will depend not only on the distance but also on the number of hills, amount of luggage and the effort the man thinks he'll have to put in. You can also negotiate an hourly rate if you plan to visit several places.

Motor-rickshaws

More sophisticated versions of rickshaws are **motor-rickshaws**, also known as auto-rickshaws (*auto* in India, *bajaj* in Indonesia, *cyclo mai* in Vietnam and *tuk tuk* in Thailand). They are noisy (*tuk tuk*s are so named because of the sound they make), smelly, unstable three-wheelers with the driver in front and enough space for a couple of passengers behind (but that doesn't stop four or five clambering aboard).

Usually powered by a feeble two-stroke engine, motor-rickshaws are useful for quick hops across town and often work out cheaper than cab fares. Like taxis they are usually supposed to have meters though it's often just as difficult to get the drivers to use them. Rides can be hair-raising; received wisdom in Bangkok is to find an elderly *tuk tuk* driver, the theory being that he must be a safe bet if he's survived long enough in this notoriously manic profession. There's only one problem – it seems impossible to find a single driver of these machines who looks older than 16.

Vehicle rental

The laws on foreigners driving **rental cars** vary throughout Asia. In China, for example, visiting foreigners may only drive in certain areas: Beijing, Shanghai and Hong Kong. However, in most countries an International Driver's Licence (get this before you leave home) will give you full access to the roads. Expect to pay from \$30–50/£18–31 per day in Cambodia or Vietnam, \$42/£25 per day in India, \$80–100/£49–61 in Laos and \$15/£8 in Bali (insurance and petrol not included) for a jeep or small saloon car from a local setup. International rental companies such as Hertz, Budget, Avis and Europcar have offices in most capital cities, which means you can book your vehicle in advance, but these places are almost always more expensive than local firms.

If you want to travel by car, you should consider **hiring a local driver** as well; even though you'll have to pay the driver's food and, if you're touring overnight, lodging costs as well, it's not usually a significant additional expense. The advantage of a local driver is that you can enjoy the scenery, leave him to find the way and deal with the local rules of the road, and you'll hopefully get good suggestions about side-trips, plus an insight into the local life and people. And, if anything goes wrong, it's far better that you aren't driving: killing a cow on the road in Nepal could cost you up to twenty years in prison, roughly the same penalty as hitting a person. An alternative is to rent a local taxi for a day, a week or whatever – a popular and economical idea in India. It's a good way to see a lot quite quickly, visit outlying districts and do it all in a bit of comfort. If you do decide to drive yourself, the following tips may help:

● Carry all relevant documentation: in Indonesia you must carry the vehicle's registration papers as well as your own. Balinese police love to stop tourists and issue on-the-spot fines if they aren't carrying the right paperwork.

● Inspect the vehicle carefully: before you accept it and make a note, also signed by the owner, of any scratches or dents, or you may get blamed for these. Check things you would take for granted in a rental vehicle at home: the lights, horn, windscreen wipers, door locks, petrol cap. Make sure you know how to get the bonnet up and check the spare tyre (is there one?), tool kit and jack.

● In some parts of Asia, insurance is not available for rental vehicles; if it is available, it's pricey. You should definitely buy insurance if you can, but make sure you know what's covered. In particular, check how much the excess is – the amount you will have to pay if there's a crash.

● Check the speed limit and rules of the road: the official version should be in any comprehensive guidebook, but spend some time observing what goes on around you – there's often a big gap between the legal and the habitual. In Beijing, nobody seems to obey red lights, while in Sumatra they are ignored if you are turning left.

Motorcycles and mopeds

Motorcycles and **mopeds/scooters** are available for rent in many places and are a great way to travel independently to out-of-the-way places at reasonable cost. All the above tips for car drivers apply to these as well, plus the following:

● Motorbike, scooter or moped riding in Asia is not for learners or novices. Check the local licensing regulations to make sure you are legally allowed to drive.

● Check that whatever you rent is insured for accidents and theft and be sure to see the documents. Make sure you know what the insurance deal is, i.e. will you have to pay an excess in the case of an accident?

- Examine the machine carefully – especially brakes, lights and tyres.
- Whatever the local laws dictate, driver and passenger should both wear helmets and always cover up. However tempting it is to feel the wind on bare limbs, it's madness not to have some sort of protection in case you come off. Consider taking or buying your own helmet – those provided are often damaged or don't fit properly.
- Be especially careful of hot exhaust pipes – many a pillion passenger ends up with a nasty burn on their calf.
- Be alert and drive defensively. Unpaved roads can be unpredictable, varying from sand to mud depending on the weather conditions; local driving styles are erratic and the rules of the road can be very alien. Hardly a day goes by on the island of Phuket in Thailand without one foreign driver racing him or herself into a crumpled smash on the roadside.

Respect

When I walked through the bazaar of one town in Pakistan, even fully robed, I was stared at, catcalled by giggly young men and felt a little vulnerable – a shameless foreign woman unaccompanied in male territory. The next day I rode into the same market on my motorbike. No giggles. No lechery. Previously disapproving old men decided I was worthy of a nod. Young men approached to make intelligent conversation and ask about the bike. Suddenly I became a person; I had respect again. The bike takes the focus off you and your marital status, opens doors and is a great conversation starter.

Nicki McCormick

Bicycles

A bicycle is the only vehicle that millions of Asians will ever own, and bikes are available for rent pretty much everywhere. Levels of sophistication vary from mountain bikes to bone-shakers that barely hold together. If you want to **rent a bike**, ask at your guesthouse or at local shops; you'll get better rates for longer rents. Security can be a problem – the exception is in Chinese cities where there are official bike parks – and you should always use a chain or lock. A few words of warning:

- Try out the bike; wonky wheels, disintegrating seats and clunking chains are hard work. Be especially careful to check the brakes. A working bell is essential all over Asia.
- Most bikes come without a helmet – take your own if you are going to do a lot of cycling.
- Be aware of potholes everywhere and anywhere on the road surface and deep storm drains at the side of streets.

- Think very carefully before cycling at night and make sure you have appropriate lights.
- Note that most other road users will behave as though you don't exist.
- Carry plenty of **water** and protect yourself from the sun.
- Don't be overambitious and overdo it in tropical conditions.

If you are intending to complete a lengthy part of your trip by bike, you'll most likely be bringing your own from home. See box on p.31 for some general hints on long-distance cycle-touring.

Hitchhiking

The cost of travel in Asia is so low that **hitching** isn't really necessary for tourists, though in out-of-the-way places, with the last bus gone, not a taxi in sight and still 40km to go to your hotel, it can sometimes become the only option. Most drivers will expect payment from their passengers. Hitchhiking carries the same risks wherever you are; just because you're on holiday, don't suspend the instincts that keep you safe at home. If you do decide to hitch a ride, bear in mind that in some areas (Tibet is one example) drivers of trucks and other private vehicles are not legally permitted to carry foreigners, and risk heavy penalties if they are caught doing so.

Walking

With the dizzying range of transport available, don't forget the pleasures of simply **walking** around – just get outside and wander where the fancy takes you. Asian life is lived on the streets – yes, there are beggars, hawkers and hustlers galore, but there are also millions of people going about their everyday lives, commuting to work, shopping at street markets, praying at tiny shrines, having a snack at food stalls, gambling or simply watching the world go by. Bear in mind that:

- Asian roads can be terrifying to cross. Walk with a local person between you and oncoming traffic. Move when they move; stop when they stop.
- Jaywalking is illegal in many places – Singapore is one, Indonesia another. Do obey pedestrian signs and use footbridges and underpasses if they exist.
- Pedestrian survival can depend on knowing the rules of the road: remember which way oncoming traffic is approaching from and be aware that drivers may interpret red stop signs differently

from you, for example, as a suggestion rather than an instruction. Other signals can also have a number of interpretations. Flashing headlights, for example, can mean, "I'm coming through" rather than "You go first".

Tours

Just as tourist bus services can take the strain out of complicated connections, so there are plenty of travel agents and **tour companies** in Asia offering organized trips, which can make things a lot smoother. You may leave home vowing to see it all and do it all independently, but it's worth bearing a few things in mind:

- A short city tour can be an excellent way to orientate yourself. It'll help you decide what you want to spend more time exploring on your own. The Bangkok Tourist Bureau even offers tours of the more traditional neighbourhoods by bicycle.
- In some places, a tour is very often the only way to get to certain parts of the country – for example, some areas of Tibet, and Mustang in Nepal, are only accessible to trekkers on organized trips.
- Not all tours are super-luxury – there are plenty of less expensive trips aimed specifically at backpackers.
- Going on a tour with a group can be an economical way to see harder-to-reach regions.
- With longer trips, make sure you find out the full details of the itinerary and what is included, as well as departure and arrival times. A common complaint is that a "three-day trip" turns out to leave after lunch on Day One and arrives home in the early morning on Day Three.

11

Accommodation

Accommodation in most parts of Asia is astonishingly cheap. In India, Nepal and much of Southeast Asia it's quite feasible to set aside just $8/£5 a day for your accommodation budget – though you'll probably get little more than a single bed and four walls for that money. You can scrape by on less if you share a double room, and less still if you sleep in dormitories with several others.

Although making the most of your money is important, you'll probably find that you're occasionally willing to pay a little more than rock-bottom rates in return for extra comforts like an attached bathroom, a quieter location, air conditioning or more attractive surroundings. After a day-long bus ride in the sweltering heat or a marathon tour of every last Kathmandu temple, a comfortable room can restore your mental health faster than a bottle of Kingfisher beer. For just $30/£20 in Malaysia you'll get a double room with TV and minibar as well as shower and air conditioning, while $100/£60 could see you installed in a chic little boutique hideaway, with pool and stylish surrounds, in, say, Ubud or Siem Reap.

Some hotels in China and Vietnam are not allowed to take foreign guests (simply because the manager hasn't submitted the requisite paperwork), so don't take offence if you're rejected on sight. Hoteliers in other countries, however, can be prejudiced – some mid-range and upmarket hotels in India won't take backpackers, regardless of how much cash you have. The suitcase-style travelpack is a useful disguise in such instances (see p.99); putting on your smartest gear helps too.

Accommodation in Asia is not confined to hotels. You may find yourself sleeping in a rafthouse on the infamous River Kwai, dossing down in pilgrims' *guruduaras* at the Golden Temple in Amritsar, doing a homestay, or even sharing a tent with other trekkers at the foot of

▲ Take your pick – guesthouse ads, India

Mount Everest. More prosaically, major Indian train stations all offer "retiring rooms" for early-morning travellers, and there's always sleeper-car accommodation on the trains themselves.

Homestays and hospitality exchange networks

In many countries, it's quite straightforward to organize a **homestay** with a local family. Not only is this usually very cheap, but it's a great way to get off the beaten track and to learn something about the lives and culture of your hosts. The home-cooked food is often a highlight. It's also a good way of putting money straight into the community.

Often, the best way to find out about homestays is through tourist offices rather than guidebooks (see individual country profiles, pp.215–340); there are also specialist organizations, such as Mongolia's Ger to Ger (Ⓦwww.gertoger.org), as well as tour operators who feature homestay programmes (see pp.343–344). Or you can do it on the spur of the moment, simply because you have no alternative, as in remote reaches of Tibet, Brunei and Sabah and Sarawak (East Malaysia).

Alternatively, you can do it for free via one of the growing number of online **hospitality exchange** networks. Most of these operate on the shared principle of promoting international friendship. You simply sign up, for free, and agree to host travellers passing through your town for an agreed maximum number of days and times per year. In exchange, you then have access to a network of members across the world, giving you free beds for the night in places as widespread as Sichuan, Islamabad and Dili. The most popular networks include CouchSurfing (ⓦwww .couchsurfing.org) and the Hospitality Club (ⓦwww.hospitalityclub.org); there are also specialist networks such as the women-only Women Welcome Women World Wide network (ⓦwww.womenwelcomewomen.org .uk), and Warmshowers.org (ⓦwww .warmshowers.org) specifically for touring cyclists.

Finding some-where to stay

Any decent **guidebook** will list a range of accommodation, and these recommendations are useful starting points – bearing in mind that prices go up, hotels change managers, and guidebook writers have preferences that you may not share. For your first few nights in Asia we strongly recommend reserving a hotel room before you leave home (see Chapter Seven for advice on this, and the Directory, p.347, for a list of accommodation booking agents). After that, you'll probably do what every other traveller does and trawl the streets yourself, especially if you're looking for budget places.

- If you're in a city, start your search in an area that has several hotels or guesthouses close together. That way you won't feel obliged to stay in the first fleapit you come across just because you've taken two buses to get there, nor will you be unduly upset if your first choice is fully booked or has closed down.

Homestay under the Great Wall

We arrived late, in the dark, having confused departure stations in Beijing and so missed our intended train to Gubeikou. Neither of us spoke Chinese but we'd managed to get a message to our homestay host, Mr Xu, and there he was, with a torch, waiting to lead us down through the terraced cherry orchards to his home. His house was brilliant: a typical adobe-walled courtyard home, beneath a section of the Great Wall, which was moonlit right there on the skyline. Someone had recommended Mr Xu's as the perfect place to overnight before and after a trek along the Wall and they were right: theirs was the best tip of our trip. We all communicated in sign language: Mr Xu's mum demonstrated precisely how we should wash our hands and feet, and any other bits we cared to, under the pump in the courtyard; and his wife made it plain that we wouldn't be allowed to bed before we'd eaten bowl after bowl of her delicious soup, stir-fries and rice. When it came to making arrangements for our hike along the Wall, Mr Xu simply phoned his English-speaking friend and we talked to him. Everything worked perfectly and our walk, from Jinshanling to Simatai, was exhilarating: we set off, well fed of course, just after dawn and saw barely another person en route. Returning to the Xus, we were welcomed back like home-coming daughters.

Dee Ridley

- Get there by mid-morning, if you can, as most places have a noon checkout time and, during peak season, may have an impromptu waiting list established by about 10am. If there are two of you, get one person to sit down and guard the packs while the other checks out two or three places to find the best deal.

- Don't ignore a hotel just because it doesn't feature in your guidebook: it's not uncommon for some books' recommendations to be overflowing while the equally pleasant outfit next door is half empty.

- The most obvious places to look for inexpensive hotels are around bus and train stations. Though in some cities these hotels may well double as brothels, business is generally discreet and you may not even realize that most of your fellow guests are booking in and out within the hour.

- If you get a bad feeling about a hotel or guesthouse, it's generally wise to trust your instincts and look for somewhere else instead: you may feel uneasy about the other "guests", you may get a bad vibe off the staff, or you may think the place looks too dirty or too much of a fire-hazard for comfort. Unfortunately you can't assume that tourist accommodation meets the health and safety regulations you may be used to at home; it's generally up to you to make that judgement for yourself.

- Finding a room in high season or at festival time can be a real problem in some places, and prices always rocket when demand outstrips supply.

- Lots of guesthouses employ touts to bring in new customers and, though you might find their persistence incredibly irritating, they sometimes come up with useful leads, especially during peak season. Touts generally hang around transport terminals (and sometimes ride the most popular routes into town to get the choicest pickings) and will flash photos and brochures at you until you agree to go and see a place with them. In some cases the tout's commission is invisibly added onto your room rate. Before going off with a tout, always get an assurance of price, facilities and, crucially, its exact location on the map.

The guesthouse circuit

Youth hostels are rare in much of Asia, so most backpackers head instead for traveller-oriented budget hotels known as **guesthouses**. These are often more welcoming and sociable than inexpensive hotels in the same price bracket, which tend to cater mainly for local businesspeople and sales reps.

Most big towns on the tourist circuit in Cambodia, India, Indonesia, Malaysia, Nepal, the Philippines, Thailand and Vietnam have a **backpackers' enclave** where you might find up to a hundred guest-houses packed into a few hundred square metres. Such concentration ensures prices are kept low and gives you plenty of choice. These areas are also good places to meet new travel companions. Travellers often say that the real highlight of their trip was the range of characters they met on the road and in the guesthouses.

On the downside, backpackers' centres do tend to take on a peculiar **ghetto character** of their own, which not only insulates travellers from the real Bangkok/Delhi/Kathmandu, but makes Bangkok, Delhi and Kathmandu seem indistinguishable. The same is true of popular backpackers' beach resorts, where travellers may hang out for weeks, if not months, without even venturing to the nearest town or mixing at all with the local population.

A **typical no-frills guesthouse** (like the ones around Bangkok's Khao San Road) has about thirty rooms packed into three or four storeys, most of them little more than white-walled cells with a ceiling fan, and a window only if you're lucky; bathrooms are shared. The big plus is the price: at just $3/£2 for a single (less if you share with other people, dorm-style), you can hardly complain about the decor. Many guesthouses also have more expensive rooms with en-suite bathrooms and air conditioning; some even have wi-fi, a swimming pool and a café. The most efficient will sell bus and train tickets, do your laundry and store left luggage as well (though beware of leaving credit cards and other valuables in these; see Chapter Fourteen).

In smaller towns, guesthouses can be far more appealing, with tropical gardens, cool central courtyards and more spacious rooms. They're often more personal than hotels, too, being family-run businesses offering just a handful of rooms. Beach accommodation is generally just as basic and cheap as city guesthouses, but looks a lot more idyllic. A standard **beach bungalow** (the usual term for guesthouses by the sea) on Malaysia's Pulau Perhentian islands, for example, is a rickety wooden A-frame hut built on stilts right on the beach, with a palm-frond roof and a verandah that looks out to sea.

Room rates

Standards of budget accommodation vary quite a lot across Asia, so it might take you a while to work out whether or not you're getting good value for money. Rural guesthouses in Thailand, for example, are often characterful places with great views, a verandah or garden, and locally made furnishings – all for around $7/£4 a double. Vietnamese budget

A few great guesthouses

Below is a very selective taster of some favourite places to stay, where you'll mostly pay well under $25/£15 a night for two people:

Ambiente, Ella, Sri Lanka ⓦ www.ambiente.lk. Featuring fabulous views across the dramatic Ella Gap and beyond, this makes a cool retreat in the hills just a short walk from the centre of the village.

Bee Bee Bungalow, Ko Lanta, Thailand ⓦ www.diigii.de/sugarbeebee. Every hut at this island hideaway is built from bamboo to its own design: with turrets, alcoves, stilts or a wonky mezzanine. They're simple of course, but en suite and right on the beach.

Bulan Baru (New Moon), Senggigi, Lombok, Indonesia Boasting spotless rooms, a swimming pool, a beautiful garden and a stunning beach close by, this is a perfect spot to relax.

Hillside Inn, Batad, Philippines Set plumb in the middle of a spectacular valley of sculpted rice terraces, this is one of just a few perfectly located guesthouses in the traditional village of Batad.

Inn of the First Bend, Lijiang, China With its charming courtyard garden and traditional wooden architecture, *Inn of the First Bend* is a pleasingly historic budget option in the old Naxi town of Lijiang in southwest China.

Jockey Club Mount Davis Youth Hostel, Hong Kong ⓦ www.yha.org.hk. Eye-popping views over Hong Kong harbour – a treat by day or night. It's set right on the top of a hill, so getting there's a trek, but you couldn't find a calmer or more panoramic spot on Hong Kong Island.

Kalsang Guest House, Dharamsala, India The best rooms at this hillside guesthouse look down over the village, and from the roof terrace you get perfect views of the snowcapped Dhauladhar mountains.

Old Hunza Inn, Karimabad, Pakistan ⓦ www.oldhunzainn.co.cc. Gaze across to six of Pakistan's most spectacular 7000-metre-plus mountain peaks from your bedroom window in this guesthouse high up along the northern stretch of the Karakoram Highway. It's basic but popular and communal meals are served nightly.

Sama's Cottages, Bali, Indonesia ⓦ www.balilife.com/sama's. A very typical, family-run Balinese hideaway, *Sama's Cottages* in Ubud are built on steep tiers that drop into the river gully. Each has its own terrace, screened by profuse tropical shrubbery, where the generous breakfasts are served.

The Shadow of the Moon at Half-Past Four, Cherating, Malaysia The timber chalets at this catchily named guesthouse are thoughtfully designed and secluded in a wooded area just a few minutes' walk from the beach.

accommodation on the other hand tends to lack personality and often costs more than it would in neighbouring countries.

Cheap travellers' guesthouses don't really exist in **Singapore**, **Hong Kong**, **Japan** and **Brunei**, so most budget tourists opt for dorm beds in youth hostels instead – although even these will set you back a minimum of $14/£8 a bed. **Camping** is cheaper, though official city campsites tend to be inconveniently located in the suburbs; elsewhere in Asia, camping is only appropriate in national parks and on treks. See Chapter Six for advice on whether or not to take camping equipment. The following tips will help you make the most of your accommodation budget:

- A dorm bed will be at least thirty percent cheaper than a single room. If no dorms are available you might want to split a double room with another traveller, again cheaper than a single room. Obviously you should only do this if you feel comfortable with the other person.
- In some places you can bargain over the price of a room (especially in low season); others might offer discounts for stays of a week or more.
- If travelling long distance, you can save a night's hotel costs by taking the overnight train or bus and making sure you get a reclining seat. Second-class berths on trains usually cost about the same as a single room in a guesthouse.
- Watch out for "luxury" service charges and taxes in mid- and up-market places (up to 21 percent extra in Indonesia, for example), and for ridiculous room-service charges as well as overpriced food in the hotel restaurant.
- Using the phone in your room to make international calls is always costly, as most hotels add a huge surcharge to phone bills. Try to get your friends or relatives to call you back. Some hotels charge a lot for wi-fi too; in others it's complimentary.
- An unorthodox way of finding cheap accommodation in Japan is to check in to a "love hotel" after all the lovers have departed for the night (usually around 10pm). These hotels are designed for secret and extramarital liaisons, but are definitely not brothels. They're completely legal and unsleazy, if a little kitsch – rooms tend to be plastered in mirrors, fake fur and romantic images – and are scrupulously clean. Because most clandestine liaisons take place during the day, overnighters get a huge discount.

Can I see the room please?

Always **look at the room** you're being offered before paying for it – this is normal practice throughout Asia and, though time-consuming, is definitely worth it. Once you've checked out a few places you'll be able to size up a room in five seconds, but for first-timers here's a checklist of essential points to look out for:

- **Is there a nicer room?** If you like the hotel but aren't sure about the room, always ask to see another one: the view might be better, the neighbours quieter and, who knows, the fan might even be working in that one.
- **Is the room secure?** Can you put your own padlock on the door? (Not always applicable in China, where rooms in cheap

hotels are locked and unlocked for you by the floor attendant.) Are the windows safe? Are there any peepholes in the door or walls?

- **Is the room clean?** Check the sheets for blood spots (blood means fleas or bedbugs), the floor for cockroaches and the walls for squashed mosquitoes. Look under the bed for rat traps (squares of cardboard sprinkled with food and smeared with glue) and examine the window screens and mosquito nets for rips.
- **Does everything work?** Try out the lights, the fan/air conditioning/heater, the flush toilet (if there is one) and the shower (ditto).
- **Do the taps run fresh or salt water?** Straight from the river? If you asked for hot water, check that it works.
- **Is it quiet?** Rooms on the main road will be noisy, but so will any place near a morning market, a night market, a mosque, a disco, a hotel kitchen or an electricity generator – which you may not discover until the next morning.

Checking in

Wherever you stay, avoid leaving your **passport** with hotel staff unless you absolutely have to do so. This is unavoidable in some parts of Vietnam, for example, where hotel managers have to present their guests' passports at the police station. If you're asked to surrender your passport as security against your bill, offer to leave a monetary deposit instead. Your passport is your only official means of identity in a strange land and should be kept on your person at all times – besides which, you'll need it for changing money and other transactions.

Most people keep their passport, airline ticket and other valuables with them whenever they leave their hotel, not least because **hotel security** can be lax. However, you could also leave these items in your room and use your own padlock on the door (if you can), or put them in a hotel safety box, again secured by your own padlock, in a lockable small box or bag, or in an envelope that you've signed over the seal. Bear in mind, though, that sawing through a small padlock is not so difficult, and be aware that not all hotel staff are scrupulously honest.

Peeping Toms

Jill and Danny were lying naked in their room in Da Nang, Vietnam, when they spotted a hole in the wall with a dirty great eye behind it, staring at them. Completely amazed, they told the person in so many words to mind their own business, and blocked up the hole with tissue and tape. Ten minutes later, they looked up to see a long pair of chopsticks penetrate the hole, free the space and the big eye return.

Chris Humphrey

www.roughguides.com

Security should also be an issue when you're inside your hotel room with your valuables. Always lock the door from the inside, even when you're awake (people have a habit of drifting in for a chat at the most inopportune moments). Wedging a tilted chair under the door handle can be a useful last resort if the lock doesn't work. And check on window access, too, in case a thief decides to climb in while you're asleep.

Bathrooms and how to use them

Though many guesthouses and hotels have Western-style showers, the traditional scoop-and-slosh method of bathing is also common right across Asia. Known in travellers' speak as a **mandi** (Indonesian for "to wash"), this basically involves dipping a scoop, jug or small bowl into a large bucket or basin of water and then chucking it over yourself – very refreshing in a chilly kind of way. The cardinal rule of the *mandi* is never to put your soap or shampoo into the basin of water and, though it often looks like a big stone bathtub, never, ever to get into it as this water might have to supply the next two weeks' worth of guests.

Washing in **cold water** is the norm throughout most of Asia, but in the high altitudes of Nepal, northern India, Tibet, Bhutan, Pakistan and north China, you'll definitely need a hot shower, so make sure it's operational before paying for your room. Some places only turn on the water heaters at certain times of day.

You'll probably come across quite a few unexpected **bathing habits** during your Asian travels:

- In rural parts of Asia, the local river, lake or well doubles as the village bathroom and everyone congregates there at the end of the day for their evening wash. Men and women nearly always have separate bathing areas and, though they may be within sight of each other, there's absolutely no ogling or communication between the two groups. Both sexes wear sarongs in the water

Lowering the tone

The staff at the five-star Mumbai hotel took one look at my scruffy T-shirt and well-travelled rucksack and said, "Sorry sir, the hotel is fully booked". I'd just finished a five-year contract in Bhutan – a country not noted for its designer clothes shops, or even its laundrettes – and was desperate for a few days of luxury. Though I waved wads of cash at the receptionist and flashed my credit card, he was just not willing to lower the tone of the establishment by admitting a backpacker: "Sorry sir, the hotel is fully booked". So I strolled down the street, found a public phone and called him up from round the corner. He didn't recognize my voice and answered, "Yes, sir, we have a room; how many nights?" Ten minutes later, I was back at the five-star, picking up the keys to my deluxe accommodation.

Gerry Jameson

and no one strips off to wash. If you bathe in the local river, you should do as they do, or find a place much further upriver.

- Traditional Japanese hotels generally have old-fashioned bathtubs. These have no running hot water, but work instead by heating up the full tub with an element, like a kettle – enabling you to sit in the water and keep warm for hours on end. The same bath water is used by several hotel guests one after the other (not as unhygienic as it sounds if you think of it like a public Jacuzzi), so it's essential to wash yourself, using the scoop-and-slosh method, before hopping into the tub.
- In Bali, the most stylish guesthouses and hotels have beautifully designed "garden bathrooms" or "rain showers", with roofs that are open to the sky, sculptured water flues and tropical plants growing round the *mandi* area.
- Most small towns in Korea have public bathhouses – a national institution that should definitely be experienced. In these you wash yourself on the side of the main pool and then climb in for a very hot soak and a chat with your neighbours. Most have separate pools for men and women.
- Traditional Bhutanese baths are heated with huge stones, which are first cooked to a high temperature in the embers of a fire and then thrown into the tub.

Toilet habits

Flush toilets and toilet paper are relatively recent arrivals in many parts of Asia and, apart from in tourist hotels, urban guesthouses and wealthier homes, it's often a question of hunkering down over a **squat toilet** like everyone else does. Asians wash their bottoms rather than wipe them, using the bucket of water provided and their left hand. This explains why eating, shaking hands and giving things is always done with the right hand – see Chapter Eight for details.

Traveller-oriented guesthouses often provide sit-down toilets that are plumbed in but don't flush. In these you're expected to do the flushing manually by pouring a bucket of water down the bowl. These plumbing systems are very sensitive and get blocked up easily as, unlike Western ones, they're not designed to take paper or tampons. Many guesthouses have signs telling you to throw your waste in the bin instead and it's selfish not to obey the rules. Even if there's no sign and no bucket, you should chuck any paper waste into a plastic bag: a blocked drain in your en-suite bathroom will attract mosquitoes and germs, and the stink will permeate your dreams.

The obvious way round all this is to adopt the Asian habit and wash instead of wipe. If that sounds a step too far, travel with your own roll of toilet paper as some places won't provide it. The one situation where it's hard to either wipe or wash is when you're out trekking in the wilderness. If you don't want to use leaves, either burn your paper with a lighter or dig a little hole and bury it – there's nothing like a ribbon of pink toilet paper for ruining a spectacular view.

Be prepared to come across a good percentage of gut-wrenchingly vile public toilets, particularly in bus and train stations, and on trains in China and India. Try and get into the habit of using hotel and restaurant facilities when you can, and don't be surprised by the following:

- Indoor bathrooms are considered unhygienic by many rural Asian communities, for whom the idea of having a toilet just a metre or so from the kitchen is quite disgusting. Indian villagers, for example, will set off for the fields every morning to do their ablutions away from the home or, if they live near the sea, they will do them on the shoreline so that the sea washes everything away. With that in mind, it pays to be careful where you swim and sunbathe on Indian beaches.

- Public toilets in remote areas of China are often very public indeed – with only a low partition between squatters, and sometimes no partition at all.

- All Chinese and Japanese hotels provide special plastic slippers for wearing in the bathroom.

- Some public toilets in Japan play piped music to mask the sound of pissing, which is considered embarrassing for Japanese women. If you're lucky, you might even come across a singing toilet-roll holder, which plays *Für Elise* every time you yank the paper.

- In Thailand, toilet attendants in upmarket restaurants massage your neck and shoulders while you stand at a urinal.

- In the "fine city" of Singapore, there's a S$500 fine for failing to flush a public toilet and should you be caught urinating in a public space, you get your picture splashed over the front page of the national newspaper.

Staying healthy

here's no advice that we can give and nothing that you can do to absolutely guarantee you don't fall sick in Asia. You are subjecting your body to different food and water, extreme heat or cold, tropical sun and there are a whole host of new creepy-crawlies to contend with. Even the air you breathe will be carrying different viruses from those you are used to. This chapter presents the facts that every visitor to Asia should know, gives advice on precautions and has suggestions to help you cope should you get ill. See p.118 for information about DVT (deep-vein thrombosis).

These points put things in perspective and help you to prepare:

- Millions of travellers go to Asia every year and return home safely, the vast majority having suffered nothing worse than a few days of travellers' diarrhoea.
- In case you do fall ill, be sure you build enough leeway into your itinerary to allow you to rest up for a few days. The last thing you'll feel like doing if you're unwell is boarding an overcrowded bus for an overnight journey.
- Read up about diseases prevalent in Asia, as symptoms that probably just indicate flu at home may be something more serious in the tropics. There are several good books on travellers' health – some people take them along, and they can make interesting if gory reading. Rough Guides' *Travel Health* and Dr Jane Wilson Howarth's *The Essential Guide to Travel Health: Don't Let Bugs, Bites and Bowels Spoil Your Trip* (Cadogan/Globe Pequot) are both packed full of vital information for before, during and after your trip. Alternatively there are several excellent websites; see the Directory, p.348, for details.

www.roughguides.com

First-aid kit

Many of the items listed here are available in Asia, but it's better to have them to hand and replace them later if required. Pre-packaged kits are available but it's usually cheaper to put one together yourself and tailor it to your needs. If you're trekking you should also consult a specialist trekking guide for additional items and keep your first-aid kit in your day sack – if you need it, you'll need it quickly.

Anti-diarrhoea tablets, anti-fungal cream, antiseptic cream, asprin/paracetamol, anti-histamine tablets, plasters small and large (fabric ones work well for blisters), bite cream (Tiger Balm, available throughout Asia, is a good alternative; it is also useful for aching muscles and headaches), cold remedy, gauze pads, insect repellent, lip salve/sun block for lips, rehydration salts, scissors, sterile dressings, sterile needles and syringes, surgical tape, thermometer, throat lozenges, tweezers.

Prescription drugs

Apart from routine prescription drugs, your doctor may be willing to give you a course of tablets to take with you if you explain where you are going. Make sure you know how and when to use them: antibiotics, for throat and bronchial infections, and for intestinal bacteria; Tinidazole, for giardia (see p.181); and Emergency treatment for malaria (see p.177)

- Things change fast; keep abreast of current developments by using the websites listed on p.348. Nasties such as SARS (Sudden Acute Respiratory Disease), bird flu and epidemics of dengue fever are prevalent in Asia.
- Go for a dental checkup before you leave home; finding dental treatment in Asia on a par with that at home can be even more difficult than finding other forms of medical care. However, private clinics in Bangkok, for example, have an excellent reputation so don't automatically assume you'll have to suffer until you get home.
- Carry a first-aid kit (see box above).
- Don't forget to take any medication you use regularly, including the contraceptive pill – enough for the whole trip; a letter from your doctor can smooth your way with suspicious customs officials.
- Make sure you have adequate medical insurance (see p.62). A medical evacuation on a special plane, for example, from Thailand back to the UK could set you back $50,000/£31,000 or more.
- Some Asian illnesses don't show themselves straight away – if you get sick within a year of returning home from Asia, make sure you tell your doctor where you've been.

Vaccinations

Get advice as early as possible about which **vaccinations** you require for your trip, as many are given as a course of two or three jabs in order to be effective. It's advisable to allow time gaps between certain vaccinations; in any case, you won't really want to subject your arm to

www.roughguides.com

four needles in one sitting. Similarly, you need to find out early about the type of malaria-preventive medication that is recommended for the areas you are visiting; you may need to start taking the tablets in advance of departure. Even if your itinerary is not finalized, compile a list of places you are planning to visit (as well as any others you may visit) and think about whether you are planning to stay in tourist resorts or off the beaten track, to travel during the monsoon, and whether you'll be camping. All of these will affect the advice you are given.

While your family doctor may offer some injections cheaply or free, you may want to contact a **private travel clinic** to make sure you get the most specialized information available. Many travel clinics have telephone information lines, are quick and convenient and, though they can be expensive, provide personalized information that's up to date and extensive (see the Directory, p.348 for contact details).

Vaccinations don't offer lifelong immunity, so keep a record so you know when you need a booster. A very few jabs can cause reactions – unpleasant but much better than getting the disease.

Different countries vary in what inoculations they insist on for visitors, but the only time you are likely to be asked for documentation is if you have recently travelled to a country in South or Central America, where **yellow fever** is endemic. In this case, you must have had a yellow fever jab (and have the certificate to prove it). It's worth taking your medical card, or a copy of it, showing which vaccinations you've had.

Diseases you should know about

Below is a rundown of diseases you might be exposed to and which vaccinations are available. Don't be unduly alarmed, however, as some of these are confined to limited regions or seasons:

- **Cholera** Vaccinations against this extremely severe diarrhoeal illness, transmitted via contaminated food and water, are generally thought to be ineffectual and short-term. The best advice is to follow the guidelines given in this chapter regarding what you eat and drink, and steer well clear of any areas where you hear there's an epidemic.
- **Dengue fever** This viral disease gives rise to severe fever and joint and muscle pain. It's spread by mosquitoes, which, unusually, bite during the day. Dengue fever is painful and unpleasant, but the more serious, life-threatening dengue haemorrhagic fever can also occur, although the latter is most usually associated with a second or later bout of the illness. There is no vaccination and the disease is currently on the increase in Asia – see precautions for avoiding mosquito bites, p.177.

- **Hepatitis** There are several strains of this disease (including Hepatitis A, B, C, D and E) in which viruses attack the liver, causing a whole raft of symptoms including yellow colouring of skin and eyes (jaundice), exhaustion, fever, joint pains, weight loss and diarrhoea. It can last for many months and can also result in serious liver problems in the long term. Hepatitis A is transmitted via contaminated food, water or saliva and the more serious Hepatitis B is transmitted through contaminated blood, needles and syringes and by sexual contact. Vaccination is possible against Hepatitis A and B. There's no vaccine against the other strains.

- **Japanese encephalitis** This is a viral illness resulting in inflammation of the brain, found across Asia, although largely restricted to rural areas. It's transmitted via mosquitoes from infected animals and is very dangerous – the death rate is high, and so is the danger of brain damage if you survive. Inoculation provides only partial protection so it's important to avoid areas if there is an outbreak.

- **Malaria** There are several strains of malaria, most causing recurring bouts of fever, headache and shivering. All are serious, debilitating and can be fatal. The parasites that cause malaria are carried by night-biting mosquitoes. All travellers to Asia should consider taking a course of preventive tablets and do everything to prevent being bitten, as none of the drugs is a hundred percent effective. See pp.175–178 for more details.

- **Meningococcal meningitis** Caused by airborne bacteria, this disease attacks the lining of the brain and can be fatal; epidemics, though rare, do affect parts of the continent. A vaccine is available.

- **Polio, diphtheria and TB** Most people will have been inoculated against these in childhood and, while they are rare in the West, they are still common in Asia. You should make sure you are still covered – you may need a booster jab.

Complementary medicine

Complementary medicine offers many alternative or additional approaches that may help combat the health risks of Asian travel. Probably one of the most useful aspects is in suggesting the value of building up your immune system before you travel. For example, echinacea is suggested as a general boost to immunity and probiotics are used by many people to increase the "good" bacteria in the gut with the aim of wiping out anything harmful that enters the digestive system. Acupressure can offer relief for travel sickness and herbal preparations can help with a variety of problems from fear of flying to stomach upsets. See Rough Guides' *Travel Health* for more information on complementary medicine.

- **Rabies** Spread via the saliva of infected cats, dogs and monkeys, rabies is prevalent throughout Asia, with ninety percent of the world's deaths from the disease occurring in India. It's also estimated that a high percentage of stray dogs in Vietnam and Thailand are rabid. If you have the course of vaccines before you go you'll still need further injections should you get bitten by an animal suspected of carrying the disease. Without previous vaccination at home, you'll need more injections if you do get bitten abroad.
- **Tetanus** Also known as lockjaw, the disease is contracted via open wounds (for example, a cut caused by stepping on a rusty nail). Most people in the West get injected at some point; make sure you are up to date before you leave home.
- **Typhoid** Spread by contaminated food and water, typhoid is characterized by extremely high fever, abdominal pains, headaches, diarrhoea and red spots on the body; patients need urgent medical help. Protection is either given by injection or a course of more expensive capsules before you leave home.

Mosquitoes

Given the number of diseases carried by **mosquitoes** (malaria, Japanese encephalitis, dengue fever), not to mention the unpleasantness of mosquito bites, you should do whatever you can to avoid getting bitten. This means wearing long sleeves and sloshing mosquito repellent on exposed skin during the dusk and darkness hours when the malarial mosquito operates, and sleeping under a mosquito net or with any open windows covered by a fine wire mesh. It's a good idea to have a shower and get changed (into light-coloured clothes) for the evening before it gets dark – mosquitoes adore sweaty skin, and also strong perfumes.

You might decide to take your own mosquito net with you – they are light and compact, and you can guarantee one brought from home won't be full of tears and cigarette burns. Ideally you want one that has been impregnated with Permethrin insecticide as an additional barrier against the bugs; you can also buy Permethrin separately to treat older nets.

Malaria

Malaria is one of the nastiest and most common tropical diseases worldwide – it affects between 300 and 500 million people each year and kills more than a million of them. Though most of these deaths occur among young children in sub-Saharan Africa, the disease is a serious risk for anyone travelling to Asia, where some of the most dangerous forms of

175

malaria lurk, especially in the Thai–Cambodian and Thai–Burmese border areas, where the parasites that cause the disease have developed resistance to several drugs.

There is currently no vaccine against malaria, but there are several **preventive drugs**, although none is a hundred percent effective. You must start taking them a specified amount of time before you arrive in a malarial area (the exact period depends on the drug) and, even more importantly, continue taking them for some time (again, determined by which drug you are taking) after you leave. It is possible to develop malaria back home if you ignore this regime – typically about 1500 British travellers return to UK with malaria every year and half a dozen of these die from the disease.

For many decades the most commonly used malaria prophylaxis has been chloroquine (sold as Nivaquine and Avloclor in the UK, and Aralen in the US), taken weekly together with daily proguanil (sold as Paludrine). However, as strains of chloroquine-resistant malaria have evolved, other drugs have come into use. Mefloquine (sold as Larium) is probably the best known due to controversy that continues to rage over side effects in some users. However there are plenty of other options: the antibiotic **doxycycline** is the drug of choice in many areas where travellers are unsuited to or choose not to take Larium. Another option, sold as Malarone, is a combination of atovaquone and proguanil and prescribed

Malaria in Asia

This is a broad overview of the malaria situation in the countries covered in this book. Be sure to check the current situation and appropriate **preventive medication** and emergency treatment with a medical specialist before you travel. Countries described as "malarial at lower altitudes" are mountainous in parts. Although they are not malarial at higher elevations, the cut-off line isn't totally clear and even transiting through lower altitudes can be risky.

Bangladesh	Malarial	Mongolia	Not malarial
Bhutan	Malarial at lower altitudes	Nepal	Malarial at lower altitudes
Brunei	Not malarial		
Cambodia	Malarial	Pakistan	Malarial at lower altitudes
China	Large areas are malarial. Seek detailed advice when you have an itinerary.	Philippines	Malarial
		Singapore	Not malarial
		South Korea	Malarial in parts. Seek detailed advice.
East Timor	Malarial		
India	Malarial	Sri Lanka	Malarial
Indonesia	Malarial	Taiwan	Not malarial
Japan	Not malarial	Thailand	Malarial
Laos	Malarial	Vietnam	Malarial
Malaysia	Malarial		

in areas where there is chloroquine resistance and other drugs may not be suitable. It's pricey but has reportedly fewer side effects.

In recent years the Chinese preparation *qinghaosu* (known as artemisi-nin in the West), a derivative of the plant sweet wormwood (*Artemesia annua*), which has been used against malaria in China for over two thousand years, has been proving highly effective in treating malaria in areas where resistance to other drugs has developed. Unfortunately, in mid-2009 information began to emerge from Cambodia of artemisinin resistance.

Before you travel, seek advice from your doctor or a specialist travel clinic about which drugs are recommended for malaria prevention in the areas you plan to visit. If you are heading a long way off the beaten track, discuss with your medical adviser whether you should carry an emergency course of treatment – though this should be used until you can get to medical help rather than instead of it. If you develop any fever up to a year after you get home, be sure to get medical advice and make sure the doctor is aware that you've been to a malarial area.

The general books on p.171 and websites in the Directory on p.348 all carry information about malaria; in addition, check out Malaria Foundation International at ⓦwww.malaria.org for the latest information.

Mosquito repellents

Hopefully all of the above has convinced you to try to avoid mosquito bites. The most effective way to do this is by applying **mosquito repellent** to exposed skin; the most widely used is called **DEET** (Diethyl Tolumide). You can buy repellent containing up to 95 percent DEET, although strengths of over 35 percent are not thought to be much more effective in any case, although below 15% the effectiveness diminishes rapidly. Wrist and ankle bands pre-soaked in the chemical are also available, or you can soak your own. Bear in mind that it's strong stuff and can cause skin reactions, especially at higher concentrations. It can also melt plastic (sunglasses, watch straps, shoes). Locally bought repellents are often very good and much cheaper than ones bought at home. They may even be the same brand – Autan, for example, is widely available throughout Asia. Some equipment companies produce travel clothing pre-treated with repellent – although the protection doesn't last indefinitely.

There's also a range of natural products available. These substances aren't quite as repugnant to mosquitoes as DEET, but avoid its disadvantages. Most of these natural repellents are based around citronella or lemon eucalyptus, geranium and soya bean or coconut oil. Preparations containing neem oil are also useful. One advantage of using a mosquito repellent though is that it will ward off leeches, ticks and sand flies, too.

Leeches

Any forays into the jungle mean potential encounters with **leeches** – tiny, thread-like blood-sucking creatures that attach themselves to your skin, zap you with an anaesthetic and anticoagulant, slurp away at the red stuff and, when they've had enough and expanded to many times their normal size, drop off and leave you dripping blood for a long time afterwards. The good news is they don't carry any nasty diseases; the bad news is that they can get through the tiniest holes, such as between the threads in most socks (and they love the eyeholes of boots). One glimpse of your ankle with a dozen or so of them attached is a short cut to hysteria.

To stop them attacking, silk socks, insect repellent and tobacco leaves in your socks are all useful, plus regular checks of your feet when you are walking. If you do fall victim, dab at the creatures with salt, a lighted cigarette or chewing tobacco (widely available across Asia) to get them to let go. Don't just pull them off in a panic – easier said than done – as this is likely to leave their sucking parts embedded in your skin, which can lead to infection.

Some travellers believe that vitamin B1 tablets or garlic capsules, taken regularly, make the blood offensive to insects and so protect against bites, though there isn't much evidence for or against this yet.

At some point in your trip you'll encounter mosquito coils. Bright green and impregnated with chemicals, they are the main Asian way of deterring mosquitoes and smoulder for about eight hours. They're useful for protecting your ankles if you are sitting outside at night, or you can put coils beside the bed while you sleep; be extremely careful, however, as the can easily become a fire risk.

The heat

The opportunity to experience a tropical climate is one of the big attractions of a trip to Asia, yet exposure to extreme heat is one of the major causes of illness for many travellers. To avoid problems, be sure to do the following when you arrive:

- Respect the heat. It isn't only mad dogs and Englishmen who go out in the midday sun, it's plenty of other travellers as well, but it's far better to stay in the shade between 11am and 2pm when the heat is most extreme, as most local people do.
- Dress sensibly – see p.104 for ideas on clothing that will help you keep cool in hot climates.
- Use plenty of high-factor **sunscreen** (particularly at high altitude), even if you are just walking around – don't forget the tops of your feet, tops of your ears and backs of your hands. Protect your head with a hat – you'll also notice many locals use sun umbrellas during the hottest part of the day.
- Heat rashes, prickly heat or fungal infections thrive in the damp, humid conditions of the tropics. Always make sure you dry

yourself carefully after bathing and use medicated talcum powder or antifungal powder (both available throughout Asia) if you are prone to suffer from these conditions.

- Drink plenty of **water**. The heat will make you sweat, so you need to increase your fluid intake to compensate. If you stop peeing or your urine is becoming dark, then you're not drinking enough.

- Increase your intake of **salt** – you also lose this when you sweat. Many travellers add a pinch of salt to fruit juices and shakes (see rehydration advice on p.181). Muscle cramps are a sign that you are lacking enough salt in your diet.

- Be aware of the symptoms of **heat exhaustion**: extreme fatigue, cramps, a rapid pulse, reddened skin and vomiting. Anyone with these symptoms needs a cool place to recover, plenty to drink and even wrapping in sheets or sarongs soaked in cold water. Hospital treatment is sometimes necessary. Heat stroke is a more serious, potentially life-threatening overheating of the body; if the patient continues to get hotter despite the treatments above or becomes confused, delirious or unconscious seek medical help fast.

- Get enough **rest**. It is very easy to get exhausted if you are racing round sightseeing in the heat all day and sampling the nightlife after dark. If you're tired, you're more vulnerable to illness.

Water

With a couple of exceptions – Singapore and Japan – **tap water** in Asia is not safe to drink, which means you should avoid ice in your drinks, too. However, there are alternatives. Bottled water is widely available. Check the seals of the bottles before you buy, as some unscrupulous dealers collect empty bottles and refill them straight from the tap; such bottles might have the seal missing or have obviously been tampered with. However, over a period of time, bottled water can make a surprising hole in your budget and you'll also have left behind a small mountain of non-biodegradable plastic. There is however an increasing awareness of this issue and travellers' restaurants and guesthouses are starting to offer **water-refill** services so you can save money and the environment at the same time.

One alternative, but not really practical outside trekking areas, is to **boil drinking wate**r to sterilize it – five minutes' boiling (ten minutes at high altitude) will kill off anything that is likely to harm you. While this is fine if you have access to cooking equipment, it is not convenient in most situations. Another option is to sterilize the water using chlorine or iodine tablets (available from outdoor-equipment shops or travel clinics). While these are cheap and easy, they are not effective against all the harmful organisms in the water and they leave the water with a definite chemical taste although neutralizing tablets are also available to get rid of

www.roughguides.com

this. Water filters also only do a partial job, and do not remove viruses. The most effective solution is to take a **water purifier**, which will both filter and sterilize the water. There are several on the market; before buying one, you should compare their sizes, weights, the speed at which they process water, and how often replacement cartridges are needed. Travel Equipment Suppliers (p.350) and Travel Clinics (p.348) stock them.

Food

The sights, smells and tastes of **Asian food** are one of the greatest pleasures of any visit to the continent. You'll be dying to try out unfamiliar fruits such as rambutans, breadfruit and mangosteens, while a walk through any Asian night market where cooks behind tiny stalls conjure up enticing, spicy meals of rice, noodles, seafood and soups will set your taste buds tingling. Though not everyone will want to tackle the crunchy fried grasshoppers of Thailand, the liberal chilli-fest of Sumatran Padang cuisine or the dog-meat delicacies of southwestern China, we guarantee you will make some unforgettable culinary discoveries.

While you should enjoy the new tastes and eating experiences to the full, it pays to exercise some control over what and where you eat:

- Avoid food that has been sitting out in the midday heat assaulted by flies, or anything that has be reheated. One of the reasons Indian food can have such a disastrous effect on foreign bowels is the common cooking style: slow-cooked casseroles and stews mean the temperature may never rise high enough to exterminate germs. Western food is often the most hazardous – ask yourself how long that cannelloni has been waiting around before its brief time in the microwave. In contrast, in a place like Thailand, stir-fries are whipped up on the spot and have no chance to languish all day in the tropical heat.

- Fruit that has already been peeled or simply chopped up such as pineapples or papaya can be a hazard. Fruit you peel yourself should be fine.

- Similarly, raw vegetables, including salad, are suspect, either because of the water they have been washed in or the human excrement that is used for fertilizer in some parts of Asia.

- Surrounded by so many unfamiliar foods, it can be difficult to get a balanced diet, especially as in some places, such as Nepal and parts of China, fresh fruit and vegetables are scarce. Consider taking vitamin tablets with you.

- Vegetarians and vegans are generally well catered for across Asia; many Asians are vegetarian on religious grounds and restaurants cater for them alongside carnivorous diners, often in delicious ways. Indeed, sources of protein such as tofu are probably more widely available in Asia than they are in the West. However, see the note about fruit and vegetables, above.

Diarrhoea and dehydration

There are numerous causes for the **diarrhoea** and vomiting that strike travellers in Asia, from a straightforward reaction to a change of water and diet to more unpleasant bacteria and viruses. Whatever the cause, the main problem you'll face is dehydration, which will make you feel exhausted and dizzy, and give you a splitting headache. It's important to focus on rehydrating the moment any stomach problems start; worry about a diagnosis later.

You should be drinking two or three litres of water a day just to cope with being in the tropics, but if you get diarrhoea you'll need a lot more. In addition, your body will be losing important minerals and so you should always carry sachets of **oral rehydration salts** (ORS) with you. These just need dissolving in clean drinking water and are available under a variety of names (such as Dioralyte) in the West and throughout Asia. Even if you're vomiting, you should sip small amounts of the solution. If you can't get hold of commercial brands, dissolve approximately one level teaspoon of salt and eight level teaspoons of sugar in a litre of clean water; it's important that the resulting mixture shouldn't contain too much salt – it mustn't be any saltier than the taste of tears. A small amount of fruit juice will improve the taste and add potassium.

Most cases of diarrhoea and vomiting run their course in two to three days, and as long as you keep drinking you'll be OK until you can start eating again; start with bland food, such as boiled rice. If the symptoms are particularly severe, persist for more than three days without abating or are accompanied by blood or mucus in your faeces, or by fever, then you should seek medical help. There are several **illnesses** you should be aware of, including bacilliary or amoebic dysentery, typhoid and a particularly common one called giardiasis (or giardia), which produces rotten-egg belches and farts – not guaranteed to help you make friends.

Anti-diarrhoea tablets should be used extremely sparingly. Diarrhoea serves a purpose in ejecting toxins from your body. These tablets, which effectively halt the movements of your digestive system, stop the diarrhoea, but they block you up, don't attack the micro-organisms responsible for the problem and can actually make you feel worse. They are useful, however, if you absolutely *have* to travel.

As bizarre as it may sound, after a few months on the road you'll be gleefully swapping stories with fellow travellers of "the yellow frothy diarrhoea I had in Nepal" – probably while tucking into a pizza in Thailand.

www.roughguides.com

Altitude

The problem of **altitude** is a serious one for anyone planning to trek in the Himalayas or visit Tibet or other high-altitude regions such as Ladakh in India, some parts of Xinjiang, Sichuan and Yunnan in China, the Karakoram region of Pakistan and Mount Fuji in Japan – anyone who usually lives at low altitude and goes over 10,000 feet (about 3000m) is at risk, whether trekking, flying in or arriving by bus or train.

The higher you go above sea level, the less oxygen there is in the air and the lower the air pressure that drives it from your lungs into your bloodstream. Your body needs time to adapt to this, and while this process is under way – probably for the first three days at altitude, especially if you have flown in – you are likely to experience headaches, shortness of breath, tiredness, loss of appetite, aches and pains, sleeping problems and nausea (collectively known as **acute mountain sickness**, or AMS). Relax totally and drink plenty of water (at least three litres daily) and the symptoms should pass, although having acclimatized you must still ascend slowly – no more than 300m per day with a rest day for every 900m climbed. If you go too fast the symptoms will return.

If your symptoms worsen, however, and especially if you start vomiting and experience loss of coordination, delirium, rapid heartbeat, breathlessness and blueness of tongue and lips, you must descend immediately. Just a few hundred metres of vertical descent can be life-saving and

▲ "Did you remember the wet wipes?" Altitude sickness can make people forgetful

usually brings about immediate recovery. Serious cases of AMS are very rare, but anyone planning to travel and especially trek over 3000m should inform themselves of the potential risks beforehand. See ⓦwww.ismmed .org/np_altitude_tutorial.htm for an Altitude Tutorial.

HIV, AIDS and contraception

Unprotected sex is as unwise in Asia as it is at home. Reliable figures are not easy to find, but **HIV and AIDS** are prevalent across the region. As an indication, there are an estimated 2.3 million people in India with HIV/AIDS. The level of AIDS education is variable throughout Asia so travellers should assume they will be the one taking responsibility for the supply and use of condoms in any sexual encounter.

Condoms, often locally manufactured, are widely available in pharmacies and supermarkets, although local brands have a fairly mixed reputation – you'd be well advised to check use-by dates and buy from air-conditioned suppliers as far as possible, as extreme heat can rot the rubber. Expatriate residents in Asia usually keep theirs in the fridge – not a service most budget hotels offer – but it is worth trying to keep them in the coolest part of your pack. Women travellers may feel conspicuous asking for condoms, especially in traditional Muslim areas, so it's

Even in paradise

Approaching the small Thai island of Ko Tao, I was mesmerized. Across the water I could see a vision of white sands, coconut palms and rickety thatched huts. As we stepped off the boat, hordes of touts appeared advertising their beach resorts. Bewildered, we followed a young, stocky Thai man by the name of Chet, who drove us to a resort. During many weeks on the island, poker playing with Chet developed into riskier games, and we started sleeping together. Armed with condoms, I didn't worry about health issues. I asked Chet if he had been tested for HIV and we discussed the chances of pregnancy. But the reality of the risks never truly set in; condoms were fast becoming an inconvenience and the belief that nothing could harm me grew. In the New Year I left for Australia but sometime in March, I began to feel ill. One morning looking in the mirror, I discovered the whites of my eyes were turning yellow. This was followed by my stomach and slowly the rest of my body. I was losing weight, my hair was falling out, and eventually I could barely stand. The doctor ordered an exhaustive series of blood tests. At last the results came: I had been diagnosed with Hepatitis B, the worst strain of the disease and one which you're destined to carry for life. Hepatitis B attacks the liver – brutally; liver cirrhosis is a distinct possibility, as is liver cancer. My world collapsed. I was treated with countless drugs and, feeling partially recovered, I left for Britain three weeks later. Back home was worse: I faced hospital appointments, HIV tests and family hysteria. I contacted Chet to warn him but he denied any knowledge of the disease and I felt angry, rejected, naive – and incredibly foolish. I have now learned to live with the disease. But it dominates my life to an extent I could never have imagined. The cost of my trip feels enormous and will continue to do so, but at least I know now that you have to be on your guard – even in paradise.

Vicky Nicholas

www.roughguides.com

preferable to carry some from home, particularly bearing in mind the quality concerns. If you don't use them for the conventional purpose, they apparently make excellent emergency water carriers with a surprisingly large capacity.

Not sure of the word in the local language? It may not be as tough as you think. While condoms are the fairly tongue-knotting *bao cao su* in Vietnamese, they are *kondom* in Indonesian and Malay, *kandom* in Hindi and Urdu, and are informally known as *meechai* in Thailand after the charismatic former Minister for Health, Mr Meechai.

Bear in mind that insect repellant and sun cream can both damage condoms so take care.

Women travellers using the **contraceptive pill** should take a sufficient supply for the entire trip; your brand may not be available locally. However, the pills can be affected by the extreme heat and if you have diarrhoea or vomiting their effectiveness is reduced, so you'll need other protection.

Health care in Asia

Millions of people in Asia have only limited access to good-quality, affordable health care. Of course, the situation varies from country to country, but don't be surprised if health facilities are few and far between and staff don't speak English or have limited training and inadequate equipment.

However, throughout much of Asia there are **private hospitals** that exist alongside the under-funded public system. In some cities with a large expatriate population or plenty of tourists, such as Kathmandu, you'll even find specialist travellers' clinics. Check locations in your guidebook, or with the embassy, if you get sick, but private places are often the best option.

You should make it clear on arrival that you can pay (many hospitals accept credit cards) and set about contacting your insurance company (see p.62 for more on insurance). In most cases, you'll end up paying the bill and reclaiming the costs later.

Throughout Asia there are plenty of pharmacies and even local corner shops selling **drugs** that in your home country would only be available on prescription, or from trained personnel. This means that on the surface it is apparently easy to self-medicate, although you'll need to know how to take the drugs, as the person selling it may not. One potential hazard is that many of the drugs distributed in Asia are fakes, possibly below strength, useless or even potentially poisonous. If you do need to buy medicine in Asia, it pays to buy from large, efficient-looking operations, whether hospitals, pharmacies or doctor's surgeries and always check that the packaging and labelling looks correct and intact, and look at the expiry date.

Traditional medicine

Many Asian countries have their own **traditional health systems**, and clinics are invariably willing to treat foreigners, although you may need to take an interpreter with you, unless you're fairly fluent in the local language. While opinions in the West vary about the efficacy of such treatments, a considerable body of anecdotal evidence suggests Eastern medicine can help in many situations where Western medicine does not.

Ayurvedic medicine, which has flourished in India for five thousand years, is a holistic medical system that looks at the whole body and detects imbalances in the system. The body is believed to be controlled by three forces – *pitta*, the sun; *kapha*, the moon; and *vata*, the wind. An imbalance in these is regarded as leading to disease; treatment, often with herbal remedies, concentrates on restoring the balance.

In **Tibetan medicine**, which derives from ayurvedic medicine, health depends on the balance of the three humours – *beken* (phlegm), *tiba* (bile) and *lung* (wind). A diagnosis is made by examining tongue, pulse and urine and by diagnostic questioning; treatment may be with herbal remedies and/or changes of diet and activity.

China has another ancient holistic medical system with largely herbal remedies, though the often bizarre ingredients in **traditional Chinese medicine** – such as snake gall bladder and scorpion oil, not to mention the notorious rhinoceros horn – have served to give it a somewhat besmirched reputation outside the country. Acupuncture, where needles are inserted at various vital points on the body, is available in clinics across China and Japan – make sure that sterile needles are used. There are also non-invasive forms of treatment, such as massage in Thailand and shiatsu in Japan, where finger pressure is used to work on much the same parts of the body as acupuncture.

Finally, bridging the gap between health care and beauty treatments are **traditional spa treatments**, available throughout Asia, especially in the more upmarket hotels of Bali, Malaysia and Thailand, where everything from mud wraps to aromatherapy massage and reflexology is on offer to soothe and detox both body and mind. Bear in mind that racing around to fit in all the sights and experience everything that a country has to offer can be exhausting. A few days or even hours out to recharge the batteries can have positive effects on short- and long-term health.

13

Staying in touch

N
ot only is it reasonable that your friends and family at home will want to keep in touch while you're away, but you may be surprised at the extent to which you are delighted by contact with them. Travelling is huge fun and wildly exciting, but it can also be stressful, disorienting and at times depressing and lonely, which is when communication with familiar people can be very comforting.

You'll find the quality of most internet, telephone and mail services in Asia very high and the main questions will be how often to stay in touch and how much it will cost. First of all bear in mind the following:

- Explain to your family and friends that while you will email/ text/call regularly there will be times when you go silent for perfectly benign reasons; you don't have internet access and/or electricity or you can't get to a phone. Always give people a rough schedule for when you *will* be in touch.

- If there has been a earthquake, coup, plane crash or any dramatic event in your area (or vaguely nearby) then make contact quickly to set minds at rest. Bear in mind that people at home won't have the intimate knowledge of Asian geography that you have. It's also a good idea to post your flight schedule on your Facebook or MySpace page so people don't assume the worst if there is a crash.

- Equally, don't get in touch just before a bungy jump or in the midst of a bout of dysentery and then not contact anybody for a few weeks.

- As well as writing, upload or email photos as much as possible. The folks at home will only really believe that you are at the Taj Mahal when they see the usual cheesy shot of you posing in front of it. See p.112 for more on photography on the road.

Internet, email and blogs

This is likely to be your most useful means of staying in touch with home, and with other travellers you meet on the road. Public **internet access** is widely available throughout Asia; in internet cafés and guesthouses in backpacker centres, the departure lounges of many international airports and in major post offices and telephone offices. However, things are much more variable outside major cities and tourist centres – check your guidebook or on travellers' forums. Internet cafés usually charge by the minute or the hour. For example, in Thailand it is as little as 50p (85 cents US) an hour in tourist centres. Wi-fi access is increasingly available, sometimes free and sometimes for a charge.

Before you go...

- Check your email can be accessed via the internet – if not, sign up for a **webmail** account from the one of the big three: hotmail, gmail or yahoo.
- If you haven't already, join a **social networking site** such as Facebook (ⓦwww.facebook.com) or Myspace (ⓦwww.myspace .com). It is an excellent way to stay in touch as you can post status updates, use instant messaging and share photos. A social messaging service such as Twitter (ⓦtwitter.com) can also be useful for sending quick updates.
- Sign up for a **Skype** account (see p.191), which enables you to talk to people worldwide via the internet rather than using a telephone; get friends and family to sign up too.

Setting up a blog

Many travellers create their own **blog** (weblog) during their trip, which are easily updated from any computer with internet access. It's a great way of keeping an online journal and you can upload photos, give links to other sites and a whole lot more. Friends and family can post their comments too, so it's a fun way to involve everyone in your adventures. And when you come home it's quite straightforward to get your blog printed into a book, leaving you with a hard-copy memento of your trip. Check out the websites ⓦwww.travelpod.com and ⓦwww.travelblog.org to see how it's done and to sign up for your own. *The Rough Guide to Blogging* also tells you how to do it.

Shall I take the laptop?

There are definite pros and cons to taking a laptop and only you can decide which side of the argument you are on:

www.roughguides.com

Advantages:

- As long as you can access wi-fi or a suitable telephone socket you have internet access wherever you are – no need to spend time and money in stuffy internet cafés. Surfing or Skype-ing on your verandah overlooking the beach is a far nicer option.
- You can download and store your photographs, editing and labelling as you go.
- With the new small netbooks weighing in at well under one kilogramme, it'll add little weight to your luggage.
- You can do your internet banking just as you would at home (see p.84).

Disadvantages:

- It's yet another thing to cart around and worry about getting dropped or stolen. By the time you've added the charger plus your camera, mobile phone and associated cables, you've lost a sizeable chunk of backpack space. See p.189 below to help you decide whether a mobile phone will meet your needs just as well.
- You'll have to decide whether it's worth paying the (probably considerable) extra premium to insure it.

With wi-fi increasingly common, although far from everywhere, it's thankfully becoming easier to avoid the whole problem of dial-up connections. However, if you are planning to spend your time in the remotest corners of the continent see ⓦwww.kropla.com for everything you'll need to know about phone plugs and modems. Also check out the forum on Gear and Gadgets at ⓦwww.travelpod.com for practical advice on taking a laptop with you.

Phones

You'll be able to **phone home** from pretty much any city or large town in Asia. Don't forget the time difference when you call, though. You'll probably get a better reception from your loved ones if you don't wake them at 3am.

Once you've thought about the many options outlined below, you might also consider getting your home phone calls automatically redirected to a number that you can access while you're travelling, a service offered by landline and mobile phone service providers. The cheapest option is to get them redirected to your Skype number; redirecting to your mobile when overseas will get costly if you're receiving a lot of calls.

▲ The online path to enlightenment

Shall I take the mobile?

Taking your **mobile/cell phone** on your Asian travels is definitely worth considering. Apart from the ease of staying in touch with people at home you'll be able to quickly book accommodation and make arrangements with any new friends on the road. The following tips should come in handy if you're using your own mobile (see p.190 for using a local SIM card):

- Speak to your phone provider before leaving home in order to get international access, or "roaming", switched on. Most pay-as-you-go phones won't work overseas so you will probably have to change contracts, which may take some time to set up. Also many US and Canadian (non-GSM) phones may not work in Asia so always check.
- Always work out the precise costs involved in making and receiving calls (including picking up voicemail) – you could easily end up bankrupting yourself. Texting is always far cheaper.
- If you are intending to use your mobile to access the internet, perhaps for emails or to update your blog or Facebook page again work out the charges – it may be cheaper to use local internet cafés.
- Don't forget you'll need to recharge your phone as usual, which means bringing an adaptor for the local electricity supply.

www.roughguides.com

- Consider taking an older handset – the latest iPhone or Blackberry may seem to answer all your needs but it will also be expensive to insure and very tempting to thieves.
- Programme useful numbers into the phone before you leave home: your embassy or consulate in the countries you'll be visiting, any hotels you have booked, etc.
- Change the numbers you have in your phone so they'll work from overseas – you'll need to add their international country code (eg +44 for the UK). Check your guidebook for this.
- Make a note of the mobile's serial number, your own phone number and your network's customer service and emergency numbers and keep this separate from the phone. If your phone gets lost or stolen you'll be able to prevent it being used.
- One advantage of taking your mobile is that you could use it for the Safety Text scheme (see p.197), which aims to encourage travellers' safety.

Using a local SIM card

If you are staying in one country for significant periods it may work out cheaper to **buy a local SIM card**, especially if making lots of domestic calls. SIM cards can cost as little as $5 (£3) in Indonesia, with top-up cards also extraordinarily cheap (for example $1 for 100 minutes). The disadvantage of using a local SIM is that your number will change with the card. You'll also need to have your phone "unlocked" in order for it to work; this may invalidate the warranty and incur a fee so it can be less hassle to buy a basic pay as you go phone in Asia. If you do change the SIM card on your own phone don't forget to store all your saved numbers in the phone memory rather than the SIM.

Public telephones

You'll find **public telephones** throughout Asia, both coin- and phonecard–operated, and many countries have phones that also accept credit cards. Don't count on them having instructions in English. In most cases, if you're calling home, it's easier to phone from post offices or telephone offices rather than phones on the street, if only to get away from the noise. Avoid making calls from hotels as they not only charge higher rates for the call, but often slap a service charge on top, too.

When **making a call** at a post office or telephone office, you'll be directed to a booth, in some cases having paid a deposit, and you can then dial your number direct. The length of the call is logged and the price calculated automatically; you pay the balance or get change from your deposit when it's all over. It's worth checking whether there is a cheaper discounted time to call (typically at weekends and in the middle of the night – which may well be more convenient for the folks at home); also check if calls are charged by the second or by the minute and whether there is a minimum call time (typically 3min).

Reverse-charge (collect) calls, charge cards and phone cards

Many telephone offices allow you to make **reverse-charge calls** but you may pay a nominal charge for these. With a reverse-charge call, the person you are calling is contacted and asked to accept the charges for that call before you are put through.

In theory you can use BT, AT&T, MCI, Telstra and other phone **charge cards** (purchased at home) to make international calls from Asia. These cards enable you to bill the cost of the call to your home number or put the cost onto a credit card account. Before applying for any of these cards, check they will work in the countries you intend to visit and get a list of the local access numbers.

There are also an increasing number of companies issuing **prepaid cards** that you can use across Asia. Typically calls are cheaper when compared with the cost of paying for a call at a phone office. However, be sure to do your research as they are not always as cheap as they first appear: many cards have an expiry limit even if you haven't used up the credit, some levy a daily service charge while others charge for every connection.

Internet phone calls (Skype)

"Voice over Internet Protocol" (**VoIP**) technology is spreading quickly throughout Asia allowing you to make calls for free or very cheaply wherever you can find a decent broadband connection. You'll have most opportunities at internet cafés in the major traveller centres; look out for signs advertising "Net 2 Phone" though be warned that the sound quality is variable. **Skype** (ⓦ www.skype.com) is the main supplier of VoIP services although Google Talk (ⓦ www.google.com/talk) is also proving popular.

Using your own laptop to make internet calls does, of course, make the whole thing more accessible but you'll probably need a headset to bump up quality and note what we've already said about carting around mountains of kit.

Fax

It's pretty old technology in the West but **faxes** can be useful in Asia if, for example, you need a document sending over to you or a hotel wants a written confirmation of a telephone booking. Facilities are widely available but take a bit more hunting out than phones. Try post offices, telephone offices and the business centres of international-class hotels (the most expensive option). Charges for faxes are usually in line with the telephone charges of the country.

Postal services

Postcards and **airmail letters** make a nice change from texts and emails and will certainly be appreciated by older relatives. Even the tiniest villages in Asia have some system of postal collection and delivery, albeit sometimes bizarre. Bear in mind the following tips when sending mail:

- If you are writing to people regularly, number the letters so they know if any have gone missing and get them to do the same if they are writing to you.
- Ask your most regular correspondent to keep your letters – they make vivid reading when you're back. Some travellers don't write a diary but keep copies of the letters they write as a record of the trip instead.
- Mail is quicker and more reliable from towns and cities, although variability in delivery time is a common complaint among travellers, taking a couple of days from Singapore but a couple of weeks on occasion from elsewhere.
- It pays to be vigilant – stick the stamps on yourself and ask for them to be franked while you wait, as there is a danger they might be steamed off and reused.
- The postage rate for postcards is often equivalent to that for an aerogramme, which can carry much more news, so check out rates when you arrive.
- Take some stamps from your home country with you – you may well meet other travellers from home at the end of their trip who'll be happy to drop a few letters in the post for you when they land.

> ## Postal deliveries Bhutanese style
>
> I lived for some time in a remote village in Bhutan. There was no road to the village and mail was delivered every two or three weeks by a "runner" whose job was literally to run between the nearest post office and all the outlying villages, delivering and collecting mail. He operated on a two-week circuit, travelling across mountain passes, over rivers, through sparsely populated forest, and sleeping wherever he was given hospitality at night. In the past, runners carried spears to fend off bears (still a considerable hazard in the area), but these days they are more likely to carry transistor radios for company. These also have a bear-scaring purpose, as it is widely believed that if a bear hears voices approaching it will run away.
>
> Lesley Reader

Poste restante

The best option for receiving mail is the **poste restante** service available at post offices in most Asian cities: you just turn up with your passport for ID and collect your mail. There is sometimes a small charge. Generally the post offices in the more popular tourist destinations are more reliable and organized – Bangkok, Singapore, Kathmandu and Kuta (Bali), for example; on the other hand, poste restante services are currently most limited in Cambodia (Phnom Penh, Siem Reap and Sihanoukville only) and Laos (Vientiane and Louang Phabang only). If you are going to be using post restante:

- Get the precise address of the post office you want to use from a good guidebook; otherwise mail bearing your name followed by "Poste Restante, General Post Office" and the name of the city should get there.

- Anyone who writes to you should print your surname in capital letters and underline it. Most places file mail alphabetically by surname, but it pays to check through under your first name as well, or any other name or title that your nearest and dearest may have used.

- Post offices usually keep mail for a month or so before either returning it or junking it. This means you have to tread a careful line between getting there too early or too late for your letters. The best plan is to get mail sent to a few key places on your itinerary for which you have reasonably fixed dates.

- Tell people at home not to send parcels – too many go astray.

- If you really must get something sent out (a vital document, for example), it's safer to use a courier company, although they aren't cheap. They won't deliver to a poste restante address so your best bet is to arrange to collect the package at their local office. Packages should take between four and seven working days to arrive from the US, UK or Australia.

Shipping stuff home

Sending parcels home is rather more time-consuming than sending letters. You should probably set aside at least half a day to get the formalities completed, but this is definitely preferable to carrying a Balinese chest or Indian rug with you on the rest of your six-month trip. Your choices are to send them by **airmail** (the most expensive option), **surface mail** or via cargo agents (see below). Many post offices in tourist areas sell boxes and tape for packing your goods; others, such as Hong Kong, even have a packing service. The Indian system involves a lengthy process where your goods are examined then laboriously stitched into white linen parcels before they are accepted for mailing.

Charges for parcels sent through the postal system are calculated by weight and can often be surprisingly expensive: a 5kg parcel sent by sea from Thailand to the UK will cost around £30 ($50) – that's the equivalent of eight nights in a cheap guesthouse. For some idea of prices, access the websites of the Hong Kong (Ⓦwww.hongkongpost .com) or Singapore (Ⓦwww.singpost.com) postal services.

Most **cargo agents**, on the other hand, ship by volume, with one cubic metre the minimum amount they'll handle. Prices depend on the destination, but, you'll be looking at around $100–200/£60–120 per cubic metre. Delivery times will be faster if you're sending from port cities than from inland towns where the goods will have to be transported to the coast first.

Bear in mind that whatever you send home is subject to examination by **customs** in your own country. They are not only looking for illegal substances, but are entitled to charge import duty/taxes on new goods that you are bringing into the country. Check the appropriate government websites before you embark on a major shopping spree or it may all end up costing more than you expect. In the UK check ⓦwww .hmrc.gov.uk, in the US ⓦwww .customs.gov, in Australia ⓦwww .customs.gov.au and in New Zealand ⓦww.customs.govt.nz

Finally, classier souvenir stores the world over will always offer to arrange shipping for you. You'll be paying them extra for the service, and there are always some rip-off merchants who take your money and send nothing, so try to go by personal recommendation if you can.

The media

It's easy to stay up to speed with home news via the internet although of more interest are local newspapers, magazines and websites some of which are published in English. Several of the magazines mentioned in Chapter Five, such as the *Far Eastern Economic Review*, as well as the Asian editions of *Time* and *Newsweek*, are published locally – airports and the bookshops in luxury hotels are usually a good source if you have any difficulty finding them. You'll even see **newspapers** from home: many outlets in resorts and capital cities use the on-demand

Suits you, sir

The tailors in Khao San Road, Bangkok, said they could make me a suit in two days for the equivalent of £30. Despite my ten-month backpacking itinerary still stretching ahead of me, I decided that a made-to-measure silk suit was something I must have. In fact, I ordered two. The process itself was fascinating: after just two fitting sessions the assortment of pieces of fabric that had been tacked inside out, draped around my body and marked up deftly with chalk lines were transformed into two superb suits – a pale cream one and a rich, deep brown one. I packaged them up at the main post office, labelling them merely as clothes being returned home – two pairs of trousers and two jackets. In hindsight, parcels like this containing clothes from Bangkok are probably viewed fairly suspiciously, or else I was just unlucky. The box was opened when it arrived several months later at Liverpool docks, and duty of £60 was imposed on these imported items. Despite costing me twice as much as I had expected, my suits were still bargains.

Jonathan Tucker

service offered by the national newspapers of Europe, Australia and North America, often selling you your daily paper in time for mid-morning coffee if not breakfast.

Television

Satellite and cable **television** have reached some very remote corners of Asia, and you'll find league soccer from England and Italy is televised throughout the region. Most mid- to top-range hotels offer CNN or BBC World, and Asian satellite networks such as Star or MTV, while some restaurants use them to lure in customers.

Radio

Worldwide **radio networks**, including the BBC World Service (Ⓦ www .bbc.co.uk/worldservice), Voice of America (Ⓦ www.voanews.com) and Radio Australia (Ⓦ www.abc.net.au/ra/) are available in Asia via short-wave radio, the internet and cable television. In addition, many countries have an indigenous English-language radio station or schedule which can offer a great insight into local culture.

If you're staying in a remote area a shortwave radio may be the only way of getting news so consider bringing one with you. Check the websites above for broadcasting schedules and frequencies.

THE BIG ADVENTURE

14

Crime and safety

While news of violent weather, kidnappings and fatalities in the region dominates the world's media, most people who run into trouble in Asia are the victims of petty theft or minor accidents. However these events have the potential to ruin your trip, especially if you lose your passport or credit cards, and the information in this chapter should help to steer you away from the potential pitfalls, and help you to cope if disaster strikes.

The underlying rule is to employ the same instincts you use to keep you safe at home. If it's your first time in Asia it's easy to overreact and be spooked without real reason. However, this is better than blithely wandering into danger with your eyes fixed on the horizon. Just because you're on holiday, doesn't mean the crooks are.

We've said it before, but nobody should set foot in Asia without adequate **insurance**; see p.62 for more information.

Get some perspective

Asia has its own **hazards**, aside from the ones that travellers encounter anywhere in the world. For example, there are landmines, terrorist groups, civil unrest, political tensions (see p.205), active volcanoes, poisonous snakes and drug-resistant malaria. However, you should always put information into perspective. If you read about rioting in Xinjiang province in China and you're heading for Shanghai, it's a good idea to stay alert, but with the distance between the two at almost 4000km, chances are you'll be out of the line of fire. If, on the other hand, one of the larger Indonesian volcanoes erupts on a small island just 20km across a stretch of ocean from where you were planning a fortnight by the sea, it may be an idea to think again.

Read up and calm down

Supplement your guidebook reading with up-to-the-minute **information** from newspapers and the internet. All Western governments offer detailed advice for travellers and country profiles online (see p.348). In the event of an emergency while you're travelling, contact your embassy or consulate abroad (see p.207 for advice on how they can help). Travellers' forums are also an excellent resource (see p.94 for some of the best).

Several non-governmental organizations also offer advice for first-time travellers: UK-based Objective Travel Safety (☎01788/899029, ⓦwww.objectivegapyear.com) runs **day-long courses** while two charities Caroline's Rainbow Foundation (ⓦwww.carolinesrainbow foundation.org) and The Suzy Lamplugh Trust (ⓦwww.suzylamplugh .org) provide a wealth of online advice.

A couple of **books** worth checking out include the in-depth *Rough Guide to Travel Survival* and the rather more lighthearted *Worst-Case Scenario Survival Handbook: Travel*; the latter details skills such as how to crash-land a plane or wrestle a crocodile.

Take responsibility

You need to be aware that in Asia you'll bear a greater **responsibility** for your own safety than you would at home. In the West official bodies oversee transport, hotels and outdoor activity companies, for example, carrying out official inspections and taking action against violators. In Asia it's probably best to assume that none of this happens, which means you need to be alert in ways that you've perhaps never thought about before. A few things to bear in mind:

- Always work out the quickest route out of your hotel/guesthouse in case of **fire**. If there is no easy way out, find somewhere else to stay.
- If you are travelling alone, consider leaving a note in your hotel room detailing your plans for the day. If you are with a group of people, watch out for each other and make sure everyone gets home safely.
- Consider signing up for the **Safety Text scheme** (ⓦwww .safetytext.com), which enables you to send a text message detailing where you are going and who with, which only gets delivered if you aren't safe and unable to cancel it.

- If the driver of your vehicle appears to be hell-bent on suicide, get out as soon as it is safe to do so – buying a new ticket is a small price to pay (for more advice on **transport safety** see p.145).

- If a local travel agent is keen to sell you a tour, are you certain the area is safe? Check official websites for up-to-date information – things can change very fast (see p.348).

- If you are **trekking** or **rafting** what are the credentials of the guides? Where is the first-aid kit and the nearest hospital? How would an injured person get there?

- If you are **diving** be sure to check the certification of your guide/instructor. Is the equipment well maintained and working correctly? Use the buddy system, check the provision of oxygen and first-aid kit on the boat and find out the location of the nearest recompression chamber.

Avoiding theft

Most crime against tourists is opportunistic theft of one sort or other. A few guidelines will help minimize the chances of it happening to you:

- **Stay alert** When you are out in public places never "zone out" listening to music or texting on your phone – you need to be aware of what's happening around you.

- Carry travellers' cheques, credit cards, most of your cash and vital documents in a concealed **money belt** (see p.102).

- Keep **photocopies** of important documents and emergency numbers (eg passport, travellers' cheque numbers, airline tickets, insurance policy, emergency telephone numbers) in a separate place, plus a small stash of cash in case of robbery. It's possible to email vital information to yourself, including scans of documents so that copies are available if needed.

- If you put valuables in **hotel safe** deposit boxes or safes keep them in a bag that you can lock with your own padlock or a stiff envelope with your signature across the seal so you'll know if it has been tampered with (see p.84). Similarly, never leave your passport, travellers' cheques and credit cards in a guesthouse safe while you go off trekking.

- Don't leave your valuables on the beach while you swim – keep them in a safety deposit box and keep the key with you in a waterproof canister (see p.102).

- Check your **credit card statement** every so often – skimming (see p.84) is common in Asia so it's wise to check whether anything untoward is happening on your account. Also, never disclose your bank account or credit card numbers to anybody you meet on the road – no matter how much you think you love them.

- Don't flaunt what you've got. Avoid wearing a lot of jewellery, use a cheap watch and carry your camera in your daypack.
- Use **padlocks** to lock your pack and attach it to immovable fittings on long-distance journeys. This also prevents anyone putting anything (such as drugs) in your pack (see p.101). Never carry important stuff in backpack pockets on your back; they are especially vulnerable to theft. Also, use your own padlock to lock your guesthouse door (see p.166).
- Beware of accepting **food or drink** from anyone. On public transport, some rogues ply the unwary with drugged food and drink and then steal everything. Others spike drinks in bars and clubs and then rob or sexually assault their victims – always keep a very close eye on your drink.
- Don't automatically trust other Westerners, and be just as careful in dormitories as you are in other situations – a small percentage of travellers fund their own journeys by thieving from others.

Common scams

Many of the common **scams** perpetrated on tourists in Asia are legendary. These scams evolve and become more sophisticated, but never go away. The best source for up-to-date versions is other travellers – they've been there, seen it, and probably been caught by it as well. Talk to people on the road, check travel forums on the Web and learn from their mistakes. You also need to be aware that some of the police in parts of Asia are less upstanding than you might expect; if you have reason to visit the police take a companion and if possible a local person to translate for you.

Watch out for:
- Miscalculation tricks when you're **changing money**, especially when dealing with hundreds of thousands of Indonesian rupiahs. There are even rigged calculators in some places. Work out what you should have and count it carefully – you should be the last person to touch the money before you leave the counter.
- **Sleights of hand** over the denomination of note you have given in payment in a shop or post office. Tricksters hide the note and produce one of a much lower denomination, telling you that you haven't paid enough. Keep your wits about you and know what you are handing over.
- **Hotel touts** and some taxi drivers, who will be desperate to get you to hotels where they either have an interest or will get a chunk

of commission (it'll go on your bill, never fear). So beware if they tell you the hotel you want is full or perhaps even that it has burned down. If they claim that the place has no beds, it is worth going to ask at reception yourself, especially as they sometimes have official-looking stooges on the steps outside, repeating the misinformation.

- Certain taxi drivers who tell you major sights are closed and that you're much better taking a **tour** with them as your driver for the day – or going to visit their brother's shop instead of the Taj Mahal. Insist they take you where you want to go.

- The classic scam in Thailand and India – persuading gullible tourists that they are being offered an amazing deal on cut **diamonds** or other gems. Travellers are attracted by the prospect of hundreds of dollars' profit to be made by selling the diamonds at home. So, despite knowing nothing about precious stones, they spend hundreds of dollars on a handful of sparklers and ten times out of ten arrive home to learn their hands are full of pretty, worthless, cut glass.

- **Rogue policemen** at Delhi railway station, who insist that to remain in Delhi you have to register with them and pay to do so. The best way to tackle this is to offer to go to the police station and fill in the forms there – but on foot; never get into an "unmarked" police car.

Indian shoeshine

At 6am on my first day in India, I arrived by airport bus in the centre of New Delhi. Not wishing to appear more vulnerable than my bloodshot eyes and untanned skin made me look, I shouldered my pack and began to walk as confidently as I could. After a few minutes my worst fears were realized when I felt a tap on my shoulder and turned round to face a scrawny man with a glint in his eye. He was frantically pointing at my feet. I looked down to discover a neat pile of dung – about the size of a molehill and as perfectly formed – resting on the top of my right shoe. As I stood awestruck, my Indian friend knelt down, produced a rag from the cloth bag slung over his shoulder, and started to wipe my shoe clean. He performed this task with a full-bodied, jerking action, which caused the bag to slip from his shoulder. When I saw its contents, the penny dropped and the mystery was solved. This man had crept up behind me, scooped a portion of dung from his bag and skilfully dolloped it on top of my shoe as I walked. Now, of course, he demanded his fee for cleaning my shoes, holding up his soiled rag as evidence of his hard work.

Ross Velton

Natural hazards

Asia is full of volcanoes that erupt, snakes that bite, rivers that flood, land that slips, and earth that moves and cracks asunder at regular intervals. Or so it can appear, if you have a disaster mentality and don't manage to temper what you read with reality.

Volcanoes, earthquakes and tsunamis

Being at the meeting point of several of the world's largest tectonic plates, Asia has a much higher level of **volcanic** and **earthquake** activity than many travellers are used to. Seismologists are unable to predict when and where the next big event will take place, but realistically the chances of being caught in a severe earthquake or a volcanic eruption are extremely slim.

If you are unfortunate enough to be involved in a strong quake, you should stay indoors if possible (corrugated-iron sheets flying off roofs are a common cause of fatalities). Stay away from windows to avoid splintering glass and shelter in a doorway if the building looks in danger of collapse (the lintel supporting a wall above a door is the strongest part of the structure).

Tsunamis and tidal waves happen when earthquakes disturb the ocean bed causing vast walls of water to race across the globe. The Asian tsunami of 2004, which devastated whole swathes of Thailand, Sri Lanka and Indonesia, has made countries much more aware of the dangers and early warning systems are being set up across the region. The best advice is to take local warnings seriously, even if it turns out to be a false alarm – if you are advised to move inland then do so, no matter how appealing your beach bungalow.

Get in touch with friends and relatives at home as soon as possible, to let them know you're safe.

▲ Head for the hills: tsunami warning sign, Thailand

Typhoons

If you know that a **typhoon** is expected in your town, the best advice is to get yourself established in a guesthouse or hotel that feels safely and solidly built (don't be stingy about paying up and moving to a better place for the night), and stay indoors. Ideally sleep in a room that is not on the ground floor, which could get submerged. Keep all windows closed and move your bed away from them if possible – flying debris might smash the glass. Expect to be stranded in your room for up to 24 hours after the typhoon hits, possibly without electricity, while you wait for the flood waters to subside, so get enough drinking water, some food, a torch and a good book before you tuck yourself away.

Dangerous animals

After human beings, the most dangerous animal in Asia is the humble **mosquito** (see p.175 for advice on avoiding bites and worse). That said there is obviously an increased chance of coming face to face with poisonous snakes or sharks in Asia than most places back home, but you should be fine if you listen to local advice and take sensible precautions:

- **Snakes** will always try to avoid human contact, but will strike if threatened. Make lots of noise when walking through jungle and tall grassland to allow them time to slither away.

Typhoon Linda

I arrived in Chumphon, South Thailand, to find preparations in full swing. Typhoon Linda was on her way, due in around 1am, and was expected to cause more damage than her predecessor who'd hit the town two months earlier. What happened then, I asked. "The water came up to here," said the guy in the restaurant, indicating a tidemark on his wall that was 1.5m above the floor, "and we all had to stay indoors for 48 hours because you couldn't get down the street without swimming." At the house next door, a lady was dragging her best teak furniture up to the first floor – she didn't want a repeat performance of the last time, she explained, showing off her own tidemarks, also 1.5m high. Her husband, meanwhile, was storing his motorbike in a neighbour's upstairs loft. Every downstairs room in the town seemed to have a tidemark. And Linda was set to be even more vicious. A crowd stood outside the TV shop, where all the sets were tuned to the weather station, and a loudspeaker van was circulating through the town, issuing official-sounding instructions. Faced with the prospect of spending two soggy days confined to my hardboard cell of a guesthouse, I decided to relocate, choosing a hotel room on the third floor, where the outside walls didn't seem likely to crumble in a Force 10. I stocked up on snacks and water, battened down the window shutters, and fell asleep wondering how things would look in the morning.

Not very different, as it turned out. A few puddles, but no obvious devastation. The guesthouse manager looked happy: Linda had diverted at the last minute, and had struck Prachuap instead, 170km up the coast. And so it was that the newspaper pictures of razed houses and submerged town centres, and the scenes of distraught families that filled the TV screens that evening, were of a town that I'd left the day before, and not of Chumphon after all.

Lucy Ridout

If you do get bitten, immobilize the limb and avoid all movement. The aim is to reduce the speed with which any toxin spreads through your body. If possible remember what the snake looks like to help with identification. Send someone for medical help. Under no circumstances contemplate anything surgical with a Swiss Army knife.

- Trek with local **guides** who know the terrain and the hazards.
- Keep fires or lanterns burning at night if you are camping in the jungle.
- Never walk without **shoes** – you're giving snakes and biting insects easy access to bare skin.
- Shake out your shoes each morning; scorpions love to sleep inside.
- They get a pretty bad press but unprovoked attacks by **sharks** are extremely rare (less than a hundred across the world each year). The best advice is to avoid swimming at night when they tend to be on the prowl and avoid spear fishing with locals which can excite sharks owing to blood being in the water.
- Other dangerous **marine animals** include jellyfish, sea urchins, Crown of Thorns starfish, moray eels and stonefish. Beginners are advised to learn what these creatures look like and give them a wide berth but if this fails it is vital to try to identify what has bitten or stung you as the treatment varies depending on the species. For more see Ⓦwww.marine-medic.com.au or Rough Guides' *Travel Health*.
- **Coral cuts** are very common amongst novice divers and snorkellers – they should be taken seriously as they get infected extremely easily. Ideally keep them dry, disinfect any time they get wet again and seek medical advice and antibiotics if infection sets in.

Sexual harassment

Thanks in large part to a diet of Hollywood films and the sight of inappropriately dressed female travellers, the local perception of Western women is of sexual availability and promiscuity. This means that **harassment**, both verbal and physical, is unfortunately alive and flourishing across Asia. As one example, there have been an increased number of reports of sexual assault on female travellers in Goa. The following tips may help:

- Make sure your hotel room is secure (if in doubt use your own padlock). Be especially careful to check door and window locks and never open the door to strangers.
- If you're in a bar, always keep an eye on your drink – spiked drinks are often a prelude to sexual assault.

- Always carry enough cash so that you can take a taxi back to your hotel if you need to.
- Observe how local women dress – if you cover up similar bits of flesh you may feel more comfortable and attract less unwelcome attention. Wearing a bra and not wearing anything too clingy can help avert some stares.
- Be aware that smiling and making eye contact with a man in certain countries, for example India, Pakistan and Indonesia, is interpreted as a distinct come-on, as is a casual touch.
- If you're being hassled by a man, ask if he'd like his sister to be treated in the same way.
- Adopt a mythical husband: some women travellers wear a ring, or carry pictures of a their "husband and kids" with which to bore potential pests.
- Even if you have set out on your travels alone, don't feel you can't join up with people you meet on the road if you feel more comfortable as part of a group; there's no right or wrong way to travel.
- Above all, don't automatically trust other Westerners because of familiarity or distrust local people because of their apparent strangeness.
- If you are placing yourself in a situation where you are potentially vulnerable, for example, engaging a trekking guide, make certain that you get recommendations from other women who have travelled with them. Consider using one of the growing number of women-run tourist operations and female guides who are available, for example, ⓦwww.3sistersadventure.com in Pokhara, Nepal.
- Don't forget it can work both ways: some men feel uncomfortable with the upfront approaches of many Asian prostitutes. The best advice is to stay polite, remain calm and walk away.

Room service

In a hotel in Danang, Vietnam, a woman walked straight into my room while I was lying there naked under my mosquito net. She didn't mess around: "Would you like sex, mouth love, touch or massage with no clothes?" When I said a polite "No, thank you", she looked at me rather despondently and added, "Do you have any washing, then?"

Chris Humphrey

The only guest at the only hotel in town, I spent the evening on the verandah listening to tales of the days of the Raj. Charming and well educated, the manager was the perfect host, until he casually slipped into the conversation, "Do you need your own room tonight or would you prefer to share mine?" I acted suitably horrified and haughty, demanded my own room and barricaded the door, just in case.

Nicki McCormick

Drugs

Many Asian governments seem to have double standards when it comes to **drugs**: they openly condemn them yet seem to turn a blind eye to the fact that they are sold to tourists in certain places, for example in *bhang* shops in parts of India. The penalties for trafficking or possession are nontheless serious: sixteen Asian countries including Malaysia, Singapore, China, Pakistan, Indonesia, Vietnam and Laos hand down the death penalty for drug smuggling, and in Thailand there are long prison sentences plus hefty fines.

Even buying drugs for your own use just isn't worth the risk; setups by dealers and the police are common. Added to that, using any drugs will make you **less alert**, less aware of your surroundings and far more likely to be the victim of other crimes such as robbery or sexual assault. The best advice is to steer clear.

There are currently around 500 Britons in prison overseas for drugs offences – it isn't worth the risk of joining them. A look at the Prisoners Abroad website (ⓦ www.prisonersabroad.org.uk) should be warning enough. Some precautions:

- Pack your own bag and check it in at the airport.
- Never check anybody else's bag in for them.
- Never carry anything across a border for anybody else – and that includes a baby, baby buggy or anything as apparently innocuous.
- Never drive anybody else's vehicle across a border for them.
- If at all possible don't sit in vehicles to cross a border – get out and walk.

Trouble spots

Below we list some of the most significant **trouble spots** for travellers to Asia. But things do change fast – check with all the sources listed in the Directory on p.348; plenty of these may have sorted themselves out by the time you travel, although new ones may well have taken their place. In addition it's best to avoid travelling during **election times** which can bring with them increased tension, violence and demonstrations. Political gatherings and strikes should also be avoided wherever possible:

- **Bangladesh** In the Chittagong Hill Tracts, the United People's Democratic Front is engaged in terrorist activity, which has included the kidnap of Westerners. Local tribal feuding has complicated the situation further.

- **China** There are long-running ethnic tensions in Tibet and Xinjiang which occasionally erupt into outright hostilities in which tourists may get accidentally involved. Certain dates may be especially volatile, such as the anniversaries of earlier uprisings, but it pays to be vigilant and check the current situation at all times.

- **India** Jammu and Kashmir have been longstanding no-go areas for tourists as militant separatist groups fight it out with government forces – kidnapping is common here. Other areas to avoid owing to attacks on travellers include Kullu/Manali in Himachal Pradesh and Manipur along the border with Burma. There is also a relatively high risk of terrorism as demonstrated by the Mumbai hotel attacks of 2008.

- **Indonesia** There is a risk of terrorist activity against foreign travellers in Indonesia as demonstrated by bombings in Jakarta in 2009 and Bali in 2002 and 2005. In addition, separatist movements are active in both West Papua and Aceh while there has been religious violence between Christians and Muslims in Maluku and Central Sulawesi. The border areas between West Timor and Timor-Leste are also considered dangerous.

- **Nepal** The Communist Party of Nepal (Maoist) fought a guerrilla war against the government for more than ten years. Following its election, the political situation has become increasingly volatile and demonstrations, strikes and informal road blocks are common.

- **Pakistan** Suicide bombings and kidnappings have increased significantly in Pakistan. Foreigners are advised to avoid much of the northwest of the country including the city of Peshawar. Sectarian violence is possible in the Punjab and Karachi.

- **The Philippines** Kidnapping has increased alarmingly in the Philippines in recent years, especially but not only in the south. It has also affected islands nearby, such as Eastern Sabah in Malaysia. It is vital to check out the situation in the Philippines and in neighbouring Malaysia and Indonesia before you travel.

- **Sri Lanka** The Tamil Tiger guerrillas (the LTTE) fought with government forces for many years for an independent state until their defeat in 2009. However, the country remains extremely unsettled with politically motivated violence a significant risk everywhere on the island. Tourists are more likely to be unwittingly caught up in violence than to be targeted but it is still important to get up-to-date information.

- **Thailand** There has been a high level of sectarian violence in some of the southern provinces bordering Malaysia for some years including terrorist attacks and bombings. Foreigners are advised to avoid Yala, Pattani, Narathiwat and Songkhla.

- **Unexploded landmines** are a real danger in a number of countries, most seriously Cambodia, Sri Lanka and Laos but also in Nepal, India, Pakistan, the Philippines, Bangladesh, and Vietnam. Take local advice and never wander off paths.

If disaster strikes

Your embassy or consulate abroad can:
- Issue emergency passports.
- Contact friends and family and ask them to help with money or tickets.
- Advise on getting money transferred.
- Help you get in touch with local doctors, lawyers and interpreters.
- Contact and visit you in local prison.
- Visit you in hospital and pass messages to your family if you wish.
- Advise on local organizations that help trace missing persons.
- Offer advice and support if you are with somebody who dies.

Your embassy or consulate cannot:
- Give you money (though they may be able to cash a cheque or give you a loan under very strict criteria).
- Pay your bills or pay to get you home, except in very exceptional circumstances.
- Intervene in legal proceedings or give legal advice.
- Get better treatment for you than for other prisoners or hospital patients.
- Get you out of prison.

You may also need to:
- Contact the police: if you are the victim of a crime they'll need to take a statement from you. See the note on p.199 about going to police stations.
- Contact your insurance company: carry your policy number and their emergency number with you and leave copies at home. There are claims procedures that you must follow in the event of theft. You will need receipts for recently bought goods and for expenses you have incurred, and you'll need a police report to support your claim. The correct procedures must also be followed for illness; if you need hospitalization you will have to inform your insurers within certain time limits. Check your policy details.
- Cancel your credit cards if they're stolen; if travellers' cheques have been stolen, contact the issuing company to order your replacements (see p.81).

www.roughguides.com

15

Coming home

E veryone expects to suffer from culture shock when they travel to distant places, but it can be even more severe when you return home. People's lives have moved on, the dog has had puppies and Uncle Toby really doesn't want to hear in graphic detail about Delhi Belly. You may feel that your experiences have totally changed your life, while those closest to you hope you've "got it out of your system" and are now ready to settle down. The following tips may help you cope:

● Before you go away, put some money aside as an arriving-home fund, and vow not to touch it during your travels – coming home can be bad enough, never mind returning without a cent.

● Make sure you keep in touch with people at home and try to paint a realistic picture about your experiences and thoughts. You can then discuss things more easily and honestly when you get home, and people won't be so surprised by the way you may have changed.

● Stay in touch with other travellers you meet on the road, who may now be going through a similar experience.

● Keep in touch with local people you meet on your travels rather than cutting yourself off from the experience – if you haven't yet sent them any photographs you may have promised, for example, then do it as soon as you get home.

● While you're still travelling, make some plans, however rudimentary, for the immediate future after you return. The worst possible homecoming is to come back to nothing. Even if it's only a plan to save up and travel some more, at least it's a plan of action.

● Compile an album, CD or file or two of your best photos, with labels to remind you of place names, people and dates. They will give you pleasure for years to come and are a great way of sharing your experiences.

Getting involved

You may well find that your arrival home throws into stark contrast the living standards and opportunities of the West compared with those in Asia and that the appalling poverty, health and educational opportunities that you have seen up close will seem all the more unfair. **Getting involved** with these issues when you return is a positive way of using your experiences to benefit others and can help you make sense of everything that you saw and did while you were away. Below are some major charities and organizations worth investigating:

- **Amnesty International** (ⓦwww.amnesty.org) campaigns for human rights worldwide. It is best known for helping speed the release of prisoners of conscience but also campaigns against the death penalty, torture and the use of child soldiers. Amnesty's website has a huge amount of information (much of it detailing things that governments would rather keep buried) and plenty of suggestions for ways to help.
- **The Burma Campaign** (ⓦwww.burmacampaign.org.uk) is involved in lobbying for sanctions against Burma and the site has excellent briefing materials on the situation in Burma, a good set of links to other sites of interest and suggestions for ways that individuals can help.
- **The Citizen's Foundation** (ⓦwww.thecitizensfoundation.org) has established 600 schools across Pakistan, focusing especially on poor areas, and emphasizing the importance of the education of girls.
- **ECPAT International** (ⓦwww.ecpat.net) works to end child prostitution, child pornography and the trafficking of children for sex. Sadly, this is a particularly relevant issue in Asia with several countries notorious for sex tourism.
- **The Environmental Investigation Agency** (ⓦwww.eia -international.org) runs campaigns for endangered species and their vanishing environments. Tigers, elephants, orang-utans and whales, dolphins and porpoises are just some of the priorities.
- **The Esther Benjamin Trust** (ⓦwww.ebtrust.org.uk) The trust works for Nepalese children, some of whom have been imprisoned, are living as street children or working in Indian circuses.
- **The Free Tibet Campaign** (ⓦwww.freetibet.org) is working towards ending the occupation of Tibet by China and allowing the Tibetan people to decide their own future; their website has excellent links for anyone interested in Tibet and plenty of suggestions for action by individuals.

www.roughguides.com

- **Greenpeace** (Ⓦwww.greenpeace.org) Probably most famous for its direct action protests, Greenpeace is concerned with all manner of environmental issues, including toxic-waste disposal, nuclear issues, climate change, genetic engineering and forest conservation, indeed any issue that relates to the state of the environment.

- **The International Campaign to Ban Landmines** (Ⓦwww .icbl.org) is global network devoted to banning landmines and cluster munitions. It also helps with the rehabilitation of victims, and works to increase awareness of the use of mines worldwide. This is highly relevant for Asian travellers as so many countries are affected (see p.207).

- **Labour Behind the Label** (Ⓦwww.labourbehindthelabel.org) is the UK arm of a global scheme aiming to improve conditions for garment workers worldwide – a key issue in Asia where so many appalling conditions persist.

- **One World** (Ⓦwww.oneworld.net) is a global community of organizations with the shared aim of fighting poverty. Their website has huge amounts of information on trade, education, climate change and debt, and plenty of suggestions for ways of getting involved.

- **Survival International** (Ⓦwww.survival-international.org) supports tribal people throughout the world. Specific projects in Asia include campaigning on behalf of the Jummas in Bangladesh's Chittagong Hill Tracts and the Wanniyala-Aetto of Sri Lanka who both face losing their land under government resettlement plans.

- **The World Society for the Protection of Animals** (Ⓦwww .wspa.org.uk) works to stop animal cruelty and to relieve animal suffering. Specific projects include improving the lives of dogs in Asia, opposing bear-baiting in rural Pakistan, bear-farming in China, bear parks in Japan and the Asian trade in marine turtles.

Making your trip work for you

Sooner or later you'll return from wandering the globe and need to consider what to do next. You will be in a better position to sell yourself to future employers, either at home or overseas, if you can not only describe your trip as an immensely enjoyable experience but can also point to **skills** that you have developed while travelling.

Don't forget that resolution to learn Hindi, Thai, Japanese, Mandarin or whatever **language** fascinated or defeated you while you were away. Local evening classes are the most sociable way of doing this or, if you live near a university with foreign students, you may be able to arrange one-to-one tuition or exchange English lessons for the language you want to learn.

Setting up a **website** about your travels, if you haven't done it on the road, can be a satisfying way of crystallizing your experiences, as well as a great way of developing computer/web-design skills. True, the net is already full of boringly self-important websites, but there are also plenty of quality personal sites too. The best travellers' sites are both entertaining and useful – see the online sections of Where To Go, pp.215–340, for some inspiration.

Working in the travel industry

In the longer term, your experiences in Asia can help prepare you for work in the **travel industry**. See *Working in Tourism* by Verite Reilly Collins (Vacation Work Publications) for an overview of the type of work that is available. While you're on the road, keep your eyes and ears open, as you may have the chance to quiz people already working in the industry; back home, travel fairs are a good place to meet potential employers and people already working in the field.

Jobs as **tour guides** with adventure travel companies are highly sought after and a great way to keep travelling. However, you'll have to qualify in first aid and convince the tour operator of your background knowledge, sense of responsibility and cool head in an emergency before they'll entrust a group of paying customers into your care. Look in the travel press for job advertisements before you go (in the UK, *Wanderlust* magazine carries these), so you have some idea of what they are after. Many of the adventure travel companies listed in the Directory (p.343) advertise for staff on their websites.

Travel writing and photography

It's a very competitive field but it may be possible to sell the story of your journey and/or photos when you get back, perhaps to student magazines, local newspapers or websites. Unless you have a track record or good contacts, you're unlikely to elicit much interest before you go, but it's worth **writing articles** on your return and submitting them "on spec" to publications – have a good look at the type of travel articles favoured by different newspapers and magazines, both regional and national. To sell your **pictures**, you'll need top quality digital images.

If you are interested in becoming a **guidebook researcher/writer**, look on the websites of the publishers of the major guidebook series – they all include guidelines on how to write for them. See ⓦwww .roughguides.com/website/aboutus/workforus if you are interested in writing for Rough Guides.

For more tips have a look at Michael Busselle's *Guide to Travel and Vacation Photography*; Lonely Planet's series of *Travel Photography* books; National Geographic's series of *Photography Field Guides*; or Barry Turners'

www.roughguides.com

The Writer's Handbook Guide to Travel Writing (Macmillan). The downloadable *Guide to Becoming a Travel Writer* and *Guide to Travel Photography* from Ⓦwww.gapyear.com are both great resources. The Royal Geographical Society runs a range of travel writing and photography courses (Ⓦwww.rgs.org). The Transitions Abroad website (Ⓦwww.transitionsabroad.com) is full of interesting material for anybody thinking of embarking on travel writing.

First-Time Asia

Where to go

Bangladesh

Capital Dhaka
Population 155 million
Language Bangla
Currency Taka (Tk)
Religion Eighty-eight percent Muslim, ten percent Hindu; the remainder are Buddhists and Christians

Climate Tropical, with the monsoon from July–October
Best time to go October–February, which avoids the monsoon and the humid build-up in the months before
Minimum daily budget US$10/£6

With its reputation for overpopulation, poverty, political instability and devastating floods (the alluvial plains, which comprise ninety percent of the country's area, are less than 10m above sea level), Bangladesh is not on many Asian itineraries. However, the country contains extensive rivers and lush forests, as well as the longest beach in the world and excellent wildlife. Bangladesh also has some fine archeological sites, including Buddhist, Hindu and Muslim monuments, remnants of empires which flourished until the seventeenth century when the Raj – British colonial rule – was established. Some grand public buildings and rajbaris, palaces built by rich Hindu landowners, are the remaining evidence of the Raj era. All of this adds up to a fascinating destination for the more adventurous.

As tourists are still rather rare here, visitors should expect more attention than usual. Bangladesh is mostly Muslim, and both men and women should dress exceptionally modestly. Women should cover arms and legs, even ankles – a *salwaar kameez*, the baggy trousers and long tunic worn by local women, is a good investment, as is a scarf for the head. Men should stay covered up also, avoiding shorts and vests. Be aware that travel can be extremely slow because of frequent ferry crossings on both road and rail routes.

Main attractions

● **Dhaka** A melting pot of over twelve million people, the Bangladeshi

Mean temperatures (°C) and rainfall (mm)

Average daily temperatures (maximum and minimum °C) and monthly rainfall (mm)

	Jan	Feb	Mar	Apr	May	June	July	Aug	Sept	Oct	Nov	Dec
Dhaka												
max °C	25	28	33	35	34	32	31	31	31	31	29	26
min °C	12	13	16	23	25	26	26	26	26	24	18	13
rainfall mm	18	31	58	103	194	321	437	305	254	169	28	2

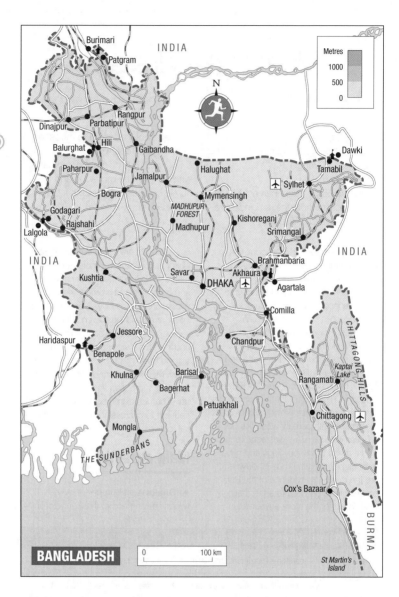

capital is a fascinating juxtaposition
of the old and the startlingly new. The
most famous ancient monuments
include the Mogul Lalbagh Fort, the
grand nineteenth-century Ahsan Manjil

(Nawab's Palace) and the Rose Garden
Mansion, a wonderful white confection.
Also here is Shankharia Bazaar, a maze
of twisting alleyways little changed
since the nineteenth century. A cruise

on the Buriganga River is a wonderful way to view the city from a different perspective and a trip to Bangsal Street (Bicycle Street) is the place to hunt for a memento of rickshaw art; paintings by the guys who decorate the rickshaws so exuberantly and characteristically.

● **Cox's Bazaar** Bangladesh's best-known tourist destination is the spot for relaxation, with plenty of accommodation and restaurants. The beach, at more than 120km long, is widely claimed to be the longest sandy beach in the world. St Martin's, Bangladesh's only coral island, is within easy reach.

● **River travel** A great opportunity to see all of Bangladeshi life as you sail past. The most useful and popular way to do this is the Rocket service from Dhaka to Khulna, on which vintage paddle steamers make the thirty-hour trip.

● **The Sunderbans** The world's largest mangrove forest, backed by freshwater swamp forests just inland. The area is inhabited by a variety of wildlife; it's the last reserve of the Royal Bengal tiger in Bangladesh (the three hundred animals thought to live here constitute about twenty percent of the world's remaining population), and also home to crocodiles, monkeys, gibbons, turtles, deer, wild boar, lizards and the Ganges river dolphin. Explore the area by boat from Mongla or arrange tours from Khulna or further afield.

● **Sylhet** Set among rolling hillsides, this tea-growing area consists of lush forests and terraced estates. The town of Srimangal is an excellent place to arrange a visit to a tea estate to see the processing of the leaves. Several tribal peoples, including the Khasi, Pangou and Manipur, live in the area, and it's possible to visit their villages.

● **Paharpur** Dating from the eighth century, these are the atmospheric remains of the largest Buddhist monastery south of the Himalayas – the most imposing archeological site in Bangladesh.

Also recommended

● **Chittagong Hill Tracts** Atypical of Bangladesh, the hill tracts, whose steep jungle-covered peaks rise to 800m, are inhabited by more than a dozen tribal groups, all of whom are Buddhists of Tibeto-Burmese descent. Unfortunately, most of the area is off limits to tourists. Rangamati, set on a peninsula overlooking the man-made Kaptai Lake, was a favoured hill station of the British; today it's an excellent centre for swimming, boating and exploring the islands of the lake. Note: check the current security situation and whether you need permits to travel here before heading off; see p.205.

● **Cycling** Much of the country being flat, Bangladesh is an interesting option for cyclists, and the bicycle is as ubiquitous here as in the rest of the Indian Subcontinent. Cycling around is a great way of getting really close to local people as well as seeing the country at a restful pace.

● **Bagerhat Area** To the north of the Sunderbans, Bagerhat is awash with historical Hindu and Muslim monuments, including the famous fifteenth-century Shait Gumbad mosque (its name means "60 domes", though it actually has 77), one of the country's most imposing.

Festivals

April Pohela Baisakh. Bangladeshi New Year is celebrated by parades and cultural events across the country but especially in Dhaka and Rangamati. **August/September** Ramadan. Month-long fast during daylight hours, but it's more than worthwhile come sunset

www.roughguides.com

when the fast ends and the delicious *iftar* meals begin.

October Durga Puja. The biggest Bangladeshi festival, celebrated with special exuberance in Dhaka. Every temple is adorned with a ten-armed statue of the goddess Durga astride a tiger, which on the tenth day is carried to the river and cast upon the waters.

Routes in and out

Zia International Airport in Dhaka has worldwide connections; Chittagong and Sylhet also have international airports. There are several overland routes between Bangladesh and India open to foreigners: between Haridaspur to the northeast of Kolkata in India and Benapole in western Bangladesh; between Lalgola in West Bengal and Godagari just north of Rajshahi; between Balurghat in West Bengal and Hili between Burimari in West Bengal and Patgram; between Dawki in Assam and Tamabil in the Sylhet region; and between Agartala in Tripura and Akhaura, due east of Dhaka. There is no overland crossing between Bangladesh and Burma.

Bangladesh online

Bangladeshi Art of the Ricksha – Ⓦ **www.asianart.com/articles/ricksha** Written by an anthropologist, this is a serious examination of rickshaw art in Bangladesh. Although it was set up some years ago, the pictures are wonderful and the site is enticing enough to make readers head straight off to book their flights.

The Daily Star – Ⓦ **www.thedailystar .net** Online edition of the national English-language newspaper.

Kazi Nazrul Islam – Ⓦ **www.nazrul .org** Dedicated to the life and works of Bangladesh's national poet, with loads of links and a forum discussing the great man's work.

Virtual Bangladesh – Ⓦ **www.virtual bangladesh.com** Pretty much everything there is to know about Bangladesh – history, geography, culture, language and literature – plus chat rooms and links to other Bangladesh-related sites.

Books

Tahmima Anam *A Golden Age* The gripping story of one family during the 1971 Bangladeshi War of Independence, a period of history that is often forgotten overseas.

David Bornstein *The Price of a Dream*. The story of the Grameen Bank, founded in Bangladesh in 1976. One of the most successful development organizations in the world, it has offered tiny loans to more than seven million village borrowers, the vast majority of them women, since its foundation. Not all the stories are rosy but it's real-life Bangladesh.

Katy Gardner *Songs at the Rivers Edge*. Travelogue, autobiography and anthropology merge in this account of a Western woman's eighteen months in a Bangladeshi village. A penetrating insight that gets under the skin of this fascinating country.

Tasalima Nasarina *Shame*. In 1992 Hindu extremists destroyed a mosque in Ayodhya, India. This novel recounts in raw and unpolished style the retaliation against a fictional Hindu family in Bangladesh. It caused an outrage in the country when it was originally published and a fatwa was pronounced against the author.

Rabindranath Tagore *Selected Short Stories*. This great Bengali writer of stories, poetry and plays, revered on the Indian Subcontinent and little-known outside, won the Nobel Prize for Literature in 1913. He lived on a houseboat in East Bengal while writing these stories and beautifully describes the lives he witnessed.

Films

The Alienation (Duratta; Morshedul Islam, 2004). This slow, thoughtful film follows the friendship between privileged Putul, street boy Antu and his sister Morium.

Bostrobalikara: Garment Girls of Bangladesh (Tanvir Mokammel, 2007). Wide-ranging and eye-opening documentary about the millions of girls and women who work in the Bangladeshi garment industry with all its dangers and hardships.

The Clay Bird (Matir Moina; Tareque and Catherine Masud, 2003). Depicting the years leading up to the birth of Bangladesh in 1971 through the story of the main character, a young student, Anu. The film beautifully explores the themes of religious tolerance, cultural diversity and the complexity of Islam through small, evocative scenes of Bangladeshi life.

A River Named Titash (Titash Ekti Nadir Naam; Ritwik Ghatak, 1973). Interlinked series of stories, often harsh and gruesome, showing life in one rural village; voted the best Bangladeshi movie of all time in 2002.

Bangladeshi tourist offices

ⓦ **www.bdonline.com/tourism**
No overseas tourist office.

Bangladeshi embassies and consulates

ⓦ **www.betelco.com/bd/bdsemb /bdsemb.html**
Australia 35 Endeavour St, PO Box 5, Red Hill, ACT 2603 ⓣ02/6295 3328.
Canada 85 Range Rd, Suite 302, Ottawa, Ontario, K1N 8J6 ⓣ613/236-0138/9.
New Zealand Contact the embassy in Australia.
South Africa 410 Farenden St, Sunnyside, Pretoria, 0002 ⓣ012/343 2105.
UK and Ireland 28 Queen's Gate, SW7 5JA ⓣ020/7584 0081. Assistant High Commissions: Birmingham ⓣ0121/643 2386; Manchester ⓣ0161/236 4853.
US 2201 Wisconsin Ave NW, Suite 300-325, Washington DC 20007 ⓣ202/342-8372. Consulate: New York ⓣ212/599-6767.

BANGLADESH

www.roughguides.com

Bhutan

Capital Thimphu
Population 670,000
Language Dzongkha
Currency Nu
Religion The state religion is
Mahayana Buddhism but there's also
a sizeable minority of Hindus
Climate Monsoonal

Best time to go Autumn (Oct &
Nov) and spring (Feb to mid-April)
Minimum daily budget All-inclusive
tours – the only way to visit the
country – cost at least US$200/£115
per person per day in the high
season (Jan–June & Sept–Dec) and
US$165/£92 per person per day in
July and August.

With Tibet to the north, Sikkim and Nepal
to the west and the far northeastern
states of India to the east, the Himalayan
Kingdom of Bhutan is geographically
remote and maintains an air of mystery
and exclusivity – only around five
thousand tourists a year are allowed to
visit, all on organized tours.

Bhutan's allure is in its distinctive
culture, which has remained largely
isolated from Western influence; most
of the people are subsistence farmers
leading a devoutly Buddhist life in
villages with distinctive architecture.
The huge, ancient dzongs – each a
combination of fortress, monastery and
administrative centre – are a feature of
every major valley, and the landscape
is dotted with evocative temples and
chortens, akin to Nepalese stupas.
National costume is worn everywhere,
and Bhutan's intricate hand-woven
textiles, their designs passed on from
mother to daughter, are gaining renown
across the world.

Travel in Bhutan, though time-
consuming, is indubitably picturesque.
Most visitors spend just a few days in
the west of the country, exploring the
valleys of Paro, Thimphu and Punakha.
Across in central Bhutan, however,
Trongsa and Bumthang are drawing
more and more visitors, while the
eastern towns of Trashigang and Trashi
Yangtse are equally fascinating, but
only feature on the itineraries of those

Mean temperatures (°C) and rainfall (mm)

Average daily temperatures (maximum and minimum °C) and monthly rainfall (mm)

	Jan	Feb	Mar	Apr	May	June	July	Aug	Sept	Oct	Nov	Dec
Thimphu												
max °C	17	14	19	23	23	26	25	24	24	22	19	17
min °C	-1	-3	5	7	11	14	17	17	15	9	0	-2
rainfall mm	40	20	10	30	10	95	105	130	55	0	0	0

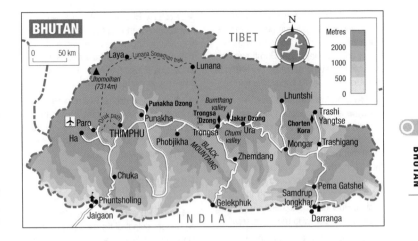

with the time (and money) to make the long trip across the country worthwhile (it's three days by road from Thimphu to Trashigang).

Main attractions

● **Thimphu** The town is one of the smallest and most relaxed capitals in Asia, with plenty to see, including Trashi Chhoe Dzong, centre of government in the kingdom and a massive, imposing presence in the Thimphu valley; several impressive temples; and the Memorial Chorten, dedicated to the memory of the third king of Bhutan. The weekly market is fabulously colourful.

● **Paro Valley** Broad and glorious, the valley contains the vast Paro Dzong near the airport, as well as Bhutan's National Museum, housed in the Ta Dzong – Paro Dzong's own watchtower, standing guard up on the hillside. At the valley's northern end, the ruined Drukyel Dzong is a popular excursion destination. The ubiquitous image of Bhutan is the temple of Takshang, or Tiger's Nest, built high up into a sheer cliff on the side of the valley – a terrific two-hour hike. It's such an

impossible location that legend tells how angels laid down their hair on the cliffside to provide the temple's foundations.

● **Punakha** Lower and warmer than Thimphu, the traditional winter capital of Bhutan has a massive dzong sitting impressively at the confluence of two differently coloured rivers. The dzong is a remarkable demonstration of the vibrancy of Bhutan's traditional woodcarving, sculpture and temple painting, having been largely rebuilt after a major fire in 1998.

● **Trongsa Dzong** The largest dzong, Trongsa is also one of the most dramatically situated, visible from many miles away. The watchtower above the dzong offers brilliant views of the area and houses Bhutan's newest museum, which contains a startling array of historical and sacred artefacts. The tiny hotels and restaurants of the town, mostly run by Tibetan refugees who have lived in Bhutan for decades, provide a relaxed welcome.

● **Bumthang Valley** For many visitors to Bhutan, the Bumthang Valley, in the centre of the country, is their favourite spot. The local dzong, Jakar, is perched

221

dramatically on a spur overlooking the valley, and there are innumerable temples in the valley, the most famous being Kurjey and Jambey. From Bumthang it is possible to visit the beautiful, high-altitude village of Ura, with its impressive temple.

- **Mongar, Trashigang, Trashi Yangtse** Accommodation in these eastern towns is sparse and the distances you need to travel to get to them can be tiring, but towering hills, thundering rivers, fascinating temples, fabulous weaving produced on simple looms in people's houses, and the ancient Buddhist monument of Chorten Kora await those who make the trip.

- **Trekking** Bhutan is sparsely populated, the countryside uncluttered; trekkers have a wide choice of routes, from the six-day Druk Path between the Paro and Thimphu valleys through to the 25-day Lunana Snowman Trek which climbs over 5000-metre-high passes across the remote north of the country. Make certain that you allow time to acclimatize to the altitude before you trek and as you climb higher; failure to do so can be very dangerous (see p.182).

Also recommended

- **The valley of Phobjikha** High up in the centre of the country, this is the winter home of rare black-necked cranes, who fly there every year from Siberia. The venerated monastery, Gangtey Gompa, is also located here, gloriously situated above the valley.

- **Local alcoholic brews** There are a huge variety of alcoholic brews cooked up by village women from locally farmed grain including the highly potent, distilled ara.

- **Bhutanese food** All visitors should try the unique, delicious red rice, aima datsi (chilli curry, as combustible as it sounds) and suja (butter tea).

- **Archery** Bhutan's national sport. Try to catch part of a contest and enjoy the yelling, singing and dancing and the attempts to deflect the opposition arrows by dodging in front of the target while the arrow is on its way.

- **Black Mountains** This remote upland area with abundant wildlife and fabulous scenery is gradually opening up to tourists who can visit isolated villages such as Nabji and Korphu.

Festivals

February Punakha Dromche. Celebrating an ancient defeat of the Tibetans by the Bhutanese, this festival features masked dances, ceremonies, a re-enactment of the event plus all the fun of a local market and fair.
March/April Paro Tshechu. Every temple celebrates an annual festival, commemorating the arrival of the Tibetan Guru Rimpoche in the eighth century and the victory of Buddhism over the indigenous evil spirits. Paro's is a vast, orchestrated affair with thousands of spectators, masked dances and the unfurling of a massive religious hanging, the thongdrel.
October/November Jambey Lhakhang Drup. A much smaller and more intimate temple festival in the picturesque Bumthang valley, featuring a dramatic night-time fire blessing (mewang).

Routes in and out

Most visitors fly into and out of Paro on Druk Air, the national airline (indeed the only airline permitted to land in Bhutan). An alternative is to enter by road, from Jaigaon in West Bengal (India), at Phuntsholing on the southern border, from where it's a six-hour drive to Thimphu. At Samdrup Jongkhar, in the far east of the country, it's possible to exit Bhutan by road for Darranga in the Indian state of Assam, though it's not permitted to enter Bhutan this way. The border between Bhutan and Tibet is closed.

Bhutan online

Bhutan Mountain Fortress of the Gods – Ⓦwww.bhutan.ethno -museum.ac.at Originally set up to accompany an exhibition of Bhutanese objects that toured Europe from 1997 to 2000 this is a great site showing some wonderful objects but also getting way below the surface of the country.
Bhutanese Refugees – Ⓦwww .geocities.com/bhutaneserefugees All is not perfect in this apparent paradise: since the 1980s over 125,000 Bhutanese people of Nepalese origin, many of whose families have been in Bhutan for generations, have left the country and become refugees in Nepal. This site explains their plight.
Bootan – Ⓦwww.bootan.com Colourful and informative general site including tourist information, news, pictures and some in-depth articles – you'll have to sort through the advertising but it's a lively, informative site.
Kuensel – Ⓦwww.kuenselonline .com The Bhutanese English-language newspaper gives a fascinating insight into the country. The juxtaposition of village stories with world events is wonderfully eccentric but gives an illuminating view of the current preoccupations of this remote land.
Women of Buddha. Nuns in Bhutan – Ⓦwww.womenofbuddha.com Light on text but the two dozen or so pictures on this site are a great illustration of the lives of these women.

Books

Terese Tse Bartholomew & John Johnston (Eds) *The Dragon's Gift*.

The Sacred Arts of Bhutan. Detailed, erudite but lovely book accompanying the exhibition of Buddhist artefacts from Bhutan that toured the world in 2009–10. Nothing beats seeing the objects for real but this is a pretty good second-best.
Gyurme Dorgje *Bhutan*. The most exhaustive, insightful guidebook to this little-visited country; it's strongest on the text and less powerful on pictures.
Rinzin Rinzin *The Talisman of Good Fortune and Other Stories from Rural Bhutan*. Wonderful and evocative tales that describe the forces and beliefs driving many of the people in the country today.
Christian Schichlgruber & Francoise Pommaret *Bhutan Mountain Fortress of the Gods*. Fabulous images and insightful text make this one of the best overall books on the country.
Jamie Zeppa *Beyond the Sky and the Earth: a Journey into Bhutan*. This enthralling read tells of the author's years as a teacher in the remote Himalayan kingdom, and is an intriguing introduction to the country, as well as a very open account of the highs and lows of life in an unfamiliar culture.

Films

The Cup (Khyentse Norbu, 2000). The first film by the only Bhutanese film director to receive Western notice. This is a small, delightful movie, about Tibetan monks in a small Himalayan monastery and the impact of the World Cup on their lives.
Golden Cup: The Legacy (Tshering Wangyel, 2007). Based on one of the stories from Rinzin Rinzin's collection, the story is a great introduction to Bhutanese myth but also stunningly shot in the central Bhutanese valley of Shingkhar.
The Other Final (Johan Kramer and Matthijs de Jongh, 2003). In 2002, as Brazil and Germany played the World

www.roughguides.com

Cup final, the two countries ranked at the bottom of world football – Bhutan at 202nd and Montserrat at 203rd – played in Thimphu. This documentary offers a fun perspective, following the the preparation, the teams and the game itself.

The Perfect Girl (Muti Thrishing; Pelden Dorji, 2005). A socially realistic drama/ love story that won plaudits as well as criticism in the country for its portrayal of prostitution.

Travellers and Magicians (Khyentse Norbu, 2004). The first feature film shot in Bhutan to make it into the West. It tells the interwoven stories of two Bhutanese men seeking to change their lives.

Bhutanese tourist offices

Ⓦ **www.tourism.gov.bt** Contact the Tourism Council of Bhutan, PO Box 126, Thimphu, Bhutan Ⓣ975-2-323251.

Bhutanese embassies and consulates

For visa information contact specialist travel agents or use the tourism contact given above.

Brunei

Capital Bandar Seri Begawan	**Religion** Islam
Population 390,000	**Climate** Tropical
Language Malay	**Best time to go** February–August
Currency Brunei dollar (B$)	**Minimum daily budget** US$50/£30

Occupying a tiny sliver of land on the northwest coast of Borneo, the Sultanate of Brunei is one of the least popular tourist destinations in Asia. This is mainly due to its size – there just aren't many attractions in the 5765 square kilometres – though it's also an expensive country to visit, with one of the highest standards of living in the region. The country's wealth comes from oil, which was first discovered here in 1903 and generates so much income that all Bruneians enjoy free health care and education, and subsidized cars, houses and pilgrimages to Mecca. The Sultan of Brunei, who rules the country, is widely acknowledged to be one of the world's richest monarchs.

Despite Brunei's dearth of tourist attractions, you may find yourself in transit here, as Royal Brunei Airlines often has good deals on its long-haul flights, some of which have connections that leave you with half a day or more to play with. Alternatively, if you're exploring the east Malaysian states of Sarawak and Sabah, which lie either side of Brunei, you can easily stop in Brunei en route between the two.

As nearly seventy percent of Brunei is covered in almost impenetrable rainforest, the country's most accessible sights are in and around the capital, Bandar Seri Begawan (often simply called "Bandar"). Accommodation will be your biggest expense if you stay here, so consider heading straight for Bandar's only youth hostel. There's a decent public bus service along the coast roads, but you'll need to rent a car to explore the southern extremities. As Brunei is a strict Muslim country, the sale of alcohol is banned (non-Muslims are allowed to import a very limited amount of alcohol but must declare it) and there's not much to do after nightfall; you should dress modestly (see p.103).

Mean temperatures (°C) and rainfall (mm)

Average daily temperatures (maximum and minimum °C) and monthly rainfall (mm)

	Jan	Feb	Mar	Apr	May	June	July	Aug	Sept	Oct	Nov	Dec
Bandar Seri Begawan												
max °C	30	30	31	32	33	32	32	32	32	32	31	31
min °C	23	23	23	24	24	24	24	24	23	23	23	23
rainfall mm	133	63	71	124	218	311	277	256	314	334	296	241

www.roughguides.com

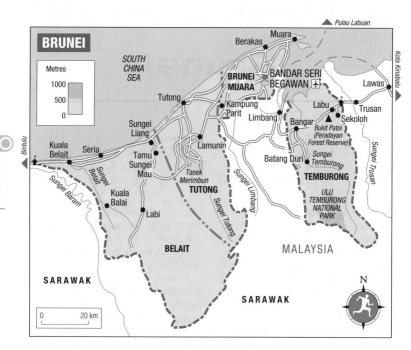

Main attractions

● **The Omar Ali Saifuddien Mosque**
The focal point of the Brunei capital,
this opulent mosque is constructed
from the finest Italian marble, with a
dome made from Venetian glass that
reflects dramatically in the surrounding
lagoon. Non-Muslims are allowed
inside the mosque except during
prayer times, and you can sometimes
persuade the caretakers to let you
ride the lift to the top of the minaret,
which gives good views over the water
villages below.

● **Kampung Ayer** Despite the
country's enormous wealth, almost half
the population of Bandar Seri Begawan
still live in traditional stilt houses built
over the city's three rivers, in the
sprawling labyrinth of wooden homes
and walkways known as Kampung Ayer.

An intriguing and photogenic sight, these
"water villages" are best explored by
water taxi.

● **Jame 'Asr Hassanil Bolkiah
Mosque** Spend a contemplative hour
or two in the elegantly manicured
gardens of Bandar's enormous mosque,
considered by some to be even more
impressive than the Omar Ali Saifuddien
Mosque.

● **Ulu Temburong National Park**
This protected swath of rainforest has a
treetop-level walkway and observation
towers for watching the resident
proboscis monkeys, plus occasional
guided night walks. On the way here
from Bandar, you get to travel through
the mangrove swamps on the famous
"flying coffin" speedboats (so called
because of their speed and shape, not
their safety record), and can visit an Iban
longhouse in Batang Duri.

Also recommended

● **The Brunei Museum** The place to bone up on the story behind modern Brunei's economic success and learn about it's lucrative relationship with oil. There's a gallery of Islamic art, displaying exquisitely designed antique Korans.

● **Stay in a village stilt-house in Sekoloh** The villagers of this remote *kampung* near Bukit Patoi offer homestay accommodation; a good way to learn about traditional Bruneian life.

Festivals

February 23 Brunei National Day. Huge parades and firework displays at Bandar's National Stadium.

July 15 His Majesty the Sultan of Brunei's Birthday Celebrations. Begins a fortnight of festivities, including parades and traditional sports competitions.

October/November Hari Raya Idul Fitri. To mark the end of the month-long Ramadan fast, the Sultan lets the public inside his fabulous palace, the Istana Nurul Iman.

Routes in and out

Most travellers fly in and out of Brunei's international airport in Bandar Seri Begawan. It's the departure point for international ferries to Lawas and Limbang in Sarawak; or you can reach both towns by bus from near Bangar in Temburong District. Boats to Pulau Labuan in Sabah leave from Bandar. Buses to the Sarawak town of Miri leave from Kuala Belait.

Brunei online

Royal Brunei Airlines Transit Tours – ⓦwww.bruneiair.com/promotion /transit/index.asp Choose from several short tours of Bandar to alleviate transit-lounge boredom.

Tourism Brunei – ⓦwww.tourism brunei.com The official site; with accommodation and tour agency links. It also covers visa requirements, embassies and duty-free allowances.

Books

James Bartholomew *The Richest Man in the World: Sultan of Brunei*. Prepare to be amazed by some mind-boggling statistics, not least concerning the Sultan's 1778-room palace.

Stanley Park *Fifa 192: The True Story Behind the Legend of the Brunei Darussalam National Football Team*. An expat Scouser takes on the role of press officer for Brunei's hopeless national team and tells the sorry, funny tale in full. Didn't go down so well with the Brunei authorities, who banned it.

Bruneian tourist offices

No overseas tourist office.

Bruneian embassies and consulates

ⓦ**www.mfa.gov.bn**
Australia and New Zealand 10 Beale Crescent, Deakin ACT 2600, Canberra ☎02/6285 4500, Ⓔbruneihc@snetspeed .com.au.

Canada 395 Laurier Ave. East, Ottawa, Ontario K1N 6R4 ☎613-234-5656, Ⓔottawa.canada@mfa.gov.bn.

UK and Ireland 19–20 Belgrave Square, London SW1X 8PG ☎020/7581 0521, Ⓔlondon.uk@mfa.gov.bn.

US 3520 International Court NW, Washington, DC 20008 ☎202/237-1838, ⓦwww.bruneiembassy.org.

www.roughguides.com

Cambodia

Capital Phnom Penh	**Main religion** Theravada Buddhism
Population 14.5 million	**Climate** Tropical
Language Khmer	**Best time to go** November–March
Currency Riel (r)	**Minimum daily budget** US$15/£9

Cambodia is attracting a burgeoning number of tourists, most of whom are drawn by the prospect of seeing the utterly compelling thousand-year-old temple ruins at Angkor. This city was the epicentre of the ancient Khmer kingdom, a Hindu–Buddhist empire that for almost five hundred years stretched right across Southeast Asia, from Vietnam in the east to China in the north and Burma in the west. These days it is a World Heritage site, and Cambodia's indisputable top attraction. Several of Cambodia's other most famous, and moving, sights are associated with the horrors inflicted by the murderous Khmer Rouge regime, which tried to force communism on its compatriots between 1975 and 1979 and in doing so drove the country back to the Stone Age and caused the deaths of at least a million people. But if you wander further afield you'll also find hill-tribe villages, trekking opportunities, Mekong River trips and relatively uncrowded beaches, all of which make Cambodia one of southeast Asia's more adventurous destinations.

Twenty-first century Cambodia has still not recovered from the devastations of the 1970s and is one of the poorest countries in the world. Public transport is excruciatingly slow and uncomfortable – though boats between Siem Reap and Phnom Penh, and around the southwest coast, offer a welcome relief from potholed roads – and outside the main tourist centres there is only very basic tourist accommodation. However, there are plenty of cheap guesthouses in Siem Reap, the town closest to Angkor, in the capital Phnom Penh and in the coastal town of Sihanoukville, and tourists generally get a good reception from the amazingly resilient Khmer people. But you'll

Mean temperatures (°C) and rainfall (mm)

Average daily temperatures (maximum and minimum °C) and monthly rainfall (mm)

	Jan	Feb	Mar	Apr	May	June	July	Aug	Sept	Oct	Nov	Dec
Phnom Penh												
max °C	31	32	34	35	34	33	32	32	31	30	30	30
min °C	21	22	23	24	24	24	24	25	25	24	23	22
rainfall mm	7	10	40	77	134	155	171	160	224	257	127	45

probably need a Khmer phrasebook to help you communicate with them outside the main tourist centres.

Gun crime continues to be a problem in Phnom Penh, so keep money and valuables hidden if you're walking around the capital after dark. Out in the sticks, landmines left over from the American-Vietnam War and the Khmer Rouge era still pose a major threat to local people, particularly in the provinces along the Thai border. The main tourist areas are clear of mines, but you should never venture off well-used tracks.

Main attractions

- **Angkor** The magnificent ruined Hindu–Buddhist temples and palaces of this ancient Khmer city, built between the ninth and fourteenth centuries, are one of Asia's top five sights – every bit as spectacular and important as better-known lost cities such as Machu Picchu in Peru. Now shrouded in jungle, the crumbling walls, intricate carvings and colossal sculpted faces of Angkor's hundred-plus temples take several days to explore. The biggest draws are the awesome complexes of Angkor Wat and Angkor Thom, but it's well worth investigating the less-visited sights, too, particularly the atmospheric jungle-encrusted remains of Preah Khan, and Kbal Spean where the actual riverbed has been carved with images of Hindu deities.

- **Siem Reap** The town nearest the Angkor temples has retained plenty of charm despite its plethora of guesthouses, tourist restaurants and tour agents. There's decent crafts shopping at the old Psar Chas market, and it's the best place in the country to see performances of traditional Khmer dance. The informal Landmine Museum on the edge of town is a heart-rending testament to the hundreds of limbs and lives that continue to be lost every year to mines hidden in fields and forests. A popular and scenic way to travel between Siem Reap and Phnom Penh is by boat; the journey takes five hours.

● **Phnom Penh** Cambodia's riverside capital is a crazy, eye-popping place to explore, with plenty of markets, temples and French colonial residences, plus a small but thriving travellers' scene. The main sights are the elegant Royal Palace; the glittering Silver Pagoda, whose floor is paved in over five thousand solid-silver tiles; the Angkor-related exhibits at the National Museum; and the unforgettable Tuol Sleng Genocide Museum, which commemorates the twenty thousand Cambodians who were tortured and murdered by the Khmer Rouge in the city's Security Prison S-21.

● **Rattanakiri** This remote province, 600km northeast of Phnom Penh, is way out in the sticks, but attracts a steady stream of tourists because of its population of hill tribes and its volcanic scenery. Most people base themselves in the provincial capital, Ban Lung, and everyone takes a tour out to nearby Yeak Laom Lake, to swim in the clear turquoise waters of this forest-encircled volcanic crater. Treks from nearby Voen Sai into the jungles of Virachey National Park include a night in a hammock and a bamboo raft trip.

Also recommended

● **Kratie** Pint-sized Kratie is a little gem of a town, set beside the Mekong River and full of colonial houses and traditional wooden Khmer homes. There's not much to do except soak up the atmosphere and make a few day-trips, including to nearby Kampie to see the Irrawaddy dolphins who frequent that part of the Mekong.

▲ Floating villages on Tonle Sap, near Siem Reap

- **Sihanoukville** Cambodia's beaches can't compare with those of neighbouring Thailand, but the country's main resort of Sihanoukville is growing fast, with half a dozen decent beaches, plenty of accommodation, very cheap beer care of the local Angkor brewery, and a fairly lively nightlife.

- **Ream National Park** The best way to enjoy this marine park is to join a tour from Sihanoukville or enlist the help of the park rangers, who can arrange informal boat trips along the mangrove-fringed Prek Toek Sap estuary and to nearby fishing islands.

- **Kampot** Scenic little town of colonial era shophouses that's rich on atmosphere and makes a handy base for trips to Bokor National Park with its otherworldly pitcher plants and giant hornbills.

- **Koh Tonsay** Tiny rustic island off Kep where, for the moment at least, there's little else but forest and a few bamboo bungalows on the white-sand beach.

Festivals

April Bonn Chaul Chhnam (Khmer New Year). Buddhist New Year is celebrated with public water fights that symbolize, in theory at least, a spiritual cleansing.
October/November Bonn Om Tuk (Water Festival). The rainy season officially ends when the waters of the Tonle Sap reverse direction and flow out into the Mekong River again. Celebrations include traditional boat parades and races, and big fireworks displays.

Routes in and out

There are no non-stop long-haul flights to Cambodia, but a number of airlines fly from Europe via Bangkok or Singapore to Phnom Penh and Siem Reap (for Angkor). Direct flights from other Asian countries are increasing all the time, and include useful routes from China, Laos, Malaysia and Vietnam.

Cambodia's overland borders are subject to unpredictable regulations, so check locally first and note that not all are open to foreigners. From Thailand there are half a dozen entry points open to foreigners; the two most commonly used are at Poipet (six hours by road from Siem Reap), and at Koh Kong (for Sihanoukville and Phnom Penh), with others near Pailin, Sam Vong and Anlong Veng. Border crossings in and out of Vietnam include useful routes between Ho Chi Minh City and Phnom Penh (via Bavet); from the Mekong Delta to Phnom Penh; and at Phnom Den and Prek Chak, for routes from the Mekong Delta and Phu Quoc island to Kampot and Kep. Access between Laos and Cambodia is at Voen Kham, with transport by minibus or boat to and from Stung Treng.

Cambodia online

Andy Brouwer's Cambodian Tales – Ⓦ andybrouwer.co.uk Famously good and regularly updated collection of blogs, features and news about Cambodia, plus an active travellers' forum.
The Angkor Guide – Ⓦ www.the angkorguide.com Maurice Glaize's seminal 1944 guide to the monuments of Angkor – available online and to download in full, for free.
Bayon Pearnik – Ⓦ www.bayon pearnik.com Online Cambodia travel and tourism magazine stacked full of features, tips and travel info.
Canby Publications – Ⓦ www.canby publications.com Digital versions of the very useful, locally published, free travel guides to Cambodia's main tourist centres.
Tales of Asia: Cambodia – Ⓦ www .talesofasia.com Especially good for overland routes and its lively forum.

Books

Francois Bizot *The Gate*. A French ethnologist tells the extraordinary story of his life in Cambodia during the Khmer Rouge years, first as a captive and later as a negotiator.

Nic Dunlop *The Lost Executioner: A Story of the Khmer Rouge.* Outstanding account of a photographer's journey through modern Cambodia in search of the Khmer Rouge commander Comrade Duch.

Carol Livingston *Gecko Tails*. Funny, touching account of how an aspiring foreign correspondent hangs out in Phnom Penh during the run-up to the 1993 elections waiting for her big break.

Dawn Rooney *Angkor: An Introduction to the Temples*. The most accessible guide, with plenty of pictures as well as temple plans and informative text.

Loung Ung *First They Killed My Father*. Harrowing autobiography of a young girl's childhood during the Khmer Rouge era.

Films

City of Ghosts (Matt Dillon, 2002). Matt Dillon plays a dodgy New York insurance salesman who flees the FBI and ends up in Phnom Penh to join his business partner in another money-making scam. The eponymous Cambodian capital is the star of the film – by turns seedy, chaotic, enervating and beautiful – with plenty of attention paid to the legacy of its tragic, violent past and to its corrupt, energetic present.

The Killing Fields (Roland Joffé, 1984). The most famous feature film about life under Pol Pot's tyrannical regime centres on journalist Dith Pran who, along with millions of others, was forced to deny his past and work for the Khmer Rouge in labour camps.

Lara Croft: Tomb Raider (Simon West, 2001). Lara Croft leaps out of the video game and on to the big screen, with Angelina Jolie doing her action-hero stuff against a backdrop of some of Angkor's most stunning monuments.

Cambodian tourist offices

Ⓦ **www.mot.gov.kh**
No international tourist offices.

Cambodian embassies and consulates

Australia and New Zealand
5 Canterbury Crescent, Deakin, ACT 2600, Canberra ☎02/6273 1154, Ⓦwww.embassyofcambodia.org.nz /au.htm.
UK and Ireland 64 Brondesbury Park, London NW6 7AT ☎020 8451 7850, Ⓦwww.cambodianembassy.org.uk.
US and Canada 4530 16th St, Washington DC 20011 ☎202/726-7742, Ⓦwww.embassyofcambodia.org.

China

Capital Beijing
Population Over 1.3 billion
Languages Mandarin, plus scores
of regional languages and dialects
Currency Yuan (¥) in China;
Hong Kong dollar (HK$) in Hong
Kong; and pataca (M$ or MOP)
in Macau
Main religions Buddhism,
Confucianism, Daoism and Islam

Climate Tropical in the south; mixed
elsewhere, including temperate
(central), desert (northwest) and
Himalayan (far west); northern and
western winters very cold, southern
and northwestern summers very hot
Best time to go April–June and
September–November for most of
the country
Minimum daily budget US$44/£27

CHINA

As the most populous country on earth, with three thousand years of recorded history and borders encompassing everything from the Himalayan plateau to tropical beaches, China exerts a huge pull on travellers to Asia. The country's scale and complexity, however, can make planning a trip a little daunting. Short visits are best confined to obvious highlights, such as Beijing, Xi'an's Terracotta Army, or the river and hill scenery around Guilin. But with more time, take advantage of the comprehensive (though often uncomfortable) transport network and explore, for example, eastern China's lush landscapes and historic towns, or the country's remoter reaches which – ethnically at least – are not even truly "Chinese".

Wherever you go, take time to try China's classic regional cooking: Northern (featuring hotpots, Peking duck and even lavish Imperial cuisine, which once graced the tables of China's emperors); Eastern (seafood and river-fish delicacies); Sichuan (pungent, spicy dishes using lots of chillies); and Cantonese (little snacks known as dim sum, and main courses using just about

any ingredient imaginable – as long as it's fresh).

Right now is an exciting time to visit, as the country is changing at breakneck speed, throwing off years of Maoist stagnation with an explosive lust for modernization under a regime that is, in economic terms at least, relatively liberal. Modern skylines are appearing as whole cities are rebuilt; roads and rail lines are spreading everywhere; and the free market is earning people wages which just a generation ago would have been unthinkable. The downsides are rising inflation, leading to poverty for those unable to take part in the boom, ingrained corruption and runaway pollution.

As its infrastructure improves, so China is becoming more accessible to foreigners than it has ever been. Though communication problems can complicate independent travel, you'll usually encounter English-speaking students in the cities who might act as guides in order to improve their language skills, and it's not impossible to learn survival Mandarin even on a brief trip. More exhausting is a complex

www.roughguides.com

Mean temperatures (°C) and rainfall (mm)

Average daily temperatures (maximum and minimum °C) and monthly rainfall (mm)

	Jan	Feb	Mar	Apr	May	June	July	Aug	Sept	Oct	Nov	Dec
Beijing												
max °C	1	4	11	21	27	31	31	30	26	20	9	3
min °C	-10	-8	-1	7	13	18	21	20	14	6	-2	-8
rainfall mm	4	5	8	17	35	78	243	141	58	16	11	3
Chongqing												
max °C	9	13	18	23	27	29	34	35	28	22	16	13
min °C	5	7	11	16	19	22	24	25	22	16	12	8
rainfall mm	15	20	38	99	142	180	142	122	150	112	48	20
Hong Kong												
max °C	18	17	19	24	28	29	31	31	29	27	23	20
min °C	13	13	16	19	23	26	26	26	25	23	18	15
rainfall mm	33	46	74	137	292	394	381	367	257	114	43	31
Lhasa												
max °C	7	9	12	16	19	24	23	22	21	17	13	9
min °C	-10	-7	-2	1	5	9	9	9	7	1	-5	-9
rainfall mm	0	13	8	5	25	64	122	89	66	13	3	0
Ürümqi												
max °C	-11	-8	-1	16	22	26	28	27	21	10	-1	-8
min °C	-22	-19	-11	2	8	12	14	13	8	-1	-11	-13
rainfall mm	15	8	13	38	28	38	18	25	15	43	41	10

bureaucracy which can make even getting a hotel room an achievement; the intensive, unabashed public scrutiny of foreigners; and the stress of trying to see too much in too short a time. If you plan to explore widely, avoid doing so on a rock-bottom budget: for long-distance travel, it's always worth spending a little bit more on a flight or for a comfortable sleeper carriage.

Main attractions

● **Beijing** With its skyscrapers and relatively wealthy population, the capital encapsulates the best of modern China. Yet the past survives in many significant icons, from the palaces of the vast Forbidden City and the charming, circular Temple of Heaven, to the notorious Tiananmen Square and Mao's Mausoleum. Downtown, look for the dwindling number of *hutong*s, the narrow alleyways which make up much of old Beijing. There are also China's foremost restaurants and nightlife to take advantage of – everything from teahouse theatres and acrobatic shows to clubs that only play deepest house.

● **The Great Wall** This extraordinary feat of civil engineering was begun in the fifth century and stretched 6000km across China. The most accessible of its remaining sections are within easy reach of Beijing, including at very popular Badaling and at less commercialized Simatai and Jinshanling, the latter offering unusually quiet and welcoming homestay accommodation.

Xi'an Made rich by the old Silk Road trade, Xi'an was one of China's former capitals. Its most famous sight is the extraordinary Terracotta Army: over eight thousand individually styled life-sized figurines guarding the tomb of the country's first emperor. Other highlights include a lively Muslim quarter and cycling right round the city atop its renovated 12-metre-high walls. The famous kung fu temple, Shaolin Si, is within a day's journey to the east, near Luoyang – it's a major tourist trap, filled with shops selling weapons and tracksuits, and with students showing off their skills.

The Li River Looking exactly like a Chinese scroll painting, a procession of tall, wonderfully weathered limestone peaks flanks 85km of the Li River in southwestern Guangxi province. Base yourself at either the package-tour city of Guilin or the more mellow village of Yangshuo, then cruise around or rent a bicycle and pedal off through the countryside.

Shanghai With over nineteen million residents, Shanghai is the world's most populous city. Its buzzy, style-conscious nightlife is matched by fantastic shopping, with good bargains for tailor-made clothes and plenty of glamorous malls. Though the city has few unmissable sights, the beautifully presented Shanghai Museum offers the perfect introduction to China's phenomenal artistic heritage.

Three Gorges The latter stage of the 6400-kilometre-long Yangzi River flows eastwards across central China and is still used as a transport artery. Catch a ferry through the Three Gorges, between the city of Chongqing and Yichang in Hubei, a two-day 250-kilometre journey past ancient towns and spectacular cliff scenery. For superlative vistas, alight at Wushan and take a half-day side cruise up the Daning River, via the pretty countryside and tiny villages bordering the Three Little Gorges.

Tibet The "roof of the world" is a place of red-robed monks and austere monastery complexes set against the awe-inspiring vastness of the Tibetan Plateau. It's also labouring under heavy-handed Chinese military rule, but even the Dalai Lama, exiled in India, encourages people to visit and see the region first-hand. Take your time and, after seeing the mighty Potala Palace in the capital Lhasa, get out to less-touristed monasteries at Shigatse and Gyantse. There's also the chance to ride the highest railway in the world, from Golmud (Qinghai) to Lhasa, nearly all of it at an altitude of 4000m or above.

Yunnan and Sichuan China's most varied region, these two provinces stretch from Tibet to the steamy tropical forests of Xishuangbanna, and also share borders with Laos, Vietnam and Burma. Top spots are Sichuan's holy mountain, Emei Shan, where you can sleep and eat in the dozen or more Buddhist temples; the giant pandas of Wolong Nature Reserve, west of Chengdu; the Yunnanese town of Dali, with its ethnic Bai population and vivid mountain and lake scenery; Lijiang, a delightful maze of cobbled lanes and wooden houses, home to the Tibetan-descended Naxi people; and the stark, dramatic scenery of Tiger Leaping Gorge, the deepest canyon in the world, with a drop of 2.5 kilometres.

Also recommended

Guangxi and Guizhou The rural regions of these provinces are among China's poorest, but it's worth exploring the minority communities dotted throughout the fabulously terraced mountains here, especially the Dong village of Zhaoxing, in northern Guangxi.

CHINA

KAZAKHSTAN

RUSSIAN FEDERATION

Altay

ALTAI MOUNTAINS

ALMATY

BISHKEK

Yining

Ürümqi

KYRGYZSTAN

Torugut Pass

TIAN SHAN MOUNTAINS

Kashgar

Korla

Turpan

Hami

TAJIKISTAN

Tashkurgan

Tarim Basin

Taklamakan Desert

Mogaô Caves

Dunhuang

Jiayuguan

AFGHANISTAN

Sost

KARAKORAM

Khotan

KUNLUN MOUNTAINS

Golmud

Qinghai Hu

Xining

Khunjerab Pass

PAKISTAN

Ali

▲ Kailash

Yangzi River

Yellow River

Lancang River

DELHI

NEPAL

HIMALAYAS

TIBET

Shigatse

Lhasa

Nu River (Salween)

Zhangmu

Gyantse

Kodari

Everest ▲

KATHMANDU

THIMPHU

BHUTAN

Tiger Leaping Gorge

Lijiang

Dali

Xiaguan

I N D I A

BANGLADESH

Kunming

Kolkota

DHAKA

Jinghong (Xishuangbanna)

Mo Han

Boten

N

BURMA

Bay of Bengal

RANGOON

VIENTIANE

THAILAND

0   600 km

BANGKOK

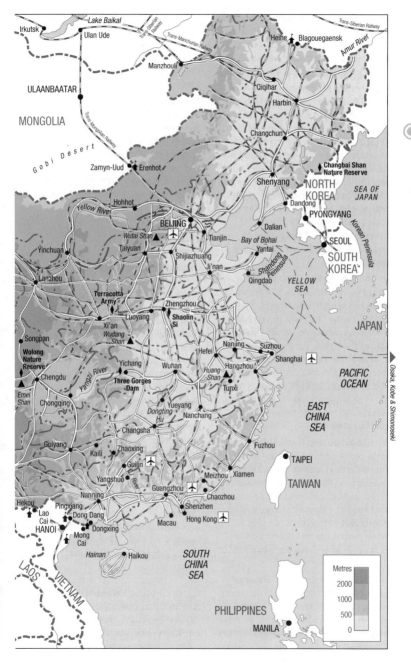

The Miao hill-tribe settlements around Kaili in Guizhou host riotous festivals through the year, featuring bull fights, dancing, dragon-boat races and fantastic outfits.

● **The Silk Road** Follow the ancient Silk Road between China and Central Asia – a 3000-kilometre-long train and bus route from Xi'an to Kashgar. On the way, you can take in remote sections of the Great Wall, the bird-watching lake Qinghai Hu, astonishing eighth-century Buddhist cave art at Dunhuang, the pleasant oasis town of Turpan and the scorching sands of the Taklamakan desert. Kashgar itself, populated by Muslim, Turkic-speaking Uigur people, is most famous for the gathering of different minorities at its enormous Sunday Bazaar – and for its remote location.

● **Hong Kong** Hong Kong's cityscape is one of the modern wonders of the world, best seen at night while crossing the harbour on the Star Ferry, though taking the famous tram up to Victoria Peak gives you another classic panorama. Shopping is a major Hong Kong pastime, at the excessively glitzy shopping malls, at the chaotic Temple Street Night Market and in the more traditional Stanley Market. Hong Kong is also the place for unrivalled *dim sum* brunches.

● **Hangzhou and Suzhou** Once a vital trade centre on the 1800-kilometre-long Grand Canal in eastern China, Hangzhou is set around the famed beauty spot of Xi Hu, or West Lake, ringed by pagodas and wooded, hilly parkland, its surface dotted with fishing boats. It's also worth making the haul 60km north to Suzhou, another canal city with a host of traditional Chinese gardens.

● **Changbai Shan Nature Reserve** Set right up on China's frontier with North Korea, Changbai Shan is hard to reach even when the road opens in summer, but the rewards are the stunning blue Tian Chi – "Heaven's Lake" – and the faint chance

you may spot Siberian tigers. More likely, you'll get to sample some of the rare fungi and medicinal herbs which locals harvest here and serve up in restaurants; Changbai Shan's ginseng is considered the best in China.

● **Chaozhou** A self-consciously traditional town in southern Guangdong province, Chaozhou has nineteenth-century streets and even older architecture, including its city walls and beautiful Kaiyuan Temple. Foodies will want to try out the famously bitter, refreshing *gongfu* tea and fruit-flavoured sauces.

Festivals

January 5 to February 5 Ice Lantern Festival, Harbin. A month-long exhibition of fabulous sculptures carved from snow and ice, including life-size figures and even exact replicas of Chinese temples.
April/May Spring Fair, Dali. A huge gathering from all Yunnan, as crowds pour in to buy and sell horses, watch wrestling matches and socialize, with much dancing and singing.
June/July Dragon-boat Festival. Traditional multi-oared dragon boats are raced along waterways in many parts of the country, especially in Hong Kong and in Yueyang in Hunan.

Routes in and out

China's main useful international airports are in Beijing, Guangzhou (capital of Guangdong), Guilin, Hong Kong, Kunming (capital of Yunnan) and Shanghai.

You can enter and depart China overland through several designated border crossings. The Trans-Manchuria and Trans-Mongolian lines of the Trans-Siberian Express run between Moscow and Beijing (see p.28) and you can also use local trains to access the border at Erenhot. Trains and buses connect Ürümqi in northwestern China with Almaty in Kazakhstan and there is road access from northwestern China into Pakistan (via Tashkurag/Sost and the Karakoram Highway, which is popular with cyclists; see p.31). Buses also connect Kyrgyzstan with Kashgar in northwest China (via the Torugut Pass) but are often off-limits to foreigners.

Entering Tibet from Nepal (via Kodari/Zhangmu) is a popular option but subject to bureaucratic vagaries, while the reverse is only possible by private tour. Far easier are the three rail and/or road crossings from north Vietnam, and the single road crossing from Boten in Laos – all of which bring you into China's southwestern provinces of Yunnan and Guangxi, from where there's regular transport to Nanning and Kunming.

There are also international ferry services to South Korea and Japan. Ferries to Incheon, near Seoul in South Korea, include services from Tianjin (near Beijing), Qingdao (Shandong) and Dalian (Liaoning). The services between China and Japan include ferries from Shanghai to Kobe/Osaka; from Tanggu near Tianjin to Kobe; and from Qingdao and Suzhou to Shimonoseki.

China online

China Expat – Ⓦ**www.chinaexpat .com** Wide-ranging site that's got plenty of interest to visitors as well as expat residents; includes features on culture and sights, guides for cities across the country; and good travel links.
The China News Network – Ⓦ**thechinanews.net** The region's headline stories.
International Campaign for Tibet – Ⓦ**www.savetibet.org** News on what's happening in Tibet, from the non-profit advocacy organization.

Smart Shanghai – Ⓦ**www.smart shanghai.com** Listings, features, maps and plenty of sassy opinionated comment about China's slinkiest city; runs classified ads for apartments too
Travel China – Ⓦ**www.travelchina guide.com** Surprisingly diverse and detailed guide to the main destinations from an online tour operator. Hotel bookings and flights too.

Books

Jung Chang *Wild Swans*. A modern-day classic that charts China's recent history as lived by three generations of women: the author, who grew up in Sichuan during the Cultural Revolution; her mother, who lived through the Japanese occupation of Manchuria and later became a Communist official; and her grandmother, who was a warlord's concubine.
Fuschia Dunlop *Shark's Fin and Sichuan Pepper: A Sweet-sour Memoir of Eating in China*. Compelling, delightful, beautifully written account of a young English woman's love affair with the strange and delicious otherness of China and its food.
Peter Hessler *River Town*. Sensitive, funny and frank, the author, a 26-year-old teacher with the American Peace Corps programme, narrates the ups and downs of his two-year stint (1996–98) in the Yangzi town of Fuling. Told with insight, warmth and intelligence, it all adds up to an outstanding introduction to China.
Peter Hopkirk *Trespassers on the Roof of the World: The Race for Lhasa*. The amazing story of how, at the start of the twentieth century, a group of Brits and Indians charted every nook of the vast High Tibetan Plateau, the most inaccessible – and hostile – place on earth.
Ma Jian *Red Dust*. It is the mid-1980s and, about to become another statistic

www.roughguides.com

▲ Li River scenery near Guilin

in the latest Campaign Against Spiritual Pollution, disaffected young Beijing photo-journalist Ma Jian sets off on an arbitrary journey around China. His wanderings, mostly done on foot, last three years and take him to remote villages and ancient minority communities that no foreign traveller could ever hope to penetrate, revealing a country of mind-blowing vastness, diversity and harshness.

Films

Crouching Tiger Hidden Dragon (Ang Lee, 2000). Despite having its roots in the martial arts genre that dominates Chinese and Hong Kong TV, this film was a big hit in the West, skilfully blending fantasy, Dao philosophy, awesome aerial stunts and strong female characters. The breathtaking scenery was filmed on location in the Ming-dynasty villages of Xidi and Hongcun in the Huang Shan mountains in eastern China, and in Xinjiang province in the remote northwest.
Hard Boiled (John Woo, 1993). Probably the most famous of the innumerable bloody, violent Hong Kong guns-and-gangsters action flicks: slick,

excessive, and with a ridiculously high body count. Stars Chow Yun Fat.
The Last Emperor (Bernardo Bertolucci, 1987). Filmed on location in Beijing's labyrinthine Forbidden City and along the bleak Manchurian frontier, this is a sumptuous retelling of early-twentieth-century history, as experienced by Pu Yi: child emperor, then puppet of Japanese-controlled Manchuria, and finally an inmate of a 1950s re-education camp in the communist People's Republic.
Lust, Caution (Ang Lee, 2007) Sexy, sophisticated psychological thriller set in 1940s Shanghai during the Japanese occupation. A young woman gets emotionally entangled with her target as she works a honeytrap for the Chinese Resistance.
Red Sorghum (Zhang Yimou, 1987), **Ju Dou** (Zhang Yimou, 1989) and **Raise the Red Lantern** (Zhang Yimou, 1991). Three stunning visual feasts by Zhang Yimou, all of them set in feudal house-holds in rural 1920s China. They're all variations on a similar theme, concerning a young woman who is sent against her will to marry an elderly and intransigent man, the elderly husband symbolizing

the inflexible Chinese state. Yimou filmed many scenes in the traditional eighteenth-century village homes around Yixian near Tunxi in Anhui province.

Chinese tourist offices

China Ⓦen.cnta.gov.cn
Hong Kong Ⓦwww.discoverhongkong.com
Australia and New Zealand 11th Floor, 234 George St, Sydney, NSW 2000 Ⓣ02/9252-9838, Ⓦwww.cnto.org.au. Hong Kong Tourism Board: Level 4, Hong Kong House, 80 Druitt St, Sydney, NSW 2000 Ⓣ02/9283 3083, Ⓔsydwwo@hktb.com.
Canada 480 University Ave, Suite 806, Toronto, Ontario M5G 1V2 Ⓣ1-416/599-6636, Ⓔcnto@tourismchina-ca.com. Hong Kong Tourism Board: 9 Temperance St, Toronto, Ontario M5H 1Y6 Ⓣ416/366-2389, Ⓔyyzwwo@hktb.com.
UK and Ireland 71 Warwick Rd, London SW5 9HB Ⓣ020/7373 0888, Ⓔlondon@cnta.gov.cn. Hong Kong Tourism Board: 6 Grafton St, London W1S 4EQ Ⓣ020/7533 7100, Ⓔlonwwo@hktb.com.
US Ⓦwww.cnto.org; 370 Lexington Ave, #912, New York, NY 10117 Ⓣ1-888-760-8218, Ⓔny@cnto.org; 550 North Brand Boulevard, Suite 910, Glendale, CA 91203 Ⓣ1-800-670-2228, Ⓔla@cnto.org. Hong Kong Tourism Board: 10940 Wilshire Blvd, Suite 2050, Los Angeles, CA 90024 Ⓣ310/208-4582, Ⓔlaxwwo@hktb.com; 115 East 54th St, New York, NY 10022 Ⓣ212/421-3382, Ⓔnycwwo@hktb.com.

Chinese embassies and consulates

For Hong Kong visa regulations, see Ⓦwww.immd.gov.hk/ehtml/hkvisas_4.htm.

Australia Ⓦau.china-embassy.org. 15 Coronation Drive, Yarralumla, ACT 2600 Ⓣ02/6273 4780. Consulates in Brisbane Ⓣ07/3210 6509 ext. 206, Ⓦbrisbane.chineseconsulate.org; Perth Ⓣ08/9222 0333, Ⓦperth.chineseconsulate.org; and Sydney Ⓣ02/8595 8002, Ⓦsydney.chineseconsulate.org.
Canada Ⓦwww.chinaembassycanada.org. 515 St Patrick's St, Ottawa, Ontario K1N 5H3 Ⓣ613/789-3434. Consulates in Calgary Ⓣ403/264-3322, Ⓦcalgary.china-consulate.org; Toronto Ⓣ416/964-8861, Ⓦtoronto.china-consulate.org; and Vancouver Ⓣ604/734-0704, Ⓦvancouver.china-consulate.org.
Ireland 40 Ailesbury Rd, Dublin 4 Ⓣ01/269 1707, Ⓦie.china-embassy.org.
New Zealand 2–6 Glenmore St, Wellington Ⓣ04/472 1382, Ⓦnz.china-embassy.org. Consulate in Auckland Ⓣ09/5713080, Ⓦauckland.china-consulate.org.
South Africa 965 Church St, Arcadia, Pretoria 0083 Ⓣ012/431 6537, Ⓦwww.chinese-embassy.org.za.
UK Ⓦwww.chinese-embassy.org.uk. 49–51 Portland Place, London W1B 1JL Ⓣ020/7299 4049. Consulates in Edinburgh Ⓣ0131/337 3220, Ⓦedinburgh.chineseconsulate.org; and Manchester Ⓣ0161/224 8672, Ⓦmanchester.chineseconsulate.org.
US 2300 Conneticut Ave NW, Washington, DC 20008 Ⓣ202/328-2500, Ⓦwww.china-embassy.org. Consulates in Chicago Ⓣ312/803-0095, Ⓦwww.chinaconsulatechicago.org; Houston Ⓣ713/520-1462, Ⓦhouston.china-consulate.org; Los Angeles Ⓣ213/807-8088, Ⓦlosangeles.china-consulate.org; New York Ⓣ212/244-9456, Ⓦwww.nyconsulate.prchina.org; and San Francisco Ⓣ415/674-2940, Ⓦwww.chinaconsulatesf.org.

www.roughguides.com

India

Capital Delhi
Population 1,166,000,000
Language Hindi, plus fourteen other main languages
Currency Rupee (Rs)
Main religions Hinduism, Islam, Buddhism, Christianity and Sikhism
Climate Tropical in south India mixed in the north, including temperate (central), desert (northwest) and Himalayan (far north); see p.65 for information on monsoon conditions
Best time to go October–March (except in the southeast); April–September (for trekking in the Himalayas, and for the southeast)
Minimum daily budget US$10/£6

For many travellers, India epitomizes the Asia experience. The country socks you in the guts with overwhelming sights, sounds and smells from the second you arrive and enthrals and appals, often both at the same time. It overflows with bizarre rituals and extraordinary characters; boasts a wealth of temples, ruined cities and dramatic landscapes; and for tourists everything you buy is bargain-priced (although it is perfectly possible to spend a fortune on luxury accommodation). However, it is also more crowded, more hassly and there is much more visible poverty than many other Asian countries.

With seven major faiths and over fifteen regional languages, India is impossible to pigeonhole. A journey from the north of India to the south is more like a trip across a dozen different countries. More than almost any other destination in Asia, India is a place to return to again and again and not somewhere that rewards a whistle-stop tour. And, because distances are phenomenal and public transport notoriously tardy, it also makes sense to confine yourself to smallish areas – aim to see something in depth and you'll have a far better experience than skittering through countless airports, stations and bus depots.

First-time visitors to India usually worry most about poor sanitation and the prospect of getting sick, but so long as you're sensible and follow the advice outlined in Chapter Twelve, you shouldn't find health is any more of an issue here than elsewhere in Asia. Modern-day India is the world's largest secular democracy, where the Hindu majority is vociferously, and occasionally violently, matched by powerful Muslim and Sikh factions, not to mention countless other religious and political groups. Tension between different groups occasionally renders some regions temporarily unsafe for visitors, so check official websites (see p.348) and travellers' forums (see p.94) for latest developments.

Main attractions

● **Taj Mahal** The world's most famous monument to love features, totally justifiably, on almost every first-timer's

Mean temperatures (°C) and rainfall (mm)

Average daily temperatures (maximum and minimum °C) and monthly rainfall (mm)

	Jan	Feb	Mar	Apr	May	June	July	Aug	Sept	Oct	Nov	Dec
Delhi												
max °C	21	24	30	36	41	40	35	34	34	35	29	23
min °C	7	9	14	20	26	28	27	26	24	18	11	8
rainfall mm	25	22	17	7	8	65	211	173	150	31	1	5
Darjeeling												
max °C	8	9	14	17	18	18	19	18	18	16	12	9
min °C	2	2	6	9	12	13	14	14	13	10	6	3
rainfall mm	13	28	43	104	216	589	798	638	447	130	23	8
Mumbai												
max °C	28	28	30	32	33	32	29	29	29	32	32	31
min °C	19	19	22	24	27	26	25	24	24	24	23	21
rainfall mm	3	3	3	0	18	485	617	340	264	63	13	3
Chennai												
max °C	29	31	33	35	38	38	36	35	34	32	29	29
min °C	19	20	22	26	28	27	26	26	25	24	22	21
rainfall mm	36	10	8	15	25	48	91	117	119	305	356	140

Indian itinerary. Built by the seventeenth-century Mogul emperor Shah Jahan to enshrine the body of his favourite wife, the vast mausoleum stands on the banks of the Yamuna River in the city of Agra, just a couple of hours' train ride from Delhi. It's worth visiting at sunrise and/or in the moonlight, when the play of light on marble is especially memorable, and the site is less crowded (more than 2.5 million visitors a year flock here).

● **Rajasthan** India's desert state is deservedly the most popular region in the country, with its glorious forts at Jaipur and Jodhpur, magnificent maharajahs' palaces, and flamboyantly clad citizens. Graceful waterside temples, exquisite mansions, and the lovely City Palace make lakeside Udaipur a must-see, and the remote desert town of Jaisalmer, built entirely of honey-coloured sandstone, is another gem – and a departure point for Rajasthan's famous camel safaris.

● **South India** The south of the country is far more relaxed than the north. The 100-kilometre-long strip of beaches in Goa has accommodation and atmosphere to suit all comers but don't forget to venture inland to the palm groves, rice fields, markets and Portuguese-style facades that characterize the heart of the Goan state. Kerala also has plenty of beach resorts but the big draw is the chance to go boating through the Kuttanad, the inland waterways that meander from Kochi in the north to Kollam in the south. The old port city of Kochi is also a prime destination to catch traditional, elaborately costumed Kathakali dance performances.

● **Ladakh** Cradled by the soaring peaks of the Himalaya and Karakoram ranges, Ladakh is a fascinating high-altitude outpost of Tibetan culture and religion. One of the furthest-flung parts of the country, this arid, stark, mountainous region offers some of the best trekking in

www.roughguides.com

243

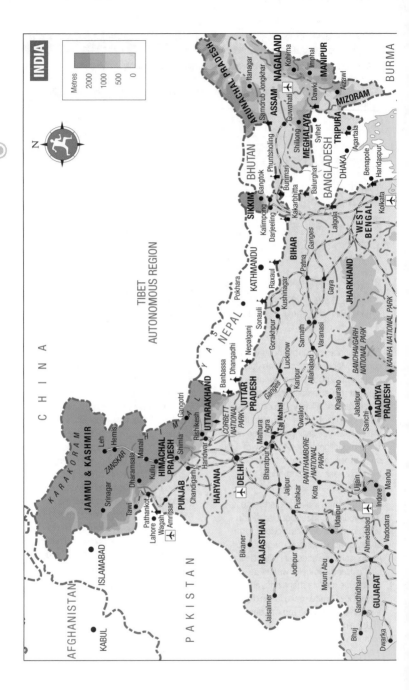

INDIA

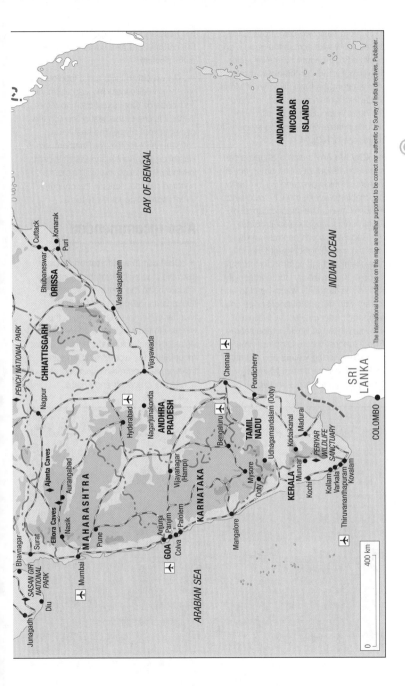

INDIA

The international boundaries on this map are neither purported to be correct nor authentic by Survey of India directives. Publisher.

www.roughguides.com

Map labels:

ANDAMAN AND NICOBAR ISLANDS

BAY OF BENGAL

INDIAN OCEAN

ARABIAN SEA

Cuttack
Konarak
Puri
Bhubaneswar
ORISSA
Vishakapatnam

PENCH NATIONAL PARK
CHHATTISGARH
Nagpur
Vijayawada

Hyderabad
Nagarjunakonda
ANDHRA PRADESH
Chennai
Pondicherry

SRI LANKA
COLOMBO

Ajanta Caves
Aurangabad
Ellora Caves
Nasik
MAHARASHTRA
Pune
Bengaluru
TAMIL NADU
Vijayanagar (Hampi)
KARNATAKA
Kodaikanal
Madurai
Udhagamandalam (Ooty)
Mysore
Ooty
Munnar
PERIYAR WILDLIFE SANCTUARY
KERALA
Kochi
Kollam
Varkala
Kovalam
Thiruvananthapuram

Mangalore

GOA
Anjuna
Panjim
Colva
Palolem

Bhavnagar
Surat
Mumbai

SASAN GIR NATIONAL PARK
Diu
Junagadh

0   400 km

India, from easy two-day strolls to treks of several weeks across the remote and spellbindingly beautiful Zanskar region. The popular two- or three-day road journey from the lively hill town of Manali to Ladakh's main town, Leh, is one of the great Asian road trips, with high-altitude passes and stunning scenery (for more, see p.143).

● **City life** Any Indian metropolis can scare the life out of a first-timer, but all visitors should have, and will probably be unable to avoid, the city experience at some point. The chaotic capital of Delhi boasts Mogul palaces inside the Red Fort, which contrast vividly with the sweeping thoroughfares in New Delhi and the ultramodern Baha'i Temple. Kipling's "city of dreadful night", Kolkata, is famously warm-hearted and literary with dozens of bookshops and a reputation for intellectual liveliness. Varanasi lines the banks of the sacred River Ganges, where pilgrims immerse themselves in the waters and cremate their dead on the banks. Mumbai boasts designer stores and some of the best, and most expensive, food in the country, but also some of the most awful poverty.

● **Go on safari** India has a fabulous variety of wildlife including wild elephants and leopards, but its real claim to fame is that it is one of the best places on the planet to spot tigers. The best known national parks for this are Ranthambore in Rajasthan and Kanha and Bandhavgarh in Madhya Pradesh, but with almost a hundred national parks in the country there's something for every taste.

Also recommended

● **Cool out in a hill station** Get away from the steamy heat of the plains in Kodaikanal in the Western Ghats, Ooty (Udhagamandalam) in the Nilgiri Hills, Munnar in Kerala or Darjeeling in the Himalayan foothills; fine scenery (stunning vistas of Kanchenjunga, the third-highest mountain in the world from Darjeeling), trekking, tea and often quaint journeys all add to the character and charm.

▲ Family fun on Chowpatty beach, Mumbai

- **Dharamsala** Through the high profile of one resident, the Dalai Lama, Dharamsala – the seat of the Tibetan government in exile – is now world famous. Thanks to the large Tibetan population and influence in the area, this is a great place to take meditation courses, shop for Tibetan trinkets, see Tibetan folk opera and even, if you get lucky, shake hands with the Dalai Lama himself. It is also easy to arrange local treks into the Dhauladhar range.

- **Amritsar** At the heart of the holy city of the Sikhs stands the sumptuous sixteenth-century Golden Temple, encircled by a sacred lake and constantly thronged by pilgrims in their finest ceremonial dress. Arrive at sunrise for the most awesome effect of gilt on water, then walk slowly through the long white marble colonnades that frame the lake; cross the causeway to enter the Golden Temple itself; and finally join the pilgrims for the free meal of chapatti and dhal, dished out to all visitors twice a day.

- **Khajuraho** The 25 Hindu and Jain temples here date back to the tenth century and are built of sandstone, with almost every facade carved into exuberantly erotic sculptures and friezes, depicting in graphic and beautiful detail a whole encyclopedia of Kamasutra-like entanglements.

- **Gangotri Glacier trek** The sacred frozen source of the River Ganges is spectacularly positioned amid spiky snow-clad peaks at 5000m above sea level, but is fairly easily reached along a seventeen-kilometre pilgrims' route.

- **Play an extra in an Indian film** India's film industry, known as Bollywood, is based in Mumbai and produces twice as many movies as Hollywood each year. Non-Indians are invariably needed to pad out the cast, so hang out at Colaba Causeway in the City where many movie hopefuls are recruited.

- **Snorkelling and diving in the Andaman islands** This glorious archipelago of two hundred picture-perfect islands lies 100km off India's east coast. Tourism is a growing industry but it's still about as far off the beaten track as you can get in India.

- **Learn meditation** From Rishikesh and Dharamsala in the north down to Kerala in the south, India is awash with well-established centres for learning and practicing meditation which are set up to cater for foreigners. See p.45 for more details.

INDIA

Festivals

January/February/March Kumbh Mela. A major three-yearly festival held in turn in the four holy cities – Nasik, Ujjain, Haridwar and Prayag (Allahabad) – where drops of nectar fell from Vishnu's pot. Each draws millions of pilgrims, including huge numbers of sadhus, to bathe in the holy river at auspicious moments. The Maha (Great) Kumbh Mela held every twelve years in Allahabad (next in 2013) is the largest of all.

April/May Thrissur Puram. Kerala's biggest temple festival involves a procession with more than a hundred fabulously ornamented elephants.

June/July Hemis Festival. Celebrating the victory of Buddhism over evil at the temple of Hemis in Ladakh; highly unusual masked dances (chaam) are the centrepiece.

June/July Rath Yatra. Puri and other Southern Indian temples celebrate Krishna's journey to Mathura; three gigantic chariots bedecked with coloured canopies are pulled through the streets by devotees.

November Pushkar Camel Fair. The largest livestock market in the world draws more than 200,000 people. The

www.roughguides.com

247

WHERE TO GO

fair coincides with a Hindu pilgrimage to Pushkar, one of the holiest of Hindu cities.

Routes in and out

There are international airports in Delhi (Indira Gandhi International Airport), Ahmedabad, Amritsar, Bangalore, Chennai, Cochin, Goa, Guwahati, Hyderabad, Kolkata, Mumbai and Thiruvananthapuram. Local politics permitting, you can also enter and depart India overland at the border crossings with Pakistan (near Amritsar); Nepal (from Banbassa, Gorakhpur, Raxaul, Kakarbhitta, Nepalganj and Dhangadhi); Bangladesh (from Haridaspur to the northeast of Kolkata, Dawki in Assam, Burimari in West Bengal, Agartala in Tripura, Balurghat in West Bengal and Lalgola in West Bengal); and Sri Lanka, which is currently only accessible by air.

India online

Best Indian Websites – Ⓦwww .bestindiansites.com If it isn't here, it doesn't exist. This is the place to start on any search for anything Indian – it's not the prettiest site in the world but it does what it says on the tin.

Indiamarks – Ⓦwww.indiamarks.com Site full of short, easily digestible guides to "everything India". The range is vast from "How to Cross an Indian Road and Live to Talk About it" via destination, hotel, restaurant and cultural guides to the more heavyweight political and economic stuff.

India Travelogue – Ⓦwww.india travelogue.com Magazine-style site with well-written, travel-oriented features, profiles and travelogues, plus plenty on destinations and activities.

The Times of India – Ⓦwww .timesofindia.com Daily news and features from the highly respected English-language daily.

Travel Intelligence – Ⓦwww.travel intelligence.net This is a global travel site partly dedicated to great travel writing. Search the "Destinations" for pieces on India by writers such as William Dalrymple, Isabella Tree and Justine Hardy.

Books

Elizabeth Bumiller *May you be the Mother of a Hundred Sons*. The life stories of many different Indian women – young brides, housewives, films stars, a traffic cop – are drawn together in this book by an American journalist.

William Dalrymple *White Moghuls*. Dalrymple is an excellent modern writer on India, and this tale– of the early European colonials who married Indian women – is an excellent introduction to his work, told with pace and panache. Follow it up with *The Last Mughal*.

Arundhati Roy *The God of Small Things*. Evocative, beautifully written story of caste, colonialism and personal tragedy in Kerala that successfully creates the dreamlike quality of the country.

Salman Rushdie *Midnight's Children*. The life story of a man born at the moment of India's independence mirrors the birth pangs of the new nation. The sheer exuberance of the language and the story-telling perfectly capture the country's wild energy.

Tahir Shah *The Sorcerer's Apprentice*. A rollicking ride through the underworld of Indian magic, miracles and sorcery. There are more desperate characters here than you'll ever believe possible.

Films

Fire, Earth and Water (Deepa Mehta, 1996, 1998, 2005). The beautiful but shocking Elements Trilogy explores themes such as sexuality, ethnic hatred and the plight of women, in moving detail which continues to provoke huge controversy in India, and which has won it accolades around the world.

Lagaan (Ashutosh Gowariker, 2001). Smash hit Bollywood movie that made a successful cross over to the West, featuring all of the usual Bollywood themes: good versus evil, heroes versus villains.

Salaam Bombay (Mira Nair, 1988). A harrowing depiction of the fight for survival by Krishna, a 10-year-old boy, who is tutored by a prostitute and drug addict.

Sholay (Ramesh Sippy,1975). Arguably the best Bollywood film ever made, its contemporary cops and robbers story broke all box office records. A great conversation subject on long journeys.

Slumdog Millionaire (Danny Boyle, 2008) Exuberant, rollercoaster of a movie that shows India in all its horror and colour, albeit through the lens of Hollywood.

Indian tourist offices

Ⓦ **www.incredibleindia.org**
Ⓦ **www.tourismofindia.com**
Australia Level 5, 135 King St, Glasshouse Shopping Complex, Sydney, NSW 2000 ☏02/9221 9555.
Canada 60 Bloor St West Suite #1003, Toronto, Ontario M4W 3B8 ☏416/962-3787.
New Zealand Contact the Sydney office or the embassy in Wellington.
South Africa PO Box 412542, Craighall 2024, Hyde Lane, Lancaster Gate, Johannesburg 2000 ☏011/325 0880.
UK 7 Cork St, London W1S 3LH ☏020/7437 3677.
US 1270 Ave of the Americas, Suite 1808, New York, NY 10020 ☏212-586-4901; 3550 Wilshire Blvd, Suite 204, Los Angeles, CA 90010 ☏213/380-8855.

Indian embassies and consulates

Australia 3–5 Moonah Place, Yarralumla, Canberra, ACT 2600 ☏02/6273 3999, Ⓦwww.hcindia-au.org. Consulates in Sydney ☏02/9223 9500, Ⓦwww .indianconsulatesydney.org; Perth ☏08/9221 1485; and Melbourne ☏03/9384 0141.
Canada 10 Springfield Rd, Ottawa, Ontario K1M 1C9 ☏613/744-3751, Ⓦwww.hciottawa.ca. Consulates in Toronto ☏416/960-0751, Ⓦwww .cgitoronto.ca; and Vancouver ☏604/662-8811, Ⓦwww.cgivancouver.org.
Ireland 6 Leeson Park, Dublin 6 ☏1/4970 843, Ⓦwww.indianembassy.ie.
New Zealand 180 Molesworth St, Wellington PO Box 4045 ☏4/473 6390.
South Africa 852 Schoeman St, Arcadia, Pretoria, 0083 ☏012/342 5392, Ⓦwww.indiansouthafrica.com. Consulates in Cape Town ☏021/419 8110; Durban ☏031/332 7020; and Johannesburg ☏011/4828 484.
UK India House, Aldwych, London WC2B 4NA ☏020/7836 8484, Visa line ☏0905/757 0045, Ⓦwww.hcilondon.net. Consulates in Birmingham ☏0121/212 2782, Ⓦwww.cgibirmingham.org; Edinburgh ☏0131/229 2144, Ⓦwww .cgiedinburg.org; and Belfast ☏028/9087 8787.
US 2107 Massachusetts Ave NW, Washington, DC 20008 ☏202/939-7000, Ⓦwww.indianembassy.org. Consulates in Chicago ☏312/595-0405, Ⓦwww .chicago.indianconsulate.com; Houston ☏713/626-2148, Ⓦwww.cgihouston.org; New York ☏212/774-0600, Ⓦwww .indiacgny.org; and San Francisco ☏415/668-0662, Ⓦwww.cgisf.org.

Indonesia

Capital Jakarta
Population 240 million
Language Bahasa Indonesia is the national language, with an estimated five hundred or more local languages and dialects
Currency Rupiah (Rp)
Religion Predominantly Muslim (88%), though animism is indigenous and widespread; there are also

Buddhist, Hindu and Christian minorities
Climate Tropical throughout, with nominal wet and dry seasons
Best time to visit During the dry season (May–Oct for most of the country, but Nov–April in northern Sumatra and central and northern Maluku)
Minimum daily budget US$15/£9

For scale and variety, Indonesia, the world's largest archipelago, is pretty much unbeatable. There's an immensely rich melange of peoples, religions and cultures and within this one country it's possible to encounter Westernized city dwellers with mobile phones as well as hunters armed with bows and arrows and clad in penis gourds. Each ethnic group has its own artistic heritage, and their textiles, music, arts, crafts and dance add a rich cultural dimension to visits to the islands. The added allure of fabulously varied scenery (from equatorial rainforest and volcanoes to white-sand beaches and desert terrain) and the equally diverse flora and fauna make Indonesia one of Asia's most rewarding

Mean temperatures (°C) and rainfall (mm)

Average daily temperatures (maximum and minimum °C) and monthly rainfall (mm)

	Jan	Feb	Mar	Apr	May	June	July	Aug	Sept	Oct	Nov	Dec
Jakarta (Java)												
max °C	29	29	30	31	31	31	31	31	31	31	30	29
min °C	23	23	23	24	24	23	23	23	23	23	23	23
rainfall mm	300	300	211	147	114	97	64	43	66	112	142	203
Makassar (Sulawesi)												
max °C	29	29	29	30	31	30	30	31	31	31	30	29
min °C	23	24	23	23	23	22	21	21	21	22	23	23
rainfall mm	686	536	424	150	89	74	36	10	15	43	178	610
Padang (Sumatra)												
max °C	31	31	31	31	31	31	31	31	30	30	30	30
min °C	23	23	23	24	24	23	23	23	23	23	23	23
rainfall mm	351	259	307	363	315	307	277	348	152	495	518	480

▲ Balinese rice terraces

destinations. Given the country's sheer enormity, though, you must be selective – with too little time and too much travel your trip could turn into a miserable, stressful race between islands.

Perhaps predictably, the problems of melding such diversity into one nation have resulted in violence and unrest. In recent years there have been civil disturbances, some lasting a couple of days, others long-running, in Maluku, Aceh, West Papua, West Timor and Sulawesi, and Indonesia is vulnerable to both manmade as well as natural disasters. However, it is important not to overstate the risks. Given the vastness of the country, difficulties in one region often barely affect another a few hundred kilometres away. Before you travel, it's vital to get up-to-date information from newspapers and the official websites listed on p.348. It's also worth noting that travel through Muslim areas (this doesn't include Bali) during Ramadan, the traditional month of fasting, can be hard going as local people don't eat, drink or smoke during daylight hours.

Main attractions

● **Bali** With its fabulous mix of beaches, volcanoes, temples, stunning scenery and artistic and cultural wealth, the island has long been the jewel in the Indonesian tourism crown. Bali is the enclave of a unique and colourful form of Hinduism, and of its thousands of temples Besakih, Tanah Lot and Uluwatu are the three most impressive. The festivals celebrated at all these shrines are a vibrant celebration of the devout traditional lifestyle that has drawn tourists to the island for decades. The gorgeous and varied beach resorts, the artistic centre of Ubud, the mountains in the volcanic centre of the island and the diving and surfing offshore are the other main draws.

● **Gunung Bromo** The obligatory sunrise views of this mountain in east Java, with the peak and its equally stunning neighbours rising from an almost other-worldly sea of sand, are simply spellbinding. There are also plenty of walks to enjoy in this cool, attractive region.

www.roughguides.com

251

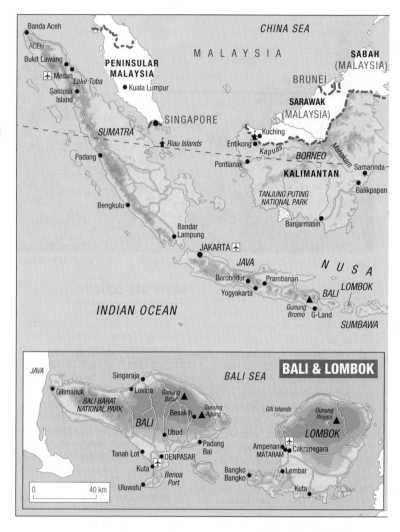

● **Borobodur** Java's number-one tourist attraction, this colossal, multi-tiered temple is the world's largest Buddhist stupa. Over a thousand years old, the temple, though now ruined, is still surprisingly evocative, with over three thousand reliefs detailing scenes from everyday life and the path followed by the soul to enlightenment.

● **Lake Toba** In northern Sumatra, this is Southeast Asia's largest freshwater lake. Its central island, Samosir, is the heartland of the Toba Batak people and offers great scenery, trekking and relaxation, with the option of visiting megalithic stone complexes, local villages and hot springs.

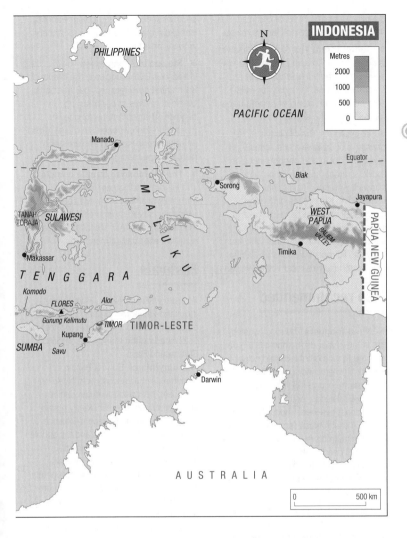

Metres
2000
1000
500
0

0   500 km

- **Orang-utans** The animals at the orang-utan rehabilitation centre at Bukit Lawang in Sumatra are arguably the most famous example of Indonesia's wildlife. The centre aims to reintroduce orang-utans into the wild that have been rescued from captivity; visitors here are welcome to watch the twice-daily feeding sessions.

- **Komodo Dragons** An apparent throwback to the age of dinosaurs, these creatures, actually the world's largest lizards, live on Komodo in Nusa Tenggara, the chain of islands stretching between Bali and West Papua.

- **Diving** The highlight of many visits, Indonesia's marine life is startling in its diversity. Current centres for diving are Bali, the Gili islands off Lombok, and Sulawesi.

• **Tanah Toraja** This region of Sulawesi is home to the Torajan people, who have a wealth of traditional architecture and ceremonies, most famously funerals. Also on offer are plenty of opportunities for trekking in the scenic highlands.

• **Yogyakarta** The city is the heartland of Javanese arts; exhibitions of art and batik, and performances of music, drama, puppetry and dance abound, with courses available for visitors. The Kraton, the old walled city, is well preserved and Yogyakarta is ideally placed for excursions into the surrounding countryside and – if it hasn't blown its lid recently – treks up Gunung Merapi, Indonesia's most volatile volcano.

Also recommended

• **Nusa Tenggara** The most westerly of this string of islands, Lombok, is a great antidote to its more developed neighbour, Bali. Its highlights include Gunung Rinjani, Indonesia's second highest mountain; the tiny Gili Islands; and the unspoilt south-coast beaches. The further east you go through Nusa Tenggara, the less tourist infrastructure there is, so the more time you'll need; highlights here include Sumba's unspoilt beaches and traditional ikat weaving and the three-coloured lake of Keli Mutu on Flores.

• **Baliem Valley in West Papua** It's time-consuming and expensive to get here, and to really explore the area you'll need to trek long distances and often sleep extremely rough. But the scenery is dramatic and splendid, and the tribes of the area are managing to retain an age-old lifestyle and culture, often despite considerable pressure from outsiders.

• **Surfing** G-Land off the south coast of Java and Desert Point off the

southwest coast of Lombok at Bangko Bangko are just two of many legendary Indonesian surf spots.

• **Staying in a longhouse** The indigenous Dyak peoples in the interior of Kalimantan have retained their traditional beliefs and ways of life to varying degrees. Their communal longhouse dwellings – long wooden structures raised on stilts – have survived and are being restored, and many welcome visitors.

• **The Prambanan temple complex** The Hindu temples here, accessed from Yogyakarta in Java, are soaring, intricately carved structures dating from the ninth century AD. Visits at dawn and dusk are especially atmospheric.

Festivals

February/March Nyale. Hundreds of thousands flock to the coasts in search of an aphrodisiac seaworm in this festival celebrated on the islands of Lombok, Sumba and Savu.
February/March Sumba Pasola. Occurring simultaneously with Nyale on the coast, the pasola features battles between hundreds of fabulously attired horsemen, and takes place to balance the sphere of the heavens and the sphere of the sea by the spilling of blood.
June–September Torajan funerals. Taking place over several days, funerals in Tanah Toraja in Sulawesi are accompanied by ceremonies, buffalo fights and sacrifices.
All year Bali temple festivals. Featuring gorgeously clad worshippers, offerings and gamelan music, temple festivals in Bali occur throughout the year.
All year Bali cremations. Ceremonial music, dance and the spectacular burning itself make this the most dramatic manifestation of religious observance on the island. Visitors are welcomed as long as they observe cultural guidelines.

Routes in and out

There are 37 designated gateways for foreigners entering and leaving Indonesia. For citizens of eligible countries visas for stays up to thirty days can be bought on entry – for a longer stay or if you are not one of the eligible nationalities you'll need a visa in advance from an Indonesian embassy or consulate. Potential visitors should check the current situation prior to travel. Indonesia boasts a huge choice of international airports, the busiest of which are in Jakarta, Denpasar (on Bali) and Medan (on Sumatra). There are fast and frequent passenger ferries from Malaysia and Singapore, mostly arriving in the Riau islands to the east of Sumatra; and an overland route from Malaysia into Kalimantan at Entikong.

Indonesia online

Bali Paradise Online – Ⓦwww.bali -paradise.com Wide-ranging site covering everything from traditional architecture to nightlife recommendations. There's also a travellers' forum.

Forum Makassar Straits – Ⓦwww .forumms.com Questions, messages, articles and photos about the coastal areas of South Sulawesi – picturesque and inspiring.

Inside Indonesia – Ⓦwww.inside indonesia.org Online topical magazine, published in Australia and detailing politics, government shortcomings and human rights and social issues across the country plus reviews of relevant books. Always interesting and hard-hitting, this is Indonesia from a different perspective.

Jakarta Post – Ⓦwww.thejakarta post.com The online version of the daily English-language newspaper that, despite its name, covers the entire country.

Orangutan Foundation International – Ⓦwww.orangutan.org This international organization is involved in the preservation of orang-utans. Their website is an excellent starting point for information on this remarkable creature.

Books

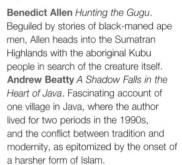

Benedict Allen *Hunting the Gugu*. Beguiled by stories of black-maned ape men, Allen heads into the Sumatran Highlands with the aboriginal Kubu people in search of the creature itself.

Andrew Beatty *A Shadow Falls in the Heart of Java*. Fascinating account of one village in Java, where the author lived for two periods in the 1990s, and the conflict between tradition and modernity, as epitomized by the onset of a harsher form of Islam.

Elizabeth Gilbert *Eat, Pray, Love*. Funny, insightful, best-selling account of a thirty-something writer's journey of self-discovery. Her quest ranges through Italy and India and climaxes in Bali, whose culture she sees as combining the spiritual and sensual in perfect harmony.

Pramoedya Ananta Toer *All That is Gone*. A wonderful introduction to an Indonesian icon, this collection of eight short stories draws on the author's childhood in east Java. His 37 books and essays have been translated into 37 languages.

Simon Winchester *Krakatoa*. Fine account of how and why the great volcano off the coast of Java erupted in 1883 and what happened afterwards.

Films

Arisan (Nia Dinata, 2004). An ensemble piece about a group of rich thirty-something Jakartans, including, rather bravely for Indonesia, two gay characters. The movie quickly dispels any idea that everyone in Indonesia is poor and needy.

Looking for Madonna (John De Rantau, 2004). A powerful mix of drama and documentary woven around HIV/AIDS in West Papua, which has the highest rates of these diseases in the country.

Opera Jawa (Garin Nugroho, 2006). Beautifully filmed, highly evocative musical based loosely on a famous scene from the Ramayana myth. The soundtrack of traditional Indonesian gamelan is glorious, as are the sets.

Pasir Berbisik (Whispering Sands; Nan T Achnas, 2001). One of the few female film directors working in Indonesia produced this dramatic film of death, destruction and violence, as a single mother and her teenage daughter flee across the desert in search of a new life.

The Year of Living Dangerously (Peter Weir, 1983). Adapted from a novel by Christopher Koch, this moody film focuses on a group of Western journalists and photographers in Indonesia to cover the upheavals of 1965, and superbly delineates the tensions and undercurrents in the country.

Indonesian tourist offices

Ⓦ www.tourismindonesia.com
Contact the information desk at the nearest embassy.

Indonesian embassies and consulates

Ⓦ www.deplu.go.id
Australia 8 Darwin Ave, Yarralumla, Canberra, ACT 2600 ☏ 02/6250 8600,

Ⓦ www.kbri-canberra.org.au. Consulates in Darwin ☏ 08/8943 0200, Ⓦ www .kri-darwin.org; Melbourne ☏ 03/9525 2755, Ⓦ www.kjri-melbourne.org; Perth ☏ 08/9221 5858, Ⓦ www.kri-perth.org .au; Sydney ☏ 02/9344 9933, Ⓦ www .indonrsianconsulatesydney.org.au.

Canada 55 Parkdale Ave, Ottawa, Ontario K1Y 1E5 ☏ 613/724-1100, Ⓦ www.indonesia-ottawa.org. Consulates in Toronto ☏ 416/360-4020, Ⓦ www .indonesiatoronto.org; and Vancouver, ☏ 604/682-8855, Ⓦ www.indonesia vancouver.org.

New Zealand 70 Glen Rd, Kelburn, Wellington ☏ 04/475 8697, Ⓦ www .indonesianembassy.org.nz. Consulate in Auckland ☏ 09/308 0842.

South Africa 949 Schoeman St, Arcadia, Pretoria 0083 ☏ 012/342 3350, Ⓦ www.indonesia-pretoria.org.za. Consulate in Cape Town 7708 ☏ 021/761 7015, Ⓦ www.indonesia -capetown.org.za.

UK and Ireland 38 Grosvenor Sq, London W1K 2HW (personal callers: 38a Adams Row, W1K 2HW) ☏ 020/7499 7661, Ⓦ www.indonesian embassy.org.uk.

US 2020 Massachusetts Ave NW, Washington, DC 20036 ☏ 202/775-5200, Ⓦ www.embassyofindonesia.org. Consulates in Chicago ☏ 312/920-1880, Ⓦ www.indonesiachicago.org; Honolulu ☏ 808/531-3017; Houston ☏ 713/785-1691, Ⓦ www.kjri-houston.net; Los Angeles ☏ 213/383-5126, Ⓦ www .kjri-la.net; New York ☏ 212/879-0600, Ⓦ www.indonesianewyork.org; San Francisco ☏ 415/474-9571, Ⓦ www .kjrisfo.org.

Japan

Capital Tokyo
Population 127 million
Language Japanese
Currency Yen (¥)
Main religions Shintoism and Mahayana Buddhism

Climate Temperate
Best time to go March–May and September–November, with cherry blossom time (April) and maple leaf season (Nov) the most rewarding
Minimum daily budget US$65/£39

Lying east off continental Asia, across the Sea of Japan from Russia, China and Korea, the Japanese archipelago comprises over six thousand volcanic islands, though the bulk of the population lives on the main island of Honshu, which is linked by bridges and tunnels to the other three main islands of Hokkaido, Kyushu and Shikoku.

Many Westerners imagine this isolated island nation to be a cold-hearted country of futuristic machinery and an obsessive work ethic, but beneath the label-conscious, hi-tech veneer, Japan is still a very traditional society, with an absorbingly ancient culture to investigate, from Zen temples to fire festivals and tea ceremonies to sumo wrestling matches. Some of the most arresting sights are the majestic Buddhist temples and the contrastingly kitsch Shinto shrines; the latter in particular are still an important focus of daily life, with devotees coming here to pray for everything from a new baby to respectable exam results. Twenty-first century Japan, meanwhile, provides the perfect contrast, full of sleek architecture, crazy fashions and intriguing technological innovations.

As the archipelago stretches over 3000km from north to south, running from the chilly end of the temperate zone to tropical Okinawa in the south, there are varied and plentiful hiking opportunities – in Honshu's Japan Alps; in the mountains, gorges and lakes of the northern island of Hokkaido; and in the national parks on the southern island of Kyushu.

Foreign tourists are rare outside the main cultural centres, but are generally welcomed warmly. Language is a problem for visitors to Japan, but foreigners usually find they can make themselves understood and there is an increasing number of signs in Roman script. Public transport is fast, efficient and extensive (this is, after all, the home of the Bullet Train).

Despite all its attractions, very few budget travellers make it to Japan, for the simple reason that they can't afford it. The cost of living is high compared with the rest of Asia, so for backpackers, one of the best ways to experience the country is to get an English-teaching job here for a few months (see p.87). Otherwise, buy a train pass, bring a tent and don't hang out in too many coffee shops or pinball parlours.

Main attractions

● **Kyoto** This historic former capital city should be at the top of every visitor's list. It has scores of breath-taking Buddhist temples, some of the country's finest Zen gardens, and lovely neighbourhoods of wooden homes and traditional tea houses. Don't miss the 1001 gilded statues of Buddha at Sanjusangen-do temple, Ginkakuji's Temple of the Silver Pavilion, or the inspirational Ryoan-ji rock garden. The modern face of Kyoto is energetic and youthful, with good bars, clubs and restaurants, and there are invigorating hill walks within day-tripping distance.

● **Tokyo** Japan's modern-day capital lacks the refined aesthetic of Kyoto, or the tranquillity of Nara, but comes up trumps with its contemporary icons, like the forest of sci-fi skyscrapers that dominates the Shinjuku district, the ever-changing gadgets exhibited in the Sony Building and the hyper-trendy street fashions and boutiques of Harajuku. Historic highlights include the country's most venerated Shinto shrine, Meiji-jingu, and the impressive Senso-ji temple, while the old-style early-morning Tsukiji fish market makes a lively contrast with the shopping malls of super-chic

Ginza, the latest gizmos on sale in Akihabara's "Electronics Town" and the cutting-edge clubs in Roppongi.

● **Hiroshima** Many visitors to Japan make a pilgrimage to Hiroshima's excellent Peace Memorial Museum, a balanced commemoration of the dropping of the atomic bomb here on August 6, 1945, and its horrific repercussions. The regenerated city has a breezy, upbeat atmosphere and is a pleasure to explore. Just a twenty-minute ferry ride away is the little island of Miyajima, site of one of Japan's most scenically located Shinto shrines.

● **Mount Fuji** Although the walk to the top of Japan's iconic snow-capped peak takes a gruelling six hours, thousands of people make it up to the 3776-metre summit every summer. Unfortunately, the tracks are always heaving with hikers, the mountainside is strewn with unattractive volcanic debris and, due to persistent haze, the views are rarely spectacular. A better way to appreciate Fuji-san is to climb nearby Mount Tenjo, which you can do in just 45 minutes, giving you the chance to admire Mount Fuji from a more

Mean temperatures (°C) and rainfall (mm)

Average daily temperatures (maximum and minimum °C) and monthly rainfall (mm)

	Jan	Feb	Mar	Apr	May	June	July	Aug	Sept	Oct	Nov	Dec
Tokyo												
max °C	10	10	13	18	23	25	29	31	27	21	17	12
min °C	1	1	4	10	15	18	22	24	20	14	8	3
rainfall mm	110	155	228	254	244	305	254	203	279	228	162	96
Sapporo												
max °C	2	2	6	13	18	21	24	26	22	17	11	5
min °C	-10	-10	-7	-1	3	10	16	18	12	6	-1	-6
rainfall mm	25	43	61	84	102	160	188	155	160	147	56	38
Nagasaki												
max °C	9	10	14	19	23	26	29	31	27	22	17	12
min °C	2	2	5	10	14	18	23	23	20	14	9	4
rainfall mm	71	84	125	185	170	312	257	175	249	114	94	81

interesting perspective. Or, more leisurely still, take a slow train ride through the surrounding Hakone region, an area of lakes and hot springs which also offers fine views of the sacred peak.

- **A night in a ryokan** These traditional inns are like a genuine step backwards in time; the rooms have *tatami* mat floors, sumptuous futons, sliding paper doors and views onto traditional Japanese gardens. Everyone pads around in their socks, and you can often ask to have dinner served on low tables in your room.

Also recommended

- **The Tono valley** For a glimpse of traditional life in rural Japan, hire a bike for a day's cycling here, visiting some of the restored eighteenth-century farmhouses and stopping in at one of the local folk museums.

- **Kenrokuen in the city of Kanazawa** Japanese gardens have inspired designers all over the world, and Kenrokuen, the country's top garden, is a classic composition of ponds, pine trees, contemplative vistas and graceful teahouses.

- **Nikko** Set in a huge forested park of mountains, lakes and waterfalls, this complex of elaborately carved and gaudily painted shrines and temples looks especially fantastical in the snow.

- **Nara** A popular side-trip from Kyoto, and also a former capital, Nara is dotted with venerable temples and shrines, in particular the historic Todai-ji temple, housing a fifteen-metre-high bronze Buddha.

- **Hiking in Kirishima National Park** The southern island of Kyushu boasts the most dramatic volcanic scenery in the country, nowhere more so than in Kirishima National Park, which has

23 peaks within its boundaries. There are plenty of bracing mountain trails here, plus waterfalls, an impressive gorge and an outdoor hot spring.

- **Hokkaido** The northernmost of Japan's four main islands is also its wildest and least populated. The volcanic landscape is dotted with lakes and forests and Shiretoko National Park is especially rewarding, with five lakes linked by forest paths, plus natural hot springs and challenging trails.

- **Naoshima: Island of Modern Art** Almost the entire tiny island of Naoshima, in the Inland Sea, is devoted to modern art. Famous names fill the wall spaces, galleries and sculpture parks of both the strikingly contemporary Chichu Art Museum, designed by Tadao Ando, and Benessse House, and there are innumerable other small art spaces and installations down alleyways, on the beaches and in the hills. There's a 007 Museum too, because the island featured in Raymond's Benson's Bond novel, The Man with the Red Tattoo.

- **A session at the onsen** Bathing in outdoor hot springs is a big thing in Japan and there are many lovely spots to enjoy some communal soaking, including popular Beppu on the southern island of Kyushu.

Festivals

February 5–11 Yuki Matsuri (Snow Festival), Sapporo. The snow sculpture competition is the highlight of this genuinely winter-wonderland event, with hundreds of extraordinary carvings of life-sized buildings and figurines made from snow and ice.

March–May Cherry blossom viewing. When the cherry trees flower there are blossom-viewing parties in parks across the country and a nightly

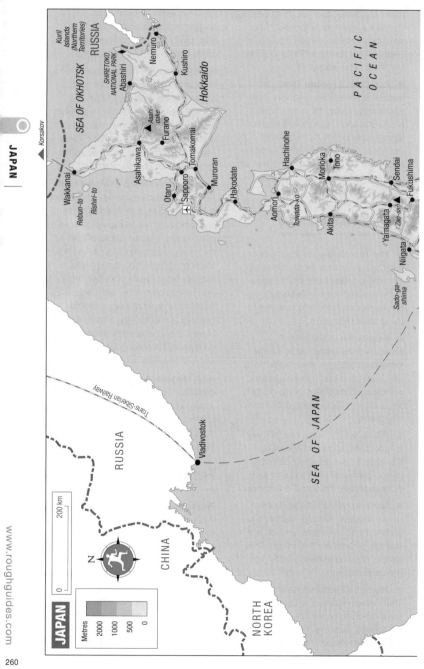

JAPAN

Metres
2000
1000
500
0

0   200 km

N

CHINA

NORTH
KOREA

RUSSIA

Vladivostok

SEA OF JAPAN

Trans-Siberian Railway

Sado-ga-
shima

Niigata

Yamagata
Zao-san

Akita

Aomori
Towada-ko

Sendai
Fukushima

Morioka
Tono

Hachinohe

PACIFIC
OCEAN

Korsakov

Kuril
Islands
(Northern
Territories)

RUSSIA

Nemuro

Kushiro

Hokkaido

SHIRETOKO
NATIONAL PARK

Abashiri

SEA OF OKHOTSK

Asahi-
dake

Furano

Asahikawa

Tomakomai

Muroran

Sapporo

Otaru

Hakodate

Wakkanai

Rebun-to
Rishiri-to

www.roughguides.com

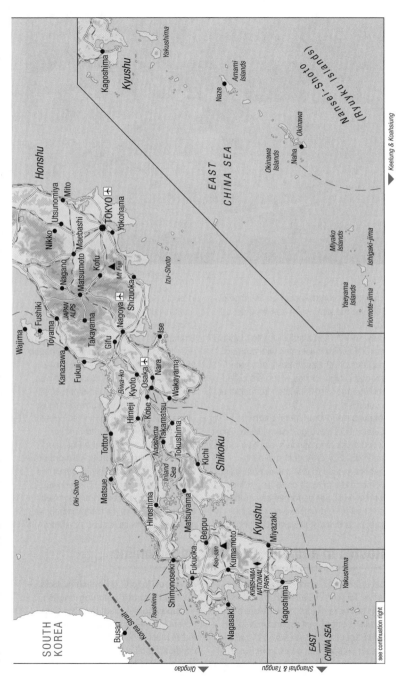

▲ *Keeling & Kaohsiung*

South Korea

Busan

Korea Strait

Tsushima

Shimonoseki

Fukuoka

Nagasaki

Aso-san

Kumamoto

KIRISHIMA NATIONAL PARK

Kagoshima

Yakushima

Kyushu

Miyazaki

Matsuyama

Beppu

Hiroshima

Matsue

Tottori

Oki-Shoto

Naruto

Takamatsu

Tokushima

Kochi

Shikoku

Inland Sea

Himeji

Kobe

Osaka

Kyoto

Biwa-ko

Nara

Wakayama

Fukui

Kanazawa

Takayama

Gifu

Nagoya

Ise

Toyama

Fushiki

Wajima

JAPAN ALPS

Matsumoto

Nagano

Kofu

Shizuoka

Mt Fuji

Izu-Shoto

Nikko

Utsunomiya

Maebashi

Mito

TOKYO

Yokohama

Honshu

Kagoshima

Kyushu

Yakushima

Naze

Amami Islands

Nansei-Shoto (Ryukyu Islands)

EAST CHINA SEA

Okinawa Islands

Naha

Okinawa

Miyako Islands

Yaeyama Islands

Iriomote-jima

Ishigaki-jima

see continuation right

EAST CHINA SEA

see continuation right

▲ *Qingdao*

▲ *Shanghai & Tanggu*

▲ Rituals of the ring: sumo wrestlers in Tokyo

cherry-blossom forecast on TV shows how far the pink wave has progressed up the country.

July 16–17 Gion Matsuri, Kyoto. Japan's cultural capital celebrates with a grand pageant of 32 sumptuously decorated six-metre-high shrines which are pulled through the streets by men in traditional costumes.

August Kodo Drummers' Earth Celebration, Sado-ga-shima Island. The world music and dance event held over three days every August makes the perfect excuse to visit this remote island, home to the famous drumming troupe, whose muscular performances at their colossal *taiko* drums are an amazing spectacle that's well worth catching.

Routes in and out

Japan's main international airports are in the Tokyo and Osaka areas, the latter convenient for Kyoto, and there are smaller international airports in Nagoya and Sapporo. You can also arrive and depart by sea, with boats from Busan

in South Korea to Fukuoka (Kyushu) and Shimonoseki (Honshu); and from China there are ferry services from Shanghai to Osaka/Kobe, from Tanggu near Tiangin to Kobe, and from Qingdao to Shimonoseki. There are also ferries from Keelung and Koahsiung in Taiwan to Okinawa (Japan's southernmost island); from Vladivostok (the terminus of the Trans-Siberian rail line in Russia, see p.28; July–Oct only) to Fushiki, near Toyama; and from the Russian port of Korsakov to Wakkanai (northern Hokkaido; July–Sept only). Consult the Japan National Tourist Office website (Ⓦwww.seejapan.co.uk/transport/sea /international.html) for a comprehensive rundown of timetables and operators.

Japan online

All About Teaching English in Japan – Ⓦ**www.all-about-teaching-english -in-japan.com** A great resource that covers everything from qualification requirements and interviews to dodgy contracts and finding an apartment.

**Japan Guide – Ⓦwww.japan-guide
.com** Impressively detailed coverage of
sights, culture and shopping, plus hostel
booking and a forum.

**Outdoor Japan – Ⓦwww.outdoor
japan.com** Especially good on cycling
and mountain-biking routes.

**Quirky Japan Homepage – Ⓦwww
.quirkyjapan.or.tv** All sorts of great
stuff here, from the downright nutty
(such as a specialist shop for people
who collect beetles) to ideas for unusual
places to visit.

**Randy Johnson's Japan Page –
Ⓦwww.ease.com/~randyj/japan
.htm** Extensive homepage with an
especially good section on getaways
in rural Japan, complete with descriptions, accommodation ideas and
directions.

Books

Shoichi Aoki *Fresh Fruits*. A style classic.
Teen street-fashion portraits from the
famously creative and style-conscious
Harajuku neighbourhood in Tokyo, culled
from the cult Japanese fanzine of the
same name.

Alan Booth *The Roads to Sata:
A 2000-mile Walk Through Japan*.
The classic travel book on Japan,
written with humour, affection and
occasional irritation by a long-time
resident who literally walked the length
of the country.

Will Ferguson *Hokkaido Highway
Blues*. The opinionated Canadian
English teacher author proves to be
good company as we follow him on his
journey across Japan, hitchhiking from
the southern tip of Kyushu to northern
Hokkaido in the wake of the cherry
blossom wave.

Haruki Murakami *The Wind-up Bird
Chronicle*. The most famous of the
novels written by Japan's best known

contemporary novelist follows an
increasingly disoriented modern-day
Japanese Everyman through a bizarre
chain of mysterious encounters.

Banana Yoshimoto *Kitchen*. A
bestseller when first published in 1988,
this modern love story was derided
by some as superficial but is still a
touching tale of bereavement and
bonding. The author has since become
one of Japan's most famous female
novelists.

Films

Akira (Katushiro Otomo, 1988).
Groundbreakingly slick – and gory –
anime based on a hugely popular manga
series, involving delinquent biker boys,
supernatural powers and corrupt power-
mongers fighting it out in post-World
War III neo-Tokyo.

Lost in Translation (Sofia Coppola,
2004). Tokyo is the real star in this story
of two unhappy, dislocated strangers
who bond during a brief stay in Japan.
The city looks great in all its sleek, high-
energy strangeness, but beware the
liberal sprinkling of clichés.

Rashomon (Akira Kurosawa, 1950).
Akira Kurosawa's classic and hugely
influential drama in which a rape and
a murder are described from the four
protagonists' different points of view.

Spirited Away (Hayao Miyazaki, 2001).
Beautifully designed animated classic
in which a sulky ten-year-old girl gets
drawn into a strange spirit world where
she faces many character-testing
challenges and difficult personalities.

Tokyo Story (Ozu Yasujiro, 1954).
This slow, rather mournful meditation
on changing values in modern Japan
follows an elderly couple as they pay an
extended visit to their grown-up children
in Tokyo.

www.roughguides.com

Japanese tourist offices

ⓦ www.jnto.go.jp

Australia and New Zealand Level 7, 36 Clarence St, Sydney NSW 2000 ☎02/9279 2177, ⓦwww.jnto.org.au.

Canada 481 University Avenue, Suite 306, Toronto, ON M5G 2E9 ☎416/366-7140, ⓦwww.jnto.go.jp/canada.

South Africa Contact the UK office.

UK and Ireland 5th Floor, 12 Nicholas Lane, London, EC4N 7BN ☎020/7398 5678, ⓦwww.seejapan.co.uk.

US ⓦwww.japantravelinfo.com. Little Tokyo Plaza 340 E. 2nd Street, Suite 302, Los Angeles, CA 90012 ☎213/623-1952; One Rockefeller Plaza #1250, New York, NY 10020 ☎212/757-5640.

Japanese embassies and consulates

Australia 112 Empire Circuit, Yarralumla, Canberra, ACT 2600 ☎02/6273 3244, ⓦwww.au.emb-japan.go.jp. Consulates in Brisbane ☎07/3221 5188, ⓦwww .brisbane.au.emb-japan.go.jp; Melbourne ☎03/9639 3244, ⓦwww.melbourne.au .emb-japan.go.jp; Perth ☎08/9480 1800, ⓦwww.perth.au.emb-japan.go.jp; and Sydney ☎02/9231 3455, ⓦwww.sydney .au.emb-japan.go.jp.

Canada 255 Sussex Drive, Ottawa, Ontario K1N 9E6 ☎613/241-8541, ⓦwww.ca.emb-japan.go.jp. Consulates in Montreal ☎514/866-3429, ⓦwww .montreal.ca.emb-japan.go.jp; Toronto ☎416/363-7038, ⓦwww.toronto.ca .emb-japan.go.jp; and Vancouver ☎604/684-5868, ⓦwww.vancouver.ca .emb-japan.go.jp.

Ireland Nutley Building, Merrion Centre, Nutley Lane, Dublin 4 ☎01/202 8300, ⓦwww.ie.emb-japan.go.jp.

New Zealand Level 18, Majestic Centre, 100 Willis St, Wellington 1 ☎04/473-1540, ⓦwww.nz.emb-japan .go.jp. Consulates in Auckland ☎09/303-4106, ⓦwww.nz.emb-japan .go.jp/auckland; and Christchurch ☎03/366-5680, ⓦwww.nz.emb-japan .go.jp/christchurch.

South Africa 259 Baines St, Groenkloof, Pretoria 0181 ☎012/452-1500, ⓦwww .japan.org.za. Consulate in Cape Town ☎021/425-1695.

UK 101 Piccadilly, London W1V 9FN ☎020/7465 6500, ⓦwww.uk.emb -japan.go.jp. Consulate in Edinburgh ☎0131/225 4777, ⓦwww.edinburgh.uk .emb-japan.go.jp.

US 2520 Massachusetts Ave NW, Washington, DC 20008 ☎202/238-6700, ⓦwww.us.emb-japan.go.jp. Consulates in Chicago ☎312/280-0400, ⓦwww .chicago.us.emb-japan.go.jp; Los Angeles ☎213/617-6700, ⓦwww.la.us.emb-japan .go.jp; New York ☎212/371-8222, ⓦwww.ny.us.emb-japan.go.jp; and San Francisco ☎415/777-3533, ⓦwww .cgjsf.org.

Laos

Capital Vientiane	**Main religion** Theravada Buddhism
Population 6 million	**Climate** Tropical
Language Lao	**Best time to go** November–March
Currency Kip (K)	**Minimum daily budget** US$15/£9

Laos is the most traditional corner of Southeast Asia, much less well known to the outside world than neighbouring Thailand and Vietnam. Though ruled by France as part of its Indochinese empire for the first half of the twentieth century, and then fatefully embroiled in the American-Vietnam War of the 1960s and 70s, Laos faded from view between 1975 and 1989 when a revolutionary communist government took over, forbidding contact with the outside world and imposing dogmatic political and economic reforms. Great hardship ensued and, despite recent liberalization, Laos continues to be much poorer and less developed than other Southeast Asian nations.

For visitors, however, the old-fashioned lifestyles and traditional rural ways of the Lao people hold great appeal, not least because tourism is still in its infancy. There are minimal tourist facilities outside the two main cities of Vientiane and Louang Phabang, and with no beaches and few historical gems to write home about, it's not everyone's idea of a great holiday destination. But those who do make it here rave about the dramatic river landscapes, the easy-going, unhurried pace of daily life, and the chance to experience a culture that's still relatively unchanged by contact with the West. It's no accident that Louang Phabang comes out top in many surveys on travellers' favourite cities in the world. If you do venture out into the sticks, you'll need to learn some Lao phrases, but you can get by in English in the main towns.

Because it has borders with Thailand, Vietnam and China, Laos works well as part of a leisurely overland trip. Indeed, journeys in Laos generally have to be leisurely, because public transport is frustratingly slow and roads are buttock-crunchingly potholed. Many visitors stick to the rivers – a more scenic, though not always more comfortable, way of getting between towns. Unfortunately, the domestic airlines are not the answer either, as they have a poor safety record on many routes, and run to an erratic schedule.

Many areas of Laos were very heavily bombed during the American-Vietnam War and, away from the main tourist areas, there is a real danger of stepping on unexploded ordnance and landmines. Always stick to well-trodden paths, and pay attention to warning signs. The other no-go area is local romances: it's illegal for foreigners to have sex with a local, unless officially married under Lao law, and suspects sometimes have their hotel rooms raided.

Main attractions

● **Louang Phabang** The former Lao capital is the most elegant and attractive city in the country, an almost village-like, UNESCO-listed gem whose riverbanks and cobblestoned lanes are lined with the graceful gilded spires of dozens of Buddhist temples. Other highlights include the Royal Palace Museum, which was home to the Lao royal family until their exile in 1975; the markets; and the view of the city from the north bank of the Mekong River.

● **The slow boat down the Mekong from Houayxai to Louang Phabang** Despite the obvious drawbacks – the trip takes two days and the boats are designed to carry cargo, not passengers – this continues to be

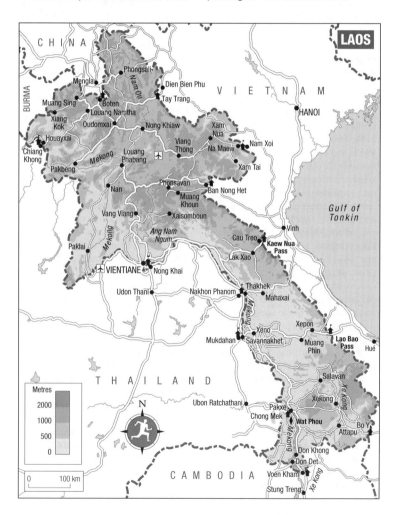

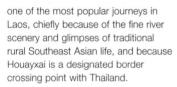

Mean temperatures (°C) and rainfall (mm)

Average daily temperatures (maximum and minimum °C) and monthly rainfall (mm)

	Jan	Feb	Mar	Apr	May	June	July	Aug	Sept	Oct	Nov	Dec
Vientiane												
max °C	28	30	33	34	32	32	31	31	31	31	29	28
min °C	14	17	19	23	23	24	24	24	24	21	18	16
rainfall mm	5	15	38	99	267	302	267	292	302	109	15	3
Louang Phabang												
max °C	28	32	34	36	35	34	32	32	33	32	29	27
min °C	13	14	17	21	23	23	23	23	23	21	18	15
rainfall mm	15	18	31	109	163	155	231	300	165	79	31	13

LAOS

one of the most popular journeys in Laos, chiefly because of the fine river scenery and glimpses of traditional rural Southeast Asian life, and because Houayxai is a designated border crossing point with Thailand.

● **Vientiane** The Lao capital is surprisingly gentle and, though lacking outstanding sights, gives a pleasant introduction to the country. Make the most of its eateries, as the city serves the best food in the country.

● **Don Det** A tiny island within the Mekong River wetlands in far southern Laos, this rural, slow-paced idyll is a backpackers' favourite, with its riverside hammocks, rare freshwater dolphins and cycling and hiking routes across adjacent Don Khon island. Life is very traditional in this area; mains electricity is still only a rumour and fishing and rice farming are the main occupations.

● **The Plain of Jars** Drawing its name from the hundreds of mysterious two-thousand-year-old stone funerary urns that lie scattered across the uplands of Xieng Khuang, the Plain of Jars is best appreciated from the air. Flying in from Vientiane gives you a gripping view of the plain's dramatic karst scenery and some of the most scarred landscape in Laos – the result of relentless bombing,

mostly by the Americans, in the 1964–73 war. Ground-level tours across the plain leave from nearby Phonsavan, but the history of the jars is more interesting than the urns themselves.

Also recommended

● **Vang Viang** Set in a spectacular landscape of limestone karst, this laid-back little riverside town is a backpackers' haven. Not far from Vientiane, it offers good-value guesthouses, interesting caves nearby and the chance to soak up the scenery while floating downriver in a huge inner tube.

● **Muang Sing** This remote little northwest town is mainly of interest for its population of hill tribespeople, who trade at the now rather overtouristed morning market and whose nearby villages are a major highlight of the burgeoning local trekking industry. There are plenty of guesthouses catering for the growing number of backpackers who visit, though the authorities have clamped down hard on opium, which is grown and smoked by local tribespeople and used to be the big draw.

● **The ruins of Wat Phou** This seventh-century temple, built by the ancient Khmers in similar style to their temples at Angkor in Cambodia, sits in a gloriously lush river valley near Pakxe, surrounded by forested mountain peaks. It's an atmospheric place, with many of the sculptures and walls half-buried, but also plenty of intact Hindu and Buddhist carvings.

● **Herbal sauna and traditional massage** Sweat out all your impurities at the Buddhist monastery of Wat Sok Pa Louang in Vientiane. In between sessions, you can sip restorative teas brewed from carambola, tamarind, eucalyptus and citrus leaves.

Festivals

April 13–16 Pi Mai Lao (Lao New Year). As in Thailand and Cambodia, the new year is heralded with water fights in the street. In Louang Phabang there's a huge parade and pagodas made of sand are built in temple grounds.
October Lai Heua Fai (Festival of Lights). Nationwide, communities decorate floats with lights and then float them on the nearest body of water to mark the end of the rainy season; it's especially pretty in Louang Phabang where each neighbourhood takes their float down to the Mekong and a fleet of boats parades them down the river.

Routes in and out

Laos has international airports in Vientiane and Louang Phabang but as there are no direct long-haul flights most visitors from Europe change planes in Bangkok. Both cities also have international connections with Chiang Mai (Thailand), Kunming (China), Hanoi, Ho Chi Minh City, Phnom Penh, Siem Reap and Taipei. Many travellers arrive overland from Thailand, most commonly at the Nong Khai/ Vientiane crossing. There are four other land crossings from Thailand; six from Vietnam; one from Cambodia at Voen Kham, near Don Det (though this is not officially open, travellers reportedly use

▲ Young monks in Louang Phabang

it without incident); and one from China at Boten (near Louang Namtha). Pay close attention to visa requirements, which differ at every entry point.

Laos online

The Boat Landing – Ⓦwww.theboat landing.laopdr.com This Louang Namtha guesthouse website is much more than a puff for their accommodation. Loads of useful info, including on overland travel into China, regional attractions and boat journeys.

Ecotourism Laos – Ⓦwww .ecotourismlaos.com Government-affiliated website about responsible and eco-conscious travel in Laos. Mostly focuses on protected areas and world heritage sites, with useful leads on lesser-known destinations, tours and interesting accommodation.

Stay Another Day – Ⓦwww.stay anotherday.org NGO with links to dozens of sustainable tourism organisations across Laos that welcome visitors and participants, from craft projects to wildlife centres and even a ballet school.

ThingsAsian – Ⓦwww.thingsasian .com The Laos section of this online writers' anthology carries some interesting travelogues and features on modern Lao life and society.

Books

Colin Cotterill *Disco for the Departed*. The latest in the series of entertaining crime thrillers set in Laos in the 1970s is the third outing for the spirit-communing hero, Dr Siri Paiboun. He's the only coroner in Laos and this case takes him into the caves of Viang Xai, former hideouts of the Pathet Lao, where his investigations uncover corruption and dirty deeds, against the backdrop of the recent communist takeover.

Natacha Du Pont De Bie *Ant Egg Soup: The Adventures of a Food Tourist in Laos*. Is deep-fried cricket really all that bad, and how should one respond to the offer of a cup of fresh turkey blood? These and many other pressing foodie questions are answered in this funny, original tour of Laos and its cuisine.

Christopher Kremmer *Stalking the Elephant Kings: In Search of Laos*. One of very few relatively recent travelogues about Laos, this one sees the author traipsing round the country in the 1990s looking for information about the Lao royal family, missing since the 1975 communist takeover, and testing the current political temperature.

Norman Lewis *A Dragon Apparent: Travels in Cambodia, Laos and Vietnam*. An elegant portrait of Laos in the 1950s from a veteran travel writer.

Christopher Robbins *The Ravens: Pilots of the Secret War of Laos*. A British journalist tells the explosive story of America's clandestine campaign in Laos during the American-Vietnam War, based on interviews with the American pilots involved.

Lao tourist offices

No overseas tourist office.

Lao embassies and consulates

Australia and New Zealand 1 Dalman Crescent, O'Malley, Canberra ACT 2606 ☎02/6286 4595, Ⓦwww.laos embassy.net.

UK and Ireland Contact the embassy in France: 74 Ave Raymond Poincaré, Paris 75116 ☎01/45 53 02 98, Ⓦwww .laoparis.com.

US and Canada 2222 S Street, NW, Washington, DC 20008 ☎202/332-6416, Ⓦwww.laoembassy.com.

Malaysia

Capital Kuala Lumpur
Population 27 million
Language Malay
Currency Ringgit (RM), aka Malaysian dollar (M$)
Main religion Islam, with significant

Buddhist, Hindu and Christian minorities
Climate Tropical
Best time to go March–July (Dec–Feb for peninsular west coast)
Minimum daily budget US$15/£9

The history of Malaysia is dominated by a succession of Portuguese, Dutch and British colonists, which means that the country's major sights tend to be rather low-key and quaintly European. Instead, the real interest comes from contemporary Malaysia's remarkably heterogeneous population, half of whom are Malays (whose culture originated in Indonesian Sumatra), a quarter ethnic Chinese, a tenth indigenous tribal people and seven percent Indians (from the Subcontinent). This dynamic mix gives great energy to the stuff of everyday life in Malaysia, with

huge variety in everything from food to festivals, places of worship to dress.

An ideal destination for first-time overlanders, Peninsular Malaysia has good transport connections with neighbouring Thailand, Singapore and Sumatra, and a well-developed tourist infrastructure. English is widely spoken, local transport is efficient, and the standard of living is among the highest in Southeast Asia. The peninsula's coast is graced with some of the most idyllic white-sand beaches in the region and plenty of rewarding offshore reefs; inland, chunks of jungle are accessible to hikers via well-maintained national-park trails and animal hides.

Six hundred kilometres east across the South China Sea from the peninsula, the East Malaysian states of Sarawak and Sabah offer a more adventurous – and more expensive – experience. They share the huge, thickly forested island of Borneo with Indonesia's Kalimantan province and the tiny sultanate of Brunei, and are only accessible from Peninsular Malaysia by plane. Once there, travel into the interior is mainly by river, particularly if you want to visit the longhouses (the traditional communal homes) of the tribal peoples, which usually stand in a remote jungle clearing beside the riverbank. Staying in a longhouse is a highlight of trips to East Malaysia, as are jungle hikes. Most travellers to Sabah also attempt to climb the fearsomely high Gunung Kinabalu.

Main attractions

● **The beaches** Peninsular Malaysia's beaches compare well with those found in southern Thailand. The biggest, most developed resorts are on the beautiful islands of Pulau Langkawi and Pulau

Mean temperatures (°C) and rainfall (mm)

Average daily temperatures (maximum and minimum°C) and monthly rainfall (mm)

	Jan	Feb	Mar	Apr	May	June	July	Aug	Sept	Oct	Nov	Dec
Kuala Lumpur												
max °C	32	33	33	33	33	32	32	32	32	32	31	31
min °C	22	22	23	23	23	23	23	23	23	23	23	23
rainfall mm	159	154	223	276	182	119	120	133	173	258	263	223
Kuching												
max °C	30	30	31	32	33	33	32	33	32	32	31	31
min °C	23	23	23	23	23	23	23	23	23	23	23	23
rainfall mm	683	522	339	286	253	199	199	211	271	326	343	465
Kota Kinabalu												
max °C	30	30	31	32	32	31	31	31	31	31	31	31
min °C	23	23	23	24	24	24	24	24	23	23	23	23
rainfall mm	133	63	71	124	218	311	277	256	314	334	296	241

Tioman, but backpackers generally prefer the cheaper, more chilled-out Perhentian Islands, which are also great for snorkelling and diving; the windsurfers' bay at Cherating, where you stay in village-style huts on stilts; and the tiny Pulau Kapas. Your best bet for a beach break from the capital is tiny Pulau Pangkor, a six-hour journey from KL.

● **Taman Negara National Park** The peninsula's biggest and most popular national park offers something for most outdoor enthusiasts. There's a spectacular canopy walkway through the tree tops, and plenty of day-hikes on well-marked trails. You could spend a night in a hide trying to spot elephants and leopards, or opt to do the guided nine-day trek through the park to the summit of 2187-metre-high Gunung Tahan, the peninsula's highest peak.

● **The Cameron Highlands** Tea plantations, colonial residences and, above all, the chance to cool down, draw scores of travellers to the hill station here. The rolling green fields are dotted with farms and country cottages, and there

are plenty of gentle walking trails through this rather quaint pastoral idyll.

● **Kuala Lumpur** You'll probably find yourself passing through the shrub-lined boulevards and rather bland malls of the Malaysian capital at some point. There's little that's special, but the variety of architectural styles is intriguing – from the traditional elegance of the Masjid Jamek mosque and its ultra-modern counterpart Masjid Negara through to the gleamingly futuristic 88-storey Petronas Towers, one of the tallest buildings in the world. There's decent shopping at the handicraft stalls of the covered Art Deco-style Central Market and in the boutiques and electronic emporia of the Golden Triangle. At the Forest Institute of Malaysia, on the outskirts of the city, you can stroll through the tree tops on a walkway that gives you elevated views of the skyscrapered skyline.

● **Georgetown** Despite being Malaysia's second largest city, this former British trading post on the island of Penang still exudes great historical charm. The elegant old European-style churches, forts and warehouses contrast appealingly with the traditional clan-houses, shophouses and markets of the Chinese community. And within easy reach of the city there's an impressive rope-and-wire canopy walkway through the treetops, bringing you close to monkeys, hornbills and clouds of butterflies.

● **Sarawak** Sarawak's most outstanding attractions are its river systems and the chance to travel by longboat along these jungle waterways, staying in tribal longhouses along the way. Gunung Mulu National Park conserves a dramatic landscape of limestone pinnacles and the largest limestone cave system in the world, with heaps of hiking and climbing potential. The Bario Loop is a challenging five-day trek through the thick jungle of the Kelabit tribal highlands near the Kalimantan border. The state capital, Kuching, is an appealing old waterside colonial outpost with excellent ethnographic collections at its Sarawak Museum.

● **Sabah** At 4101m, Gunung Kinabalu, in Kinabalu National Park, is Sabah's biggest draw; its summit is accessible to any reasonably fit hiker willing to undertake the day-and-a-half's climb up. Sabah's other highlights are the Sepilok Orang-utan Rehabilitation Centre, where you can watch the baby orang-utans learning to swing and swagger, the forests around the Kinabatangan River, famous for their proboscis monkeys, and the chance to shoot the rapids on the Sungei Padas, near Beaufort.

Also recommended

● **Diving and snorkelling off Pulau Sipadan** Exceptionally rich reefs and marine life grace the waters around this island off eastern Sabah, where highlights include fabulous shore diving,

underwater caves, barracudas, white-tip sharks and masses of turtles. It's a protected area, so visitor numbers are limited and you have to base yourself at off the island, at Semporna.

● **Riding the jungle railway** If you have plenty of time, it's worth travelling the entire length of this fourteen-hour route, which starts in Gemas, near Melaka, and meanders through the mountainous landscapes of the peninsula's scenic jungle interior all the way up to Kota Bharu. But most people break the journey at Jerantut, which is three hours from Gemas and convenient for Taman Negara.

● **Melaka** This cosmopolitan old port town wears its history on its sleeve, with self-consciously prettified churches and town squares from its days under Portuguese and then Dutch colonial rule. More interesting are the 300-year-old ancestral homes and temples of the Peranakan, the descendants of the Chinese merchants who settled here and married local Malay women. Melaka is also a great place to sample Peranakan cuisine, known for its distinctive blending of sour sauces and coconut milk.

Festivals

January or February Thaipusam, Batu Caves, Kuala Lumpur. Devout Hindus do penance for past sins by parading to the Batu Caves with skewers and hooked through their flesh.

January or February Chinese New Year. Across Malaysia, Chinese communities welcome in their new year with parades of lion dances and street performances of Chinese opera.

June Gawai Dayak (Harvest Festival), Sarawak. The Iban people celebrate the end of the rice harvest with rowdy parties and excessive drinking at their open-to-all longhouses.

October or November Kota Belud Tamu Besar, Kota Belud, Sabah. The huge annual version of the weekly market draws big crowds of tribespeople and is a good chance to buy handicrafts and catch cultural performances.

Routes in and out

Malaysia's main international airport is near Kuala Lumpur, and is also the hub for Asia's major low-cost carrier, Air Asia (Ⓦwww.airasia.com), but some travellers fly in or out of Singapore, which is a short bus ride from the southern Malaysian city of Johor Bahru. A limited number of Asian airlines also cover regional routes into Penang airport. Peninsular Malaysia has several land border crossings with Thailand, served by buses, boats and trains, but because of ongoing separatist violence in far southern Thailand the safest routes are via Satun and Ko Lipe rather than Hat Yai. There are good boat connections between west-coast Peninsular Malaysia and the Indonesian island of Sumatra, as well as a Weesam Express ferry service between Sandakan, in Sabah, and Zamboanga (Mindanao) in the southern Philippines. Most people fly to Sabah and Sarawak from Kuala Lumpur or Singapore, but you can also cross overland from Brunei and Indonesian Kalimantan.

Malaysia online

Masak-masak – Ⓦmasak-masak .blogspot.com The energetic blogs of an enthusiastic Kuala Lumpur foodie open up a whole new culinary world.
Sabah Tourism – Ⓦsabahtourism .com The official Sabah tourism website features well-researched information on upcoming festivals, diving, trekking and cultural destinations, plus general travel tips and links.

Visitor Guide Malaysia – Ⓦwww .visitorsguide.com.my Decent general guide to the country and its attractions, with features and blogs.
Wild Asia – Ⓦwww.wildasia.net Although it covers nature conservation and responsible tourism across the whole of Southeast Asia, this site is particularly strong on Malaysia. It includes feature articles, short guides to wilderness areas of Malaysia, and tips on eco-friendly accommodation.

Books

Tash Aw *The Harmony Silk Factory*. The prize-winning debut from Malaysia's most successful novelist is set in 1940s British-ruled Malaya just as the Japanese are about to invade. Most of the action takes place in the Kinta Valley of the western peninsula, where three different characters weave together the story of the mysterious central character, silk merchant and part-time inventor Johnny Lim.
Tan Twan Eng *The Gift of Rain*. This gripping, beautifully written novel takes on big themes in its story of a young Chinese-English boy in wartime Penang and his friendship with a martial-arts-practising Japanese diplomat.
CS Godshalk *Kalimantaan*. A sweeping novel about ambitious, empire-building British colonials in tribal, nineteenth-century Borneo that painstakingly re-creates the world of James Brooke, the first White Rajah of Sarawak.
Redmond O'Hanlon *Into the Heart of Borneo*. The hilarious true story of two erudite, but not terribly fit, Englishmen as they search the impenetrable Borneo jungle for the elusive two-horned rhinoceros. There's a memorable passage on a typical Dyak party (involving much drunkenness and buffoonery) and off-puttingly graphic descriptions of leeches, Dyak cuisine and jungle trekking.

Film

Entrapment (Jon Amiel, 1999). Hi-tech pre-Millennium bank-heist caper starring Catherine Zeta Jones, Sean Connery – and Kuala Lumpur, where much of the action takes place, leaving room for plenty of glamorous shots of the slinky Petronas Towers.

Karaoke (Chris Chong, 2009). One of only a handful of Malaysian films ever to have been screened at the Cannes Film Festival, this is the quirky story of Betik, newly returned from the city to help run his mum's karaoke bar, and his village neighbours. By day the villagers work on the oil-palm plantation; by night they reveal their loves and longings through the karaoke machine microphone.

Return to Paradise (Joseph Ruben, 1998). Three young Americans party together in Malaysia and then go their separate ways. One stays on to do some conservation work with orang-utans but gets busted for the group's stash of recreational hash and ends up on Death Row. Will the other two acknowledge their responsibility and return to paradise to face the music, share the jail term and get him off Death Row?

Malaysian tourist offices

Ⓦ www.tourism.gov.my

Australia and New Zealand Level 2, 171 Clarence St, NSW 2000 ☎02/9299-4441, Ⓔmtpb.sydney@tourism.gov.my; 355 Exhibition St, Melbourne ☎03/9654 3177; 56 William St, Perth, WA 6000 ☎09/481-0400, Ⓔmtpb.perth@tourism.gov.my.

Canada 1590-1111, West Georgia St, Vancouver, BC V6E 4M3 ☎604/689-8899, Ⓦwww.tourismmalaysia.ca.

South Africa 1st Floor, Building 5, Commerce Square, 39 Rivonia Rd, Sandhurst, Johannesburg ☎011/268-0292, Ⓔmtpb.johannesburg@tourism.gov.my.

UK and Ireland 57 Trafalgar Square, London WC2N 5DU ☎020/7930 7932.

US 818 West 7th St, Suite 970, Los Angeles, CA 90017 ☎213/689-9702, Ⓔmtpb.la@tourism.gov.my; 120 East 56th St, Suite 810, New York, NY 10022 ☎212/754-1113, Ⓔmtpb@aol.com.

Malaysian embassies and consulates

Ⓦ www.kln.gov.my

Australia 7 Perth Ave, Yarralumla, Canberra, ACT 2600 ☎02/6273 1543, Ⓦwww.kln.gov.my/perwakilan/Canberra. Consulate in Perth ☎08/9225 7055, Ⓦwww.kln.gov.my/perwakilan/perth.

Canada 60 Boteler St, Ottawa, Ontario K1N 8Y7 ☎613/241-5182, Ⓦwww.kln.gov.my/perwakilan/ottawa. Consulate in Vancouver ☎604/685-9550, Ⓦwww.kln.gov.my/perwakilan/vancouver.

Ireland Level 3A-5A, Shelbourne House, Shelbourne Rd, Ballsbridge, Dublin 4 ☎01-667-7280, Ⓦwww.kln.gov.my/perwakilan/Dublin.

New Zealand 10 Washington Ave, Brooklyn, Wellington ☎04/385 2439, Ⓦwww.kln.gov.my/perwakilan/wellington.

South Africa 1007 Schoeman St, Arcadia, Pretoria 0083 ☎012/342 5990, Ⓦwww.kln.gov.my/perwakilan/Pretoria.

UK 45 Belgrave Square, London SW1X 8QT ☎020/7919 0251, Ⓦwww.kln.gov.my/perwakilan/london.

US 3516 International Court, NW, Washington, DC 20008 ☎202/572-9700, Ⓦwww.kln.gov.my/perwakilan/washington. Consulates in Los Angeles ☎213/892-1238, Ⓦwww.kln.gov.my/perwakilan/losangeles; and New York ☎212/490-2722, Ⓦwww.kln.gov.my/perwakilan/newyork.

Mongolia

Capital Ulaanbaatar (also spelt Ulan Bator)
Population 2.6 million
Language Mongolian
Currency Tug
Religion Mahayana Buddhist. There is a small minority of Muslims in the Kazakh population.

Climate Extreme continental. Very cold winters of minus 20–40°C. Warm/hot summers of plus 20–40°C.
Best time to go June–September.
Minimum daily budget
In Ulaanbaatar US$10/£6. To travel outside the capital US$80/£49

Larger than France, Spain and Germany combined and with less than half a million tourists a year, it's unsurprising that Mongolia is hardly overrun with visitors. Yet there is a great deal to interest visitors and if your aim is to get as far from the twenty-first century as possible, then this is the place for you. The nomadic lifestyle, little changed since the days of Genghis Khan, is still the way of life of nearly half the population. Even in the cities (of which there are only three) many of the people prefer to live in traditional "gers", round white felt tents, rather than the concrete blocks that were introduced during eighty years of socialist (Russian) development. Ulaanbaatar has fine temples (Ganden Monastery is the biggest and most

important), art galleries and museums but outside the city this is the country for vast open landscapes – the mountains, desert and open steppe, inhabited only by nomadic families with their herds of horses, camels and reindeer. There are less than two people per square kilometer so you can travel for hours meeting only a few horsemen, a family on a motorbike, or the occasional truck overloaded with sheepskins travelling towards the capital.

For many visitors one of the greatest pleasures is the lack of other tourists. Foreigners are never hassled, and the local people are delighted to show off their beautiful country and heritage. Although much of the country is open grassy steppe, each province has its

Mean temperatures (°C) and rainfall (mm)

Average daily temperatures (maximum and minimum °C) and monthly rainfall (mm)

	Jan	Feb	Mar	Apr	May	June	July	Aug	Sept	Oct	Nov	Dec
Ulaanbaatar												
max °C	-19	-13	-4	7	13	21	22	21	14	6	-6	-16
min °C	-32	-29	-22	-8	-2	7	11	8	2	-8	-20	-28
rainfall mm	0	0	3	5	10	28	76	51	23	5	5	3

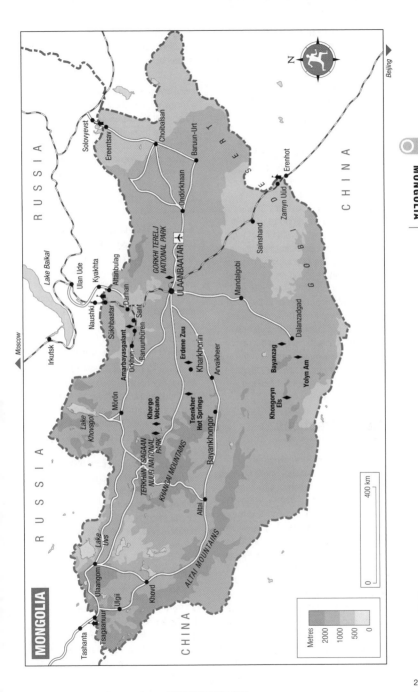

MONGOLIA

www.roughguides.com

own ancient monuments, unusual geographical features or rare wildlife that make it worth visiting. In the south next to the border with China lies the fabled Gobi Desert where dinosaur remains are frequently found. In the west is the high Altai mountain range, and in the central region the Khangai mountains. On the northern border with Siberia is "Mother Ocean", Lake Khovsgol, which is outstandingly peaceful and beautiful.

This is a difficult country for backpackers. The best way to enjoy Mongolia fully is to organize your trip before you go, either with one of the local travel companies in Ulaanbaatar, or with a foreign travel company; most of the latter can be found on the Internet. Be prepared for long-distance travel, either by plane or by jeep. In the most important visited and beautiful places, traditional ger camps with toilet and washing facilities have been set up for travellers. Elsewhere camping is the only option, with rivers or lakes to cleanse yourself and minimal toilet facilities. Expect a wild trip!

Main attractions

● **Gobi Desert** Straddling the southern border between Inner Mongolia (an autonomous region of China) and Outer Mongolia, this vast expanse of sparsely populated wilderness is the habitat of a surprising variety of wildlife, including several rare species such as snow leopards, Gobi bears, wild sheep and camels. Apart from the handful of sites visited by most tourists, which include an ice-filled canyon (Yolyn Am), the "Flaming cliffs" at Bayanzag (where many dinosaur remains have been discovered) and Khongoryn Els at the far western side, where big golden sand dunes meet the end of the high Altai

mountain range, the main attraction of the Gobi lies in the astonishing amount of empty space.

● **Kharkhorin** This quiet valley was once the centre of the great Mongol Empire. On the site where Genghis Khan built his capital in the thirteenth century, a monastery was later founded which became the centre of Buddhism in Mongolia. Erdene Zuu monastery is now the main attraction in this otherwise unexceptional town, and is visited by foreigners and Mongolians throughout the year.

● **Visit a ger** Hospitality is an important tradition in this sparsely populated land, and anyone passing by, be they Mongolian or foreign, will be invited into the traditional white felt ger and enjoy the traditional bowl of "airag" (fermented mare's milk). Increasingly, nomadic people are supplementing their income by providing hospitality for visitors – try to spend at least some time with them.

● **Lake Khovsgol** Situated on Mongolia's northern border with Siberia, this huge inland sea (over 130km long) is surrounded by mountains, forests and meadows of wild flowers. It's a perfect place to relax, or to enjoy a few days trekking, horse-riding, mountain biking, fishing or boating. Along the western shore are a growing number of facilities for tourists, including ger camps and lodges located at the water's edge. This is also the area where the isolated nomadic reindeer herders, the Tsataan people, roam.

Also recommended

● **Terelj** Only 80km from Ulaanbaatar, the Gorkhi Terelj National Park boasts granite mountains, lush green valleys and fast-flowing rivers. Towards the end of the road are several ger camps tucked away in the side valleys, but beyond this it is as remote as anywhere in Mongolia.

- **Hot springs** There are many hot mineral springs dotted about the country, visited mainly by Mongolians for their health-giving properties. Relatively accessible is Tsenkher in Arkhangai province where you can stay in traditional gers and relax in outdoor hot pools while admiring the surrounding forested mountains.

- **Riding** Take the opportunity to ride, whether it be mountain bikes, horses, camels, yaks or even reindeer – check with travel companies to see what they can offer. Gallop across the open steppe like one of Genghis Khan's warriors or ride over the mountains in a yak and cart.

- **Amarbayasgalant Monastery** One of the largest and most beautiful monasteries in Mongolia. The temples and pavilions were largely spared the fate of other similar institutions during the Stalinist purges of the 1930s.

Festivals

End January–March Tsagaan Sar. The forced consumption of delicious buuz (steamed dumplings) and vodka marks the Lunar New Year, the end of winter and the beginning of spring.

July Naadam. Three-day annual festival celebrating "the three sports of men" (horseracing, archery and wrestling), held in every town or village on or around July 11.

October Eagle Festival. Celebrating the culture, lifestyle and spirituality of the Kazakh people within Mongolia, the festival takes place in the province of Bayan-Ulgii, in the far west of the country, accessible from the state capital of Ulgii, and includes traditional hunting with eagles, parades, costumes and sporting events.

Routes in and out

Chinggis Khaan Airport, just outside Ulaanbaatar, receives international flights. An alternative is to enter Mongolia on the Trans-Mongolian Railway, a branch line of the Trans-Siberian Railway with train border crossings at Naushki (Russia) and Sukhbaatar and Erenhot (China) and Zamyn-Uud. There are overland road borders that foreigners can use between Tashanta (Rusiia) and Tsagaanuur in the far northwest, Kyakhta (Russia) and Altanbulag in the north, Solovyevsk (Russia) and Ereentsav in the northeast and Erenhot (China) and Zamyn-Uud in the southeast. It's possible that other land crossings are open and accessible to foreigners, but information is extremely sparse, and the best advice is to check government sources, local travel agents and travellers' bulletin boards.

Mongolia online

Amarbayasgalant Monastery – Ⓦwww.amarbayasgalant.org Small site created and maintained by the monastery with plenty on its history, Buddhist philosophy and day to day life.

Blue Peak – Ⓦwww.bluepeak.net The site of photographer Roger Gruys who lived and travelled extensively in Mongolia. The images are fabulous and there's interesting background and travel information as well.

Mongolian Artist – Ⓦmongolianartist .com Excellent, up-to-date site introduction on all aspects of Mongolian art and culture including art, film and photography, plus a smattering of general info.

Ulaanbaatar – Ⓦwww.ulaanbaatar .net A gateway to the city, including plenty of links to news, background and practical stuff.

www.roughguides.com

Books

Benedict Allen *Edge of Blue Heaven*. A fine travelogue detailing the adventurous author's intrepid horse trek in the west of the country and a solo camel trek across the Gobi.

Stephen J Bodio *Eagle Dreams: Searching for Legends in Wild Mongolia*. This renowned naturalist, hunter and writer traces his fascination with the eagle-hunters of Mongolia and the realization of his dream to hunt with them.

John Man *Genghis Khan*. Popular, recent history of the most famous character in Mongolian history.

Stanley Stewart *In the Empire of Genghis Khan*. This prize-winning account of the author's 1000-mile journey across Mongolia brilliantly melds history and anecdote.

Louisa Waugh *Hearing Birds Fly*. Having spent two years in Ulaanbaatar, Louisa Waugh heads off to experience the harshness of village life in remote western Mongolia, living in a ger, breaking the ice in winter for her daily wash, and moving up into the Altai mountain pastures to help care for the sheep and goats in the summer.

Films

Chinggis Blues (Roko & Adrian Belic, 1999). This documentary traces the journey of a blind American blues singer from the West Coast to the wilds of Mongolia in search of the secret of khoomi (throat singing).

Nohoi Oron (State of Dogs; Peter Brosens & Dorjkhandyn Turmunkh, 1998). Prize-winning mystical travelogue following the life of Bassar, one of the twelve thousand stray dogs in Ulaanbaatar.

The Story of the Weeping Camel (D Byambasuren & Luigi Falami, 2004). Documentary that mixes drama, nature film and ethnographical study as it follows a Mongolian nomad family seeking to reunite a baby camel with its mother. This was followed up by *The Cave of the Yellow Dog*.

Wild East: Portrait of an Urban Nomad (Michael Haslund-Christensen, 2002). Set in Ulaanbaatar, this documentary traces two friends, Jenya and Sasha, as they try to find work. It explores issues of identity, tradition versus modernity, science versus religion and the struggle of life under the new capitalism.

Mongolian tourist offices

Ⓦ**www.mongoliatourism.gov.mn**
No overseas tourist office.

Mongolian embassies and consulates

Canada 151 Slater St, Suite 503, Ottawa, K1P 5H3 ☎613/569-3830, Ⓦwww.mongolembassy.org.

UK 7-8 Kensington Court, London W8 5DL ☎020/7937 0150, Ⓦwww.embassyofmongolia.co.uk.

US 2833 Main St NW, Washington, DC 20007 ☎202/333-7117, Ⓦwww.mongolianembassy.us. Visas can also be applied for at the Permanent Mission of Mongolia to the UN, 6 East 77th St, NY 10021 ☎212/861-9460, Ⓦwww.un.int/Mongolia.

Nepal

Capital Kathmandu
Population 28 million
Language Nepali plus 47 other languages and dialects spoken by the 55 separate ethnic groups that make up the population
Currency Rupee (Rs)
Religion Hindu and Buddhist with a small Muslim minority

Climate Monsoonal
Best time to go Autumn (Oct & Nov) and spring (Feb to mid-April)
Minimum daily budget US$6/£10 though organized treks and adventure sports add significantly to the cost

Sandwiched between the enormous land masses of Tibet and India, Nepal is a relatively small country, but what it lacks in size it more than makes up for in dramatic scenery and the vast range of experiences on offer. Nepal contains a huge stretch of the Himalayas so it's unsurprising that trekking is the main draw. Other attractions include Kathmandu, whose very name conjures up images of mountains and mysticism; the wildlife reserves of the lowland jungles in the south; Buddhist and Hindu temples and festivals; white-water rafting and mountain-biking. Many visitors also come in pursuit of bodily calm and spiritual truth, and Nepal has plenty of practitioners of massage,

Ayurvedic and Tibetan medicine and astrology, plus courses in meditation and yoga.

Nepal remains one of the poorest countries in the world, facing not just a population explosion but also enormous environmental degradation, including the deforestation of much-tramped treks; visitors should do what they can (see the KEEP website listed on p.285 for suggestions) to avoid further damage to the fragile mountain ecosystem.

Tourism provides an important source of foreign exchange but tourist numbers plummeted in the wake of the Maoist rebels' battle against the government, which began in 1996. However, the war ended in 2006 and Nepal became a

Mean temperatures (°C) and rainfall (mm)

Average daily temperatures (maximum and minimum °C) and monthly rainfall (mm)

	Jan	Feb	Mar	Apr	May	June	July	Aug	Sept	Oct	Nov	Dec
Kathmandu												
max °C	18	19	25	28	30	29	29	28	28	27	23	19
min °C	2	4	7	12	16	19	20	20	19	13	7	3
rainfall mm	15	41	23	58	122	246	373	345	155	38	8	3

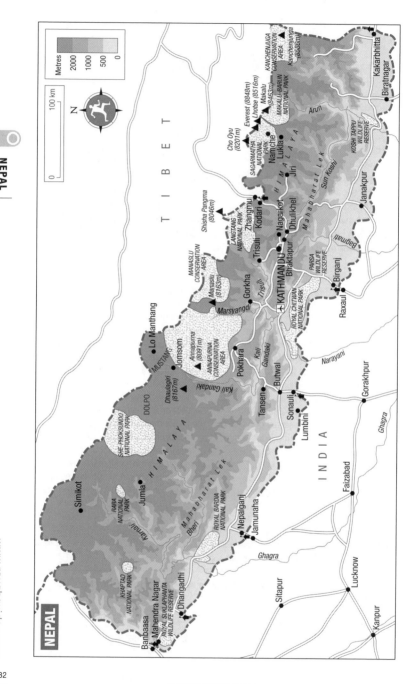

republic and held elections in 2008. The monarchy was abolished and the country is now ruled by a Maoist-dominated government. However, all is not well in the Himalayan state and political unrest continues; potential visitors should check the security situation before finalizing plans for a visit (see p.348).

Main attractions

- **Himalayas** The north of the country is occupied by the highest mountain range in the world with scores of spellbindingly dramatic peaks. Whether it is from near or far, during a hard trek or from the comfort of an aeroplane seat, the one obligatory aim for every visitor to the country is to catch sight of these amazing mountains at least one time. For the less mobile, mountain flights leave daily from Kathmandu between May and September; you pass just 25km from Everest and get to eyeball a couple of dozen of the world's highest peaks.

- **Kathmandu** Nepal's bustling, sprawling capital city is noisy, traffic-clogged and appallingly polluted, but also vibrant, excellent for shopping and eating and a great place to arrange trips out into the wilderness. Durbar Square, in the heart of the city, is the location of innumerable temples and ancient monuments, most notably the Hanuman Dhoka (Old Royal Palace) and the Kumari Chowk; the latter is the home of Nepal's pre-eminent living goddess, the Kumari, a prepubescent girl worshipped as the living incarnation of the Hindu goddess Durga. The other obligatory sights, on the outskirts of the city, are the huge Buddhist stupas at Swayambunath and Boudhanath from where the stylized eyes of the Buddha gaze out in all directions on the world, and the Hindu shrines at Pashupatinath.

- **Kathmandu Valley** Some of the best-preserved historic buildings and temples in the area are found in the ancient city of Bhaktapur, which has its own Durbar Square, featuring the five-storey Nyatapola pagoda. Patan, just south of Kathmandu, is the valley's most Buddhist city, with a calmer, less frantic feel than elsewhere; there's yet another Durbar Square here, with a fine Royal Palace dating from the seventeenth century and a number of temples. Easily accessible from Kathmandu, although strictly speaking outside the valley itself, are Nagarkot and Dhulikel, both great excursions for stunning mountain views, and excellent bases for treks.

- **Pokhara** One of the most popular destinations in Nepal, Pokhara is excellent for simply relaxing amid great scenery and in plenty of comfort; the views of the unforgettable Machhapuchhre (or "fish-tail peak") and the Annapurna and Manaslu mountain ranges are stunning. Pokhara is the starting point for many treks, most notably those in the Annapurna region, and there are also plenty of local excursions, including hikes to the mountain viewpoint of Sarangkot, boating or kayaking on Phewa lake, horse-riding and cycling.

- **Trekking** Nepal has an enormous variety of treks on offer, varying in length and difficulty and the amount of comfort available along the way. It's worth researching the options, especially if you want to get away from the most popular routes. The three-week Annapurna circuit through gloriously diverse scenery involves climbing up to a heady 5416m; you'll need to be reasonably fit to tackle it, though there's plenty of accommodation and eating places en route, and other trekkers for company. Everest treks, which get you close to the world's tallest peak, are very strenuous, the cold and high altitude being serious

▲ Teahouse on the Everest trek

concerns; you'll need to allow three weeks to do one of these, unless you fly into or out of Lukla, partway along the route. This is another route that gets pretty crowded. Those with less time may want to consider the eight-day Helambu trek or the seven to twelve day Langtang trek which are both closer to Kathmandu. If you have plenty of time, and real money, the Mustang and Dolpo regions are way off the beaten track.

Also recommended

- **Royal Chitwan National Park** On the plains in the far south of the country, the park is the jungle home of the famed Bengal tiger and the Indian rhinoceros, as well as plenty of deer and wild oxen, crocodiles and over 450 species of birds – among other creatures. Elephant rides, jeep tours, canoe trips and walks are all available, though Chitwan's fame and accessibility mean that it can be hard to escape the crowds; Royal Bardia National Park and Royal Suklaphanta Wildlife Reserve, further to the west, are alternatives.

- **White-water rafting and kayaking** Nepal's picturesque rivers offer both beginners and the more advanced plenty of opportunities to try these activities. Two- or three-day trips on the Trisuli River west of Kathmandu, and three- or four-day excursions out of Pokhara or on the upper Kali Gandaki are among the most popular. Agents in both Kathmandu and Pokhara can arrange trips.

- **Courses in meditation, yoga or Nepali** The Kathmandu valley, and to a lesser extent Pokhara, are ideal places to enrol yourself on a course.

- **Lumbini** A place of pilgrimage for devotees from across the globe, the spot where Buddha was born in 543 BC has ancient archeological monuments as well as modern Tibetan and Theravadan monasteries.

- **Mountain biking** Organized tours, geared to any level of fitness and ability, provide all equipment and accommodation – and a lift if you get tired. Kathmandu and Pokhara are the main centres to arrange trips.

Festivals

February/March Shiva Raatri. Nepal's best known religious fair or *mela*, "Shiva's Night" attracts thousands of pilgrims and *sadhus* (Indian ascetic holy men) to Pashupatinath on the eastern edge of Kathmandu for worship and mind-boggling yogic demonstrations.

August/September Indra Jatra. An eight-day confection of music, dance and drama, in which the living goddess, the Kumari, is towed in a chariot through Kathmandu.

September/October Dasain. Nepal's longest and biggest festival lasts fifteen days. The best day for onlookers is Vijaya Dasami, the tenth evening, which celebrates the hero Rama's victory over the evil king Ravana, as detailed in the great Hindu epic, the Ramayana; it is marked by processions, including Kharga Jatra, a sword procession, and masked dances.

October/November Mani Rimdu. Masked dances celebrate the victory of Buddhism over the ancient Bon religion in Tengboche Monastery in the Everest region.

Routes in and out

Kathmandu's international airport, Tribhuvan, is served by several major carriers. There are a handful of well-used overland routes from India, arriving into Mahendra Nagar (from Banbassa; convenient if you're coming from Delhi), Dhangadhi (north of Sitapur), Nepalganj (north of Faizabad), Sonauli (from Gorakhpur), Birganj (from Raxaul) and Kakarbhitta. The crossing from Tibet is between Zhangmu and Kodari; however, only tour groups are allowed into Tibet via this route (though independent travellers can leave Tibet this way) – check the situation at the time of travel.

Nepal online

Everest News – ⓦwww.everestnews .com This site offers up-to-date and extensive coverage of news from Everest and the other big Himalayan peaks. There's a huge amount of information here about current expeditions, plus plenty of detail about history, facts, gear – almost everything you'd want to know about the highest mountain on earth.

Himalayan Art – ⓦwww.himalayanart .org Fabulous site dedicated to Himalayan art that displays more than 35,000 images from museum, university and private collections around the world, including paintings, sculpture and textiles. There's excellent information on all the images here as well.

International Porter Protection Group – ⓦwww.ippg.net This group campaigns for a safe and fair deal for porters who work in the trekking business. Their thought-provoking site has plenty of sad examples of what can go wrong for the people who carry the loads and advice for trekkers on how to make sure the porters get a decent deal.

Kathmandu Environmental Education Project (KEEP) – ⓦwww.keepnepal .org Excellent site for tourist information, plus images of some popular treks. There are good links to other environmental organizations and plenty of good ideas about how to visit Nepal without doing more harm than good.

Yeti Zone Web Himalayan Trekking Guide – ⓦwww.yetizone.com Offers brilliantly detailed, day-by-day accounts of the Annapurna Circuit and Sanctuary, Everest and Khumbu regions, Langtang and Helambu treks, plus ample inspirational images. You can order DVD or MPEG versions or simply read it all on the site, which is packed with information and also features a bulletin board if you're looking for a trekking partner.

Check out the Yeti Cam to search for the elusive creature.

Books

Eva Kipp *Bending Bamboo, Changing Winds: Nepali Women Tell Their Life Stories*. Moving oral histories and photographs from across the country detailing every aspect of women's lives.

Jon Krakauer *Into Thin Air*. Harrowing and thought-provoking description of the events of May 1996, the deadliest season ever on Mount Everest.

Peter Matthiessen *The Snow Leopard*. Fabulous and now classic read, describing the author's two-month hike into the remote Inner Dolpo region of northwest Nepal. Alongside beautiful descriptions, Matthiessen talks about his emotional ups and downs, as he oscillates between exhaustion and exhilaration and tries hard to make sense of his Zen Buddhist training.

Manjushree Thapa *Tilled Earth*. The latest volume of work, this time short stories, by one of Nepal's best known writers. The stories cover people from the cities, rural areas and the Nepalese diaspora abroad; through the small dramas of Nepalese lives the author movingly illustrates deeper truths.

Samrat Upadhyay *Arresting God in Kathmandu*. This is a volume of short stories by one of the first Nepalese authors to be published in the West; tales of traditional expectations are set against a Kathmandu backdrop of urban life and a changing society.

Films

Himalaya (Eric Valli, 2000). The Oscar-nominated story of a struggle for power between the generations in an isolated mountain village in the Dolpo region, played out on the annual salt trek across the Himalayas.

Starkiss Circus Girls in India (Chris Relleke & Jascha de Wilde, 2003). Documentary detailing the lives of girls from desperately poor Nepalese families who are essentially sold to the Great Rayman Circus, the oldest in India. It's a bleak look at their lives, work and future options.

Nepalese tourist offices

Ⓦ www.welcomenepal.com
No overseas tourist office.

Nepalese embassies and consulates

Ⓦ www.immi.gov.np/location.php
Australia and New Zealand Suite 2.02, 24 Marcus Clarke St, Canberra City, ACT 2601 ☏2/6162 1554, Ⓦwww .necan.gov.np;
Canada Contact US Embassy
South Africa No diplomatic representation.
UK 12A Kensington Palace Gardens, London W8 4QU ☏020/7229 1594, Ⓦwww.nepembassy.org.uk.
US 2131 Leroy Place NW, Washington, DC 20008 ☏020/667-4550, Ⓦwww .nepalembassyusa.org.

Pakistan

Capital Islamabad
Population 158 million
Language Urdu is the official
language, though it is largely used as
a second language alongside other
native tongues, including Punjabi,
Sindhi, Pashto, Saraiki and Baluchi
Currency Pakistani Rupee (Rs)
Religion 96% Muslim mostly Sunni
Climate There are three climatic
zones: dry (which covers most of
the country), humid subtropical
(from Lahore to Peshawar) and
highland (the climate of the northern
mountains)
Best time to go The south is best
from November–March, when it
is cooler; the north is best from
April–October (main trekking season
June–Sept), which avoids the
harshest winter snows
Minimum daily budget US$10/£6

Relatively few tourists make it to Pakistan, but those that do generally describe it as being like Nepal without the crowds or like India without the hassles. The country has many attractions, including spectacular mountain and desert landscapes, and ancient ruins and fabulous mosques – the legacy of prehistoric civilizations and successive Persian, Arab, Mogul and Sikh empires. Travellers generally head for the north, either using the Karakoram Highway and its offshoots, or visiting Peshawar, the Khyber Pass and Chitral. Hiking is the most popular activity, and there are plenty of treks to suit all levels of fitness and aspiration.

Although the tourist industry in Pakistan is embryonic, there's a fair choice of hotels, especially in towns and cities, but electricity and water supplies can be unreliable. Trains and buses are generally slow, and can be uncomfortable. English is spoken by most educated Pakistanis, and foreigners who respect the local culture are warmly welcomed as honoured guests. Women should dress appropriately for a Muslim country, in long loose clothes. During Ramadan, the Islamic month of fasting, eating, drinking and smoking are banned during daylight hours; many restaurants are closed,

Mean temperatures (°C) and rainfall (mm)

Average daily temperatures (maximum and minimum °C) and monthly rainfall (mm)

	Jan	Feb	Mar	Apr	May	June	July	Aug	Sept	Oct	Nov	Dec
Islamabad												
max °C	16	19	24	31	37	40	36	34	34	32	28	20
min °C	2	6	10	15	21	25	25	24	21	15	9	3
rainfall mm	64	64	81	42	23	55	233	258	85	21	12	23

The accession of Jammu and Kashmir to Pakistan or India remains to be decided.

offices work short hours and tempers can get rather frayed.

Some parts of Pakistan are considered dangerous for travellers, most notably rural Sindh, the tribal areas of the Northwest Frontier province and Balochistan, and rural areas of Punjab. However, the situation can change very fast, and travellers planning to visit Pakistan should check the current situation with their own government advisory body before they go (see p.348) and, once in the country, with local tourist offices and/or the police. There are also parts of the country that are off-limits to foreigners, so it is vital to get up to date information.

Main attractions

● **Trekking in Northern Pakistan**
The meeting point of the Himalaya, Karakoram and Hindu Kush mountain ranges, the region offers some of the best scenery and best trekking in the world, ranging from gentle day-long strolls to extremely strenuous affairs lasting several weeks and involving glaciers, fast-flowing rivers and passes 5500m up. Trekking centres are Shigar near Skardu, Gilgit, Chitral and, further afield, the Hunza, Nagar and nearby valleys. As the trekking infrastructure is much less developed

than in Nepal, the need for self-sufficiency is far greater, though there are now trekking companies organizing treks. Be sure to read p.182 for information on acclimatisation to altitude.

● **Hunza Valley** Whether you are trekking or sightseeing, the Hunza valley is especially recommended - many of the greatest peaks are nearby and the Ismaili (Shia) people are especially welcoming. The valley is famous for its fertility; the water channels that irrigate the land are excellent pathways for exploration and there's the dramatic Baltit Fort to explore.

● **Karakoram Highway** To travel along this 1300-kilometre-long road – linking Islamabad with Kashgar in China (see p.143) via the Khunjerab Pass – is to experience some of the most spellbinding scenery in the world, as the highway leaves the plains of the Punjab, climbs through forest to barren slopes where it weaves between towering mountains, over huge passes, beside thundering rivers and along apparently impenetrable valleys. With a visa for China, and as long as you collect your return visa for Pakistan in Sost, you could travel the full length of the highway from Islamabad, spend a few days sightseeing in Kashgar and then head back.

● **Islamabad and Rawalpindi** Built in the 1960s, Islamabad, Pakistan's planned capital, is laid out on a grid design, without the chaos (and the character) usually associated with Asian cities. Faisal Masjid, one of the largest mosques in the world, is worth a visit, as are the nearby Margalla hills, which offer opportunities for walks and treks. Just 15km away, the traditional city of Rawalpindi has both chaos and character aplenty. Rajah Bazaar, the commercial heart of its old market area, is a maze of tiny alleyways lined with shops and workshops of every type.

Although the two cities have little to detain visitors for long, they do make a convenient gateway to Pakistan if you're visiting the north.

● **Peshawar** Though it's long had a reputation as a frontier town, Peshawar these days is a thriving city, though the buzz and excitement of the twisting alleyways and bazaars of the Old City remain. A popular excursion from Peshawar is 40km south to the village of Darra Adam Khel (usually just called Darra), centre of arms manufacture and trading in the region. Here, gunsmiths' shops line the road, and you'll be invited to test-fire home-made imitation Kalashnikovs.

● **Khyber Pass** In Western minds, the pass has mystical status, symbolizing a time when travellers were real adventurers. Travel there by road or steam train from Peshawar (the Khyber Steam Safari runs a couple of times a month), and gaze down into Afghanistan through the barren, desolate hills. The pass may be closed if security concerns are high.

● **Lahore** The most worthwhile of Pakistan's cities, Lahore has numerous fine examples of Mogul architecture, while a walk through the atmospheric alleyways of the Old City takes in mosques, bazaars and markets. The Lahore Museum is a treasure trove of items from throughout Pakistan's history.

● **Moenjo Daro** The Indus Valley civilization, at its peak four thousand years ago, was centred here; a great deal remains of the original city, much of it brilliantly preserved and well restored.

Also recommended

● **Tombs of Uch Sharif** These are some of the most beautiful – albeit partially ruined – tombs in the country. Fabulously decorated, the tombs, the

www.roughguides.com

oldest of which is thought to date from the tenth century, are lasting memorials to the prominent figures of Sufi Islam who are buried here.

● **Camel safari** Venturing into Pakistan's largest desert, the Cholistan, by camel, you'll visit forts built along the ancient trading route across the sands, most famously the eighteenth-century Fort Derawar.

● **Mountain flights** Take a flight from Islamabad to Gilgit or Skardu, or from Peshawar to Chitral; the planes fly between rather than above the peaks, so you get fantastic views – especially as the pilots are only allowed to fly in fine weather.

● **Take the road between Gilgit and Chitral** The two- to three-day journey, crossing the Shandur Pass, is one of the roughest but most impressive in the country, with awesome mountain scenery. The most flexible way to do it is by hiring a jeep, and there are some great spots along the way to camp rough.

● **Deosai Plains** Located above 4000m, this is one of the highest plateaus in the world. Snow-bound for half the year (visit between May and November), the area is famed for its wildlife (including the Himalayan Brown Bear and Tibetan Wolf) and springtime flowers.

Festivals

March Basant. Annual spring kite-flying festival in Lahore accompanied by traditional food, dance, costume and music.
July Shandur polo tournament. Annual event between Gilgit and Chitral, played out among fabulous, remote scenery at the world's highest polo ground, 3775m up on the Shandur Pass. Some authorities claim the game was invented in the north of the country, and matches in Pakistan are far more enthusiastic and

raucous than in the West. The Shandur polo tournament is accompanied by cultural events and golf and fishing tournaments.
October Lok Mela, Islamabad. Pakistan's National Folk Festival is held over ten days and showcases the best of Pakistani culture, food and music from every corner of the country, and also features groups from overseas.
December Chaomos. The solstice festival of the Kalasha people in Chitral region features feasting, sacrifices and dancing.

Routes in and out

Karachi, Islamabad, Lahore, Quetta and Peshawar have international airports, the first three offering the most worldwide connections. Overland routes link Pakistan with China (via the Karakoram Highway); India (the only crossing is between Wagah on the Pakistani side and Attari on the Indian side); Iran (the only official crossing is at Taftan, more than 600km west of Quetta); and Afghanistan (between Torkham on the Khyber Pass and Jalalabab, and at Chaman between Quetta and Kandahar). Be aware that the land borders with India, Iran and Afghanistan are subject to political tensions and changing regulations regarding their use by foreign nationals. Check the situation carefully before setting off.

Pakistan online

All Things Pakistan – Ⓦpakistaniat .com This site does what it says on the tin and has vast amounts of information – follow the 'Places' links for some inspirational travel features
Pakistan Positive – Ⓦwww.pak positive.com Operated by a Pakistani living in Karachi, this site specializes in

ordinary news from around the country –
it's a great antidote to all the bad media
the country gets.

Waqas Usman – ⓦ www.pbase.com
/waqas/pakistan Photographer's site
with some great images from around
the world – his Pakistan pictures are
excellent and a great inspiration for any
trip. The Deosai Plateau is especially
appealing.

Wildlife of Pakistan – ⓦ wildlifeof
pakistan.com Inspirational site with
great articles and features on all aspects
of Pakistani wildlife from the coasts to
the highest of the mountains.

Women of Pakistan – ⓦ www.jazbah
.org This site celebrates the achievements
of Pakistani women and includes plenty
of profiles, articles, essays, interviews and
suggestions of books worth reading.

Books

Kathleen Jamie *The Golden Peak:
Travels in Northern Pakistan*. Not a
great deal happens on the author's
journey through Pakistan but this
woman is a poet and it shows in her
fabulous descriptions.

Eric Newby *A Short Walk in the Hindu
Kush*. This book's iconic status as a
classic of travel writing is well deserved
as the author details his adventures
in the Hindu Kush. It's a great tale,
told hilariously, and is pretty much a
handbook on how not to venture into the
mountains.

Bapsi Sidhwa *The Pakistani Bride*.
Sidhwa is one of Pakistan's best
regarded authors writing in English. This
is her first book and a great introduction
to her themes of colliding worlds and the
appalling outside forces that may impact
on an individual.

Kamila Shamsie *Kartography*. Set in
Karachi in the 1980s and 90s, following
the civil war of 1971, which created an

independent Bangladesh, this is the
story of Raheen and Karim and childhood friendship growing into adult love.

Khushwant Singh Train to Pakistan.
One of the best books about the awful
human cost of the 1947 Partition of the
continent into Hindu India and Muslim
Pakistan. Ten million people were
relocated and by the end of it a million
had been slaughtered in the accompanying bloodshed.

Films

Choorian (Syed Noor, 1998). This
smash hit single-handedly revived
Punjabi film-making, although the story
of good versus evil is pretty standard
"Lollywood" fare (the Pakistan film
industry being based in Lahore).

Khamosh Pani (Silent Water; Sabiha
Sumar, 2003). Set in 1979, just as
Pakistan is subject to martial law, with
flashes back to the time of Partition. This
is the tale of the village of Charkhi in the
Punjab and the widow Ayesha whose
son becomes a fundamentalist. As
Sikh visitors seek to unearth the hidden
past, the tensions of martial law form an
eloquent backdrop.

Ramchand Pakistani (Mehreen
Jabbar, 2008) Successful on the film
festival circuit, this beautifully filmed
story depicts the events of 2002 when
India and Pakistan were on the brink of
war and tells how one innocent family
became victims.

Yeh Dil Aap Ka Hua (Javed Sheik,
2004). Love, marriage and business
rivalry are the themes of this modern
smash hit. A great topic of conversation
for those long bus journeys.

1947: Earth (Deepa Mehta, 1999). An
adaptation of the novel *Cracking India*
(or *The Ice Candy Man*) by novelist Bapsi
Sidhwa, this film looks at Partition through
the eyes of a young Parsi girl in Lahore.

Pakistani tourist offices

Ⓦ www.tourism.gov.pk
No overseas tourist office.

Pakistani embassies and consulates

Ⓦ www.mofa.gov.pk
Australia 4 Timbarra Crescent, O'Malley, Canberra, ACT 2606 ☏02/6290 1676, Ⓦ www.pakistan.org.au. Consulate in Sydney ☏2/9222 1806.
Canada 10 Range Rd, Ottawa, Ontario K1N 8J3 ☏613/238-7881, Ⓦ www.pakmission.ca. Consulates in Montreal ☏514/845-2297; Toronto ☏416/250-1255; and Vancouver ☏604/643-1748.
New Zealand 182 Onslow Rd, Khandallah, Wellington, 6035,

☏4/479 0026. Consulate in Auckland ☏9/307 2238.
South Africa 312 Brooke St, Menlo Park, Pretoria 0081 ☏12/362 4072, Ⓦ www.fortunecity.com/skyscraper /techiw/754.
UK 35–36 Lowndes Square, London SW1X 9JN ☏020/7664 9200, Ⓦ www .pakmission-uk.gov.pk. Consulates in Birmingham ☏0121/233 4123; Bradford ☏01274/661114; Glasgow ☏0141/427 5755; Manchester ☏0161/255 1786.
US 3517 International Court NW, Washington, DC 20008 ☏202/243-6500, Ⓦ www.pakistan-embassy.org. Consulates in Chicago ☏312/781-1831; Houston ☏281/890-2223, Ⓦ www .pakistanconsulatehouston.org; Los Angeles ☏310/441-5114, Ⓦ www .pakistanconsulatela.org; and New York ☏212/879-5800, Ⓦ www.pakistan consulateny.org.

The Philippines

Capital Manila
Population 88 million
Language Tagalog
Currency Peso (P)
Main religion Roman Catholic
Climate Tropical

Best time to go November–April for the western half of the archipelago, but avoid the eastern islands between November and January
Minimum daily budget US$20/£12

The Philippines is an outdoors destination, with world-class – and good-value – diving off many of its 7107 islands, as well as plenty of white-sand beaches and hundreds of hiking trails across its lush volcanic terrain. Because of its Spanish colonial history, which lasted over 300 years, its subsequent half-century as an American colony, and its Catholic heritage, there are fewer indigenous cultural sights here than in Indonesia or Thailand, but this is more than compensated for by the exuberant, easy-going Filipino attitude to life, once summed up as "that rare blend of Asian grace and Latin fire". The Filipinos hold great fiestas – their calendar is packed with religious occasions that are celebrated with pageants, fancy-dress parades, music and dancing in the streets, the inevitable beauty-queen contest, and plenty of beer and spit-roasted pork; foreigners are warmly welcomed at these events and offered characteristic Filipino hospitality.

In spite of its obvious attractions, the Philippines are still a relatively unusual backpackers' destination, in part because accommodation and travel are about fifty percent more expensive than in Thailand, but also because you can't get to the archipelago overland. For many travellers, this comparatively low-key tourist development is a big plus, and a welcome relief from some of the more clichéd Southeast Asian havens. English is widely spoken and the transport system is generally easy to fathom, if a bit flexible in its timetabling, though you'll be spending a lot of time on boats unless you budget for a few fast but pricey internal flights.

The last few years have seen an alarming number of kidnappings in the Philippines, many of them by Muslim separatist groups. Most governments are currently advising against travel to central, southern and western Mindanao, where the separatists are most active, and to the Sulu archipelago.

Main attractions

- **The beaches** Filipino beaches are some of the finest in Asia, and with almost 60,000km of coastline, there's plenty to choose from. You'll find the very best in the chain of islands known as the Visayas, which stretches from the southern tip of Luzon all the way down to Mindanao, and includes the major islands of Samar, Leyte, Bohol, Cebu, Negros and Panay, as well as hundreds of alluring pint-sized islets in between. The most famous island in the set is tiny Boracay, a beautiful but

www.roughguides.com

293

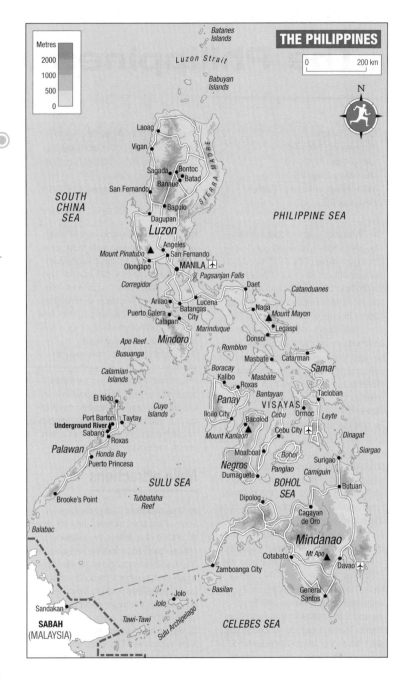

THE PHILIPPINES

Metres
2000
1000
500
0

0   200 km

N

Batanes Islands

Luzon Strait

Babuyan Islands

Laoag

Vigan

SOUTH
CHINA
SEA

Sagada   Bontoc
Banaue   Batad

San Fernando

Baguio

Dagupan

Luzon

Angeles

Mount Pinatubo   San Fernando

Olongapo   MANILA

PHILIPPINE SEA

SIERRA MADRE

Pagsanjan Falls

Corregidor

Arilao   Lucena

Puerto Galera   Batangas
Calapan   City

Daet

Catanduanes

Naga   *Mount Mayon*

Legaspi

Marinduque

Donsol

Apo Reef   *Mindoro*

Busuanga

Romblon

Masbate   Catarman

Calamian Islands

Boracay

Kalibo

Roxas

Masbate

Samar

El Nido

Cuyo Islands

Port Barton   Taytay

Underground River

Sabang

Roxas

Panay

Iloilo City

Bantayan

VISAYAS

Cebu

Bacolod   Cebu City

Tacloban

Leyte

Ormoc

Palawan

Honda Bay

Puerto Princesa

Mount Kanlaon

Moalboal   *Bohol*

Negros

Panglao

Dumaguete

Surigao

Dinagat

Siargao

Camiguin

*BOHOL
SEA*

Butuan

Brooke's Point

Tubbataha Reef

SULU SEA

Dipolog

Cagayan
de Oro

Balabac

Mindanao

Cotabato   *Mt Apo*   Davao

Zamboanga City

Jolo

Basilan

General
Santos

Sandakan

Jolo

SABAH
(MALAYSIA)

Tawi-Tawi   *Sulu Archipelago*

CELEBES SEA

FIRST-TIME ASIA

pricey resort island with a major party scene. Quieter, equally lovely Visayan islands include Romblon, Bantayan, Panay, Bohol, Malapascua and Panglao, all of which offer the perfect combination of luxuriously soft sand, a decent choice of beachfront accommodation, and laid-back fishing villages.

● **Diving** With all that fabulously clear tropical water around, it's not surprising that the Philippines is one of Asia's premier diving destinations. You'll find some of the richest reefs off Boracay, Palawan and Mindoro, but there are also spectacular underwater walls, drop-offs and coral arches at Moalboal on Cebu, and hammerhead sharks and manta rays near Panglao and Cabilao islands.

● **Manila** Cursed with traffic and pollution that make Bangkok seem like a nature reserve, Manila is one of those capitals that just has to be endured between flights or ferry connections. You can cheer yourself up, though, with a visit

to the Chinese cemetery – it's literally a ghost town, with streets and two-storey houses for the departed. Elsewhere, parts of Intramuros, the Old City, date back to the sixteenth century and the early years of Spanish occupation and combine well with a browse around the galleries of the twin national museums in Rizal Park, which focus on tribal people and colonial history. Otherwise, Manila is best for shopping and drinking, with colossal malls in every neighbourhood, and a trendy nightlife scene in Malate.

● **Puerto Galera** With stunning beaches, thirty major dive sites along a reef so rich in marine life that it's UNESCO-listed, and heaps of reasonably priced accommodation, Puerto Galera, on the north coast of Mindoro, is the perfect beach break away from Manila.

● **Banaue** This little town in northern Luzon occupies a stunning landscape of mountains, steep-sided valleys, and breathtakingly beautiful amphitheatres of

Mean temperatures (°C) and rainfall (mm)

Average daily temperatures (maximum and minimum °C) and monthly rainfall (mm)

	Jan	Feb	Mar	Apr	May	June	July	Aug	Sept	Oct	Nov	Dec
Manila												
max °C	30	31	33	34	34	33	31	31	31	31	31	30
min °C	21	21	22	23	24	24	24	24	24	23	22	21
rainfall mm	23	13	18	33	130	254	432	422	356	193	145	66
Iloilo												
max °C	29	31	31	33	33	32	31	31	31	31	31	30
min °C	23	23	23	24	25	24	24	24	24	24	24	23
rainfall mm	64	46	33	43	158	264	447	386	315	269	211	119
Surigao												
max °C	28	29	29	31	31	31	31	31	31	31	29	28
min °C	23	23	23	23	24	24	24	24	24	24	24	23
rainfall mm	544	376	506	254	158	125	178	130	168	272	427	620
Zamboanga												
max °C	31	31	32	31	31	31	31	31	31	31	31	32
min °C	23	23	23	23	24	24	23	24	23	23	23	23
rainfall mm	64	46	33	43	158	264	447	386	315	269	211	119

www.roughguides.com

sculpted rice-terraces. To make the most of the scenery, follow the popular walking trail between Banaue and the traditional village of Batad. The bus journey up to Banaue is a scenic highlight in itself, as it takes you along the Halsema Highway, one of the most awesome roads in Southeast Asia.

● **Palawan** Graced with peaceful shores, thickly forested crags and a gorgeous rugged natural beauty, the large, remote island of Palawan is probably the single most rewarding destination in the Philippines. It's got everything: snow-white beaches at Taytay, Port Barton, Sabang and Roxas, breathtaking scenery in the Bacuit archipelago, unrivalled diving at El Nido and Tubbataha Reef Marine Park, hiking trails through the jungle, intact tribal culture, and a noticeable lack of tourists. And there's also the famous eight-kilometre boat ride through the spooky, bat-infested caves of the Underground River in Saint Paul's Subterranean Cave.

● **Sagada** This charming hill village in northern Luzon is the home of the Igorot tribe, who are famous for their hanging coffins – suspended high in caves out of the reach of wild animals – as well as for their weavings. There are plenty of hiking possibilities and a distinctly bohemian ambience to the village, all of which make it a really nice place to hang out for a few days.

Also recommended

● **Siargao Island** Kayaking is the perfect way to explore the shapely coastline of this undeveloped island off northeastern Mindanao, with its secret coves, hidden lagoons and peaceful crystal-white beaches. There's famously good surfing here too and a rustic interior full of coconut palms and tiny villages.

● **Camiguin Island, off northern Mindanao** Famous for its exceptionally sweet and succulent *lanzone* (lychee) fruits, this little gem of an island offers heaps of variety, including sugar-fine beaches, seven volcanoes, exceptional trekking and rock-climbing, hot springs and waterfalls.

● **Shooting the rapids at Pagsanjan Falls** The scenery along this stretch of the Bombongan River is impressively dramatic, and it's a genuine thrill to race the fourteen rapids as you squeeze between the jungle-clad canyon walls. This is an immensely popular day-trip from Manila, but you can avoid the crowds by staying nearby and doing an early-morning boat ride before the coaches pitch up.

Festivals

January Ati-Atihan, Kalibo, Panay Island. Everyone dresses up in outrageous costumes for Southeast Asia's biggest three-day street party, which is held in honour of the Holy Infant Jesus and climaxes with a masquerade ball.

March or April Holy Week Crucifixions, Pampanga province, Luzon. Held every year near San Fernando, these are real crucifixions of real people. Under the rapt gaze of hundreds of spectators, a dozen or so pious penitents flagellate themselves before being nailed onto crosses, believing that this earthly suffering will ease their eventual passage into heaven. Although the penitents are taken off the crosses after only a few seconds, it's a disturbing spectacle with plenty of genuine blood – and an act of piety that is not endorsed by the Catholic Church.

October Lanzones Festival, Camiguin Island. Ribald festival in honour of the lychee, Camiguin's most famous product, which sees islanders parading through the streets dressed only in lychee leaves.

Routes in and out

Most long-haul travellers fly into the Philippines via Hong Kong and land in Manila, though there are alternative connections via Southeast Asian capitals; both Cebu and Davao also have international airports. Weesam Express operates international ferries from Sandakan in Sabah (East Malaysia) to Zamboanga (Mindanao).

Philippines online

Bundok Philippines – www.geocities.com/Yosemite/3712 Specialist site all about hiking in the Philippines, with lots of good hike reports.

Click the City – Ⓦwww.clickthecity .com The best online guide to what's on in Manila, with some recommendations for other cities too.

Dive Buddies Philippines – Ⓦwww .divephil.com A commercial website, but it carries a decent roundup of the archipelago's best dives.

Jens Peters' Philippines Guide – Ⓦwww.travelphil.de Comprehensive travel site created by a travel guide author. Alongside links and summaries on everything from ferry travel to motorcycling, there's also a fun "Who's Who" section with links to homepages and biogs of Filipino bands, actors and other celebs.

Tanikalang Ginto – Ⓦwww.filipino links.com Links to scores of interesting Philippines-related sites, including travel, unusual destinations, books and hotels.

Books

Alan Berlow *Dead Season: A Story of Murder and Revenge*. Famously gripping account of the real facts behind three murders – of a soldier, a peasant and a plantation owner – on the sugar-producing island of Negros,

which reveals a depressing picture of the powerlessness of ordinary Filipinos in the face of entrenched interests and far-reaching corruption.

Jessica Tarahata Hagedorn *Dogeaters*. Gritty contemporary novel by a Filipino-American set in Marcos-era Manila and peopled with a cast of prostitutes, DJs, clubbers and hustlers.

James Hamilton-Paterson *Playing With Water: Passion and Solitude on a Philippine Island*. The beautifully lyrical account of the several extended periods the author spent living alone on a tiny uninhabited island near Marinduque, befriended by local fishermen and learning to dive and fish as they did. His descriptions of these underwater forays are breathtaking.

F Sionil José *Dusk*. The Philippines' most famous and widely read author writes in English and has won numerous awards. His best known works are the five Rosales Saga novels, an accessible, socially conscious, historical epic of Philippine history. *Dusk* is the opener, set at the end of the nineteenth century during the time of the fateful Spanish-American War.

Hiroo Onoda *No Surrender: My Thirty-Year War*. The incredible true story of the Japanese lieutenant who did not know World War II was over until he emerged from the jungle on Lubang Island (northwest off Mindoro) almost thirty years later, in 1974. His account tells how he continued to wage his one-man guerilla campaign in the Philippines, despite repeated rescue attempts, including by his own relatives, all of which he dismissed as trickery and enemy propaganda.

Films

Back to Bataan (Edward Dmytryk, 1950). Patriotic dramatization of the infamous Bataan Death March in World War II, when seventy thousand Filipino and US POWs were marched by their Japanese captors from Mariveles to San Fernando, an arduous trip of 100km across the Batan Peninsula west of Manila. Some seven thousand soldiers died along the way, with around another seven thousand escaping into the jungle. John Wayne takes the role of the US soldiers' leader, opposite Anthony Quinn as leader of the Filipino guerilla fighters.

Manila in the Claws of Neon (Lino Brocka, 1975). Classic noir depiction of a hellish Manila by one of the Philippines' most acclaimed film directors, as a young, bewildered innocent from the provinces heads to the scary metropolis in search of his beloved.

Small Voices (Gil M Portes, 2002). Multi-award winning heart-warmer from one of the Philippines' most important directors. Faced with a corrupt and apathetic education system, an idealistic young teacher enters her class of young, impoverished pupils into a singing contest.

Woman of the Breakwater (Mario O'Hara, 2003). By turns a warm, funny, depressing and heart-warming story of life on the streets for the slum-dwellers of Manila Bay.

Philippines tourist offices

Ⓦ www.tourism.gov.ph
Ⓦ www.wowphilippines.com.ph
Australia and **New Zealand** Suite 401, 4th Floor, Thakral House, 301 George St, Sydney, NSW 2000 ☎02/9279 3380, Ⓦ www.philippinetourism.com.au.
UK and Ireland 146 Cromwell Rd, London SW7 4EF ☎020/7835 1100, Ⓦ www.wowphilippines.co.uk.
US and Canada Ⓦ www.wowphilippines .ca; 30 North Michigan Ave, Suite 913, Chicago, IL 60602 ☎312/782-2475, Ⓔ pdotchi@aol.com; 3660 Wilshire Blvd, 900 Suite 216, Los Angeles, CA 90010

☎213/487-4525, Ⓔ pdotla@aol.com; 556 Fifth Ave, New York, NY 10036 ☎212/575-7915, Ⓔ pdotny@aol.com; 447 Sutter St, Suite 507, San Francisco, CA 94108 ☎415/956-4060, Ⓔ pdotsf @aol.com.

Philippines embassies and consulates

Ⓦ dfa.gov.ph
Australia 1 Moonah Place, Yarralumla, Canberra, ACT 2600 ☎02/6273 2535, Ⓦ www.philembassy.au.com. Consulate in Sydney ☎02/6273 7377, Ⓦ www .philippineconsulate.com.au.
Canada 130 Albert St, Suite 606, Ottawa, Ontario K1P 5G4 ☎613/233-1121, Ⓦ www.philippineembassy.ca. Consulates in Toronto ☎416/922-7181, Ⓦ www.philcongen-toronto.com; and Vancouver ☎604/685-7645, Ⓦ www .vancouverpcg.net.
New Zealand 50 Hobson St, Thorndon, Wellington ☎04/472 9848, Ⓔ embassy @wellington-pe.co.nz.
South Africa 54 Nicolson St, Muckleneuk, Pretoria 0181 ☎012/346-0451 Ⓦ www.philippineembassy -pretoria.com.
UK and Ireland 6-8 Suffolk St, London SW1Y 4HG ☎020/7451 1800, Ⓦ www .philembassy-uk.org.
US 1600 Massachusetts Ave NW, Washington, DC 20036 ☎202/467-9300, Ⓦ www.philippineembassy-usa.org. Consulates in Chicago ☎312/332-6458, Ⓦ www.chicagopcg.com; Honolulu ☎808/595-6316, Ⓦ www.philippine consulatehonolulu.com; Los Angeles ☎213/639-0980, Ⓦ www.philippine consulatela.org; New York ☎212/764-1330, Ⓦ www.pcgny.net; and San Francisco ☎415/433-6666, Ⓦ www .philippineconsulate-sf.org.

Singapore

Population 4.5 million
Language Malay, Mandarin, Tamil and English are the official languages; various Chinese dialects also spoken
Currency Singapore dollar (S$)
Religion Buddhism, Islam, Hinduism, Sikhism, Christianity

Climate Tropical
Best time to go Singapore is extremely hot and humid all year; November–December is slightly cooler, but also has the highest rainfall
Minimum daily budget US$32/£18

Though some monuments and buildings from its British colonial days remain, Singapore is more a showcase for gleaming modern architecture than a memorial to times past, and the speed and ruthlessness of development on the tiny island are quite breathtaking. As the region's transport hub, most visitors to Southeast Asia pass through here at some point. While many love the orderly efficiency of the place after a few weeks in wilder parts, others miss the feel of "real" Asia among the high-rises, shopping centres, seamless transport systems and booming economy. But it doesn't take too much to discover the older parts of Singapore such as Little India which are less shiny and feel a bit more exotic.

It's easy to mock the authoritarian regulations that have accompanied Singapore's development – don't bring in any chewing gum, don't jaywalk and always flush the toilet after use – but Singapore is the Asia that most Asian nations aspire to, a well-ordered and safe environment both day and night for residents and foreigners alike. It isn't cheap when compared to the countries around it, though, and anyone on a tight budget should try to stay as short a time as possible. Fortunately, the island is compact enough that you can explore the highlights – downtown Singapore, the zoo and Sentosa – in just a few days. Singapore has a well-deserved reputation as a foodie mecca, which owes much to the different cuisines of

Mean temperatures (°C) and rainfall (mm)

Average daily temperatures (maximum and minimum °C) and monthly rainfall (mm)

	Jan	Feb	Mar	Apr	May	June	July	Aug	Sept	Oct	Nov	Dec
Singapore												
max °C	31	32	32	32	32	32	31	31	31	31	31	30
min °C	21	22	23	23	23	23	22	22	22	22	22	22
rainfall mm	146	155	182	223	228	151	170	163	200	199	255	258

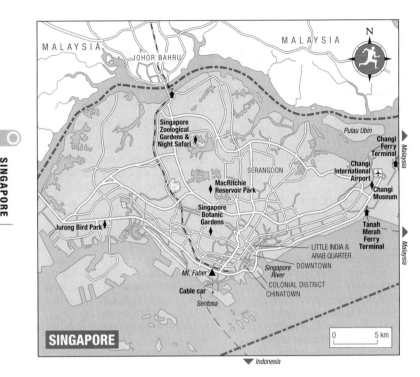

the rich ethnic mix on the tiny island, with Chinese in the majority and sizeable minorities of Malays and Indians.

Main attractions

● **Chinatown, Little India and the Arab Quarter** Towered over by the new Singapore skyline, these remaining ethnic enclaves are relatively untouched by modern development. Some of their tiny, terraced shophouses are still in operation – the shop operates from the front downstairs rooms, while the inhabitants live behind and above. Not surprisingly, traditional places of worship remain most evocative of times past. The Sri Mariamman Hindu temple, with its exuberant carvings; the graceful domes and dignified interior of the

Sultan Mosque; and the Thian Hock Keng Chinese temple are especially atmospheric and picturesque.

● **Singapore Zoological Gardens** A shining example of a zoo with a worldwide reputation: most of the bigger animals are kept in huge enclosures, separated from visitors by deep moats. Also on offer is a brilliant Night Safari for viewing nocturnal animals.

● **Food** Head for the food courts, lined with numerous stalls selling their own specialities; you put your meal together from whichever stalls take your fancy. The surroundings at these places may be pretty uninspiring, but the range of Asian cuisines on offer is amazing, from Malay satay to Indian biriyanis via Thai tom-yam soup. Those missing more familiar tastes will be pleased to find that Singapore also offers everything from Italian and French to Mexican, and American coffee-bar chains have hit the city big-time.

- **Raffles Hotel** The luxurious atmosphere of this colonial-era institution is still much in evidence, and a visit is considered a must for tourists, though much of the site has been turned into a shopping arcade. You can even have a Singapore Sling at the very bar where the cocktail was created – though it'll cost you more than a night in one of the city's budget guesthouses (Ⓦwww.raffles.com).

- **Sentosa** This offshore-island amusement park has plenty of rides, exhibitions and museums. Underwater World, where a moving walkway carries you through a transparent underwater tunnel with sharks and other sea creatures swimming around outside, is hard to beat, as are the views of the city's skyscrapers you get as you ride the cable car here.

- **Jurong Bird Park** This superlative park does nothing by halves; with over six hundred species of bird it is the largest collection in Southeast Asia. It has the world's tallest man-made waterfall in one of the four walk-in aviaries and the largest walk-in aviary in the world which means that it's possible to see African birds flying. There's even a penguin enclosure that keeps those feathered friends at Antarctic temperatures.

- **Changi Museum** The most thought-provoking spot on the island; a record of what life was like for the World War II prisoners of war.

- **Ride the Singapore Flyer** The world's largest observation wheel (165m tall) is located next to the Esplanade and offers great views of Singapore, Indonesia and Malaysia (Ⓦwww.singaporeflyer .com.sg).

Also recommended

- **A cruise on the Singapore River** A chance to see the city's fabulously modern high-rises, gentrified warehouses and Chinese shophouses from a different angle.

- **Shopping** Singapore's number-one hobby. The island's shopping malls are certainly on a grand scale, and boast

▲ The Singapore Skyline

aggressive air-conditioning – useful if the heat gets too much. You'll find the greatest concentration of malls along Orchard Road. If you're on a wider trip through Asia, though, you'll usually find better prices elsewhere.

● **MacRitchie Reservoir Park** There are excellent walking trails out here and the HSBC Tree Top Walk way up in the forest canopy offers great views of the forest.

● **Drink at the Swissotel's City Space Bar** From this seventieth-floor bar you can see as far as Indonesia to the south and Malaysia to the north.

● **Pulau Ubin** Just 7km long and 2km wide, this tiny island tucked into the waters between Singapore and Malaysia gives a glimpse into a rural Singapore long gone elsewhere, with Malay stilt houses, shady roads through rubber plantations and secluded beaches.

● **Asian Civilizations Museum** If you're looking for inspiration for the next leg of your journey you'll surely find it here, in this stylish, perfectly judged introduction to the cultures, arts and faiths of Southeast Asia, the Indian Subcontinent, China and Islamic Asia.

● **Esplanade** Singapore's high-profile entertainment complex is a must, not least for its startlingly futuristic design. It's known locally as "the durian" because of its spiky covering (Ⓦwww .esplanade.com).

Festivals

January/February Thaipusam. In honour of the Hindu god of bravery, Lord Murugan, devotees have their bodies pierced and are encased in *kavadi*, heavy metal spiked cages.
January/February Chinese New Year. Dragon and lion dances, Chinese opera and a riverside carnival all topped off with

the Chingay Parade, Singapore's biggest, in which floats, martial arts troops and stilt walkers parade through the City Hall – Marina Bay area of the city.
October/November Thimithi. At the Sri Mariamman Temple, Hindu devotees sprint across burning coals in honour of Draupathi, a legendary heroine and incarnation of the goddess Mariamman.

Routes in and out

Singapore's Changi airport is one of the busiest in Asia and is served by all major international carriers. As well as long-haul flights, there are excellent links to all parts of Asia. A causeway connects Singapore with the Malaysian city of Johor Bahru, and there are direct buses to destinations throughout Malaysia with connections on to Hat Yai and Bangkok in Thailand; trains also link Singapore with Johor Bahru, Kuala Lumpur, Butterworth and Ipoh in Malaysia. There are ferries to Tanjung Belungkor in Malaysia, and to the islands of Batam and Bintan in the Riau Archipelago of Indonesia, from where there are connections to Sumatra.

Singapore online

Esplanade – Ⓦ**www.esplanade.com** Singapore's biggest and best arts complex hosts a great website. Detailing everything you can do here – and that's a lot.
Makansutra – Ⓦ**www.makansutra .com** Leaving no doubt that Singapore is foodie heaven, this website features articles, reviews and listings about every aspect of eating in Singapore – there's also an excellent discussion forum where you can ask specific advice on where to eat.
Official Gateway to Singapore – Ⓦ**www.sg** Awesome in its scope and efficiency, this portal has links to more

than 16,000 Singaporean sites on every imaginable aspect of Singapore and is updated daily – if it isn't here, the chances are it doesn't exist.

Talking Cock – Ⓦ www.talkingcock .com To 'talk cock' means to talk nonsense or engage in idle banter in Singlish, the street language of Singapore, which is officially discouraged. This is Singapore's best known satirical website which campaigns for free speech, including the right to talk Singlish. A lot of it is obscure for visitors but the Coxford Singlish Dictionary is a great read.

Books

Maurice Collis *Raffles*. This biography describes the amazing life of Raffles, the British founder of modern Singapore.

Su-chen Christine Lim *A Bit of Earth*. Following the friendship between a Malay chef and a Chinese refugee, this moving novel, by one of Singapore's best known novelists, subverts the stereotypes that exist within the culture.

Vyvyane Loh *Breaking the Tongue*. The Fall of Singapore is told from a local perspective in this chilling story. The Chinese central character, Claude Lim, has been brought up to be British, and this book is also about identity, as relevant to Singapore today as it was at that time.

Lau Siew Mau *Playing Madam Mao*. The complex plot involves an actress, Chang Ching, who shares a name with Mao's third wife and also plays her on the stage. The instability of identity is set against the backdrop of uncertainties in Singapore in the 1980s – including media censorship and the repression of political opposition.

Hwee Hwee Tan *Foreign Bodies*. One of Singapore's best known authors tackles nine frenetic days in the lives of the three central characters taking on culture clash in the city-state head on.

Films

Chicken Rice War (Cheah Chee Long, 2001). A riff on Romeo and Juliet, this tells the story of Fenson Wong and Audrey Chang whose feuding parents operate neighbouring stalls in a hawker centre.

Eating Air (Zhi Feng, 1999). This is the story of less than model Singaporeans, the tatooed bikers who smoke, drink, trade porn and drive fast motorbikes. But there's a touching love story here as well – and a rousing rock soundtrack.

I Not Stupid (Jack Neo, 2002). A big box office success in Singapore, this comic drama tells the story of three 12-year-old classmates and their families.

Money No Enough (Tay Teck Lock, 1998). A pointed look at the grasping ruthlessness of modern Singapore society, this film garnered praise, and a huge box-office income, at home.

Twelve Storeys (Eric Khoo, 1997). The lives of ordinary Singaporeans are dissected in this scathing criticism of the island's heart and soul. An oldest son, an elderly lady and a henpecked husband tell their tales and illustrate the dark side of Singaporean culture and life.

Singaporean tourist offices

Ⓦ **www.visitsingapore.com**

Australia Level 11, AWA Building, 47 York St, Sydney, NSW 2000 ☎02/9290 2888.

Canada Contact the closest US office.

New Zealand c/o Vivaldi World Ltd, 1340-C Glenbrook Rd, RDI, Waiuku, Auckland ☎0800/608 506 (Freecall NZ only).

UK Grand Buildings, 1-3 Strand, London, WC2N 5HR ☎020/7484 2710.

US 5670 Wilshire Blvd #510, Los Angeles, CA 90036 ☎323/677-0808; 1156 Ave of the Americas #702, New York 10036 ☎212/302-4861.

Singaporean embassies and consulates

🌐 **www.mfa.gov.sg/internet**
Australia 17 Forster Crescent, Yarralumla, Canberra, ACT 2600 ☎02/6271 2000, 🌐www.mfa.gov.sg /canberra.
Canada 44th Floor, One First Canadian Place, Toronto, Ontario M5X 1B1 ☎416/863 5597.

New Zealand 17 Kabul St, Khandallah, Wellington ☎04/470 0850, 🌐www .mfa.gov.sg/wellington.
South Africa 980 Schoeman St, Arcadia, Pretoria, 0083 ☎012/430 6035, 🌐www.mfa.gov.sg/Pretoria.
UK 9 Wilton Crescent, London SW1X 8SP ☎020/7235 8315, 🌐www.mfa .gov.sg/london.
US 3501 International Place NW, Washington, DC 20008 ☎202/537-3100, 🌐www.mfa.gov.sg/washington; consulates in Chicago ☎312/853-7555; Miami ☎305/858-4225; New York ☎212/223-3331; and San Francisco ☎415/543-4775.

South Korea

Capital Seoul	Buddhism and Christianity
Population 48 million	**Climate** Temperate
Language Korean	**Best time to go** September–
Currency Won (W)	November; also April–June
Main religions Mahayana	**Minimum daily budget** US$35/£21

Overshadowed as a tourist destination by neighbouring China and Japan, South Korea features on backpackers' itineraries more as a place to find work than as somewhere to explore for its own sake. English-teaching jobs are fairly easy to land in Seoul and Busan (check the adverts in the local English-language newspapers), and the cost of living is less prohibitive than in Japan, though still a lot higher than nearly everywhere else in Asia. Being so close to China and Japan, South Korea also works well as part of a journey between the two, and there are useful ferry services in both directions.

The same is not true of its immediate neighbour, North Korea, with whom virtually all contact – including transport links – has been banned since 1950, when civil war erupted between the communist, Soviet-backed North and the US-backed South. Though overt hostilities ended in 1953, no peace agreement has yet been signed, so the two countries are still theoretically at war. Indeed the ceasefire line between them – the Demilitarized Zone (DMZ) – is a major tourist attraction. During the early years of the new millennium there was unprecedented dialogue between the two governments and a few of the eleven million separated North–South families were reunited for the first time in fifty years. However, relations have soured once more and North Korea remains a very difficult and expensive place to visit. Visas are not granted to nationals of South Korea or the US; other nationalities can only apply once they've paid for a tour and had it approved of by the government: all visitors are obliged to be accompanied by a tour guide throughout their stay in this reclusive, autocratic, communist state. Access is generally by plane or train from Beijing but, should North–South relations thaw further, restored rail links between the two countries would make South Korea accessible by rail all the way from Europe, via the Trans-Siberian terminus in Vladivostock.

The dominant force in contemporary South Korean culture is Confucianism; more of a philosophy than a religion, it originated in China 2500 years ago and is essentially a moral code of family duty and social obligations. The most widespread religion in South Korea is Mahayana Buddhism, and you will find traditional Buddhist temples all over the country, in the heart of the city as well as hidden away on remote mountain sides.

For tourists, South Korea's greatest attractions are the thousands of hiking trails through the forests of its mountainous national parks. Around seventy percent of the country is mountainous, and the autumn colours on the trees that carpet the mountains are at their most spectacular in late October; springtime brings a similarly impressive display of cherry blossom, followed soon after by azaleas. Try to avoid major sights, national parks and hiking trails at weekends, when you'll

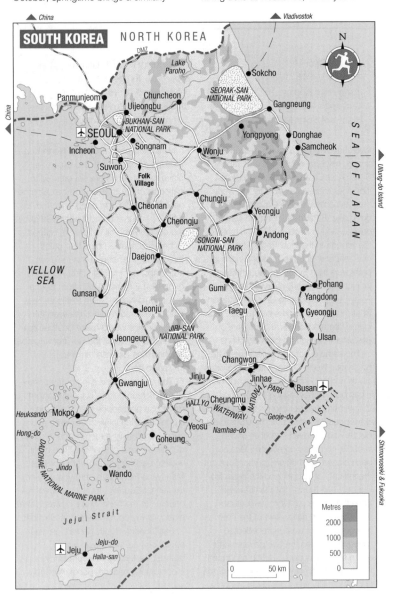

www.roughguides.com

Mean temperatures (°C) and rainfall (mm)

Average daily temperatures (maximum and minimum °C) and monthly rainfall (mm)

	Jan	Feb	Mar	Apr	May	June	July	Aug	Sept	Oct	Nov	Dec
Seoul												
max °C	0	3	8	17	22	27	29	31	26	19	11	3
min °C	-9	-7	-2	5	11	16	21	22	15	7	0	-7
rainfall mm	31	20	38	76	81	130	376	267	119	41	46	25
Busan												
max °C	6	7	12	17	21	24	27	29	26	21	15	9
min °C	-2	-1	3	8	13	17	22	23	18	12	6	1
rainfall mm	43	36	69	140	132	201	295	130	173	74	41	31

be competing for space with thousands of city dwellers. Public transport within South Korea is fast and efficient, and the country is so compact that you can cross from coast to coast in half a day.

Main attractions

● **Gyeongju** Korea's ancient capital, Gyeongju, is the country's big must-see, and rates as one of the ten most important ancient cultural cities in the world. In among the shops and markets of the modern-day city you'll find abundant relics of its two-thousand-year history, including colossal fifth-century tombs and burial mounds, a seventh-century stone observatory, and the royal pleasure gardens of Anapji, which were designed in 674 AD. Other quarters of Gyeongju are rich with elegant pagodas and historic wooden Buddhist temples, and numerous trails take you up the slopes of the sacred mountain, Nam-san, which dominates the south of the city.

● **Hiking in the national parks** South Korea is full of exhilarating national parks, all of which are crisscrossed by clearly marked trails and dotted with good camping spots (and the occasional mountain hut). The cream of the crop is Seorak-san, and in particular Naeseorak

(Inner Seorak), an exceptionally tranquil stretch of forested peaks, rivers, waterfalls and Buddhist temples – and some established rock climbs too. Also well worth seeking out are Jiri-san, which boasts a 65-kilometre-long ridge trail and lots of historic temples; the popular and fairly gentle trails of Songni-san; and Bukhan-san, which is on the edge of Seoul.

● **Seoul** South Korea's modern-day capital has a reasonable number of sights to keep you entertained for a few days. Most interesting are the five imposing royal palaces, some of which date back to the fifteenth century. Inside the Changdokkung Palace you'll find one of South Korea's loveliest gardens, the Piwon, a haven of ponds and pavilions. In the modern part of town, check out the Kimchi Museum, dedicated to the fiery pickled cabbage that is South Korea's national dish, browse the cutting-edge Leeum Museum of Modern Art, and spend the evening in the trendy nightlife district of Sinchon or at the enormous Namdaemun Market, which opens from around 10.30pm until dawn and sells everything from handicrafts to live fish, plus great hot food.

● **Panmunjeom** On the 38th parallel, the 1953 ceasefire line between North

www.roughguides.com

and South Korea – a four-kilometre-wide strip of land spiked with guardposts – is still in force today, and the village of Panmunjeom, which stands on the DMZ just 56km north of Seoul, is a popular day-trip from the capital. Unless you can afford the cost of joining an organized tour around North Korea this is the closest you can get to the repressive, desperately impoverished totalitarian state. There's no border crossing here (or anywhere between the two countries) but Panmunjeom attracts busloads of tourists, all of whom are required to dress smartly (no jeans, T-shirts or combat trousers).

● **The Korean Folk Village** It may sound like a coach-tour nightmare, but the Korean Folk Village is well worth a day-trip from Seoul, especially if you've not got time to explore the rest of the country. A reconstruction of a typical nineteenth-century village, it's complete with Buddhist temple, Confucian school, pottery and weaving workshops, blacksmiths and traditional farmhouses. The people you see in the village do actually live and work here, even if they might look like actors dolled up in traditional outfits.

Also recommended

● **Dadohae National Marine Park**
A collection of dramatic little archipelagos off the southwestern coast between Mokpo and Wando, the Dadohae National Marine Park is of such importance it's been UNESCO-listed as a biosphere reserve. Among the tiny specks of islands dotted across the sapphire sea the obvious bases are Heuksando and Hong-do, where you can join boat tours through this extraordinary seascape.

● **The island of Ullung-do** Rugged, remote and starkly beautiful, this tiny volcanic outcrop – accessed by ferry from Samcheok – has hardly any roads and is best explored on foot. It takes two days to walk round the island, giving you ample opportunity to enjoy the temples, forested ridges, waterfalls and famous 2000-year-old juniper tree.

▲ Chokseongnu Pavilion, Jinju

- **Taking an open-air bath with a view at Seorak Waterpia** Soak up the glorious mountain vista while wallowing in the natural hot springs at this spa resort in Seorak-san National Park, where you can also bathe in a lemon-flavoured pool, go skinny-dipping, and brave a shower under a near-boiling waterfall.

- **The fifteenth-century village of Yangdong** Prettily set beside a river and beneath a wooded hill, Yangdong is of such historic importance that villagers are forbidden to modify or knock down their antique wooden houses, many of which are magnificent structures, with sweeping roofs, beautifully carved beams and capacious verandahs.

- **Staying in a yogwan** If you're on a budget, make a beeline for these ubiquitous traditional guesthouses: they're cheap, family-run, and usually have lots of character. You sleep on a futon on the floor – a special treat in winter when the underfloor heating system kicks in and acts like a huge electric blanket.

Festivals

March or April Jinhae Cherry Blossom Festival, Jinhae, near Busan. The cherry blossoms are particularly gorgeous in Jinhae, where they're celebrated with a week of parades and blossom photo contests, but you also get a good show in Incheon and in Seorak-san National Park.
May or June Dano Festival, Namdaecheon, near Gangneung. Very traditional festival of the spirits in which shamen pray for a good harvest and there are public displays of traditional wrestling, martial arts, dance and masked drama.
October Chungju World Martial Arts Festival. Groups from across the world gather to demonstrate their special martial arts skills in this week-long sporting spectacle in Chungju, credited as the spiritual home of modern taekwondo.

Routes in and out

Most international flights arrive at Seoul's Incheon Airport, 60km west of the capital, though there are a limited number to Busan and Jeju-do. South Korea has good international ferry connections with Japan, China and Russia. Ferries and hydrofoils connect Busan with the Japanese port towns of Shimonoseki, Fukuoka and Osaka. Ferries to China all arrive at and depart from Incheon (near Seoul), running regularly to Tianjin (near Beijing), Qingdao and Weihai (both in Shandong), Dalian and Dandong (both in Liaoning), and Lianyungang (Jiangsu). There's also at least one ferry a week between Sokcho and Vladivostok, the terminus of the Trans-Siberian rail line in Russia (see p.28). See ⓦenglish.visitkorea.or.kr for a detailed guide to all South Korea's international ferry timetables.

There has been no legal border crossing between South and North Korea since the Korean War.

South Korea online

Discovering Korea – ⓦwww .discoveringkorea.com Interesting, wide-reaching travel and culture blog from a young Korean-American, Matt Kelley, living in Seoul. He broadcasts a radio show on the same subject and is planning a book too.
Korea in the Clouds: A Guide to Hiking Korea's Mountains – ⓦkoreaclimbs.blogspot.com Useful resource of hikers' accounts of their climbs and trails in Korea, with maps, tips, access information and updates.

www.roughguides.com

The Korean Blog List – Ⓦkorea .banoffeepie.com Over five hundred blogs about Korea, written in English by expats, emigrés and tourists.
Life in Korea – Ⓦwww.lifeinkorea.com Plenty of useful and interesting stuff here, from culture and travel to forums and language exchange.

Books

Kang Chol-Hwan *The Aquariums of Pyongyang: Ten Years in the North Korean Gulag*. The horrifying account of Kang Chol-Hwan's childhood, which was spent from ages 9 to 19 in a North Korean labour camp, because his grandfather was suspected of harbouring counter-revolutionary tendencies. The family was released in 1987 and the author, a journalist, now lives in South Korea.

Jennifer Barclay *Meeting Mr Kim: Or How I Went to Korea and Learned to Love Kimchi*. Lively and engaging account of how a young British woman ends up living in South Korea for a while. While her musician boyfriend entertains the barflies at Seoul's Grand Hyatt, she does lots of random exploring in the countryside and along the coast.

Bruce Cumings *Korea's Place in the Sun: A Modern History*. An accessible, opinionated, introduction that includes a controversial account of the twentieth-century North–South split.

Simon Winchester *Korea: A Walk Through the Land of Miracles*. An updated version of a 1988 journey around South Korea by one of Britain's most erudite travel writers.

Films

Chihwaseon: Strokes of Fire (Im Kwon-Taek, 2002). Beautifully shot story of the troubled life and loves of an impassioned, alcoholic nineteenth-century artist. It won the already famous Korean director Kwon-Taek Im best director award at the Cannes Film Festival.

Memories of Murder (Boon Jun-Ho, 2003). Phenomenally popular, way above-average suspense thriller based on the real unsolved case of ten serial rapes and murders in a small village in the late 1980s.

JSA: Joint Security Area (Yeong-Ae Lee, 2000). A huge smash at the Korean box office, this pertinent North-South psychological thriller is set around Panmunjeom in the DMZ and tells the stories of two soldiers, one from each side of the border.

Spring, Summer, Autumn, Winter... and Spring (Kim Ki-Duk, 2004). Gentle Buddhist fable about a troubled young man and an elderly monk who live in a floating temple on a lake encircled by forested slopes. The breathtakingly beautiful setting – Juwangsan National Park – is stunning, shot in its different seasonal guises.

A Tale Of Two Sisters (Kim Ji-Woon, 2004). Scary, brilliantly crafted psycho-supernatural thriller about two sisters returning to live with their father and cruel stepmother after a stint in a mental-health hospital. Updated version of a traditional ghost story.

South Korean tourist offices

Ⓦwww.visitkorea.or.kr
Australia and New Zealand Level 18, Australia Square Tower, 264 George St, Sydney, NSW 2000 ☎02/9252 4147, Ⓔvisitkorea@knto.org.au.
Canada 700 Bay St, Suite 1903, Toronto, Ontario M5G 1Z6 ☎416/348-9056, Ⓔtoronto@knto.ca.
UK and Ireland 3rd Floor, New Zealand House, Haymarket, London SW1Y 4TE

①020/7321 2535, ⓔlondon@mail.knto
.or.kr.
US Two Executive Drive, Suite 750,
Fort Lee, NJ 07024 ①201/585-0909,
ⓔny@kntoamerica.com; 737 N.
Michigan Ave, Suite 910, Chicago, IL
60611 ①312/981-1717, ⓔchicago
@kntoamerica.com; 5509 Wilshire Blvd,
Los Angeles, CA 90036 ①323/634-
0280, ⓔla@kntoamerica.com.

South Korean embassies and consulates

ⓦ**www.mofat.go.kr**
Australia 113 Empire Circuit, Yarralumla
ACT 2600 ①02 6270 4100, ⓦaus-act
.mofat.go.kr. Consulate in Sydney
①02/9210 0200.
Canada 150 Boteler St, Ottawa,
Ontario K1N 5A6 ①613/244-5010,
ⓦcan-ottawa.mofat.go.kr. Consulates in
Montreal ①514/845-2555, ⓦwww
.koreanconsulate.qc.ca; Toronto
①416/920-3809, ⓦwww.korean
consulate.on.ca/en; and Vancouver

①604/681-9581, ⓦwww.can-vancouver
.mofat.go.kr.
Ireland 15 Clyde Road, Ballsbridge,
Dublin 4 ①01/660-8800, ⓦirl.mofat
.go.kr.
New Zealand 11th Floor, ASB Bank
Tower, 2 Hunter Street, Wellington,
①04/473 9073, ⓦnzl-wellington
.mofat.go.kr. Consulate in Auckland
①09/379 0818.
South Africa Greenpark Estates No.
3, 27 George Storrar Drive, Groenkloof,
Pretoria 0181 ①012/460-2508, ⓦzaf
.mofat.go.kr.
UK 60 Buckingham Gate, London
SW1E 6AJ ①020/7227 5505, ⓦgbr
.mofat.go.kr.
US 2320 Massachusetts Ave NW,
Washington, DC 20008 ①202/939-
5663, ⓦwww.koreaembassyusa.org.
Consulates in Chicago ①312/822-9485;
Los Angeles ①213/385-9300,
ⓦkoreanconsulatela.org; New York
①646/674-6000, ⓦwww.korean
consulate.org; and San Francisco
①41/921-2251, ⓦwww.korean
consulatesf.org.

www.roughguides.com

Sri Lanka

Capital Colombo
Population 20 million
Languages Sinhala, Tamil
Currency Rupee (Rs)
Religion Buddhists are in the
majority (70%), with Hindu (15%),
Christian and Muslim minorities

Climate Tropical, with two distinct
monsoons
Best time to go November–April
for the south and west coasts;
January–April for the hills; May–
September for the east coast
Minimum daily budget US$10/£6

A small country, Sri Lanka nonetheless
offers an enormous variety of quintes-
sentially Asian experiences. The island is
dotted with ruins from ancient Buddhist
empires, including serene, gigantic
Buddha figures and *dagobas*, white-
painted domed shrines ranging from just
a few metres tall to immense, imposing
structures; variations of those are found
in India, Thailand, China and other Asian
countries. Other architectural features
worth keeping an eye out for are buildings
dating from the Portuguese, Dutch and
British colonial periods, which lasted from
the first European arrival in 1505 through
to Independence in 1948.

Sri Lanka also boasts glorious
landscapes, with lovely beaches, cool
rolling hills, mountains and huge tracts
of rainforest, excellent for spotting

wildlife. Many bird species like it here
too, spending the winter on Sri Lanka's
southern coasts before returning to
temperate zones. Outside Colombo and
Kandy – the main cities – the island has
a rural feel, making it more manageable
than chaotic India to the north.

Civil war raged across the island for
decades between the Hindu Tamil minority
and the Buddhist Sinhalese majority until
mid-2009 when the Government declared
the Tamil Tigers defeated and their leaders
dead. The disputed territories were
essentially the whole of north and east Sri
Lanka, and throughout the conflict these
areas were too dangerous to visit. As the
fighting intensified in the months leading
up to the end of the war, the numbers of
dead, wounded and displaced soared
leaving a humanitarian crisis in its wake

Mean temperatures (°C) and rainfall (mm)

Average daily temperatures (maximum and minimum °C) and monthly rainfall (mm)

	Jan	Feb	Mar	Apr	May	June	July	Aug	Sept	Oct	Nov	Dec
Colombo												
max °C	30	31	31	31	31	29	29	29	29	29	29	29
min °C	22	22	23	24	26	25	25	25	25	24	23	22
rainfall mm	89	69	147	231	371	224	135	109	160	348	315	147

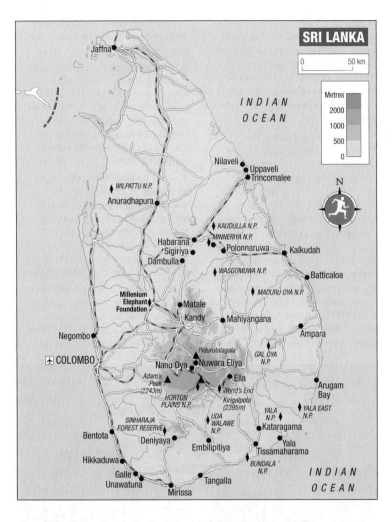

SRI LANKA

0   50 km

Metres
2000
1000
500
0

INDIAN OCEAN

Jaffna

Nilaveli
Uppaveli
Trincomalee

WILPATTU N.P.
Anuradhapura

N

KAUDULLA N.P.
MINNERIYA N.P.
Habarana
Sigiriya
Polonnaruwa
Kalkudah
Dambulla

WASGOMUWA N.P.
Batticaloa

MADURU OYA N.P.

Millenium
Elephant
Foundation
Matale
Kandy
Mahiyangana

Negombo
Ampara

✈ COLOMBO
Pidurutalagala
GAL OYA N.P.
Nanu Oya
Nuwara Eliya
Adam's
Peak
(2243m)
Ella
World's End
Arugam
Bay
HORTON PLAINS N.P.
Kirigalpota
(2395m)
YALA N.P.
YALA EAST N.P.
SINHARAJA FOREST RESERVE
UDA WALAWE N.P.
Bentota
Kataragama
Deniyaya
Embilipitiya
Yala
Hikkaduwa
Tissamaharama
Galle
BUNDALA N.P.
INDIAN OCEAN
Unawatuna
Tangalla
Mirissa

that will take many years to resolve. It remains to be seen whether peace finally returns to this lovely island and whether it manages to shake off the legacy of so much war and bloodshed.

To add to the misery huge swathes of coastal Sri Lanka were destroyed by the Asian tsunami of December 2004, and rebuilding from that disaster has been slow, especially in the east.

You should check with government travel advisories (see p.348) before travelling to the north.

Main attractions

● **Colombo** Though this is where everyone arrives, most visitors don't linger long in the capital. However, the National

313

Museum and the Dutch Period Museum are worth a look, while the Raja Maha Vihara, 13km from the city centre, is the most visited Buddhist temple on the island. For retail therapy, there are stylish shops selling modern Asian chic gifts, homewares, soft furnishings and clothes, making the city an ideal last stop.

● **Adam's Peak (2224m)** The mountain is a place of pilgrimage for Muslims, Hindus and Buddhists, who believe that the metre-long foot-like imprint in a rock on the peak belongs to Adam, Shiva and the Buddha, respectively. The less devout can also make the three- to four-hour ascent (up a total of 4600 steps) from the village of Dalhousie to see the sunrise and marvel at the Shadow of the Peak a few minutes later, when the perfectly triangular silhouette of the mountain is distinctly visible on the countryside below. These are best seen under the clearer skies of January to April, which is also the height of the pilgrimage season, although trekking at other times of the year is perfectly possible.

● **Anuradhapura** The island's capital from the fourth century BC until the ninth century AD, Sri Lanka's holiest town has much of historical interest and some fabulous monuments including the Ruwanwelisiya dagoba, which is over 50m tall and surrounded by a wall of carved elephants.

● **Polonnaruwa** Set beside a huge artificial lake, Polonnaruwa was the medieval capital of the island, after the decline of Anuradhapura. The town is the site of numerous well-preserved monuments but best known are the sublime Buddhist images, the Gal Vihara, carved out of a towering granite rock face.

● **Millennium Elephant Foundation** Elephants are a pervasive Sri Lankan image, whether painted or sculpted. Millennium offers a great chance to see live ones at close quarters; old or sick

▲ Sigiriya

ones are cared for when they retire from forestry work.

- **Kandy** Situated on the hills surrounding a huge artificial lake and reachable by a scenic train ride from Colombo, Sri Lanka's cultural capital is a cool place to hang out. It is also the home of one of the most venerated temples in Sri Lanka, the Dalada Maligawa or Temple of the Tooth – so named because it holds what's believed to be a tooth of the Buddha, rescued from his funeral pyre.

- **Sigiriya** Built on top of a massive 200-metre-high granite monolith, this fifth-century fortress stands sentinel over the surrounding plains. The stronghold was created by the murderous King Kassapa who, after killing his father to grab the throne, feared retribution from the rightful heir, his brother, and took refuge here. A sheltered overhang in the rock face contains well-preserved fresco paintings. Much of the climb is up a rather exposed staircase but the views from the top make it worth the effort.

- **South coast beaches** The resorts further north such as Bentota and Hikkaduwa are better known and busier but the smaller, charming Mirissa, Tangalla and Unawatuna in the south are the real gems. On the coast near Unawatuna, you can see one of Sri Lanka's most iconic images – the stilt fishermen.

Also recommended

- **Ella** A small, peaceful, attractive village set at around 1000m in the hills. It is cool but not cold and has some fabulous views down to the plains. There are plenty of local walks; the most energetic can climb nearby Ella Rock for even more spectacular views, and the train journey from Ella to Nanu Oya is one of the most picturesque in the country.

- **Sunrise over World's End** The highest plateau in Sri Lanka has a viewpoint over a one-thousand-metre drop, from where you can admire the clouds several hundred metres below.

- **Galle** Enclosed inside the ramparts of the old Dutch Fort, this port town retains much of its colonial ambience. It is possible to walk most of the way around the ramparts for great views across the town and out to sea, which are especially lovely at sunset.

- **Cricket** Sri Lankans are mad about the game, and there's often a foreign side on tour. Go to a match and experience the wild atmosphere and loud, exuberant crowd.

- **The flamingoes of Bundala National Park** The park is Sri Lanka's best area for bird-watching at any time of year, with thousands of flamingoes crowding its lagoons and wetlands from January to April.

- **Ude Walawe National Park** Elephants are the main draw here, easily spotted in the open grassland of the park than more densely forested areas, but the scenery is great, with dramatic hills rising behind the plains, and there are also leopards, crocodiles, jackals and plenty of birds of prey.

- **Tea** Sri Lanka is the world's biggest tea exporter and in the upland areas around Nuwara Eliya the hillsides are covered with its brilliant green bushes. Visit one of the tea factories to learn about the intricate process that gets the leaves from the field to the pot.

- **Sinharaja Forest Reserve** This is the last remaining area of undisturbed rainforest in Sri Lanka with a vast profusion of flora and fauna including the elusive leopard – although far less elusive are the myriad of leeches that feast on visitors.

www.roughguides.com

Festivals

February Navam Poya. Celebrating Buddha's announcement of his impending death, this is one of the island's biggest festivals, taking place at Gangaramaya temple in Colombo, and featuring parades of dancers, drummers and elephants.

July/August Esala Perahera. Sri Lanka's most extravagant festival, honouring Buddha's sacred tooth relic from the Temple of the Tooth, takes place over ten days and nights in Kandy. The great final procession includes fabulously bedecked elephants, accompanied by dancers and drummers.

July/August Kataragama. Fire-walking and self-mutilation are the most famous aspects of the annual Hindu celebration at Kataragama temple.

July/August Vel. Colombo's most important Hindu festival includes a procession of the chariot of Skanda, God of War, across the city.

Routes in and out

Although Sri Lanka is separated from India only by the narrow Palk Strait, there is no ferry route between the two countries and the construction of a bridge has been under discussion for decades. All arrivals and departures are through Bandaranaike International Airport at Colombo.

Sri Lanka online

Ari Withanage's Welcome to Sri Lanka – Ⓦ **withanage.tripod.com** Run by Ari, a Sri Lankan living just outside London, this excellent site gives a thorough introduction to all aspects of the island, with plenty of detail and fine pictures.

Art Sri Lanka – Ⓦ **www.artsrilanka .org** Informative, well-illustrated site on anything you ever wanted to know about Sri Lankan art, both ancient and modern.
Infolanka – Ⓦ **www.infolanka.com** General umbrella site with excellent links to articles and other sites on every aspect of Sri Lankan life, including religion, politics, travel, sport and cooking.
Sacred Sites of Sri Lanka – Ⓦ **lankabhumi.org** Serious and fascinating site about all aspects of the sacred places in Sri Lanka. There are some fabulous images and useful links: the ones to Adam's Peak and Sigiriya are especially fruitful.
WWW Virtual Library Sri Lanka – Ⓦ **www.lankalibrary.com** Excellent general site with a monster number of links to sites on Sri Lankan tourism, culture and religion, as well as up-to-the-minute news. There are also several forums.

Books

Romesh Gunesekara *Reef*. Evocative, moody tale of a house boy, his mentor and their obsessions with cooking and the underwater world, by one of Sri Lanka's most well-known and accomplished authors.
Michelle de Kretser *The Hamilton Case*. Set in the time around Independence, this historical thriller, excellent for period detail, follows the story of lawyer Sam Obeysekere, who gets involved in the murder of a British tea planter.
Michael Ondaatje *Running in the Family*. This is a memoir of the author's eccentric Burgher family during the first half of the twentieth century.
A. Sivanandan *When Memory Dies*. Insightful but somewhat gruelling tale of three generations of one Tamil family in the years from the ending of the

Colonial era to the descent into civil war. The author writes powerfully of the destruction of harmony between the Tamils and Sinhalese.

Nirupama Subramanian *Sri Lanka: Voices from a War Zone*. This is a collection of terrible and powerful essays by an Indian journalist who spent years reporting on the war; she gives voice to what she calls the "little histories" of ordinary people on both sides of the ethnic divide caught up in cataclysmic events.

Films

Death on a Full Moon Day (Pura Handa Kaluwara; Prasana Vithnage, 1998). One of Sri Lanka's best-known directors tackles the war, with this tale of a blind father who refuses to believe that his soldier son is dead. See also his Ira Madiyama ("August Sun") which juxtaposes the stories of a Muslim refugee, a Sinhalese widow and a government soldier in the maelstrom of the war.
Mansion by the Lake (Wekanda Walauwa; Lester James Peries, 2002). Set in rural Sri Lanka in the 1980s, Sujata Rajasuriya and her daughter return from years in London to sell the family mansion. One of Sri Lanka's few directors to have made his name in the West returns to his usual themes of families as a microcosm of social, political and economic changes in the world outside.
A Mother Alone (Duvata Mawaka Misa; Sumitra Gunawardena, 1997). This film tells the story of Thushari, unmarried and pregnant, as she is shunted around the family to try to avert the shame of her situation; the film tellingly illustrates the lives of women in Sri Lankan society.
Saroja (Somaratne Dissanayake, 1999). This controversial story of a wounded Tamil Tiger fighter who takes refuge in a Sinhalese village explores themes of reconciliation, friendship and humanity in the time of war.

Uppalavana (Sunil Ariyaratne, 2008). Buddhist nun, Sister Upuli, discovers a wounded rebel fighter and slowly learns that religious devotion is no protection against the complications of life, thrown into sharp focus by the complexities of the civil war.

Sri Lankan tourist offices

Ⓦ**www.srilankatourism.org**
Australia 29 Lonsdale St, Braddon, ACT 2612 ☏6/2306 002.
Ireland 59 Ranelagh Road, Dublin 6 ☏3/1496 9621.
New Zealand Contact the Australian office.
UK 3rd Floor, 1 Devonshire Square, London, EC2M 4WD ☏0845/880 6333.

Sri Lankan embassies and consulates

Ⓦ**www.visitsrilanka.org/other /abroad.html**
Australia 35 Empire Circuit, Forrest, Canberra, ACT 2603 ☏02/6239 7041. Consulate in Sydney ☏2/9223 8729, Ⓦwww.slcgsyd.com.
Canada Suite 1204, 333 Laurier Ave W, Ottawa, Ontario K1P 1C1 ☏613/233-8449, Ⓦwww.srilankahcottawa.org. Consulate in Toronto ☏416/323-9133.
New Zealand Contact the embassy in Canberra.
South Africa 410 Alexander St, Brooklyn, Pretoria 0181 ☏12/460 7690, Ⓦwww.srilanka.co.za.
UK 13 Hyde Park Gardens, London, W2 2LU ☏020/7262 1841, Ⓦwww .slhclondon.org.
US 2148 Wyoming Ave NW, Washington, DC 20008 ☏202/483-4026, Ⓦwww .slembassyusa.org. Consulate in Los Angeles, CA 90010 ☏213/387-0210, Ⓦwww.srilankaconsulatela.com.

www.roughguides.com

Taiwan

Capital Taipei
Population 23 million
Language Mandarin, Chinese
dialects including Taiwanese and
Hakka, and ten tribal languages
Currency New Taiwanese dollar (NT$)
Religion Buddhism, Daoism and
Confucianism

Climate Subtropical, with a rainy
season in May and June
Best time to go Good at any
time but be aware that at festival
time, especially Chinese New Year,
transport is booked solid and hotel
prices soar
Minimum daily budget US$20/£12

Taiwan has had a turbulent history, with
Chinese dynasties and foreign powers
seeking sovereignty over the island.
Today its situation is ambiguous: at the
end of the civil war on mainland China in
1949, with the communists set to win,
the leader of the nationalist Kuomintang,
Chiang Kai-shek, led an exodus of
soldiers, merchants and scholars to
Taiwan. They proclaimed the island the
Republic of China, the official name it
retains today. China views Taiwan as
a dissident province, while Taiwan has
never declared independence from the
mainland but views itself as the legitimate
government of China. While relations
have thawed to some extent, military
intimidation by the mainland and a war of
words between the two continue.

Taiwan today is home to some of
the noisiest, most frantic cities in Asia,
but also offers gorgeous mountain,
coastal and inland scenery and a vibrant
religious and cultural life. It's a startling
mixture of a modern industrial nation at
the cutting edge of computer technology
and production, alongside age-old
beliefs and practices, with literally
thousands of atmospheric temples.

There are also plentiful opportunities to
get out into the countryside, either to take
it easy and admire the views along with
the rest of the day-trippers, or to get off
the beaten track and take advantage of
opportunities for trekking and camping.
While the mountain scenery is serene and
tranquil, bear in mind that Taiwan is one
of the most densely populated countries

Mean temperatures (°C) and rainfall (mm)

Average daily temperatures (maximum and minimum °C) and monthly rainfall (mm)

	Jan	Feb	Mar	Apr	May	June	July	Aug	Sept	Oct	Nov	Dec
Taipei												
max °C	19	18	21	25	28	32	33	33	31	27	24	21
min °C	12	12	14	17	21	23	24	24	23	19	17	14
rainfall mm	86	135	178	170	231	290	231	305	244	122	66	71

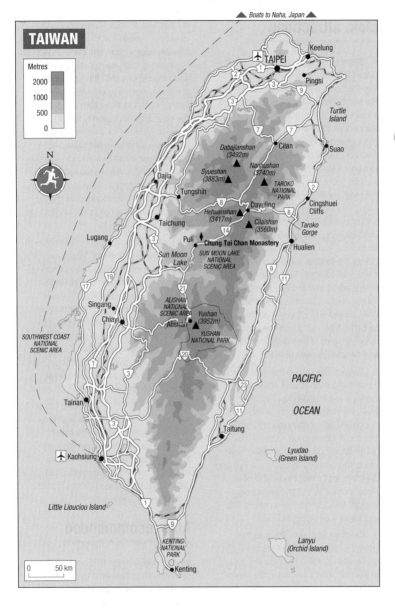

TAIWAN

Metres
2000
1000
500
0

N

Boats to Naha, Japan

Keelung

✈ TAIPEI

Pingsi

Turtle
Island

Suao

Cilan

Dabajianshan
(3492m) ▲

Nanhushan
(3740m) ▲

Syueshan
(3883m) ▲

TAROKO
NATIONAL
PARK

Dajia

Tungshih

Dayuling

Cingshuei
Cliffs

Taichung

Hehuanshan
(3417m) ▲

Ciiaishan
(3560m) ▲

Taroko
Gorge

Lugang

Puli

Chung Tai Chan Monastery

Hualien

Sun Moon
Lake

SUN MOON LAKE
NATIONAL
SCENIC AREA

Singang

ALISHAN
NATIONAL
SCENIC AREA

Yushan
(3952m)

Chiayi

Alishan ▲

YUSHAN
NATIONAL
PARK

SOUTHWEST COAST
NATIONAL
SCENIC AREA

PACIFIC

OCEAN

Tainan

Taitung

Lyudao
(Green Island)

✈ Kaohsiung

Little Liouciou Island

Lanyu
(Orchid Island)

KENTING
NATIONAL
PARK

0   50 km

Kenting

TAIWAN

in the world – you'll be hard pushed to get away from everybody. And as you won't come across many other Western

tourists or a backpacker circuit, you'll have ample opportunity to mingle with and meet local people.

www.roughguides.com

Main attractions

- **Taipei** The capital is a congested place, with three million people in the city itself and another three million in the surrounding countryside. That said, it has plenty of attractions, including atmospheric temples, museums, historic monuments and teeming night markets. If you do nothing else here, visit the National Palace Museum, featuring the world's finest array of Chinese artefacts, moved here in 1948 by the Kuomintang. Other must-see sights are Taipei 101, one of the world's tallest buildings, with a mind-blowing observatory on the eighty-ninth floor; the weekend Jade Market, one of the largest jewellery markets in the world; Wistaria Teahouse, Taipei's oldest teahouse; and the Huaxi Street Tourist Night Market featuring Snake Alley, where you can try a drink of snake blood and bile (and optional venom), removed from specimens freshly killed and skinned in front of you.

- **Taroko Gorge** On the east coast, the island's main tourist attraction features the thundering Liwu River, towering cliffs and plenty of excellent opportunities for camping and trekking. The most picturesque route to the gorge is via one of the central cross-island routes from Taichung via Puli and Dayuling that passes near the peak of Hehuanshan, with fabulous scenery – tropical valleys, mountain panoramas and lakes – all along the way.

- **Kenting National Park** In the sunny, fertile lowlands of the far south of the island, this park, near the town of Kenting, has white beaches, forests, an attractive coastline, waterfalls, hot springs and plenty more to explore. The coast is an ideal area for snorkelling and diving, there are watersports to try by day, and pubs, clubs and karaoke bars to choose from at night.

- **Alishan** At 2190m, the best of the island's mountain resorts doesn't merely offer an escape from the lowland heat; it's a gorgeous spot, surrounded by cedar and pine forests, with the blossoming of the cherry trees a special feature in the spring. Among the numerous treks here, the obligatory excursion is the one to the peak of 2489-metre Jhushan (Celebration Mountain), where several thousand people jostle every morning for views of the sunrise. The narrow-gauge Alishan Forest Railway from Chiayi to Alishan is an especially picturesque route there, taking three and a half hours to climb up through the rolling hills.

- **Tainan** Temples are the main reason to visit the old capital of Taiwan, which is said to contain around two hundred of them. The most famous is Tiantan, one of the oldest temples in Taiwan, dedicated to the Jade Emperor, where a constant stream of visitors comes to pray in a highly atmospheric setting: every wall, ceiling and door is adorned with detailed carvings and frescos, and spirit mediums are often involved in rituals in which they attempt to contact the dead on behalf of the living.

- **Taking the east coast highway from Suao to Hualien** The most dramatic part of this scenic road are the Cingshuei Cliffs, a 21-kilometre stretch of road that is carved out of cliffs that drop a sheer 1000m into the crashing surf below.

Also recommended

- **Lugang** A major harbour from the seventeenth to twentieth centuries, this small west-coast town preserves the traditional architecture and heritage of Taiwan. In the centre of town, the Longshan Temple is renowned for its fabulous woodcarvings and Tianhou Temple is one of the oldest on the island.

▲ Alishan

The craftsmen in Lugang still produce furniture, fans, lanterns and incense using traditional techniques, and the Lukang Folk Art Museum is a good place to view fine, historic examples of their art.

● **Chung Tai Chan Monastery** This modern temple/monastery complex is about as stunning as modern religious architecture gets. Designed by C.Y. Lee, architect of Taipei 101, the scale is vast, featuring a central building of 37 floors and a 150-metre central tower.

● **Scaling Yushan** At 3952m this is the highest peak on the island and the highest in northeast Asia. To reach the summit you'll probably need to spend a night on the mountain, watching the sunrise from the top.

● **Sun Moon Lake** Set 750m up in the hills, this popular tourist spot is the largest freshwater lake on Taiwan. The surrounding forests and bamboo groves contain many excellent treks.

● **Orchid Island (Lanyu)** Just 45 square kilometres in size, the island is home to the indigenous Tao people, who still lead a seafaring lifestyle. Reached by ferry from Taitung, Lanyu has excellent coastal scenery and volcanic countryside, fabulous snorkelling and traditional Tao villages to explore.

Festivals

January/February Lantern Festival. Nationwide celebration marking the end of the Chinese New Year festivities that varies from area to area but reliably includes fireworks, paper lanterns, lion and dragon dances. It is especially picturesque in Pingsi, where paper lanterns are launched into the sky and in Yanshuei near Chiayi where huge fireworks the size of trucks are part of the fun.

April/May Birth of Mazu. Mazu is the most popular goddess on the island (there are more than five hundred temples dedicated to her). More than a week of celebration includes the eight-day, 300-kilometre, Dajia Mazu Pilgrimage from Jhenlan Temple in Dajia to Fongtian Temple in Singang, featuring parades, dragon and lion dances, and enormous excitement and drama.

June Dragon Boat Festival. Nationwide exuberant one-day festival, one of Taiwan's most important, in which fabulously decorated boats race in remembrance of the suicide of poet Chu Yuan.

Routes in and out

International airports serve Taipei (Taoyan International Airport) and Kaohsiung. Ferry services operate into Kaohsiung and Keelung from Naha, Japan. There's no direct travel between mainland China and Taiwan; Hong Kong is a popular transit point.

Taiwan online

Forums – ⓦ www.forumosa.com Forums about every imaginable aspect of Taiwanese life, including plenty of interest to visitors such as travel, driving, events and volunteering.
National Palace Museum – ⓦ www .npm.gov.tw Extensive and colourful site illustrating many of the treasures of this amazing museum – inspirational if you're thinking of a trip and some consolation if you'll never make it there.
Pashan – ⓦ hikingtaiwan.blogspot .com Excellent site by a Taiwan resident and travel-writer about hiking in the island, from short day hikes to longer ones, and with some great links.
Taiwan Photographers – ⓦ taiwan photographers.wordpress.com Stunning photographs from around the island by amateurs and professionals that will have you booking your ticket pronto.
Travel in Taiwan – ⓦ www.tit.com.tw /e_home.htm A bi-monthly travel magazine featuring heaps of information for visitors, with articles and excellent photos covering every area and every facet of the island – from serious history through to sights, shopping and dining.

Books

Ann C Carver and Sung-Sheng Yvonne Chang (Eds) *Bamboo Shoots After Rain: Stories by Women Writers of Taiwan*. Ranging from the 1920s until modern times, this is a good introduction to the literature of a society in transition.
Hsien-Yung Pai *Crystal Boys*. This controversial story about a gay Taiwanese man was the first Taiwanese novel to tackle homosexuality. It offers keen insights into Asian family dynamics often inaccessible to Western readers.
Li Qiao *Wintry Night*. This is an abridged translation of the three-volume saga by one of Taiwan's most prolific authors, following the history of the Peng family of Chinese settlers from the 1890s through to World War II, alongside the history of the island from the nineteenth century.
Wang Chen-ho *Rose, Rose I Love You*. A social satire on the Taiwanese love of money, told in the distinctive voice of a pedantic teacher who is trying to teach English to a crowd of prostitutes so they can extract money from American GIs visiting the island for R&R during the Vietnam War.
Wang Wen-hsing *Family Catastrophe*. This book caused a sensation when it was published in 1972. It details the undoing of a traditional family and is now regarded as a modern classic.

Films

20,30,40 (Sylvia Chang, 2004). The lives of three very different women are dissected (somewhat unevenly it must be said) by one of Taiwan's very few women directors.
Eat Drink Man Woman (Ang Lee, 1994). Now a mainstream Hollywood director, this was one of Lee's earliest films to make an impression on Western audiences. It investigates the relationship

between an ageing chef and his daughters via the Chinese obsession with food.

The Time to Live and the Time to Die (Hou Hsiao-hsien, 1985). Partly autobiographical story, by one of Taiwan's best-known directors, of childhood in a poor rural family set against a background of war, displacement and urbanization in the 1950s.

Vive L'Amour (Tsai Ming-liang, 1994). Prize-winning but ultimately bleak look at the lives of three isolated people in Taipei.

Yi Yi (Edward Yang, 2000). Arguably Yang's best film so far, this replays his constant theme of the problems of modern city life, this time looking at the middle-class Jian family as they struggle with the rush of time.

Taiwanese tourist offices

ⓦwww.tbroc.gov.tw
Canada Contact the US office.
UK c/o The Saltmarsh Partnership, 25D Copperfield St, London, SE1 0EN ⓣ020/7928 1600.
US 1 East 42nd St, 9th Floor, New York, NY 10017, New York ⓣ212/867-1632; 555 Montgomery St #505, San Francisco, CA 94111 ⓣ415/989-8677; and 3731 Wilshire Blvd, Suite 780, Los Angeles, CA 90010 ⓣ213/389-1158.

Taiwanese embassies and consulates

ⓦwww.tbroc.gov.tw
ⓦwww.taiwanembassy.org
Australia Taipei Economic and Cultural Office, Unit 8, Tourism House, 40 Blackall St, Barton, Canberra, ACT 2600 ⓣ02/6120 2025, ⓦwww.teco.org.au. Consulates in Brisbane ⓣ07/3229 5168, ⓦwww.taipeieco.org.au; Melbourne,

VIC 3000 ⓣ03/9650 8611; and Sydney ⓣ02/9223 3233.
Canada Taipei Economic and Cultural Representative Office, World Exchange Plaza, 45 O'Connor St, Suite 1960, Ottawa, Ontario K1P 1A4 ⓣ613/231-5080, ⓦwww.taiwan-canada.org. Consulates in Toronto ⓣ416/369-9030, ⓦwww.taiwanembassy.org; and Vancouver ⓣ604/689-4111, ⓦwww.taiwan-vancouver.org.
Ireland 8 Lower Hatch St, Dublin 2 ⓣ1/678 5413.
New Zealand Level 21, 105 The Terrace, Wellington ⓣ4/473 6474, ⓦwww.taiwanembassy.org/nz; consulate in Auckland ⓣ9/303 3903.
South Africa 1147 Schoeman St, Hatfield, Pretoria, 0001 ⓣ012/430 6071; Consulates in Cape Town ⓣ21/418 1188; and Johannesburg 2196 ⓣ11/883 3120.
UK Taipei Representative, 50 Grosvenor Gdns, London SW1W OEB ⓣ020/7881 2650, ⓦwww.roc-taiwan.org/uk; and Edinburgh ⓣ0131/220 6886.
US 1 East 42nd St, 4th Floor, New York 10017 ⓣ212/486-0088, ⓦwww.taiwanembassy.org/US/NYC; Atlanta ⓣ404/870-9375, ⓦwww.taiwanembassy.org/US/ATL; Boston ⓣ617/259-1350, ⓦwww.taiwanembassy.org/US/BOS; Chicago ⓣ312/616-0100, ⓦwww.taiwanembassy.org/US/CHI; Guam ⓣ671/472-5865, ⓦwww.taiwanembassy.org/US/GUM; Houston ⓣ713/626-7445, ⓦwww.taiwanembassy.org/US/HOU; Kansas ⓣ816/531-1298, ⓦwww.taiwanembassy.org/US/MKC; Los Angeles ⓣ213/389-1215, ⓦwww.taiwanembassy.org/US/LAX; Miami ⓣ305/443-8917, ⓦwww.taiwanembassy.org/US/MIA; San Francisco ⓣ415/362-7680, ⓦwww.taiwanembassy.org/US/SFO; and Seattle ⓣ206/441-4586, ⓦwww.taiwanembassy.org/US/SEA.

Thailand

Capital Bangkok	**Climate** Tropical
Population 63 million	**Best time to go** November–
Language Thai	February (but March–Sept for
Currency Baht (B)	peninsular east coast)
Main religion Theravada Buddhism	**Minimum daily budget** US$15/£9

The perfect place to start a cross-Asia trip, Thailand has a well-established tourist infrastructure, with good transport links, plenty of backpacker-oriented guesthouses and a thriving travellers' scene. Hard-core travellers dislike the place for those very reasons, considering it too easy, too popular, and over-explored – in short, not cool enough. But to most visitors it's simply a great holiday destination.

Bumming around on tropical beaches is the most popular tourist activity, with trekking in the northern hills a close second. Further south, swaths of intact rainforest have been conserved as national parks, offering a good chance of seeing monkeys, tropical birds and even elephants from the trails. Thailand also has plenty of cultural highlights, including well-preserved ruined cities from almost every major period in its history, the finest of which are the Hindu-Buddhist temples built by the ancient Khmers of Cambodia a thousand years ago. In contemporary Thailand, over eighty percent of the population are Buddhist, so there are also plenty of working temples to explore.

Thai food is another highlight – pungently laced with chilli and delicately flavoured with lemongrass and coconut, it's also deliciously inexpensive. English is spoken by Thais working in the tourist industry, but not off the beaten track.

Most Western governments advise against visiting Thailand's far southeastern provinces of Songkhla, Pattani, Yala and Narathiwat, where sectarian violence has caused thousands of deaths in recent years. These areas don't anyway hold much interest to tourists; the beautiful nearby provinces of Trang and Satun are not affected, and access into Malaysia via Satun is safe and easy.

Main attractions

- **Bangkok** Most people spend a few days in the Thai capital, but many find the pollution, traffic congestion and chaotic street life extremely wearing. There's plenty to take you off the street, however, including the glittering Grand Palace compound and its beatific gigantic Reclining Buddha; the comprehensively stocked National Museum; the massive Chatuchak weekend market, with over eight thousand stalls to peruse; and a happening nightlife that runs the full range from depressing strip joints to cutting-edge clubs.

- **Beaches** Thailand's beaches are among the world's best. You'll find the most developed and expensive resorts,

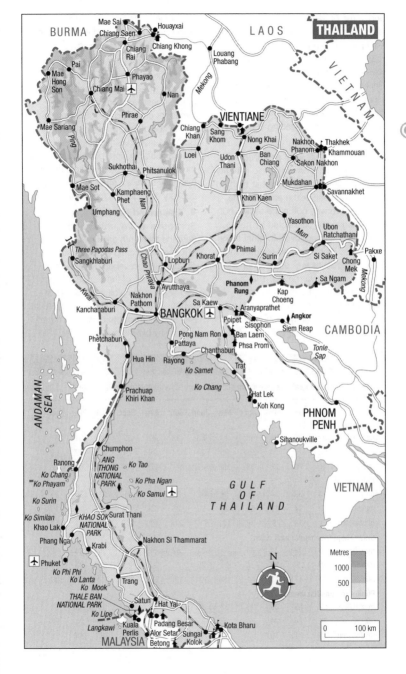

WHERE TO GO

and some of the finest sands, on the islands of Ko Samui and Phuket, while backpackers tend to head for the more budget-oriented Ko Pha Ngan, Ko Tao, Ko Phayam and Ko Lipe. Ko Phi Phi's beaches are nothing short of stunning, Ko Samet makes an easy break from Bangkok and Ko Chang is handy for travellers heading in or out of Cambodia.

● **Trekking** Thailand's so-called "hill-tribe treks" focus on the ethnic-minority villages that you walk to, rather than on the walking itself or the scenery. The hill tribes live way out in the sticks, but their villages are connected by tracks, so the hiking is not difficult. Most treks last two to four days and feature nights in the villages, as well as an elephant ride and some river rafting. The main trekking centres are the northern cities of Chiang Mai and Chiang Rai, but routes out of both are hugely oversubscribed, so it's better to start

from Mae Hong Son, Pai, Kanchanaburi or Umphang instead, where trails are quieter and more rewarding.

● **Chiang Mai** Best known as the hub of the trekking industry, Thailand's second city is also an attractive and popular destination in its own right, famed for charming traditional temples, its hill-tribe museum, and delicious Burmese-style cuisine. Guesthouses are plentiful, the night bazaar is great for shopping, and many visitors prolong their stay to take a short course in Thai cookery or traditional massage.

● **The ruined former capitals of Sukhothai and Ayutthaya** Dating from the thirteenth century, Sukhothai is a beautiful example of thoughtful city planning enlivened by lakes and elegant statues of the Buddha. The 300-year-old temples and palaces of Ayutthaya display a refined mix of Hindu and Buddhist sculpture, and are fun to explore by bicycle and river boat.

Mean temperatures (°C) and rainfall (mm)

Average daily temperatures (maximum and minimum °C) and monthly rainfall (mm)

	Jan	Feb	Mar	Apr	May	June	July	Aug	Sept	Oct	Nov	Dec
Bangkok												
max °C	32	33	34	35	34	33	32	32	32	31	31	31
min °C	20	22	24	25	25	24	24	24	24	24	22	20
rainfall mm	8	20	36	58	198	160	160	175	305	206	66	5
Chiang Mai												
max °C	29	32	34	36	34	32	31	31	31	31	30	28
min °C	13	14	17	22	23	23	23	23	23	21	19	15
rainfall mm	0	10	8	36	122	112	213	193	249	94	31	13
Surat Thani (peninsular east coast)												
max °C	30	33	34	35	34	32	32	32	31	30	28	32
min °C	20	20	22	24	25	25	25	25	25	25	23	23
rainfall mm	40	11	18	67	184	121	120	112	205	261	304	98
Phuket (peninsular west coast)												
max °C	32	33	33	33	32	31	30	31	30	30	30	31
min °C	24	24	24	26	25	25	25	25	24	24	24	24
rainfall mm	35	31	70	148	281	299	283	274	323	368	204	71

THAILAND

www.roughguides.com

▲ Big Buddha pier, Ko Samui

● **Kanchanaburi** Sited on the banks of the River Kwai, Kanchanaburi is most famous for its role as a POW camp in World War II and for its bridge. There are plenty of sobering World War II sights in the town, as well as a reasonable range of trekking, rafting and cycling options that make the most of the fine river scenery, plus some appealing rafthouse accommodation too.

Also recommended

● **Khao Sok National Park** Here you can sleep in a tree house under limestone karst, wake to the sound of hooting gibbons, and take an adventure tour via waterlogged caves and jungle trails to a vast, scenic lake.

● **The ancient Khmer temple of Phanom Rung** This exquisite pink sandstone complex was built in the tenth century as a blueprint for the Angkor temples across the border in Cambodia.

● **Thai massage** Enjoy a traditional massage at Bangkok's Wat Pho temple,

then learn the techniques yourself at a course in Bangkok or Chiang Mai.

● **Snorkelling and diving off the remote Similan Islands** The turquoise water, powdery sand and banks of coral are regularly visited by sharks, rays and turtles.

● **The Mae Hong Song loop** Rent a motorbike and spend as many days as you can on the circular 600-kilometre route through the glorious upland scenery of the remote northwest.

● **Kayaking the Krabi coastline** An exhilarating way of exploring the spectacularly craggy outcrops and remote uninhabited islands off the southwest coast.

● **Pai** This laid-back little northern town has a distinct New Age air and is the perfect place to take some courses in alternative therapies, browse the art shops and hike the surrounding valleys.

● **Full-moon beach party** Join the hordes for the monthly full-moon parties on Ko Pha Ngan, an infamous backpackers' beach rave that attracts up to thirty thousand clubbers.

www.roughguides.com

Festivals

W www.thailandgrandfestival.com
April 13–15 Songkhran. The Thai New
Year is an excuse for a massive nationwide waterfight, with everyone dousing
each other in the streets.
October or November Ngan Kin Jeh
(Vegetarian Festival) in Phuket and Trang.
Chinese devotees celebrate their New
Year by purifying themselves for nine
days and then parading through town
performing acts of self-mortification such
as pushing skewers through their cheeks.
November Loy Krathong. Beautiful
nationwide festival to honour the water
spirits and celebrate the end of the rainy
season. Baskets of flowers and lighted
candles are floated on rivers, lakes,
canals and seashores.

Routes in and out

Thailand's main international airport is in
Bangkok, but some international flights
also use the airports in Ko Samui and
Phuket in the south and in Chiang Mai in
the north. There are lots of buses linking
major cities and tourist resorts in Thailand
and Malaysia, and you can also travel
between the two countries by train and
boat; take heed however of the warnings
against travel through some of the border
areas and opt for routes through Satun
instead. Overland travel to Laos is also
straightforward; the most popular border
crossing is the Friendship Bridge which
connects the Thai town of Nong Khai with
Vientiane in Laos, but you can use several
other crossings in the north and northeast. There are half a dozen legal overland
routes in and out of Cambodia, of which
the most used are from Aranyapathet to
Poipet (for Siem Reap), and from Trat via
Koh Kong to Sihanoukville (for Phnom
Penh and the south). There is no overland
access from Burma.

Thailand online

Ajarn – W www.ajarn.com Thinking of
stretching your travel budget by working
as an English teacher in Thailand?
This site will tell you how, where – and
perhaps why not.
Khao San Road – W www.khaosan
road.com The "community website"
for Southeast Asia's most notorious
backpackers' ghetto gives a good
taste of Thailand's travellers' scene,
and includes guesthouse listings and
a forum.
Paknam Web Network – W www
.paknamweb.com Amazing spread of
websites, blogs and forums about all
things Thai, from top tourist sights to
local movies, language lessons to life in
a Thai prison.
Thailand Travel Forum – W travel
forum.org/thailand Active forum that
gets lots of traffic and has a core of
regular contributors.
Thai Visa – W www.thaivisa.com
Expat-oriented network of forums on
living in Thailand, but has plenty of
relevant threads for visitors too.

Books

Mischa Berlinski *Fieldwork*. Funny,
perceptive literary thriller involving an
anthropologist, a clan of missionaries,
hill-tribe villagers and a journalist, played
out in and around the hills of northern
Thailand.
Karen Connelly *Touch the Dragon*.
The true story of a 17-year-old Canadian
schoolgirl's one-year stay in a small town
in northern Thailand.
Alex Garland *The Beach*. Gripping cult
thriller (made into a film in 1999) that
uses a Thai setting to explore the way in
which backpackers' ceaseless quest for
"undiscovered" utopias inevitably leads
to them ruining the idyll.

Sandra Gregory with Michael Tierney
Forget You Had a Daughter. The candid and shocking account of a young British woman who was imprisoned in Bangkok's notorious Lard Yao prison after being caught trying to smuggle 89 grammes of heroin out of Thailand.
Phra Peter Pannapadipo *Phra Farang: An English Monk in Thailand*. The frank, funny and illuminating account of a former businessman's life as a Thai monk.

Films

Bridge on the River Kwai (David Lean, 1957). This classic movie wasn't actually made in Thailand and the story it tells is hugely embellished – but Allied POWs did build a Thailand–Burma railway in World War II and the site of the real bridge, in Kanchanaburi, is much visited.
Iron Ladies (Youngyooth Thongkonthun, 2000). Warm-hearted, off-beat Thai comedy based on the often hilarious true-life adventures of a volleyball team from north Thailand that was made up of transsexuals and transvestites.
Ong Bak (Prachya Pinkaew, 2003). Martial arts action classic filmed in Bangkok and northeast Thailand. Lead kickboxer Tony Jaa performed all his own stunts and was such a hit that he became official Cultural Ambassador for Thailand.
Tears of the Black Tiger (Wisit Sasanatieng, 2000). A gentle send-up of the Thai action films of the 1960s and 1970s, using exaggerated acting styles and comic-book colours to tell the story of handsome bandit Dum and his love for upper-class Rumpoey.

Thai tourist offices

ⓦwww.tourismthailand.org
Australia and New Zealand Suite 2002, Level 20, 56 Pitt St, Sydney 2000 ☎02/9247 7549, ⓦwww.thailand.net.au.

South Africa Contact the UK office.
UK and Ireland 1st Floor, 17–19 Cockspur St, London SW1Y 5BL ☎0870/900 2007, ⓦwww.tourism thailand.co.uk.
US and Canada 611 North Larchmont Blvd, 1st Floor, Los Angeles, CA 90004 ☎323/461-9814, ⓔtatla@tat.or.th; 61 Broadway, Suite 2810, New York, NY 10006 ☎212/432-0433, ⓔinfo@tatny.com.

Thai embassies and consulates

ⓦwww.mfa.go.th/web/10.php
Australia 111 Empire Circuit, Yarralumla, Canberra ACT 2600 ☎02/6273 1149, ⓦcanberra.thaiembassy.org. Consulate in Sydney ☎02/9241 2542, ⓦthaiconsulatesydney.org.
Canada 180 Island Park Drive, Ottawa, Ontario K1Y 0A2 ☎613/722-4444, ⓦwww.magma.ca/~thaiott. Consulate in Vancouver ☎604/687-1143, ⓦwww.thaicongenvancouver.org.
New Zealand 2 Cook St, Karori, Wellington ☎04/476 8618, ⓦwww.thaiembassynz.org.nz.
South Africa 428 Pretorius/Hill St, Arcadia, Pretoria 0083 ☎012/342 5470, ⓦwww.thaiembassy.co.za.
UK and Ireland 29–30 Queens Gate, London SW7 5JB ☎020/7589 2944, ⓦwww.thaiembassyuk.org.uk. Consulates in Hull ☎01482 581668, ⓦwww.thaiconsul-uk.com; and Dublin ☎01/478-6412, ⓦwww.thaiconsulate ireland.com.
US 1024 Wisconsin Ave NW, Suite 401, Washington, DC 20007 ☎202/944-3600, ⓦwww.thaiembdc.org. Consulates in Chicago ☎312/664-3129, ⓦwww.thaichicago.net; Los Angeles ☎323/962-9574, ⓦwww.thai-la.net; and New York ☎212/754-1770, ⓦwww.thaiconsul newyork.com.

Timor-Leste

Capital Dili	**Best time to go** May–July is
Population 1.2 million	when temperatures are mildest,
Languages Tetum and Portuguese	but the dry season runs from
Currency US dollar (US$)	June–October
Main religion Roman Catholic	**Minimum daily budget** US$25/£15
Climate Tropical	

Timor-Leste (East Timor) is a very young nation: having finally been give the chance to vote for independence from Indonesia in 1999, the East Timorese finally achieved it on May 20, 2002. For tourists, the fledgling country is very much a new frontier, and with stunning beaches, world-class diving and a ruggedly mountainous interior – not to mention a culture fed by numerous animist cults as well as a strong dose of Portuguese heritage – there's plenty to keep you interested. Plus, being less than 500km west of Australia and just a two-hour flight from Darwin, it makes an ideal final stop on a leisurely overland trip from Europe to Australia. Timor-Leste's dogged courage in the face of its appalling recent history is also part of its appeal to adventurous tourists. Where supporting Timor-Leste was once a question of lobbying for global attention,

you can now help the local economy by holidaying there.

As the eastern half of the island of Timor, which sits at the easternmost point of the Indonesian archipelago, Timor-Leste endured a long history of colonial rule. It was a Portuguese colony for four hundred years (West Timor, meanwhile was bagged by the Dutch and is now part of Indonesia) until 1975 when, just as independence loomed, the world looked the other way as Indonesia invaded. For the next 24 years, the Fretilin resistance movement, led by Xanana Gusmão (subsequently Timor-Leste's first president), waged a guerrilla war against the occupiers, and the Indonesians were brutal in their response, killing some 250,000 people. They even refused to leave quietly, killing hundreds more people, forcing thousands into West Timor as refugees, and systematically

Mean temperatures (°C) and rainfall (mm)

Average daily temperatures °C and monthly rainfall (mm)

	Jan	Feb	Mar	Apr	May	Jun	Jul	Aug	Sep	Oct	Nov	Dec
Dili												
°C	27	27	27	27	27	25	25	24	25	25	27	27
rainfall mm	140	128	139	82	77	51	25	13	18	23	64	141

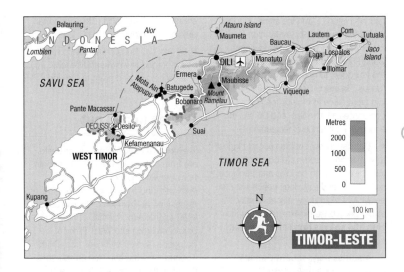

destroying the country's infrastructure on their way out – damage that is still evident in places today.

With help from around the world, Timor-Leste is recovering and rebuilding but the country is desperately poor. Tourism is in its infancy and facilities are sparse though by no means nonexistent. Hotel accommodation is often fairly pricey for what you get, and is found mainly in the capital, Dili, and at a few beachfront towns along the north coast; for travel elsewhere, a tent would be useful, especially as there are no restrictions on camping on the beach. Public transport is limited so renting a motorbike in Dili is a good idea, though be prepared for some rough rides away from the north coast. Beware of travelling to remote areas in the rainy season (Nov–April) when floods often render parts of central and southern Timor-Leste inaccessible. Political unrest flares into violent demonstrations on occasion, predominantly in Dili. Though Tetum is the national language, English is widely spoken, as is Portuguese and Indonesian.

Main attractions

- **Atauro Island** Just a couple of hours by boat from Dili, this 25-kilometre-long island of fishing and farming families offers fabulous diving, almost guaranteed dolphin sightings, great snorkelling and hiking, and a few accommodation options.

- **Diving** There are unparalleled wall dives off the eastern tip of Timor-Leste, especially around the coast between Com and Tutuala, with plenty of manta rays, sharks and turtles as well as dugongs. Similarly impressive wall dives can be found close to shore along the coast between Dili and Manatuto, and can be organized from Dili.

- **Dili** Timor-Leste's beachfront capital has many battle scars among its faded Portuguese-style houses and wooden homes but is also by far the liveliest place for restaurants and nightlife. The museum and cultural centre at the Xanana Gusmão Reading Room is one of the few must-sees; housed in a beautiful colonial-style building, its exhibitions will fill you in on the

www.roughguides.com

nation's history. Climb the steps up to the feet of the towering 27-metre-high statue of Christ for a grand coastal view over Cape Fautacma and beyond, then take the trail down to one of its quietest bays, "Jesus' Backside Beach". The Tais Market is a great place to browse for Timor-Leste's beautiful textiles, and Dili has the country's best range of restaurants.

● **Baucau** Timor-Leste's second biggest town has an attractive old quarter, scenic local hikes through paddies and traditional settlements and a glorious beach just 5km away. As it's got a few places to stay, it's also a good base for explorations further east. The scenery along the coast road from Dili to Baucau is spectacular.

● **Maubisse and Mount Ramelau** Even if you don't make the three-hour climb up Timor-Leste's highest peak, Mount Ramelau (2962m), you should take a trip into its foothills for breathtaking upland scenery, beautiful valleys and pretty, traditional villages. This is also the main coffee-growing region in the country. Base yourself at the hill town of Maubisse, which has great views.

Also recommended

● **Ikat textiles** Timor-Leste is justly famous for its beautiful hand-woven heavy cotton textiles whose characteristic dark reds and blue are made from natural plant dyes; the yarn is tie-dyed using the ikat process and the *tais* (sarongs) often feature stylized figures and animals. Dili market is a good pace to look for *tais*, or try the villages of Viqueque in the southeast or Bobonaro in the west, both of which are especially renowned for their weaving.

● **Jaco Island** This tiny national park islet is fringed with white-sand beaches, breathtakingly pale blue water and rich shallow reefs that are perfect for snorkelling. Catch a lift with a fisherman or join a dive tour.

● **Com** This burgeoning beach resort has a gorgeous white-sand beach, a decent hotel, and great diving and snorkelling close by.

Routes in and out

The only direct flights into Timor-Leste are from Bali in Indonesia (with Merpati), from Darwin in northwest Australia (AirNorth) and from Singapore (AustAsia); flights land at Presidente Nicolau Lobato International Airport in Dili. There's a border crossing into West Timor at Batugede, served by buses from Dili to Kupang, and you can also cross into Oecussi, the Timor-Leste enclave in West Timor, via Oesilo. Ferries connect Dili with Oecussi.

Timor-Leste online

Discover East Timor – Ⓦ www .discoverdili.com Introduces the main tourist destinations and activities, points you in the right direction for various hotels, bars and restaurants and gives some background info too.
Dive Timor Lorosae – Ⓦ www .divetimor.com Lots of useful info plus tempting under- and above-water pictures on this site belonging to an Australian-run dive shop in Dili.
East Timor Action Network – Ⓦ www .etan.org This US-based grassroots organization has been working in solidarity with the people of Timor-Leste for decades; its website highlights its current campaign issues.
East Timor Directory – Ⓦ www.east timordirectory.net News headlines, blogs, features, forums, an online bookstore and cultural insights all make this one of the best general-purpose Timor-Leste sites.

Books

Luis Cardoso *The Crossing: A Story of East Timor*. Though the author grew up on Atauro Island under Portuguese rule, he was studying in Lisbon when Indonesia invaded in 1975 and remained trapped there in exile until Independence. This is the story of his exile and of his father's life in Timor during under Indonesian rule.

Irena Cristalis *Bitter Dawn: East Timor – A People's Story*. A Dutch journalist tells the recent history of Timor-Leste's struggle for independence through the life stories of some of the extraordinary people – among them guerilla fighters, nuns, students, politicians and farmers – whom she met there during Indonesia's final vicious attempt to hold on to the fledgling nation.

Daniel J. Groshong *Timor-Leste: Land of Discovery*. Timor-Leste's first coffee-table book is full of beautiful photographs of the country, its people and even its underwater landscapes; the pictures are accompanied by insightful text.

Timothy Mo *The Redundancy of Courage*. The island of Danu is the barely disguised fictional alter ego of Timor-Leste in this gritty, thought-provoking 1991 novel about a self-serving gay Chinese hotel owner who reluctantly gets drawn in to the brutal guerrilla war against the country's colonial occupiers. Many of the characters are easily identifiable as members of the resistance.

John Pilger *Distant Voices*. Bestselling 1994 anthology of investigations by the multi-award-winning campaigning journalist. At the heart of the book is an extraordinary exposé of Indonesia's murderous policies in Timor-Leste.

Timor-Leste tourist offices

Ⓦ www.turismotimorleste.com
No overseas offices.

Timor-Leste embassies and consulates

Ⓦ www.mfac.gov.tp
Australia 25 Blaxland Crescent, Griffith ACT 2603 ☎02/6260-8800, Ⓔ TL_Emb .Canberra@bigpond.com. Consulates in Melbourne ☎03/9248-1169; and Sydney ☎02/9239-0060.
UK and Ireland Contact the embassy in Portugal: Avenida Infante Santo, 17-6 1350-175 Lisbon ☎00-351-21-393-3730, Ⓔembaixada.rdtl@mail.telepac.pt.
US and Canada 3415 Massachusetts Ave, NW, Washington, DC 20007 ☎202-965-1515, Ⓔembtlus@earthlink .net.

Vietnam

Capital Hanoi	**Climate** Tropical with monsoon
Population 85 million	conditions between May and
Language Vietnamese	October
Currency Dong (d)	**Best time to go** Late September–
Main religions Mahayana	December, and March and April
Buddhism and Catholic	**Minimum daily budget** US$15/£9

There is so much of cultural interest in Vietnam, from the intriguing diversity of hill tribes and other ethnic minorities in the northern hills and central highlands, to the classically Southeast Asian orchards and ricefields of the southern Mekong Delta. The capital, Hanoi, buzzes with markets, conical-hatted soup vendors and a swarm of motor-bike traffic, while its dynamic southern counterpart Ho Chi Minh City (formerly Saigon) fizzes with twenty-first century entrepreneurship and glitz. Though North and South have been at peace now for thirty years, following two decades of vicious civil war, the Vietnam War (referred to by the Vietnamese as the American War) of the 1960s and 1970s still figures strongly in visitors' agendas. But when you've had your fill of crawling through guerrilla tunnels and posing beside downed helicopters, there are eleventh-century Hindu ruins, historic old towns, and 300-year-old Confucianist temples to explore. The Chinese heritage is a particular highlight, its influence apparent in everything from atmospheric shrines and courtyard homes to elegant imperial mausoleums.

Despite all these attractions, Vietnam doesn't always elicit the rave reviews enjoyed by its near neighbours Thailand and Malaysia. This is partly because the tourist industry is still finding its feet, but also because the laid-back, smile-inducing, typical Southeast Asian welcome is sometimes absent too. Interactions tend to be more abrasive and overtly business-minded in Vietnam, and travellers soon weary of the constant haggling, often becoming obsessive about the seemingly endless scams and rip-offs. However, if you arrive prepared not to take the cons personally and, most importantly, if you can stop yourself from automatically branding everyone a swindler, Vietnam's many other qualities will get the chance to shine through.

As the old-style communist approach is enthusiastically shoved aside by the new socialist market economy, Vietnam's infrastructure is developing fast, bringing an explosion of attractive tourist accommodation and entrepreneurial tour operators. The country's long thin shape and many useful overland border-points mean that it works well as a stepping stone between China and either Laos or Cambodia, and transport options are improving all the time. The famous "Reunification Express" trains travel the country from top to bottom, taking a minimum of thirty hours to connect Hanoi with Ho Chi Minh City,

Metres	
	2000
	1000
	500
	0

Red River

Ha Giang

Nanning

Hekou
Lao Cai
Cao Bang

CHINA

Sa Pa

Lai Chau

Da River

Dong Dang
Lang Son

Pingxiang

Dongxing

Son La

Thai
Nguyen

Mong Cai

Tay Trang

Dien
Bien Phu

Hong
Gai

Oudomxai

HANOI

Mai Chau

Haiphong

Ha Long Bay

Hoa
Binh

Hainan
Island

Louang
Phabang

Na Maew

Nam Xoi

Nam Dinh
Ninh Binh

Ban Nong Het

Thanh Hoa

Gulf of
Tonkin

L
A
O
S

Vinh

Cau Treo
Kaew Nua

Ha Tinh

VIENTIANE

Dong Hoi
DMZ

Mukdahan

Savannakhet

Dong Ha

Lao Bao
Hué

Da Nang
Hoi An

THAILAND

My
Son

Ubon
Ratchathani

Quang Ngai

Altapu

Bo Y

Khorat

Kon Tum

Plei Ku

Qui Nhon

Ban Lung

Le
Tanh

Buon Ma Thuot

Tonle
Sap

Mekong River

Nha Trang

CAMBODIA

Da Lat

Phan Rang

PHNOM PENH

Tay Ninh

Moc Bai

Cu Chi

Phan Thiet

Kampot

K'am Samnar
Bavet

Chau Doc

Cao
Lanh

My
Tho

Ho Chi Minh City

Sihanoukville

Ha Tien

Tinh
Bien

Vinh Long

Long Hai

Phu Quoc
Island

Rach Gia

Can
Tho

Ben Tre

Vung Tau

Gulf of
Thailand

Tra Vinh

SOUTH CHINA SEA

Mekong Delta

Ca Mau

Bac Lieu

Con Dao
Archipelago

N

0   200 km

VIETNAM

and there is an expanding network of tourist buses that follow routes designed specifically for budget travellers.

Main attractions

- **Hanoi** Vietnam's capital, in the north of the country, enjoys a relatively cool climate and is a surprisingly pleasant place to linger. Highlights include the historic Confucian-style Temple of Literature, the chaotically traditional alleys of the Old Quarter, and the rather macabre Ho Chi Minh Mausoleum, where the embalmed body of the communist hero and North Vietnam president is displayed in a glass box. The outstanding Museum of Ethnology is well worth an afternoon: it introduces the cultures of Vietnam's 52 main hill tribes and other minority groups with excellent displays and a park full of reconstructions of typical homes.

- **Taking a boat tour round the dramatic Ha Long Bay** Peppered with hundreds of bizarrely shaped limestone outcrops and yawning caves, this vast bay is so spectacular that it's listed as a World Heritage Site. A boat tour is the best and most popular way to appreciate the beauty and drama of the bay, and the fishing island of Cat Ba makes the most interesting departure point.

- **Ho Chi Minh City** More famously known as Saigon, HCMC, the former capital of South Vietnam, is a modern, hectic contrast to Hanoi, stuffed with venerable temples, classy restaurants and hundreds of bars. Most visitors make the "war sights" a priority, in particular the absorbing War Remnants and Ho Chi Minh City museums, and the former American Embassy.

- **The Mekong Delta** Southeast Asia's greatest river, the 4184-kilometre-long Mekong, rises on the Tibetan plateau and runs down through China, Laos, Thailand and Cambodia before reaching journey's end in Vietnam, where it fans out into dozens of smaller rivers to water the vast alluvial plains of the Mekong Delta. The scenes here are quintessential Southeast Asia: emerald rice paddies, fruit orchards, sugar-cane fields and coconut palms, tended by conical-hatted

Mean temperatures (°C) and rainfall (mm)

Average daily temperatures (maximum and minimum °C) and monthly rainfall (mm)

	Jan	Feb	Mar	Apr	May	June	July	Aug	Sept	Oct	Nov	Dec
Hanoi												
max °C	20	21	23	28	32	33	33	32	31	29	26	22
min °C	13	14	17	20	23	26	26	26	24	22	18	15
rainfall mm	18	28	38	81	196	239	323	343	254	99	43	20
Da Nang												
max °C	24	26	27	30	33	34	34	34	31	28	27	25
min °C	19	20	21	23	24	25	25	25	24	23	22	20
rainfall mm	102	31	12	18	47	42	99	117	447	530	221	209
Ho Chi Minh City												
max °C	32	33	34	35	33	32	31	31	31	31	31	31
min °C	21	22	23	24	24	24	24	24	23	23	23	22
rainfall mm	15	3	13	43	221	330	315	269	335	269	114	56

farmers and crisscrossed by waterways that are chock-a-block with sampans and rowing boats. You can explore the area and its floating markets on day-trips from Ho Chi Minh City, or stay in one of the delta villages such as Can Tho, My Tho or Ben Tre.

- **Hué** During the nineteenth century, this attractive city reigned as Vietnam's capital, and its walled citadel still contains evocative relics from the Imperial City. A short boat ride along the Perfume River brings you to the mausoleums of Hué's seven emperors, each constructed to a different design and set in an elegantly landscaped memorial park of pagodas, pavilions and pleasure gardens. In complete contrast, Hué is also the most convenient departure point for day-trips to the infamously bleak stretch of land known as the DMZ, or Demilitarized Zone, 100km north of Hué on the Seventeenth Parallel, which served as the border between North and South Vietnam until reunification in 1975.

- **Hoi An** This captivating historic port town is characterized by narrow streets and a clutch of beautifully preserved 200-year-old merchants' shophouses, some of which are still inhabited by family descendants and can be visited. It's also a famously good place to get silk outfits tailor-made at bargain prices. And if you're here on the night before the day of the full moon, in any month, you'll experience the highly atmospheric monthly Full-Moon Festival, when the town's electricity is temporarily switched off, the streets are illuminated by lanterns and there's traditional dance performed in the streets.

- **Hill-tribe treks** The cool, misty and extremely scenic region around the northern hill town of Sa Pa is inhabited by a variety of hill tribes and is a hugely popular, in many cases oversubscribed, destination for hikes between minority villages. Most of the hill tribes arrived in

the region about two hundred years ago, when persecution in their native China prompted a mass migration into the northern hills of Vietnam, Laos and, most famously, Thailand. For a more authentic trekking experience, head for Bac Ha, which is famous for its spectacular Sunday market attended by crowds of exuberantly dressed Flower Hmong hill-tribespeople, but in the week is very quiet.

- **The Cu Chi tunnels near Ho Chi Minh City** These are among the most visited sights from the American War. Scores of communist Viet Cong guerrillas spent weeks in this 250-kilometre network of underground hideouts, where facilities included rudimentary subterranean hospitals, kitchens and classrooms, relics of which can still be seen today. Above ground, the place has become something of a war theme park, with fake tripwires and a shooting gallery where visitors can play with M-16s and Kalashnikovs.

Also recommended

- **Tam Hoc and Hoa Lu** Glowing red- and gold-lacquered temples plus a sampan ride up the meandering waterways of the Red River Delta, through entrancing inland karst scenery, make this region a great day out from Hanoi, though you can also stay in the area, in the friendly town of Ninh Binh. With extra time it's well worth renting a bicycle to explore the tracks through the peaceful rice-growing landscape.

- **Beaches** Vietnam may not be renowned for these, but the sands that ring remote little Phu Quoc island, close to the Cambodian border, are splendid. Other low-key beaches that are easier to get to and reasonably near Ho Chi Minh City include modest Long Hai, and the beautiful, and rather more upmarket, Mui Ne, near Phan Thiet.

www.roughguides.com

▲ Black Hmong women, Sa Pa

● **Drinking freshly brewed bia hoi** Pull up a tiny plastic stool and join the crowd round the barrel of *bia hoi* (draught beer) in one of the makeshift streetside joints in Hanoi or Ho Chi Minh City.

● **The Cham temples of My Son** Dating back to the eleventh century, these evocative jungle-clad ruins of a group of Hindu temples still retain some carvings and statues despite the best efforts of countless American B52s.

Festivals

February Water Puppet Festival, Thay Pagoda, near Hanoi. A three-day extravaganza of water-puppet performances, organized as part of the Vietnamese New Year celebrations.

May/June Tet Doan Ngo. The summer solstice is marked across the country by parades and traditional dragon boat races.

Routes in and out

With Ho Chi Minh City and Hanoi both served by international flights, it's quite feasible – and very popular – to enter the country via one city and leave via the other; coming direct from Europe it's generally cheaper to get a flight to Bangkok or Singapore and then a budget connecting flight. Da Nang airport also runs flights to a few Asian countries, including Korea and Singapore.

There are many overland options into Vietnam. From China, the obvious route is by train: Beijing–Hanoi, for example, takes 43 hours; alternatives are from Kunming by bus to the border at Lao Cai, near Sa Pa, then train to Hanoi; and from Guilin and Nanning by bus to Moc Bai and then hydrofoil to Ha Long City. Coming from Laos, the main route is the bus from Savannakhet (on the Thai-Lao border) to Dong Ha and Da Nang, via Lao Bao; other options include access to Vinh (via Cau Treo or Ban Nong Het); to Nam Xoi (via Na Maew); from Attapu to Kon Tom, via Bo Y; and from Oudomxai to Dien Bien Phu (via Tay Trang). In recent years, many new border crossings with Cambodia have opened, and more may follow, making it possible to journey by bus from Phnom Penh to Ho Chi Minh City (via Moc Bai); by boat and taxi from Phnom

Penh to Chau Doc and the Mekong Delta; by taxi and bus from Kampot or Kep to Phu Quoc island or HCMC; and by bus and taxis from Ban Lung in northeast Cambodia to Plei Ku.

Vietnam online

Hitchhiking Vietnam – Ⓦwww .pbs.org/hitchhikingvietnam Funny, straight-talking homepage that's a refreshing introduction to the country, with excerpts from the author's journal and photo album describing her seven-month trip around Vietnam.

Saigon and Hanoi ESL – Ⓦwww .saigonesl.com Designed for English teachers in HCMC and Hanoi, this site also includes a mass of info and links on Vietnamese life, culture and travel, plus a forum.

Terra Galleria: Vietnam – Ⓦwww .terragalleria.com/vietnam A photographer's guide to the photo opportunities of Vietnam, with a stunning gallery of shots.

Things Asian – Ⓦwww.thingsasian .com Vietnam is a major focus of this pan-Asian site, with hundreds of well-written stories on all areas and aspects of travel in the country, plus a photo gallery and travel tips.

Books

Maria Coffey *Three Moons in Vietnam.* Things have moved on a lot since Maria Coffey researched her book in 1994, shortly after Vietnam began welcoming foreign tourists. These days, you'd have to stray way off the standard route to experience a fraction of the discomfort and wide-eyed stares that greeted the author on her trip, by boat and bicycle, from the Mekong Delta to Halong Bay. But many of her observations remain pertinent and the humour and warmth

of her account have lost none of their currency.

Duong Van Mai Elliott *The Sacred Willow: Four Generations in the Life of a Vietnamese Family.* The author illuminates the history of her country from the late nineteenth century to the end of the twentieth through the characters and experiences of her own extended family, among them a mandarin at the Imperial court and an anti-French Viet Minh resistance fighter.

Bao Ninh *The Sorrow of War.* An award-winning modern classic that follows a very young North Vietnamese army captain through the American War and into the post-war years as he works as part of a team that searches for the bodies of lost comrades. Though the novel is fiction, the author was born in Hanoi and was one of the few from his North Vietnamese Army brigade who survived the war.

Tim O'Brien *Going After Cacciato.* What does war do to people? Novelist Tim O'Brien has made his name as an eloquent chronicler of the emotional, physical and moral effects of the American-Vietnam War on the people involved on both sides and the land it destroyed. This one starts with the notion that one American soldier in Vietnam, Cacciato, would, all things considered, prefer to be in Paris than fighting in Vietnam; he sets out to walk the 8600 miles necessary to get there, pursued by the men in his squad.

Andrew X Pham *Catfish and Mandala: A Two-Wheeled Voyage through the Landscape and Memory of Vietnam.* A Vietnamese American whose family fled to the US when he was 10 returns – by bicycle – to the country of his birth. As he travels he ponders the questions of identity, cultural bonds and memory that fill his head, interweaving them with vivid descriptions of the Vietnam he experiences in the late 1990s.

Films

Apocalypse Now (Francis Ford Coppola, 1979). The most famous of all the films about the American-Vietnam War, this operatic, psychedelic extravaganza shows us the war from inside the heads of some of the American soldiers who fought it.

Cyclo (Tran Anh Hung, 1995). Dubbed the Vietnamese *Pulp Fiction* by some critics, this is a shockingly graphic thriller set in 1990s' Ho Chi Minh City that paints a recognizable portrait of modern-day city life. It follows a desperately poor young cycle-rickshaw driver as he gets drawn ever deeper into S&M prostitution, drug smuggling and gang warfare. Tran Anh Hung's other films have quite different tones, most famously The Scent of Green Papaya (1993), which is set in 1950s and 60s Saigon and follows a young woman from the country who comes to the city to work as a maid.

Heaven and Earth (Oliver Stone, 1993). Based on the autobiography of Le Ly Hayslip, who grew up with the war, was tortured by the Viet Cong and eventually fled to Saigon. The film ends with Le Ly in rural US, struggling to cope with life as the wife of a damaged and violent former GI.

Indochine (Régis Wargnier, 1991). Catherine Deneuve stars in this beautifully shot three-cornered 1930s love-story set during the final years of French colonial rule in Indochina.

The Quiet American (Philip Noyce, 2002). Michael Caine is the jaded foreign correspondent in this brilliant adaptation of Graham Greene's famous novel about cross-cultural romance, geopolitics and misguided American interests in 1950s Saigon.

Vietnamese tourist offices

Ⓦ **www.vietnamtourism.com**
No overseas offices; contact the visa section of your nearest embassy.

Vietnamese embassies and consulates

Ⓦ **www.vnembassy.net**
Australia and New Zealand 6 Timburra Crescent, O'Malley, Canberra, ACT 2606 ☏02/6286 6059, Ⓦwww.vietnamembassy.org.au. Consulate in Sydney ☏02/9327 2539, Ⓦwww.vietnamconsulate-sydney.org/en.
Canada 470 Wilbrod St, Ottawa, Ontario K1N 6M8 ☏613/236-0772, Ⓦwww.vietem-ca.com.
South Africa 87 Brooks St, Brooklyn, Pretoria 0181 ☏012/362 8119, Ⓦwww.vietnamembassy-southafrica.org.
UK and Ireland 12 Victoria Rd, London W8 5RD ☏020/7937 1912 Ⓦwww.vietnamembassy.org.uk/consular.html.
US 1233 20th St NW, Suite 400, Washington, DC 20036 ☏202/861-0737, Ⓦwww.vietnamembassy.us. Consulate in San Francisco ☏415/922-1577, Ⓦwww.vietnamconsulate-sf.org.

First-Time Asia

Directory

Discount travel agents

Airtreks US & Canada ☎1-877/AIRTREKS; ⓦwww.airtreks.com. Round-the-world specialist.

Flight Centre US ☎1-866 967 5351, Canada ☎1-877 967 5302, UK ☎0870/499 0040, Australia ☎13 31 33, New Zealand ☎0800/243 544, South Africa ☎0860 400 727; ⓦwww.flightcentre.com. Guarantee to offer the lowest international air fares.

Harvey World Travel Australia ☎1300/855492, ⓦwww.harveyworld.com.au; New Zealand ☎0800/758787, ⓦwww.harveyworld.co.nz. Discounted flights.

North South Travel UK ☎01245/608 291, ⓦwww.northsouthtravel.co.uk. Discounted fares worldwide. Profits are used to promote sustainable tourism.

STA Travel US ☎1-800/781-4040, UK ☎0871/2300 040, Australia ☎134 782,

New Zealand ☎0800/474 400, South Africa ☎0861/781 781; ⓦwww.statravel.com. Good discounts for students and under-26s, plus round-the-world tickets.

Trailfinders UK ☎0845/058 5858, Ireland ☎01/677 7888, Australia ☎1300/780 212; ⓦwww.trailfinders.com. Large, efficient agent for independent travellers.

Travel Cuts US ☎1-800/592-CUTS, Canada ☎1-866/246-9762; ⓦwww.travelcuts.com. Specialists in budget travel, including student and youth discount offers.

USIT Ireland ☎01/602 1906, Northern Ireland ☎028/9032 7111; ⓦwww.usit.ie. Ireland's main outlet for discounted, youth and student fares.

Specialist tour operators

Above the Clouds Trekking US ☎802/482-4849, ⓦwww.abovecloulds.com. Treks in Nepal, Bhutan and India.

Allways Dive Expeditions Australia ☎1800/338239, ⓦwww.allwaysdive.com.au. Dive and accommodation packages to Indonesia, Malaysia, Thailand and the Philippines.

Amerispan US ☎800/879-6640, Worldwide ☎215/751 1100; ⓦwww.amerispan.com. Language courses and packages in China, Japan, Korea, Taiwan and Thailand.

Backroads US ☎800/462-2848 or 510/527-1555, ⓦwww.backroads.com. Cycling, hiking and multi-sport tours in Bali, Bhutan, Cambodia, China, India, Nepal, Thailand, Tibet and Vietnam.

Cactus Language UK☎0845/130 4775, US ☎212/601 9343; ⓦwww.cactus language.com. Language courses and packages in Japan and China for all levels and durations, from one week.

Dragoman UK ☎01728/861133, ⓦwww.dragoman.com. Short and

extended overland journeys plus small group adventures.

Exodus UK ☎0845/863 9600, ⓦwww.exodus.co.uk. Adventure tour operators and overland expedition specialist with a huge range of Asian trips including cycling, trekking. They are UK based but have agents throughout the world; see website.

Explore UK ☎0845/013 1539, ⓦwww.explore.co.uk This adventure specialist offers a vast array of trips throughout Asia including North Korea.

Footprint Adventures UK ☎01522/804929, ⓦwww.footprint-adventures.com. Adventure travel specialists offering trekking, wildlife, camping and birding trips to many Asian destinations.

Imaginative Traveller UK ☎0845/077 8802, From outside UK ☎+44 1473/667 337; ⓦwww.imaginative-traveller.com. Adventurous tours throughout Asia, including photography and culinary special interest trips plus trekking cycling and camping.

D

DIRECTORY | Discount travel agents • Specialist tour operators

www.roughguides.com

343

Intrepid Travel UK ☎020 3147 777, Australia ☎1300/364 512, New Zealand ☎0800/600 610, US ☎01800/970 7299, Canada ☎1 866/360 1151, South Africa ☎3/9473 2626; ☯www.intrepidtravel.com. A vast array of small-group tours from short to long and from basic to luxurious throughout the continent.

Kumuka Expeditions Australia ☎1300/667277, New Zealand ☎0800 440499, Ireland ☎1800/946843, UK ☎0800/092 9595, US & Canada ☎1800/517-0867, South Africa ☎0800/991503; ☯www.kumuka.com.au. Specializes in adventure tours and overland expeditions to Asia including Japan, Mongolia and South Korea.

Mir Corps US ☎1-800/424-7289, ☯www.mircorp.com. Trans-Siberian-Express trips, plus tours to China, Tibet and Mongolia.

Off the Map Tours UK ☎0116/240 2625, ☯www.mongolia.co.uk. Mongolia specialist, featuring trekking, mountain-biking, motorcycling, horse-riding and Trans-Siberian trips.

Red Spokes Cycle Adventure Tours UK ☎020/7502 7252, ☯www.redspokes.co.uk. Small-group cycle trips along the classic routes – Karakoram Highway, Manali–Leh – and in Laos, Vietnam, India, Nepal and Thailand.

REI Adventures US ☎1-800/622-2236, ☯www.rei.com/travel. Climbing, cycling, hiking and multisport tours throughout Asia.

Responsible Travel UK ☎01273/600030, ☯www.responsibletravel.com. Online agent for over three hundred tour operators that have been hand-picked and screened for their positive environmental, economic and socially responsible policies.

The Russia Experience UK☎0845/521 2910, ☯www.trans-siberian.co.uk. Experts on Trans-Siberian and Mongolian travel.

Surf Travel Company Australia ☎2/9222 8870, ☯www.surftravel.com.au. Flights and accommodation packages to the best surf spots throughout Indonesia and beyond.

Travel Indochina Australia ☎1300/138755, ☯www.travelindochina.com.au. Goes beyond the more obvious sights in Thailand, Laos, Vietnam, China, India, Japan and Cambodia.

Village Ways ☎01223/750049, ☯www.villageways.com. Community-based tour company arranging for tourists to visit and stay in the Indian Himalayas.

Vodka Train Australia ☎03/9672 5353, New Zealand ☎0800/174 073, UK ☎020/8877 7650; ☯www.vodkatrain.com. Budget two- to three-week Trans-Siberian and Trans Mongolian rail packages, for 18–35-year-olds.

Worldwide Quest Adventures US ☎1-800/387-1483, ☯www.worldwidequest.com. Nature, adventure and cultural travel throughout Asia including some innovative food and wine trips.

Volunteering and placements

Global resources

Earthwatch ☯www.earthwatch.org. Large, long-established, organizer of volunteer placements on scientific projects, such as assessing Mongolian wildlife, exploring the roots of the Angkor civilization in Cambodia, and documenting the coral reefs of Thailand.

Go MAD: Go Make A Difference ☯www.go-mad.org. Designed by and for travellers who want to volunteer at small, local organizations. No fees or forms. Links to volunteer organizations, mostly orphanages and

schools, in Cambodia, India, Indonesia, Laos, Nepal, Thailand and Vietnam.

Hands Up Holidays UK ☎0800/783 3554 or 020/8871 0341, US & Canada ☎201/984-5372, New Zealand ☎06/347 1189; ☯www.handsupholidays.com. Mostly two-week trips (or tailor-mades) combining luxury sightseeing with three to five days' volunteering in India, Bali, Vietnam and Thailand.

i to i ☯www.i-to-i.com. Short-term voluntary placements teaching English or doing care, community work, construction or work with

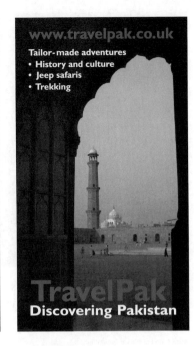
D

www.roughguides.com

345

www.roughguides.com

wildlife in Cambodia, China, India, Malaysia, Nepal, Philippines, Sri Lanka, Thailand and Vietnam.

Australia and New Zealand

Youth Challenge Australia ☎2/9514 5512, ⓦ www.youthchallenge.org.au. Runs volunteer programmes including short-term youth placements (for 18–30-year-olds) of ten weeks in India, Costa Rica and Guyana.

UK and Ireland

Coral Cay Conservation ☎020/7620 1411, ⓦ www.coralcay.org. Reef and rainforest conservation projects, including coral reef surveying in the Philippines and Cambodia.

Greenforce ☎020/7384 3343, ⓦ www .greenforce.org. Charity that offers volunteer placements of varying lengths in teaching, conservation, community development and work with children throughout Asia.

Indian Volunteers for Community Service (IVCS) ☎020/8864 4740, ⓦ www.ivcs.org .uk. Inexpensive, three-week to six-month visitors' programme at a rural development project in India.

Projects Abroad ☎01903/708300, ⓦ www.projects-abroad.co.uk. Volunteer and intern placements from two weeks upwards in teaching, care, conservation, medical fields, journalism and the field of human rights in Cambodia, China, India, Mongolia, Nepal, Sri Lanka and Thailand.

Travellers Worldwide ☎01903/502595, ⓦ www.travellersworldwide.com. Placements from two weeks to a year on a huge number

of projects in Brunei, China, India, Malaysia, Sri Lanka and Thailand.

Working Abroad ☎01273/711406, ⓦ www .working abroad.com. Offers a personalized search service that compiles a list of volunteer projects tailored to individual requirements.

Year Out Group ☎01380/816696, ⓦ www .yearoutgroup.org. Umbrella organization representing more than thirty-five different gap-year and year-out placement finders.

US and Canada

Crooked Trails ☎206/383-9828, ⓦ www .crookedtrails.com. Not-for-profit community-based organization offering volunteer work and homestays in Thailand, Nepal and India.

Global Volunteers ☎1-800/487-1074, ⓦ www.globalvolunteers.org. One- to three-week projects at in China, Vietnam and India.

Go Abroad.com ⓦ www.volunteerabroad .com. Online agency for volunteer placements, internships and study and teaching opportunities across Asia.

One! International ☎780/467-6254, ⓦ www.one-international.com. Canadian-based organization needing volunteers for placements working with street children in Mumbai.

Projects Abroad US ☎1-888/839-3535, Canada ☎1-877/921-9666; ⓦ www .projects-abroad.org. Voluntary placements from two weeks upwards in a huge number of types of work throughout Asia.

Accommodation resources

Asia Hotels ⓦ www.asia-hotels.com
Asia Hotels Network ⓦ www.asiahotels.net
Couch Surfing ⓦ www.couchsurfing.org
eLong ⓦ www.elong.net
Hospitality Club ⓦ www.hospitalityclub.org

Hostel World ⓦ www.hostelworld.com
HostelBookers ⓦ hostelbookers.com
Hostelling International ⓦ www.hihostels .com
TripAdvisor ⓦ www.tripadvisor.com

www.roughguides.com

347

Health information and clinics

health.yahoo.com Information on specific diseases and conditions, drugs and herbal remedies, as well as advice from health experts.

www.cdc.gov The US government's official site for travel health.

www.fitfortravel.scot.nhs.uk Scottish NHS website with useful advice on travel-related diseases and how to avoid them.

www.tripprep.com Comprehensive database of necessary vaccinations for most countries, as well as destination-specific info on medical services.

www.who.int The World Health Organization website includes travel and health advice, disease outbreak news and and detailed A–Z of countries.

Australia, New Zealand and South Africa

Travellers' Medical and Vaccination Centre ☎1300/658 844, **www.tmvc.com.au**. Lists travel clinics in Australia, New Zealand and South Africa.

UK and Ireland

Hospital for Tropical Diseases Travel Clinic ☎0845/155 5000, 020/7388 9600 (Travel Clinic), **www.thehtd.org**.

MASTA (Medical Advisory Service for Travellers Abroad) ☎0870/606 2782, **www.masta.org** for the nearest clinic.

Travel Medicine Clinic ☎028/9031 5220.

Tropical Medical Bureau ☎1850/487 674, **www.tmb.ie**. Ireland.

US and Canada

Canadian Society for International Health ☎613/241-5785, **www.csih.org**. Extensive list of travel health centres.

CDC ☎1-800/232 4636, **www.cdc.gov/travel**. Official US government travel health site.

International Society for Travel Medicine ☎1-770/736-7060, **www.istm.org**. Has a full list of travel health clinics.

Official advice on trouble spots

Australia Department of Foreign Affairs **www.smartraveller.gov.au**

Canada Foreign Affairs & International Trade Department **www.voyage.gc.ca**

Ireland Department of Foreign Affairs **www.dfa.ie**

New Zealand Ministry of Foreign Affairs **www.safetravel.govt.nz**

South Africa Department of International Relations and Cooperation **www.dfa.gov.za**

UK Foreign and Commonwealth Office **www.fco.gov.uk**

US State Department **travel.state.gov**

Travel book and map stores

Australia and New Zealand

Mapland 408 Centre Rd, Bentleigh, Melbourne, Vic 3204 ☎03/9557 8555, **www.mapland.com.au**.

Map Shop 6–10 Peel St, Adelaide, SA 5000 ☎08/8231 2033, **www.mapshop.net.au**.

Map World Australia: 280 Pitt St, Sydney, NSW 2000 ☎02/9261 3601; 136 Willoughby Rd, Crow's Nest, Sydney, NSW 2065 ☎02/9966 5770; Jolimont Centre, 65 Northbourne Ave, Canberra, ACT 2601 ☎02/6230 4097; 900 Hay St, Perth WA 6000 ☎08/9322 5733; **www.mapworld.net.au**. New Zealand: 173 Gloucester St,

D

DIRECTORY

www.roughguides.com

349

Christchurch ☎0800/627 967, ⓦwww.map world.co.nz.

UK and Ireland

Blackwell's Map Centre 50 Broad St, Oxford OX1 3BQ ☎01865/333677, ⓦmaps.blackwell.co.uk. Branches in Aberdeen, Bristol, Cambridge, Cardiff, Leeds, Liverpool, Newcastle and Sheffield.

Daunt Books 83 Marylebone High St, London W1U 4QW ⓦwww.dauntbooks .co.uk. Plus several branches across London.

National Map Centre Ireland 34 Aungier St, Dublin 2 ☎01/476 0471, ⓦwww.map centre.ie.

Stanfords 12–14 Long Acre, London WC2E 9LP ☎020/7836 1321, ⓦwww .stanfords.co.uk. Also at 29 Corn St, Bristol BS1 1HT ☎0117/929 9966.

The Travel Bookshop 13–15 Blenheim Crescent, London W11 2EE ☎020/7229 5260, ⓦwww.thetravelbookshop.com.

US and Canada

Distant Lands 56 S Raymond Ave, Pasadena, CA ☎626/449-3220, ⓦwww .distantlands.com.

Get Lost Travel Books 1825 Market St, San Francisco, CA ☎415-437-0529, ⓦwww.getlostbooks.com

Globe Corner Bookstore 90 Mt Auburn St, Harvard Sq, Cambridge, MA ☎617/497-6277, ⓦwww.globecorner.com.

Idlewild Books 12 West 19th St, New York, NYC ☎212/414-8888, ⓦwww.idlewildbooks .com

Longitude Books ⓦwww.longitudebooks .com.

Map Town 400 5 Ave SW #100, Calgary, AB T2P 0L6 ☎1-877/921-6277, ⓦwww .maptown.com.

Travel Bug Bookstore 3065 W Broadway, Vancouver, BC V6K 2G9 ☎604/737-1122, ⓦwww.travelbugbooks.ca.

World of Maps 1235 Wellington St, Ottawa, ON K1Y 3A3 ☎1-800/214-8524, ⓦwww.worldofmaps.com.

Travel equipment suppliers

Australia and New Zealand

Kathmandu Outlets in all major Australian and New Zealand cities; Australia ☎03/9267 9999, New Zealand ☎03/373 6110; ⓦwww .kathmandu.com.au.

Mountain Designs Shops across Australia and in New Zealand ☎07/3114 4300; ⓦwww.mountaindesigns.com.

Paddy Pallin Branches across Australia ☎1800/805398, ⓦwww.paddypallin.com.au.

UK

Cotswold Outdoor Over 30 branches across the UK ☎0844/557 7755, ⓦwww .cotswold-outdoor.co.uk.

Field and Trek Branches across the UK ☎0870/333 9622, ⓦwww.fieldandtrek.com.

Itchy Feet 162 Wardour St, London W1F 8ZX ☎020/7292 9750; also 4 Bartlett St,

Bath BA1 2QZ ☎01225/442618, ⓦwww .itchyfeet.com.

US and Canada

Campmor 810 Route 17, North Paramus, New Jersey ☎1-888/226-7667, ⓦwww .campmor.com.

Mountain equipment Co-op (MEC) Thirteen stores across Canada ☎1-888/847-0770, ⓦwww.mec.ca.

The North Face Twenty stores across the US ☎1-866/715-3223, ⓦwww.thenorth face.com.

Recreational Equipment Inc (REI) Stores in 28 states ☎1-800/426-4840, ⓦwww .rei.com.

Sierra Trading Post Outlets in Meridian NV, Reno NV, Cheyenne WY and Cody WY ☎1-800/713-4534, ⓦwww.sierratrading post.com.

A final checklist

See Chapter Six for details on what to take, and for some suggested optionals.

Documents

- airline/travel tickets
- confirmation printouts (hotels/flights)
- debit/credit card
- guidebooks
- insurance policy
- international driver's licence
- International Student Card (ISIC)
- International Youth Hostel Card
- maps
- passport
- passport photos
- phrasebook
- photocopies of vital documents
- travellers' cheques

Basic odds and ends

- camera and memory cards
- contact lens solution/glasses
- contraceptives
- earplugs
- first-aid kit
- flashlight (torch)

- mobile phone
- moneybelt/ neck pouch
- mosquito net
- mosquito repellent
- MP3 player
- notebook/journal and pens
- padlocks
- penknife
- photos of home
- rain gear/umbrella
- sewing kit
- sink plug
- sunglasses
- sun hat
- sunscreen
- tampons
- toilet paper
- toiletries
- towel/sarong
- travel plug adaptor
- water bottle, water purifier or purification tablets

Travel store

Books change lives

Book Aid International
www.bookaid.org

Poverty and illiteracy go hand in hand. But in sub-Saharan Africa, books are a luxury few can afford. Many children leave school functionally illiterate, and adults often fall back into illiteracy in adulthood due to a lack of available reading material.

Book Aid International knows that books change lives.

Every year we send over half a million books to partners in 12 countries in sub-Saharan Africa, to stock libraries in schools, refugee camps, prisons, universities and communities. Literally millions of readers have access to books and information that could teach them new skills – from keeping chickens to getting a degree in Business Studies or learning how to protect against HIV/AIDS.

What can you do?

Join our Reverse Book Club and with your donation of only £6 a month, we can send 36 books every year to some of the poorest countries in the world. For every two pounds extra you can give, we can send another book!

Support Book Aid International today!

 Online. Go to our website at www.bookaid.org, and click on 'donate'

 By telephone. Start a Direct Debit or give a donation on your card by calling us on 020 7733 3577

Book Aid International is a charity and a limited company registered in England and Wales.
Charity No. 313869 Company No. 880754   39-41 Coldharbour Lane, Camberwell, London SE5 9NR
T +44 (0)20 7733 3577   F +44 (0)20 7978 8006   E info@bookaid.org   www.bookaid.org

Travel

Andorra The Pyrenees, Pyrenees & Andorra Map, Spain

Antigua The Caribbean

Argentina Argentina, Argentina Map, Buenos Aires, South America on a Budget

Aruba The Caribbean

Australia Australia, Australia Map, East Coast Australia, Melbourne, Sydney, Tasmania

Austria Austria, Europe on a Budget, Vienna

Bahamas The Bahamas, The Caribbean

Barbados Barbados DIR, The Caribbean

Belgium Belgium & Luxembourg, Bruges DIR, Brussels, Brussels Map, Europe on a Budget

Belize Belize, Central America on a Budget, Guatemala & Belize Map

Benin West Africa

Bolivia Bolivia, South America on a Budget

Brazil Brazil, Rio, South America on a Budget

British Virgin Islands The Caribbean

Brunei Malaysia, Singapore & Brunei [1 title], Southeast Asia on a Budget

Bulgaria Bulgaria, Europe on a Budget

Burkina Faso West Africa

Cambodia Cambodia, Southeast Asia on a Budget, Vietnam, Laos & Cambodia Map [1 Map]

Cameroon West Africa

Canada Canada, Pacific Northwest, Toronto, Toronto Map, Vancouver

Cape Verde West Africa

Cayman Islands The Caribbean

Chile Chile, Chile Map, South America on a Budget

China Beijing, China, Hong Kong & Macau, Hong Kong & Macau DIR, Shanghai

Colombia South America on a Budget

Costa Rica Central America on a Budget, Costa Rica, Costa Rica & Panama Map

Croatia Croatia, Croatia Map, Europe on a Budget

Cuba Cuba, Cuba Map, The Caribbean, Havana

Cyprus Cyprus, Cyprus Map

Czech Republic The Czech Republic, Czech & Slovak Republics, Europe on a Budget, Prague, Prague DIR, Prague Map

Denmark Copenhagen, Denmark, Europe on a Budget, Scandinavia

Dominica The Caribbean

Dominican Republic Dominican Republic, The Caribbean

Ecuador Ecuador, South America on a Budget

Egypt Egypt, Egypt Map

El Salvador Central America on a Budget

England Britain, Camping in Britain, Devon & Cornwall, Dorset, Hampshire and The Isle of Wight [1 title], England, Europe on a Budget, The Lake District, London, London DIR, London Map, London Mini Guide, Walks In London & Southeast England

Estonia The Baltic States, Europe on a Budget

Fiji Fiji

Finland Europe on a Budget, Finland, Scandinavia

France Brittany & Normandy, Corsica, Corsica Map, The Dordogne & the Lot, Europe on a Budget, France, France Map, Languedoc & Roussillon, The Loire, Paris, Paris DIR, Paris Map, Paris Mini Guide, Provence & the Côte d'Azur, The Pyrenees, Pyrenees & Andorra Map

French Guiana South America on a Budget

Gambia The Gambia, West Africa

Germany Berlin, Berlin Map, Europe on a Budget, Germany, Germany Map

Ghana West Africa

Gibraltar Spain

Greece Athens Map, Crete, Crete Map, Europe on a Budget, Greece, Greece Map, Greek Islands, Ionian Islands

Guadeloupe The Caribbean

Guatemala Central America on a Budget, Guatemala, Guatemala & Belize Map

Guinea West Africa

Guinea-Bissau West Africa

Guyana South America on a Budget

Holland see The Netherlands

Honduras Central America on a Budget

Hungary Budapest, Europe on a Budget, Hungary

Iceland Iceland, Iceland Map

India Goa, India, India Map, Kerala, Rajasthan, Delhi & Agra [1 title], South India, South India Map

Indonesia Bali & Lombok, Southeast Asia on a Budget

Ireland Dublin DIR, Dublin Map, Europe on a Budget, Ireland, Ireland Map

Israel Jerusalem

Italy Europe on a Budget, Florence DIR, Florence & Siena Map, Florence & the best of Tuscany, Italy, The Italian Lakes, Naples & the Amalfi Coast, Rome, Rome DIR, Rome Map, Sardinia, Sicily, Sicily Map, Tuscany & Umbria, Tuscany Map, Venice, Venice DIR, Venice Map

Jamaica Jamaica, The Caribbean

Japan Japan, Tokyo

Jordan Jordan

Kenya Kenya, Kenya Map

Korea Korea

Laos Laos, Southeast Asia on a Budget, Vietnam, Laos & Cambodia Map [1 Map]

Latvia The Baltic States, Europe on a Budget

Lithuania The Baltic States, Europe on a Budget

Luxembourg Belgium & Luxembourg, Europe on a Budget

Malaysia Malaysia Map, Malaysia, Singapore & Brunei [1 title], Southeast Asia on a Budget

Mali West Africa

Malta Malta & Gozo DIR

Martinique The Caribbean

Mauritania West Africa

Mexico Baja California, Baja California, Cancún & Cozumel DIR, Mexico, Mexico Map, Yucatán, Yucatán Peninsula Map

Monaco France, Provence & the Côte d'Azur

Montenegro Montenegro

Morocco Europe on a Budget, Marrakesh DIR, Marrakesh Map, Morocco, Morocco Map,

Nepal Nepal

Netherlands Amsterdam, Amsterdam DIR, Amsterdam Map, Europe on a Budget, The Netherlands

Netherlands Antilles The Caribbean

New Zealand New Zealand, New Zealand Map

DIR: Rough Guide **DIRECTIONS** for short breaks

Available from all good bookstores

Nicaragua Central America on a Budget
Niger West Africa
Nigeria West Africa
Norway Europe on a Budget, Norway, Scandinavia
Panama Central America on a Budget, Costa Rica & Panama Map, Panama
Paraguay South America on a Budget
Peru Peru, Peru Map, South America on a Budget
Philippines The Philippines, Southeast Asia on a Budget,
Poland Europe on a Budget, Poland
Portugal Algarve DIR, The Algarve Map, Europe on a Budget, Lisbon DIR, Lisbon Map, Madeira DIR, Portugal, Portugal Map, Spain & Portugal Map
Puerto Rico The Caribbean, Puerto Rico
Romania Europe on a Budget, Romania
Russia Europe on a Budget, Moscow, St Petersburg
St Kitts & Nevis The Caribbean
St Lucia The Caribbean
St Vincent & the Grenadines The Caribbean
Scotland Britain, Camping in Britain, Edinburgh DIR, Europe on a Budget, Scotland, Scottish Highlands & Islands
Senegal West Africa
Serbia Montenegro Europe on a Budget
Sierra Leone West Africa
Singapore Malaysia, Singapore & Brunei [1 title], Singapore, Singapore DIR, Southeast Asia on a Budget
Slovakia Czech & Slovak Republics, Europe on a Budget
Slovenia Europe on a Budget, Slovenia
South Africa Cape Town & the Garden Route, South Africa, South Africa Map
Spain Andalucía, Andalucía Map, Barcelona, Barcelona DIR, Barcelona Map, Europe on a Budget, Ibiza & Formentera DIR, Gran Canaria DIR, Madrid DIR, Lanzarote & Fuerteventura DIR Madrid Map, Mallorca & Menorca, Mallorca DIR, Mallorca Map, The Pyrenees, Pyrenees & Andorra Map, Spain, Spain & Portugal Map, Tenerife & La Gomera DIR
Sri Lanka Sri Lanka, Sri Lanka Map
Suriname South America on a Budget
Sweden Europe on a Budget, Scandinavia, Sweden
Switzerland Europe on a Budget, Switzerland
Taiwan Taiwan
Tanzania Tanzania, Zanzibar
Thailand Bangkok, Southeast Asia on a Budget, Thailand, Thailand Map, Thailand Beaches & Islands
Togo West Africa
Trinidad & Tobago The Caribbean, Trinidad & Tobago
Tunisia Tunisia, Tunisia Map
Turkey Europe on a Budget, Istanbul, Turkey, Turkey Map
Turks and Caicos Islands The Bahamas, The Caribbean
United Arab Emirates Dubai DIR, Dubai & UAE Map [1 title]
United Kingdom Britain, Devon & Cornwall, Edinburgh DIR England, Europe on a Budget, The Lake District, London, London DIR, London Map, London Mini Guide, Scotland, Scottish Highlands

& Islands, Wales, Walks In London & Southeast England
United States Alaska, Boston, California, California Map, Chicago, Colorado, Florida, Florida Map, The Grand Canyon, Hawaii, Los Angeles, Los Angeles Map, Los Angeles and Southern California, Maui DIR, Miami & South Florida, New England, New England Map, New Orleans & Cajun Country, New Orleans DIR, New York City, NYC DIR, NYC Map, New York City Mini Guide, Oregon & Washington, Orlando & Walt Disney World® DIR, San Francisco, San Francisco DIR, San Francisco Map, Seattle, Southwest USA, USA, Washington DC, Yellowstone & the Grand Tetons National Park, Yosemite National Park
Uruguay South America on a Budget
US Virgin Islands The Bahamas, The Caribbean
Venezuela South America on a Budget
Vietnam Southeast Asia on a Budget, Vietnam, Vietnam, Laos & Cambodia Map [1 Map],
Wales Britain, Camping in Britain, Europe on a Budget, Wales
First-Time Series FT Africa, FT Around the World, FT Asia, FT Europe, FT Latin America
Inspirational guides Earthbound, Clean Breaks, Make the Most of Your Time on Earth, Ultimate Adventures, World Party
Travel Specials Camping in Britain, Travel with Babies & Young Children, Walks in London & SE England

For more information go to www.roughguides.com

So now we've told you about the things not to miss, the best places to stay, the top restaurants, the liveliest bars and the most spectacular sights, it only seems fair to tell you about the best travel insurance around

WorldNomads.com

keep travelling safely

Recommended by Rough Guides

Small print and
Index

A Rough Guide to Rough Guides

Published in 1982, the first Rough Guide – to Greece – was a student scheme that became a publishing phenomenon. Mark Ellingham, a recent graduate in English from Bristol University, had been travelling in Greece the previous summer and couldn't find the right guidebook. With a small group of friends he wrote his own guide, combining a highly contemporary, journalistic style with a thoroughly practical approach to travellers' needs.

The immediate success of the book spawned a series that rapidly covered dozens of destinations. And, in addition to impecunious backpackers, Rough Guides soon acquired a much broader and older readership that relished the guides' wit and inquisitiveness as much as their enthusiastic, critical approach and value-for-money ethos.

These days, Rough Guides include recommendations from shoestring to luxury and cover more than 200 destinations around the globe, including almost every country in the Americas and Europe, more than half of Africa and most of Asia and Australasia. Our ever-growing team of authors and photographers is spread all over the world, particularly in Europe, the US and Australia.

In the early 1990s, Rough Guides branched out of travel, with the publication of Rough Guides to World Music, Classical Music and the Internet. All three have become benchmark titles in their fields, spearheading the publication of a wide range of books under the Rough Guide name.

Including the travel series, Rough Guides now number more than 350 titles, covering: phrasebooks, waterproof maps, music guides from Opera to Heavy Metal, reference works as diverse as Conspiracy Theories and Shakespeare, and popular culture books from iPods to Poker. Rough Guides also produce a series of more than 120 World Music CDs in partnership with World Music Network.

Visit www.roughguides.com to see our latest publications.

Rough Guide travel images are available for commercial licensing at www.roughguidespictures.com

SMALL PRINT

www.roughguides.com

Rough Guide credits

Text editor: Andy Turner
Layout: Nikhil Agarwal
Cartography: Karobi Gogoi, Ashutosh Bharti
Picture editor: Emily Taylor
Production: Rebecca Short
Proofreader: Helen Castell
Editorial: Ruth Blackmore, Keith Drew, Edward Aves, Alice Park, Lucy White, Jo Kirby, James Smart, Natasha Foges, Róisín Cameron, Emma Traynor, Emma Gibbs, Kathryn Lane, Monica Woods, Mani Ramaswamy, Harry Wilson, Lucy Cowie, Amanda Howard, Lara Kavanagh, Alison Roberts, Joe Staines, Peter Buckley, Matthew Milton, Tracy Hopkins, Ruth Tidball; **Delhi** Madhavi Singh, Karen D'Souza, Lubna Shaheen
Design & Pictures: London Scott Stickland, Dan May, Diana Jarvis, Mark Thomas, Nicole Newman, Sarah Cummins; **Delhi** Umesh Aggarwal, Ajay Verma, Jessica Subramanian, Ankur Guha, Pradeep Thapliyal, Sachin Tanwar, Anita Singh, Sachin Gupta
Production: Vicky Baldwin

Cartography: London Maxine Repath, Ed Wright, Katie Lloyd-Jones; **Delhi** Rajesh Chhibber, Rajesh Mishra, Animesh Pathak, Jasbir Sandhu, Alakananda Roy, Swati Handoo, Deshpal Dabas
Online: London George Atwell, Faye Hellon, Jeanette Angell, Fergus Day, Justine Bright, Clare Bryson, Aine Fearon, Adrian Low, Ezgi Celebi, Amber Bloomfield; **Delhi** Amit Verma, Rahul Kumar, Narender Kumar, Ravi Yadav, Debojit Borah, Rakesh Kumar, Ganesh Sharma, Shisir Basumatari
Marketing & Publicity: London Liz Statham, Niki Hanmer, Louise Maher, Jess Carter, Vanessa Godden, Vivienne Watton, Anna Paynton, Rachel Sprackett, Laura Vipond, Vanessa McDonald; **New York** Katy Ball, Judi Powers, Nancy Lambert; **Delhi** Ragini Govind
Manager India: Punita Singh
Reference Director: Andrew Lockett
Operations Manager: Helen Atkinson
PA to Publishing Director: Nicola Henderson
Publishing Director: Martin Dunford
Commercial Manager: Gino Magnotta
Managing Director: John Duhigg

Publishing information

This fifth edition published February 2010 by
Rough Guides Ltd,
80 Strand, London WC2R 0RL
14 Local Shopping Centre, Panchsheel Park, New Delhi 110017, India

Distributed by the Penguin Group
Penguin Books Ltd,
80 Strand, London WC2R 0RL
Penguin Group (USA)
375 Hudson Street, NY 10014, USA
Penguin Group (Australia)
250 Camberwell Road, Camberwell, Victoria 3124, Australia
Penguin Group (Canada)
195 Harry Walker Parkway N, Newmarket, ON, L3Y 7B3 Canada
Penguin Group (NZ)
67 Apollo Drive, Mairangi Bay, Auckland 1310, New Zealand
Cover concept by Peter Dyer.

Typeset in Bembo and Helvetica to an original design by Henry Iles.
Printed in Singapore

368pp includes index
A catalogue record for this book is available from the British Library
ISBN: 978-1-84836-474-5

The publishers and authors have done their best to ensure the accuracy and currency of all the information in **The Rough Guide to First-Time Asia**, however, they can accept no responsibility for any loss, injury, or inconvenience sustained by any traveller as a result of information or advice contained in the guide.

1   3   5   7   9   8   6   4   2

Help us update

We've gone to a lot of effort to ensure that the third edition of **The Rough Guide to First-Time Asia** is accurate and up-to-date. However, things change – places get "discovered", opening hours are notoriously fickle, restaurants and rooms raise prices or lower standards. If you feel we've got it wrong or left something out, we'd like to know, and if you can remember the address, the price, the hours, the phone number, so much the better.

Please send your comments with the subject line "**Rough Guide to First-Time Asia Update**" to ⓔmail@roughguides.com. We'll credit all contributions and send a copy of the next edition (or any other Rough Guide if you prefer) for the very best emails.

Have your questions answered and tell others about your trip at ⓦwww.roughguides.com

Acknowledgements

Thanks to the following people for their anecdotes about travelling in Asia:

Juliet Acock, Shannon Brady, Locky Brennan, Sasha Busbridge, Daniel Gooding, Chris Humphrey, Gerry Jameson, Debbie King, Karen Lefere, Mark Lewis, Laura Littwin, Sang Man, Jean-Louis Martin, Nicki McCormick, John McManus, Jo Mead, Neil Poulter, Nicholas Reader, Dee Ridley, Laura Stone, Andrea Szyper, Chris Taylor, Jonathan Tucker, Andy Turner, Ross Velton and Bob Williams.

Photo credits

All photos © Rough Guides except the following:

SMALL PRINT

Introduction
Potala Palace, Lhasa, Tibet © moodboard/Corbis

Reasons to go
02 Masked dancers, Indian Himalayas © Pictures Colour Library
03 Sea kayaking, Thailand © Bruce Clarke/ Photolibrary
06 Clown anenome fish, Philippines © Richard Lindie/iStock
07 Full Moon Party, Thailand © James Pomerantz/Corbis
09 Surfer off Sumatra, Indonesia © Sean Davey/ Aurora Photos/Corbis
12 Bromo and Semeru volcanoes, Java, Indonesia © Bruno Morandi/Photolibrary

13 Malaysian longhouse © Lucid Images/ Photolibrary
16 Orang-utans, Indonesia © ImageState/Tips Images

Black and whites
p.72 Mongolian Horseman at Naadam festival © Reuters/Corbis
p.92 Tourists at Angkor Wat, Cambodia © Hugh Sitton/Corbis
p.106 Hiking boots © Yan Liao/Alamy
p.201 Tsunami warning sign, Thailand © Havet/ iStock Photos
p.240 Li River scenery, Guilin, China © Robert Churchill/iStock

Index

Map entries are in colour.

A

accommodation 15, 115, 121, 259, 309
accommodation booking agents........................347
adaptors, travel 107
AIDS 183
air passes 141
air travel......................25
air-conditioning.............65
airline tickets 55–61
airports
  arrivals.....................119–122
  checking-in 117
  sleeping in.......................120
  transit 118
  transport from 122
altitude sickness...........182
Angkor (Ca)..................229
Annapurna Circuit (N)...283
Asia...................................4
ATMs.....................82, 121

B

backpacks 98–101
Bali (In)..........................251
Banaue (Ph).................295
Bandar Seri Begawan (Br)
 226
Bangkok (T) 324
BANGLADESH..... 215–219
Bangladesh..................216
  best time to go.................215
  books 218
  climate chart 215
  costs 215
  embassies........................219
  festivals 217
  films..................................219
  routes in and out.............218
  security............................205

  tourist offices 219
  visas 51
  websites..........................218
banking, internet 84
bargaining......................79
bathrooms 167, 168–170
batik courses.................46
beaches
  Bali (In) 251
  Boracay (Ph)................... 293
  Com (TL) 332
  Cox's Bazaar (Ba) 217
  Goa (I)............................. 243
  Kenting (Ta) 320
  Ko Lipe (T)....................... 326
  Ko Pha Ngan (T)............... 327
  Ko Phi Phi (T) 326
  Ko Samui (T) 326
  Langkawi (M)................... 271
  Mirissa (SL) 315
  Perhentian Islands (M) 272
  Phu Quoc (V).................. 337
  Phuket (T)........................ 326
  Puerto Galera (Ph).... 151, 295
  Siargao Island (Ph).......... 296
  Sihanoukville (Ca)............ 231
  Tioman (M) 272
  Unawatuna (SL)............... 315
beggars 133, 138
Beijing (Ch) 234
BHUTAN........ 12, 220–224
Bhutan.........................221
  best time to go................ 220
  books 223
  climate chart 220
  costs 220
  embassies........................ 224
  festivals 222
  films.................................. 223
  routes in and out............. 222
  tourist offices 224
  trekking 36, 222
  visas 51
  websites........................... 223
blogging........................187
boats 150–152
Bollywood......................13

books, country specific
  ......see *individual country subindexes*
books, general...............94
bookshops, travel........348
Boracay (Ph)................293
border crossings 32, 50–55
Borobodur (In) 252
Bromo, Mount (In) 14, 251
BRUNEI................ 225–227
Brunei..........................226
  best time to go 225
  books 227
  climate chart 225
  costs 225
  embassies........................ 227
  festivals 227
  routes in and out............. 227
  tourist offices 227
  visas 51
  websites........................... 27
Buddha statues 16
budgeting 7, 75–79
Burma...........................10
buses........... 142–146, 152

C

CAMBODIA......... 228–232
Cambodia 229
  best time to go................ 228
  books 232
  climate chart 228
  costs 75, 228
  embassies........................ 232
  festivals 70, 231
  films.................................. 232
  routes in and out............. 231
  security....................207, 229
  tourist offices 232
  visas 51
  websites........................... 231
cameras............... 111–113

DISCARD